Bob L.
36240 Enfield dr
Newark Ca
94560
U.S.A .

Finance:

Environment and Decisions

Finance:
Environment and Decisions

George A. Christy
North Texas State University

Peyton Foster Roden
Louisiana State University, New Orleans

Canfield Press
San Francisco

A Department of Harper & Row, Publishers, Inc.

New York · Evanston · London

Cover photography by David Keller
Color conversion by John Hall
san francisco photo factory

Design by Gracia A. Alkema

Finance: Environment and Decisions

Copyright ⊙ 1973 by George A. Christy and Peyton Foster Roden

International Standard Book Number: 0-06-382503-1

Library of Congress Catalogue Card Number: 72-7630

75 76   10 9 8 7 6

Preface

The table of contents indicates that this is a new kind of business finance book, whose content and sequencing arose from three convictions. First, we believe that an understanding of financial management logically begins with a discussion of the financial system and the changing environment within which the financial manager works and to which he must continually adjust. Second, an introductory course in finance should reflect mainly the needs of non-finance majors, who ordinarily comprise 90 per cent of a class. Third, experience has taught us that a realistic account of financial management is more likely to engage the student's interest and lasting recall than an abstract and overly mathematical approach.

Thus, our opening chapters, Part I, review what every businessman should know about monetary policy, interest rates, security prices, financial markets and institutions, and international money flows. These external factors are the data of most financial decisions; without a grasp of their nature and behavior, the study of business finance becomes an academic exercise, largely devoid of real content or applicability. Particularly is this true of decisions concerning sources of finance or the timing of financial policy. Experience demonstrates that economic debacles stem at least as often from faulty forecasts of the economy and financial markets as from formal violations of financial rules and precepts.

While texts on principles of economics describe some features of the financial environment, and texts on money and banking take up others, neither treatment ordinarily proceeds from the businessman's standpoint. By contrast, we have attempted at all times to see the financial scene through the corporate manager's eyes.

Besides delineating the financial system, Part I serves a second purpose. It introduces and illustrates many of the terms and ideas on which the theory of financial decisions fundamentally depends: suitability, liquidity, discount, present value, interest-rate risk, and others. The attentive student will approach chapter 13, "The Three A's of Financial Management," with a solid conceptual foundation.

Our second conviction is that a first-course book should not be directed at finance majors. Length, selection of topics, and intensity of treatment should reflect an awareness that, for some 90 per cent of the students using it, this book is likely to represent a sole and final exposure to finance. In planning our book, this awareness guided us to several conclusions.

Since not everything can be taught in an introductory course, the text should be held to teachable size. This is most readily accomplished by excluding subjects of professional interest to finance specialists but of minor importance to businessmen generally. For the same reason, the book should carry a broad-based emphasis. It should view the financial system and financial manager's task from the standpoint of an accountant, operating manager, or sales executive; it should emphasize those aspects of finance which any businessman will encounter in his daily job and which he must increasingly understand as he progresses upward through management ranks.

With confined space, we have preferred to develop a limited number of important issues in significant detail, rather than undertaking a sketchy survey of a wider range of subjects. Our book does not attempt a complete account of either the financial system or business finance. Instead, it offers a selective treatment of centrally important topics, with at least some pretension to systematic order and plausible sequence.

Our third effort has been to avoid unnecessary complication. We will exclude technical jargon wherever possible, and will present most theories and principles in the language and terminology of everyday business. Many will be illustrated with numerical examples; far fewer will be presented in simple algebraic equations. In only one instance will a simple use of calculus be made. In an introductory course, clear descriptions seem preferable to any severe test of the student's verbal or mathematical skills.

In contrast to many authors, we have not professed to shun value judgments in this text. These are unavoidable in the business of living—and in the living of business. It seems artifical to exclude them from the study of a subject which is, after all, more of an imperfect art than a rigorous science. (Indeed, the practice of finance in the 1960s appears in retrospect to be a very crudely practiced art: witness the financial shambles made of Penn-Central and Lockheed, and the net fruits of seven years' Federal Reserve policy, 1965 through 1971.)

It also has been our hope to incorporate in these chapters some tangible feeling for the real, workaday world of business. We would hope our efforts lead to an appreciation of the fact that monetary policy, business financial management, investment, and so forth, consist ultimately of flesh-and-blood people struggling to get things done. The notion, sometimes conveyed in textbooks, that finance, or any other art of business or economic decision, lies in sets of abstract principles or mathematical models functioning in disembodied isolation from individual hopes, fears, intelligence, stupidities, intuitions, and uncertainties, has always impressed us as misleading and fatuous. It seems far better to admit that finance is full of rough edges and confusing befuddlements rather than picturing to the student a kind of well-oiled machine, permitting of precise decisions. This is a spurious impression of the real world which firsthand experience will quickly obliterate.

Although we have made many simplifications in order to make a more readable introductory book, we have also tried to avoid oversimplification. We have not hesitated to present complicated theories (in simple language) when they were necessary. Chapters 5 and 6, dealing with interest, are an example. Nor have we refrained from using elementary mathematical models when we believed these gave the briefest and clearest exposition of important theory. We have also tried to give both sides of important open controversies.

The foundation of any discipline is the knowledge of its terms. The glossary we have provided at the end of the book is neither sophisticated nor comprehensive, but it should be genuinely useful to the student struggling to grasp the meaning of a new system of knowledge.

In short, this book is only intended to scratch the surface of finance, but to scratch it significantly.

Plan of This Book. The plan and sequencing of this book conform with the important divisions of the field of finance and with the recognition that most students using this text will be business administration majors. Money, the most fundamental subject, begins our study of the financial manager's environment, which occupies chapters 2 through 12. The object of this section is to give a clear, high-relief picture of how the financial system works and what its moves mean to the businessman. These chapters systematically delineate the financial forces which surround the business enterprise and help shape the decisions *all* managers must make—production and sales executives as well as accountants and money managers.

Chapters 13 through 28 deal with the basic functions of financial management. We have called these the "Three A's" of business finance: (1) anticipating financial needs, (2) acquiring financial resources, and (3) allocating funds optimally within the enterprise. These chapters are concerned with the basic decisions which the financial manager must make correctly to ensure adequate support for his colleagues in production, marketing, purchasing, engineering, and so on.

Six further topics complete our introductory view of finance. Corporations acquire long-term funds by selling stocks and bonds; the new-issues market and investment bankers' services are described in chapter 29, "Marketing New Security Issues." The special problems generated by financial difficulties and the need to finance rapid growth are summarized in chapter 30, "Financial Difficulties and Financing Growth." The ups and downs of debt-security markets form an important, specialized part of the environment that the financial manager must monitor, and chapter 31 deals briefly with fluctuations in "The Money, Bond, and Mortgage

Markets.'' Equity investment and equity price behavior are treated in chapter 32, ''The Stock Market.'' The business cycle is of supreme importance to everyone in business, forming the external backdrop against which all business is carried on and all decisions are made. Its special significance to the financial manager, and ways he should react to its recurring ups and downs, are delineated in chapter 33, ''The Business Cycle.'' Finally, in a world where an ever-rising percentage of trade and investment flows across national boundaries, ''Financing International Business Transactions'' has become a key part of the financial manager's work in many companies. Chapter 34 introduces this task to the reader.

We wish to thank the many people who played a role in the book's development. Students have insisted on relevance and clarity; colleagues have spurred us to be current and precise. In addition, we owe much to Gracia Alkema of Canfield Press and to Sally Giovinco, whose efforts in production and editing of the text have made the book a readably pleasant surprise to us. We are sure that all users—students and faculty—will benefit immeasurably from their efforts. Finally, we applaud our families for their patience and encouragement. Without them, this book would never have been completed.

George A. Christy

Peyton Foster Roden

Contents

1

The Environment of of Business Finance

1

Finance — The Subject

Definition of Finance — Scope and Divisions — *Money* — *Business Finance* — *Investment* — *Other Branches* — Study Viewpoints in Finance — *The Specialist* — *The Businessman* — *The Informed Citizen* — *The Philosopher* — *Broad Links of Finance* — Science or Art? — Basic Principles in Finance

To finance something means to arrange payment for it. In civilized life, most things are paid for with money. At first glance, finance seems to be the study of money management. Important phases of finance deal with the ways businessmen, investors, governments, financial institutions, and families handle their money: how they budget, save, lend, spend, and invest it. And since money is the "stuff" of which financial decisions and moves are usually made, a study of finance must also include the study of money itself: its nature, creation, behavior, regulation, and problems. Finance includes, too, the study of many institutions and phenomena that have arisen in money-using societies: interest rates, inflation, stocks and bonds, banks, stock exchanges, and credit.[1]

Definition of Finance

Why then shouldn't we define finance simply as the study of money and ways people use it? There are three objections

---

[1]For technical terms unfamiliar to you, see the glossary.

to thus narrowing the definition: (1) Many activities associated with finance—saving, paying for things, giving or getting credit—do not necessarily require money; in a barter economy, for example, all these acts could be performed with goods. (I can save food till tomorrow, pay for a new goatskin with arrowheads, lend five bushels of wheat now for six at harvest-time.) (2) Money isn't what ultimately pays for things. One of the co-authors may pay $4,000 for a new car, but what really pays for the car is three months' sweat and toil in the classroom. In fact, if we think of things too much in terms of money, our view of economic life and values becomes distorted. If the price of the car increases to $6,000 but the co-author still makes only $4,000 for three months' teaching, he'd better wake up and demand a raise. (3) Money, like goods and services, can be bought and sold. That is, while we ordinarily think of using money to buy other things, it is equally possible to use other things to buy money. If one thinks the bottom is going to fall out of a certain stock or house prices, he may be well-advised to sell his shares and home for money and buy them back again after prices have fallen. Money is an asset of fluctuating value; in the increasingly popular theory of asset-choices, it is an asset on a par with all others. Thus the problem of "financial choices" involves more than money alone.

These considerations suggest a broader, more fundamental definition of finance, not limited rigidly to money and the way it is used. What finance actually involves, whether money is used or not, is paying for things. Most stored wealth (what people could raise to pay out, if they had to) does not even consist of money; it comprises their various assets and investments: houses, stocks, bonds, owner-operated businesses, real estate, insurance policies, and so on. Thus a more inclusive definition is the following: Finance is *the study of the nature and uses of the means of payment.*

This definition still leaves money center-stage, the star performer in the financial drama. But it allows for the fact that things other than money can serve as a means of payment. A promise to pay, for example, can procure the immediate use of goods or services; thus IOUs and credit play a huge role in financing production, consumption, and the exchange of goods.

Scope and Divisions

The problems finance deals with can be classified and divided into an indefinite number of subjects. Three branches of finance, however, stand out above all others in importance. These are (1) money, (2) business finance, and (3) investment. Other more specialized branches—commercial banking, international finance, and mortgage lending, for example—are based largely upon principles derived from these three primary divisions. For a more concrete idea of the subject matter finance wrestles with, let us look briefly at each of these main divisions and its central problems.

Money

An understanding of what money is and does is the foundation of financial knowledge. Three aspects of the study of money are particularly important to the business student: (1) the connection between the total supply of money, on one hand, and price-levels and business activity, on the other, (2) the structure and behavior of the financial system, which is based on money, and (3) the role of the financial system as a barometer of business conditions. Let us say a word here about each aspect.

The essential requirement for "good" money seems to be that its supply is carefully controlled. The important questions about money itself revolve around its *supply* and *value,* two factors that seem to be inversely related.[2] Theoretically, just the right size money supply will produce prosperity without inflation; too much money will bring on boom and inflation, and too little money will result in recession and deflation.

Thus money is linked in certain ways to the business cycle—the ups and downs of output, employment, and incomes. It is also linked to the price level. Money is not necessarily stable or dependable over time, either as a measure of value or a store of buying power. The theory and practice of finance therefore pay close attention to forecasting trends in money's buying power in order to profit from timely shifts between money and other assets.

A nation's well-being and even survival may depend on adequate control of the value of money. The rise of Naziism was a main consequence of the Great German Inflation of 1923, which impoverished the middle class and inclined it toward desperate political choices. On an individual level, well-being and comfortable retirement may depend on a person's ability to forecast the direction of money's value and act accordingly. In the United States, for example, people who have held bonds or mortgages since 1939, instead of investing in real estate or common stocks, have seen two-thirds of their stored buying power evaporate in rising prices. Many observers now fear that unless the country halts the long-standing inflationary trend, an eventual debacle will bankrupt the economy and jeopardize basic liberties.

After looking at money itself, one needs to review the parts and phenomena of the money-using system. This introduces the study of such elements as near-monies (such as savings deposits), interest rates (the yield and cost of money), banks (which create money), non-bank financial intermediaries (which link lenders and borrowers), central banks (such as the Federal Reserve System, which regulate money and credit supplies), international payments (which involve exchanging one nation's money for another's), and, finally, the behavior of the financial system as a whole.

Out of the financial system come both problems and cues for the businessman. Problems related to tight money, more stringent standards of credit-worthiness, rationing of funds by banks or other lenders, congested bond markets, and collapsing stock prices, for example, bring painful anxieties and often dire risks to firms afflicted by them. Such developments are warnings to businessmen that the business environment is becoming less favorable: the financial barometer indicates that it is time to pull in one's economic horns. Conversely, easy

---

[2]Two factors are inversely related if an increase in one brings a decrease in the other. For example, chapter 3 uses an algebraic formulation, the Equation of Exchange, to illustrate how—if other factors remain the same—a rise in money's supply diminishes its buying power.

money, ready availability of loans, and a rising stock market usually signal clear weather ahead and a good time to expand business commitments. Thus knowing how to monitor and interpret the financial system and its signals is an indispensable skill for anyone in business.

Business Finance

If gold was "the sinews of war" in Frederick the Great's time, modern money is the sinews of business enterprise. Most business failures are announced by a firm's running out of money. Dun & Bradstreet statistics, gathered over the years on business failures, show that the most frequent cause after inexperience is poor financial management. Without adequate financial support no business can survive; without sound financial management, no business can prosper and grow.

The head of a firm or its financial manager must know how to do three things well: (1) to anticipate a firm's needs for money—to support inventories and receivables as sales rise, to build or renew plant and equipment, and to meet bills in general; (2) to assure the availability of funds when needed, either through the firm's own cash inflows or from various external sources—banks, commercial paper, or investors who will buy the company's stock and bonds; and (3) to allocate funds to their most profitable uses within the enterprise—the problem of how much to put into such assets as cash reserves, inventory, credit to customers, buildings, different kinds of machines, research outlays on new products, and the like. In assuring the availability of funds (step 2), the financial manager must aim for a safe yet profitable mix of financing sources; monies raised in different ways (through stocks, bonds, bank loans, and so forth) have very different kinds of obligations, costs, restrictions, and hazards attached.[3]

The shrewd financial manager always tries to finance his company in the least costly way consistent with the degree of uncertainty his management is willing to accept. Finding this balance is often referred to as the "eat well or sleep well" dilemma. Great profits are typically compatible only with a large assumption of uncertainty, while a preference for reduced uncertainty necessarily brings a shrinkage of profit possibilities. Thus with large profit prospects coupled with a high degree of uncertainty, management eats well but sleeps restlessly. A more cautious financial structure may bring sounder sleep but fewer gourmet meals.[4]

Investment

Broadly, investment means the commitment of money to any kind of earning asset, so the term needs further distinction. The purchase of a machine, factory, or house constitutes real investment, or investment in tangible property. Financial investment consists of buying intangibles—stocks, bonds, or other paper claims

---

[3]Another way of structuring the basic problems of business finance is to say the financial manager must make two main decisions: (1) what assets to acquire (number and kind), and (2) what liabilities to finance these assets with. Some business finance texts distinguish these two areas as the investment decision and the financing decision, respectively.

[4]It should be observed that the term "risk" is misused in the context where we have written "uncertainty." Accurately used, risk refers to a situation in which the various possible outcomes follow a known probability distribution. But the probabilities of the different results of financing a company in various ways are never known and can rarely be estimated accurately. Thus, although many authors refer to risk in describing the "eat well or sleep well" dilemma, the term is mistakenly applied.

to wealth. Real investment enters into the study of business finance mostly by way of capital budgeting, or the allocation of a firm's money to investments that will last more than one year. The distinction between the two can be overemphasized, however, for from the standpoint of any person or business, investment is a unified problem: an individual's invested position includes his real estate and owner-operated business as well as his common stocks and insurance policies.[5]

The three main problems in investment are (1) selection (what to buy), (2) timing (when to buy it), and (3) what combination to buy (the so-called portfolio problem).[6] Solutions to these problems lie partly in a sound knowledge of valuation: being able to estimate what future income an investment will produce under various conditions and what, consequently, it is likely to be worth.

Investment is generally thought of as buying securities or real property for a combination of income-return and gradual capital gains. Opposed to this conservative approach is speculation, or "trading": the attempt to profit from fluctuations in prices. The word *speculate* comes from the Latin *speculare,* meaning "to see ahead," and successful speculators are those who perceive future values ahead of investors and the general public.

Other Branches

Other branches of financial study can be elaborated almost endlessly, ranging from personal finance to the specialized management of central banks, such as the Bank of England or the Federal Reserve System. The following subjects are of considerable interest to businessmen. *Investment banking,* or the underwriting and marketing of new issues of stocks and bonds, undergirds the raising of funds for corporations, state and local governments, and, in limited degree, for federal agencies. *Security analysis,* aimed at appraising the real worth and price possibilities of stocks, bonds, and other securities, importantly aids investment. *Business cycles* are so largely financial in origin, and affect business finance, investment, and money supplies so vitally, that they need to be considered a branch of finance. *International finance,* incorporating such matters as foreign exchange, the nation's balance of payments, and the work of the International Monetary Fund, forms an indispensable backdrop for the nation's financial system. Other areas of finance not discussed here—for example, mortgage lending, commercial bank management, financial statement analysis, credit management, the public finance of governmental bodies, and the management of investment portfolios—are of major interest to various financial specialists.

Study Viewpoints in Finance

A knowledge of finance, in different degrees and from different standpoints, is useful to people in at least four stations of life. It helps (1) the financial specialist,

---

[5]For fuller discussion of this point, see John C. Clendenin and George A. Christy, *Introduction to Investments* (New York: McGraw-Hill Book Company, 1969), chapters 1 and 28, especially p. 4.

[6]Although current study of portfolio strategy is often packaged in rather complex mathematical equations and sophisticated jargon, the basic principle involves getting either the highest expected return for a given level of uncertainty, or getting a given expected return at the least possible uncertainty. To do this, the investor tries to construct a security portfolio in which (1) a single adverse change will not affect a large part of his holdings, and (2) a factor that depresses one part will increase the value of another.

(2) the average businessman, (3) the informed citizen, and (4) the philosopher or broad student of human affairs.

The Specialist

Many business people earn above-average livings as financial specialists: as treasurers and controllers of companies, as bankers, brokers, mortgage lenders, or stock and bond analysts. Obviously, such experts require an intensive preparation in the theory and practice of finance, particularly the phase by which they support themselves.

The Businessman

Everyone in business—salesman, personnel manager, production manager, and so on—feels the impact of financial forces on his work, pay, and opportunities. Within a firm, financial considerations underlie and shape many business decisions. "Why won't the controller approve credit on that order I wrote? What right does he have to monkey in the sales department's affairs?" External financial events also affect one's business career. "What's this about a 'tight bond market' knocking out the company's expansion program and my promotion? I thought we could always borrow from the bank!" This book suggests answers to these and similar questions.

The Informed Citizen

The citizen, businessman and non-businessman alike, is continually affected by broad changes in the financial system around him. Tight money may bring economic slowdown and job loss; inflation, interest-rate changes, and swings in credit standards and availability may significantly affect his living standard and economic security; a balance of payments crisis may leave him stranded as a traveler in a foreign country. An understanding of these phenomena and what underlies them leads to more informed and effective choices in daily life.

The Philosopher

A reflective person may well find finance a fascinating philosophic study because it reveals much about human nature and motives. It is often said that people's money dealings, more than any others, lay naked their character and basic morals.[7]

History suggests that the integrity of financial bargains and soundness of money itself are among the most dependable barometers of quality of life and rise or fall of a civilization. All declining civilizations, it might be noted, have "polluted" their money supplies through debasement of currency or coinage, and persistent price inflation has often been a seal of doom on a society. Athens went this way from the time of Solon's reforms, and Rome as well, from the

---

[7]Ralph Waldo Emerson, the American philosopher, wrote: "Money is representative, and follows the nature and fortunes of the owner. The coin is a delicate meter of civil, social, and moral changes . . ." See *The Complete Works of Ralph Waldo Emerson*, 12 vols., ed. Edward Waldo Emerson (Boston: Houghton-Mifflin Co., 1904), vol. 6, p. 101.

beginning of decadence in the Empire. By this yardstick, the outlook for the United States is hardly encouraging.

Broad Links of Finance

Ultimately, the study of finance is as wide as human life itself. Only for the blinker-wearing, tunnel-visioned technical drudge is finance a narrow, mind-shrinking specialty. It is true that the understanding and practice of any branch of finance requires specialized knowledge. But success in finance also requires a wide range of general knowledge. For, as we shall see—particularly in chapter 12—the financial system is so widespread in its relations, so linked with all phases of human society, that very little happens which does not affect money or people's use of it. The state of the financial system reflects not only what businessmen and bankers are doing but also the whole range of a society's values, ethics, ideals, goals, politics, customs, and morals. Thus the financial system is a web spreading through practically the entire realm of human affairs, alert and reacting to the rustles and tremors that affect people's attitudes and behavior. He whose finger is sensitive to financial events and trends has a firm grip on the pulsebeat of his society and times.

In presenting finance as a philosophic and humanistic subject as well as a technical one, this book will demonstrate the linkage of finance with the broad range of human knowledge, and not only with economics and accounting, management and statistics, or even with the social sciences generally. Rather, we propose to show connections between finance and literature, politics, history, philosophy, and ethics—the liberal and mind-widening arts—as well. These relations suggest that the more broadly based your education is, the more readily you will understand and appreciate what goes on in finance, and the more discerningly and successfully you are likely to make financial decisions.[8]

Science or Art?

Because finance describes and classifies the phenomena of the payments system, it is often called a science. Since it deals with people, it is a social science, a branch of the wider social science of economics. It is also an applied science: one using classified and tested knowledge as a help in practical affairs. In fact, most branches of finance are "how to do it" subjects: business finance (how to raise and manage the money needed in a business), investment (how to make income and capital gains by putting money in stocks and bonds), money and banking (how government agencies and the banking industry try to manage the

---

[8]The superiority of generalists over specialists has often been asserted. Francis Bacon, the English philosopher, observed that ". . . expert men [specialists] can execute, and perhaps judge of particulars, one by one; but the general counsels, and the plots and marshalling of affairs, come best from those that are learned [generalists]." Francis Bacon, *Essays* (New York: E. P. Dutton & Co., Inc., 1958), Everyman's Library, p. 150. A recent echo of this view, applying specifically to finance, comes from Sigmund G. Warburg, England's most successful merchant (investment) banker of the past generation. Warburg declares that the study of Greek and Latin classics is a better preparation for merchant banking than finance, economics, and accounting. See Joseph Wechsberg, *The Merchant Bankers* (New York: Little, Brown, and Company, 1968), p. 166.

nation's money supply to produce healthy economic activity without inflation or other bad side-effects).

It is true, as we shall see, that finance contains a nucleus of systematic principles, some of which can be stated in mathematical equations, like the laws of physics and chemistry. It contains a much larger body of rules or tendencies that hold true "in general and on the average." Most practical problems of finance, however, have no hard and fast answers that can be worked out mathematically or programmed on a computer; they must be solved by judgment, intuition, and the "feel" of experience. Thus, despite its frequent acceptance as an applied science, finance remains largely an art. In playing the piano, knowledge of the keyboard and ability to read music are important, but this knowledge alone cannot produce a Van Cliburne. It goes similarly with a great treasurer, banker, or stock trader. Knowledge of facts and principles is the foundation, but high achievement calls for intuitive judgment. Success in any art is personal to the practitioner.

Basic Principles in Finance

Although finance, like other business and economic disciplines, divides and subdivides into specialized fields, you will soon see that there are common principles that work the same way in *all* fields of finance. Two such principles, briefly explained, will suffice here for illustration.

The first of these principles is known as *the financial manager's dilemma.* It means simply that, in any financial decision, profitability (how much you stand to make) is generally opposed to liquidity (how easily you can get your money back if you need to). This principle holds true whether the decision concerns an investment in corporate assets, a personal venture in securities, or what to buy for a bank's investment portfolio.

A second principle is *suitability,* or the preservation of time-balance between assets and liabilities. This principle means that the assets in which money is invested should not have a longer maturity than the liabilities through which the money is raised. A vigorous paraphrase of this principle runs, "Never borrow short and lend—or invest—long." Old as this principle is, it was the most consistently violated of all financial rules during the era of wheeler-dealer speculation that preceded the 1969–70 credit crunch. In fact, most enterprises that went to the wall in this squeeze did so precisely because they borrowed money at short term and invested it in long-term assets that could not return to cash till after the borrowings fell due. When the credit squeeze made it impossible for the borrowers either to renew their loans or reborrow from other sources, they were forced into default and bankruptcy.

Financial principles, as you can see, are often simply common sense applied to money-related problems. Of course, the principles can be wrapped in complicated jargon and formidable mathematics. But this does not have to be the case, and we shall try to avoid unnecessary complication wherever possible.

To Remember

Definition of finance
Branches of finance
Financial manager's dilemma
Suitability

Questions

1 Can things be financed without money? Explain.
2 Why is the value of money said to be inversely related to its supply?
3 What sort of cues does a businessman derive by watching the financial system?
4 What are the three principal tasks of the financial manager in a business?
5 Distinguish between real and financial investment.
6 In what ways do smart speculators concern themselves with values?
7 Discuss the relations of finance to other fields of knowledge.
8 Is finance a science or an art? Explain.
9 Give an illustration of how the manager of a manufacturing enterprise might violate the principle of suitability.

2

What Money Is

Definition of Money — *Why Money?* — *Real vs. Money Flows* —
Money's Four Functions — *A Medium of Exchange* — *A Standard
of Value* — *A Store of Value* — *A Standard of Deferred Payment* — **The
Value of Money** — **Near-Money** — *Liquidity* — *The Money-to-Assets
Ratio* — **Credit and Velocity**

Definition of Money

Since finance deals largely with money, a definition of
this central item logically commences our study. A thing can
be defined according to what it is, what it does, or what it
consists of, and money is no exception. As we shall see, money
serves several functions in economic life. But one in particular
marks the essential attribute of money: that of serving as a
general medium of exchange. Money is thus defined as anything
that is generally acceptable in payment for goods and services,
or in discharge of debts.

General acceptability, not being made of a particular
"stuff," is the essential characteristic of money. In the past,
many things have served their turn as money: decorative shells,
beads, stone axes, metal bars; bronze, gold, and silver coins;
and the engraved notes of banks and governments. Today,
by widespread agreement, the U.S. money supply consists of
three components: (1) coin, (2) currency (non-interest-bearing

notes of the Treasury and the twelve Federal Reserve Banks), and (3) demand deposits in commercial banks (which are transferable from one person to another through that familiar written order, the check.) Some writers would also include time deposits in commercial banks as a fourth component because they are so quickly and dependably converted into cash. Table 2–1 shows that as of November 30, 1971, the nation's total money supply, as customarily measured, was approximately $237.5 billion.[1]

Table 2–1.   U.S. Money Supply, November 30, 1971

Item	Millions of Dollars
Coin	6,715
Paper Currency	
Treasury Currency	615
Federal Reserve Notes	53,306
Demand Deposits	176,900
Total	237,536

Source: Derived from *Federal Reserve Bulletin,* January 1972.

Why Money?

Why did money come into use? The answer is convenience. The use of money enriches economic life by broadening the scope of exchange, production, and consumption. Money is generalized purchasing power. It is a common denominator of buying power and economic choice. It broadens the scope of exchange by eliminating the need for a "double coincidence of wants" necessary in barter. (If A makes fishhooks and B grows yams, no barter is possible—except through an appropriate third party—unless B wants fishhooks at the same time A desires yams.) It amplifies the range of goods and services people can produce by making possible a wider specialization and division of labor. Wider markets and greater time devoted to production become possible when one can sell his labor or output for money instead of seeking out barter trades with those who have what he needs. Finally, money adds flexibility to economic consumption. It enables each consumer to distribute his spending as he wishes: he can pick the kinds and amounts of goods he personally desires, and he also can save part of his money income, thus exercising the option of transferring some of his consumption to the future when he may enjoy it more.

---

[1] Recent years have witnessed much debate over the best measure of money supply. Almost certainly, there is no single best measure for all purposes. Consequently, to get a number of readings on money supply, economists have defined various measures with serialized names: M_1 (coin, currency, and demand deposits), M_2 (M_1 with time deposits in commercial banks added), and so on. Many studies of the effect of changes in money supply on economic activities revolve around statistical tests in which economic changes are correlated with (or regressed on) money supply defined in various ways. The goal is to find which kind of the various measures of money-supply is more closely linked in its ups and downs with fluctuations in economic activity.

Real vs. Money Flows

All economic activity can be represented as two matching flows. These flows take place on two levels, as shown in Figure 2–1. The upper level consists of the economy's real flows: the flow of labor, materials, and machine-services into products and the final flow of goods and services from producers to consumers. These flows account for the satisfaction of wants and needs, or utilities, that are the end-purpose of economic effort. Below them is the lower level, consisting of money flows. These flows involve the innumerable payments of currency or checks that assist the production, exchange, and consumption of the real wealth moving above. Figure 2–1 indicates that almost every economic transaction involves a double movement. One part is the movement of goods from seller to buyer. The other is the movement of money from buyer to seller. Thus, it is easy to think of money as a "fluidizer" of economic life: flows of money are a kind of river on which goods and services pass quickly and frictionlessly through their various stages of production to their final destination in consumption and human satisfaction.

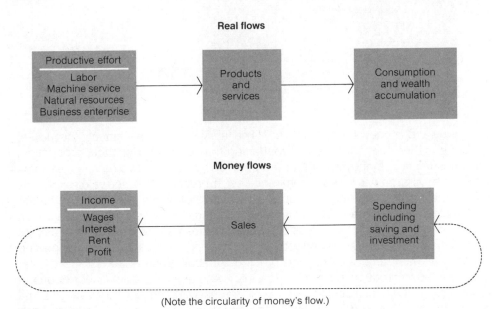

(Note the circularity of money's flow.)

Figure 2–1. Economic Flows

Given the complex structure and intricate functioning of modern economic life, money's role as a common denominator of buying power and economic choice is indispensable. Without money we would find it hopelessly cumbersome to hire labor, buy machines, raise capital, pay interest, make savings, keep accounts, reckon costs, compare spending alternatives, and perform innumerable other behind-the-scenes functions that make possible the mass-production, mass-marketing, and mass-consumption that support today's high living standards.

Despite its indispensability, money is still only a facilitating agent. It cannot logically be an end in itself because, in the final analysis, money is only good for what it will buy. A million dollars in cash on a desert island would be less valuable to the castaway than a single glass of water. Another trillion dollars added to the U.S. money supply, with no increase in the volume of goods and services, would only bring on a disastrous inflation of prices. Thus, while money is an indispensable vehicle for financing, exchanging, distributing, or saving wealth, it is not wealth itself. Money, in short, is a necessary but not sufficient condition for prosperous economic life.[2]

Money's Four Functions

Formally, money serves four purposes. It functions as (1) a general medium of exchange, (2) a standard of value (or price), (3) a store of value, and (4) a standard of deferred payment. How reliably money serves these purposes determines how effectively it contributes to economic life and whether or not a society is free from money-related problems.

A Medium of Exchange

We have seen that money as a medium of exchange makes possible many of the complex efficiencies of modern economic life. The varied services of money depend, however, on its having purchasing power. It must have an acceptability in exchange for goods and services that is based ultimately on people's confidence that, when they get around to spending it, it will also be acceptable in exchange for the goods and services *they* want to buy. In other words, money must have what economists call value in exchange, since—usually consisting only of a piece of paper—it has no value in use. We shall see a few paragraphs onward that money's value ordinarily depends on one property: relative scarcity.

A Standard of Value

In modern societies, most values are prices, or values expressed in money. Money provides a convenient unit for comparing values, regardless of size or kind, and for reducing them by a common denominator. Money is thus the common yardstick by which people keep their accounts, determine incomes and profits, prepare their budgets, and regulate and apportion their spending, savings, and investments. In serving this function, too, money contributes to superior accuracy, flexibility, and efficiency in economic life.

Since money is the yardstick by which economic choices are measured, it is important that this yardstick be as fixed and unchanging as possible. When the value of money—its buying power—fluctuates too rapidly, or moves up or down too far, financial planning becomes extremely difficult, and poor decisions and mistaken economic policies are likely to result. Suppose that a businessman pays $1,000 for a machine that brings him $1,500 in sales. If there are no other costs, he may count—and pay taxes on—$500 in profit. But if, over the machine's life, the dollar's buying power is cut in half, the businessman has actually incurred a loss (if he has not doubled his prices). It will cost him $2,000 to replace the

---

[2]A necessary condition must be present before an effect will take place. A sufficient condition insures that an effect will take place. Oxygen is a necessary condition for fire, but not a sufficient one since its presence does not produce fire if combustible materials and sufficient heat are not present.

machine, and his real loss, or the loss measured in purchasing power, is $500 in depreciated money, plus the income tax he was obliged to pay. You can see that money-value comparisons and accountings hold true only so long as money's buying power remains relatively stable. To continue thinking in terms of dollars when the value of the dollar itself is changing is a common and often costly mistake, one which an American economist has labeled the "money illusion."[3]

A Store of Value

The receiver or holder of money can choose between spending his purchasing power (immediate enjoyment) or saving it (deferred enjoyment). Saving money assumes various forms but the commonest involve holding either money itself (currency or demand deposits) or money substitutes (savings deposits, E-bonds, Treasury bills, and so forth), which pay interest on the money borrowed and repay—or permit withdrawal of—fixed dollar sums. Both forms of saving have their advantages and disadvantages. Keeping one's savings in cash assures him of instantly available spending power, but he collects no interest. Money substitutes pay interest, but have various disadvantages: delay or inconvenience in getting cash, fluctuation in market price prior to maturity, and (if the issuer of the money substitute should have difficulty) freezing, or even loss of principal and interest.

With either form of saving—holding a money substitute or holding money itself—the store of value depends for its effectiveness on a stable price level. In recent years, money and money substitutes have performed very poorly as stores of value because of persistent price inflation. Based on the rise in consumer prices, today's dollar will buy only about one-third as much as 1939's "heavyweight" dollar.

A Standard of Deferred Payment

Debts arise when people receive goods or services, or borrow economic resources (including money) on promises to pay (or repay) in the future. Debts are ordinarily expressed in money, giving rise to money's fourth and final function as a standard of deferred payment. Deferred payments measured in money range from short-term obligations such as accounts payable, six-month promissory notes, and Treasury bills, to very long-dated IOUs such as bonds and mortgages. Their common characteristic is that the principal owed and the interest, if interest is formally payable, are denominated in dollars.[4]

Money's efficiency as a standard of deferred payment, like its efficiency as a store of value, suffers from price-level changes which alter money's purchasing power. Assuming other factors are constant, good financial strategy calls for borrowing to the limit of one's ability when prices are expected to rise, for then the borrower can pay off his debts in cheaper dollars. Lenders, of course, need additional compensation for loss of purchasing power when inflation takes place.

---

[3]See Irving Fisher, *The Money Illusion* (New York: Adelphi Co., 1928).

[4]Some IOUs are not formally interest-bearing. Investors in these get their interest by paying less than face (maturity) value for them, or discounting them. An investor, for example, would be getting interest at approximately a 6 per cent per year rate by buying a U.S. Treasury bill (which matures at $1,000 in 3 months) at a price of $985.

In the past few years, they have increased their interest charges, and this has helped offset the cheaper dollars in which they are being repaid. However, a dollar whose value fluctuates is much less fair and reliable for business purposes than a dollar whose buying power remains stable. With a stable dollar, businessmen, lenders, and debtors need only concern themselves with the value of goods bought or sold; with a fluctuating dollar, one must try to outguess the acrobatics of money value as well. This is not easy to do, and a changing dollar always leads to the windfall gains and severe losses which are unintended or involuntary parts of business transactions. In short, unstable money is a hindrance to orderly economic life.

The Value of Money

What has been said above suggests that money today has value only for what it will buy. This is, indeed, the common definition of the value of money: its purchasing power. But what does purchasing power depend on? In answering this question, we need to note that the present age has broken sharply with the past on what it will accept as money. This break accounts for many of today's money problems.

In former times, money consisted of objects that had intrinsic value: notably, gold and silver coins. This gave money a double assurance of purchasing power because its value depended not only on its stated worth as money but also on its precious metal content. It is true that late in the seventeenth century paper money began to appear. But until about forty years ago, paper money in most countries was redeemable in gold or silver coin. Often it was simply a "warehouse receipt" for precious metal coin or bullion on deposit at the national treasury or central bank. So governments in those days did not dare, as a rule, to overissue paper money. If too much paper money was issued, people became suspicious that the government was polluting, or debasing, the money supply. So they would take their paper dollars, pounds, or francs to the banks and redeem them in gold or silver coin. This threat to clean out the nation's supply of precious metal (on which, as we shall see, its *international* buying power ultimately depended) ordinarily sufficed to keep the government "honest" in issuing paper money. Inflation was thus much less a threat than it has since become.

Using paper money alone, as we do today, money's value is regulated only by its scarcity. Once people become used to accepting irredeemable paper money, it works well enough so long as its supply is conscientiously controlled by the monetary authority. (Have *you* ever thought to worry about what is actually behind the dollars you spend?) As we shall see in chapter 3, if the supply of paper money were permitted to increase only as fast as the nation's real output of goods and services expanded, the value of money would remain constant; there would be no inflation, and therefore no need to scramble to take advantage of it or to protect oneself against it. All over the world, however, governments have found that inflating the money supply is a seemingly easy way to pay for expenditures without arousing voter resentment through increased taxes, and (so they long thought) without running up interest rates by competing with other borrowers for people's savings. A great deal of government spending is therefore quietly financed by inflating the money supply, usually by having the central bank create deposit or "checkbook'' money for the government. When the government spends its new deposits, they become part of the public's money supply. Soon more money is chasing the same amount of goods, and a new cycle of inflation has started.

Inflation is often called America's number one economic problem. As Figure 2–2 shows, the post-World War II inflation has differed from all others in the nation's history. Eras of price inflation have always accompanied our major wars, from the Revolutionary War on, because the government has always issued large volumes of new paper money to finance the war. But until World War II, each war-time inflation was followed by an interval of price deflation. Then, money regained its lost value and lenders of money recouped what they had temporarily lost through rising prices. These post-war price declines were caused largely by the public's unwillingness to accept paper money, which had depreciated relative to gold and silver coins. People who had been foolish or unlucky enough to accept quantities of paper currency found themselves saddled with money of inferior purchasing power; paper money thus became unpopular. So the government gradually got rid of it, or at least did not let the supply increase.[5] But the gold standard, which gave citizens the right to demand gold in exchange for paper dollars, was aban-

Figure 2–2. Price Inflation in the United States 1820–1971 (1913 = 100)

[5]It took fourteen years after the Civil War ended in 1865 before the paper dollar got back to full equality with the gold dollar. At one time during the war, a gold dollar was worth three paper ones. Actually, the Treasury ceased its issue of additional paper money, and the nation's economy, expanding rapidly, grew up by 1879 to its enlarged money supply. The lapse from the gold standard during World War I was brief and scarcely noticeable, but after the war the Federal Reserve contracted the supply of checkbook money so sharply in 1919 that a major depression followed in 1920.

doned by our government in 1933. After World War II, therefore, no gold coin was in circulation to make paper money look bad by comparison, and no check existed on the government's ability to keep on issuing paper money to pay for war, welfare, aid to education, and other public services. Thus, while the value of money curve on Figure 2–2 fell back after previous wars, you can see that it has risen steadily since World War II.

Near-Money

Only money can act as a general medium of exchange, but its store of value function is shared by many other kinds of assets. Recall that most of a man's stored wealth is represented not by currency and demand deposits, but by stocks, bonds, notes, savings accounts, and so on, as well as a house and perhaps an owner-operated business. Some of these assets may take considerable time to sell—the house or business, for example—and some, such as stocks and bonds, have values that fluctuate unpredictably. But others are either quickly redeemable in cash at the owners demand—savings accounts and E-bonds, for example—or ordinarily resellable at a reasonably certain price not less than the owner originally paid. In this second class one would find U.S. Treasury bills and negotiable time certificates of deposit in commercial banks, popularly known as CDs. These quickly cashable dollar claims are called *near-money* because they are the closest thing to cash which can still earn interest.

Liquidity

The key to whether or not an asset is near-money is whether it is convertible into cash, quickly and with little chance of loss. This quality of assets is called *liquidity*. We also speak of a person, business or bank being liquid when they have on hand or can readily raise enough cash to meet their maturing obligations.

Behind liquidity, however, must stand some apparatus to insure easy encashment of these near-money claims. Deposit-type financial intermediaries—savings and loan associations, mutual savings banks, savings departments of commercial banks, and credit unions, for example—all maintain cash reserves normally equal to a certain percentage of their deposit liabilities. This percentage of cash will be set by the institutions' managers, or required by regulatory agencies, on the basis of experience. Fundamentally, this percentage reflects two principles: (1) that only a small percentage of depositors is likely to cash its claims at any one time, and (2) that over any substantial interval deposits of cash will exceed withdrawals as the institution grows.

Short-term marketable securities like Treasury bills and CDs have three circumstances favoring their easy encashment. First, the underlying promise to pay is very reliable, which gives them wide acceptability as investments. Second, their time to maturity is relatively short—one year or less—so their market value can never diverge far from their face or maturity value. For example, if the prevailing discount on Treasury bills is 6 per cent, a $1,000 bill with one year to maturity will sell for approximately $943.40, and a three-month bill will sell for about $985.22. Third, they have an active resale market with almost assured demand. So—like savings accounts, savings and loan share accounts, E-bonds, and the cash value of one's life insurance policy—Treasury bills, CDs, and other high-grade, short-term marketable claims have high liquidity. In the short run, at least, they make dependable stores of value.

The Money-to-Assets Ratio

Usually, this practice of putting one's purchasing power "on ice" in near-money form works smoothly and dependably. Ordinarily, only a small fraction of the nation's holders of near-money will demand cash (or have their near-money mature) on any single day. This permits an enormous volume of near-money claims to be piled on a much smaller supply of actual money. How large this ratio of near-money to money is can be seen in Table 2–2.

Table 2–2. Money and Near-Money: Comparative Amounts,[1]
November 30, 1971

Item	Billions of Dollars
Money Supply[2]	237.5
Near-Monies	
Deposit-type	
Time and Savings Deposits in Commercial Banks	265.5
Savings and Loan Share Accounts	171.4
Mutual Savings Bank Deposits	80.2
Money-market Securities	
U.S. Treasury Bills	89.8
Commercial and Finance-Company Paper	31.2
Bankers Acceptances	7.5
Total near-money	645.6

[1]Note: this list of near-money is far from exhaustive.

[2]For composition of money supply on this date see Table 2–1.

Source: Selected from various tables in *Federal Reserve Bulletin*, January 1972.

We can formulate a ratio M/A (money-to-assets) or A/M (assets-to-money) to measure the economy's potential liquidity. A look at such a ratio should quickly abolish the illusion that everyone in the economy could get liquid at once. If all near-money claims were simultaneously presented for cashing or offered for sale, their prices would obviously fall close to zero, since enough money would be available to redeem or buy only a small fraction of them. Thus, a claim that the economy as a whole is liquid depends on the assumption that only a small fraction of near-money claims will be offered for cash at any one time.[6]

The ratio of money to near-money (and to other assets in which people

---

[6]This assumption is based on the law of large numbers, and is the principle on which fractional reserve banking is based. The law of large numbers states that as populations grow numerically larger, their probability distribution becomes increasingly stable and predictable.

store their purchasing power) plays an important part in regulating economic activity. For it measures the degree of ease or strain with which people can convert their stored purchasing power back into readily spendable money balances.

When strain develops in the ratio of near-money to money, its first symptom is rising interest rates. If a growing proportion of near-money holders now decide they need or would prefer to hold cash, sellers of bills, paper, and other promissory notes used to raise money will try to attract new holders by offering higher rates of interest. Similarly, deposit-type intermediaries will increase their interest rates to arrest withdrawals and attract new holders.

As we shall see, rising interest rates and tight money do not go on forever. At some point, the shortage of money and cost of borrowing it will become severe enough to slow down the boom in economic activity that has caused the rising demand for cash. This slowdown, typically accompanied by rising unemployment and some fall in output, will restore a better balance between money supply and the total amount of spending people are attempting to make. At this point, interest rates will fall because reduced economic activity will once more create surplus money, or money looking for interest-bearing near-money investments.

The momentary significance of the money-to-assets ratio depends, in fact, on whether there are more money-holders looking for assets than asset-holders looking for money. So long as money-holders are actively storing their buying power in near-monies, even a low ratio of money-to-assets may not bring immediate strain. Conversely, if asset-holders are actively dumping assets to raise money, a much higher money-to-assets ratio may still be accompanied by acute strain. Thus the economy's "feeling" of liquidity, and the trend of interest rates, depend not only on the M/A ratio but on whether people are currently moving from money into assets, or vice versa.

Credit and Velocity

What has been said concerning liquidity and near-money suffices to illustrate the two further notions of credit and velocity. Credit, of course, has different meanings, such as being worthy of trust with other people's money or having the ability to obtain a loan when needed. But the tangible evidence of credit is simply a loan of money, so when we speak in this book of "credit outstanding," we mean the volume of loans made and still unrepaid.

Credit arises when someone who has ready purchasing power lends it to a borrower in exchange for an IOU, typically an interest-bearing promise to pay. Over the term of the loan—the time interval in which the credit is outstanding—the borrower uses the money and the lender holds the borrower's promise to pay. Or, if the promise is transferable, he may sell it to some third party and, in effect, get his money back ahead of time, possibly to relend again.

The important points to recognize about credit are the following: (1) Extending credit by a lender involves giving up his purchasing power and accepting a paper promise to pay. (2) A very large part of the economy's claims to wealth are tied up in such promises to pay, or credit instruments. (3) Since credit claims are not spending power, but have to be converted into spending power under various uncertainties, their prices are less certain than, to put it quaintly, the price of cash. (4) The freedom with which credit is granted varies widely, depending on economic conditions, people's confidence in the future and in would-be borrowers, and on the potential lenders' own need for their cash. (5) Finally, the ease or tightness of credit obviously affects the spending ability of all who must borrow in order to spend, and is thus an important force regulating the economy's activity.

The notion of *velocity,* which simply means the turnover rate of money, is also illustrated in the preceding discussion. Suppose the following sequence: McTavish deposits $10,000 in a savings and loan association. The savings and loan lends the $10,000 to Earnest, who is buying a house. Earnest pays the $10,000 to Clawhammer, who built the house. The same $10,000 has turned over three times, twice in credit transactions and once in payment of a debt. As you can see, credit and velocity are often linked. The first two transactions described above led to the creation of credit claims. McTavish got a $10,000 passbook entry to hold (while his money was doing other work), and the savings and loan got a $10,000 mortgage note signed by Earnest. Earnest's payment extinguished another credit claim: his debt to Clawhammer.

As we shall see in the next chapter, rising velocity, which means that the money supply is being worked harder, is a symptom of strain in the credit system. So also, of course, is a rise in interest rates. The two signs normally occur together.

To Remember

Money	Value of money
Real vs. money flows	Near-money
Medium of exchange	Liquidity
Standard of value	Money-to-assets ratio
Store of value	Credit
Standard of deferred payment	Velocity

Questions

1 Could savings and loan deposits serve as money? Discuss.

2 Does more money mean more wealth and higher living standards? Why or why not?

3 Explain money's role as a medium of exchange. What does its function here depend on?

4 What problems arise in connection with money's service as a store of value? Is money the only store of value? Explain.

5 What is the value of money? How is it decided?

6 Is near-money as liquid as money? Explain.

7 What does the liquidity of a savings and loan deposit depend on? What does the liquidity of a Treasury bill depend on?

8 Explain how changes in the money-to-assets ratio produce changes in liquidity.

9 Distinguish between money and credit. Which is there more of in the U.S. economy? Why?

10 Would you expect the velocity of money to rise or fall during a business boom? Why?

3

What Money Does

We have reviewed money's role as a "fluidizer" of economic activity. Goods will not flow in the stream of trade unless money is offered for them, and they will not be manufactured for long either, because businessmen must have money coming in to meet their costs of labor, materials, and capital. Money must also be available to cash people's near-monies and other financial assets, or they can not spend freely. So, though money is not a sufficient condition for a smooth-running economy, it is a necessary condition.

How, in principle, does money function in the economy? In this chapter we shall look at two simple models, or conceptual representations, of how it operates.

The Equation of Exchange

We begin by defining four symbols. Let:

M = money supply,
V = velocity, or the turnover rate of money,
P = the average price level, and
O = the economy's real output of goods and services.

Then we can write the simple equation

$$M V = P O, \tag{Eq. 3-1}$$

to show that money supply times velocity equals output times price level. As you can see, the equation is actually a truism: it simply says that the total outlays spenders make equal total receipts obtained by sellers for their goods and services.

This equation, a modification of Irving Fisher's well-known Equation of Exchange, brings home some basic truths about money and the economy. Let us examine them.

Money's Two Dimensions

How much economic activity money can support depends, as Eq. 3-1 shows, both on how much money there is and on how fast that money turns over. Thus money is sometimes said to have two dimensions: supply and velocity. An old saying (coming, we believe, from sixteenth century England) asserts that "A nimble shilling can do the work of a lazy crown."[1] In other words, a small amount of money turning over rapidly can serve an economy as effectively as a large amount of money turning over sluggishly.

How fast money turns over depends on many factors. Some of them are: (1) the current and prospective level of people's incomes, (2) the strength of their incentives to spend (including willingness to go into debt), (3) the availability of credit, (4) the ease of cashing near-money, and, of course, (5) the existing supply of money (since that will partly determine how hard the money supply needs to be worked). Clearly, much depends on people's optimism about the future and what they expect prices to do: it is wise to try to buy quickly to beat rising prices, and to postpone spending if prices are expected to fall. Institutional arrangements are also important: if well-developed financial markets, trustworthy banks, and highly liquid non-bank financial intermediaries encourage people to lend money with little fear of loss or illiquidity, then velocity will be much higher. Table 3-1 shows how one measure of velocity in the United States has risen since the end of World War II, an interval of remarkable development in our financial institutions.

Velocity can be defined primarily in two ways. If we ask how often a dollar (of demand deposits or currency) turns over physically, we speak of *transactions velocity, V_t.* If we ask how often a dollar turns over in creating income for someone, in generating gross national product, we speak of *income velocity, V_y.* The velocity in Eq. 3-1 is income velocity since the economy's output, O, times its average price level, P, equals its income. Transactions velocity can only be guessed at. Statisticians can measure demand deposit turnover through debits (reductions) to checking accounts, but there is no way to measure currency turnover.

---

[1]The crown, no longer minted or circulating, was a five-shilling piece.

Table 3-1. Income Velocity of Money in the United States 1945–1970, By Five-Year Intervals

Year	Money Supply (billions of $)	National Income (current $)	Income Velocity Y/M
1945	94.1	181.2	1.92
1950	110.2	241.9	2.20
1955	130.6	330.2	2.53
1960	141.0	415.5	2.95
1965	163.4	620.6	3.80
1970	209.4	800.1	3.82

Sources: Derived from various issues of *Federal Reserve Bulletin; Historical Statistics of the United States.*

Which sort of velocity we use depends on our purpose. Ordinarily, transactions velocity is probably a rather steady multiple of income velocity.[2] How many transactions it takes to produce a dollar's worth of income depends on how long a chain of processors and middlemen stands between first producer and final consumer. If twenty stages separate the farmer who raises the calf from the grocer who finally sells the consumer his dollar's worth of hamburger, then it may take $10 to $12 worth of transactions to produce the final $1 of income.

If we are interested in transactions velocity, then we must rewrite Eq. 3–1 to read

$$M V_t = P T,$$ (Eq. 3–1A)

where V_t replaces V, and T (a measure of total transactions) replaces O. For the rest of this book, however, we shall use Eq. 3–1, in which V stands for V_y, income velocity.

Effects of Spending

Although Eq. 3–1 is a truism, it is nevertheless informative. Since each side is broken down into two factors, these can explain how particular changes take place. What, for example, accounts for a rise in spending? Is it an addition to money supply, which monetary authorities can largely control? Or is it a rise in velocity, which is much harder to restrain? What result does the rise in spending produce? Does it increase output, which is good, or the price level, which is ordinarily bad? Eq. 3–1 illustrates the meaning of analysis, or the breaking down of something into its components, for further study.

Let us look at MV, or total spending. We see that a rise in spending can result from various combinations of change in both money supply and velocity. For example, money supply may increase while velocity remains constant. Or, with no increase in M, a step-up in V may still increase total spending. Both M and V can rise, or a fall in V can cancel a rise in M. Eq. 3–1 suggests that money supply managers must take careful note of changes in both M and V

---

[2]This would seem to hold true unless bank debits were swollen by stock-market or other financial speculation, or unless currency payments rose abnormally as a result of income tax evasion, narcotics traffic payments, or other illicit transactions.

if they hope to regulate successfully the public's spending. The goal of monetary management, as we shall see, is to provide just enough spending power to keep the economy fully employed at constant prices. Monetary managers, however, can only regulate, within limits, the supply of money; they have little influence over its velocity. Therefore, they must basically guess the velocity factor, and then provide the money supply they think will permit maximum employment without inflation. Often they are wrong because velocity may temporarily behave unpredictably. In general, velocity has been in a rising trend since the end of World War II. Table 3–1 shows that in 1970 the average dollar turned over (as income to someone) about 3.8 times, compared with 1.9 times in 1945.

What effects will a rise in MV, or total spending, exert? Eq. 3–1 tells us that this must raise either output, O, or price level, P, or both. Traditional theory teaches that the precise effect depends on whether or not the economy is fully employed. That is, if substantial reserves of unemployed labor and excess plant capacity exist, then added spending will theoretically put these unemployed resources to work and add to output (and real income) without much effect on prices. If the labor force and plant are already fully employed, then prices will increase much more than output will. Even before full employment is reached, bottlenecks—shortages of key skills or particular kinds of plant capacity or materials—have often precipitated a price rise. This was particularly noticeable in the 1936–37 business recovery. Similarly, at points in the sixties, probably all productive grades of labor were employed, even though joblessness ran high among the poorly trained or poorly motivated. In both cases, skills in demand were in short supply and provided a bargaining lever for higher wage rates at the same time that less employable categories showed high unemployment.

Different effects theoretically take place if spending falls, as it may when the Federal Reserve inaugurates a tight money policy to halt inflation. Since wages and many prices are difficult to cut,[3] the main impact of a slowdown in spending is typically on O instead of $P;$ output and employment usually fall while prices continue to rise.

Of course, if presidents and monetary authorities had the courage to risk voter disapproval and allowed unemployment to increase for a while, the price rise, according to traditional theory, would ultimately slow down. It would slow down because unemployed workers and plants would keep wages and prices down by competing for scarce jobs and sales. But since 1945, the nation has been increasingly unwilling to endure prolonged spells of unemployment. In that year, Congress passed the Employment Act, making maximum employment, economic growth, and purchasing power national objectives. Maximum employment has been an objective politically more profitable to pursue than purchasing power. Inflation has thus been a chronic worry. Table 3–2 shows the price level's steady rise and the dollar's steady decline in purchasing power since 1945.

---

[3]It has been an economic dogma since the 1950s that wages and most administered prices are *inflexible in a downward direction.* How true this is, is open to debate. That they have shown little downward flexibility since World War II cannot be denied. However, since 1945, no one has seriously expected money supply managers to tighten money to an extent that would force wages and prices down (as tight money usually succeeded in doing in earlier decades). So downward inflexibility may simply reflect a general expectation that the authorities will not put them down, rather than an *inherent* resistance to decline.

Table 3–2. Buying Power of the Dollar, Selected Years, 1939–1971

Year	Consumer Price Index	Dollar's Buying Power in 1939 Cents
1939	100	100
1945	129	78
1950	172	58
1955	194	52
1960	213	47
1965	226	44
1971	291	34

Source: Derived from various issues of *Federal Reserve Bulletin.*

Kinds and Causes of Inflation

If inflation results from too much money chasing too few goods, it is known as *demand-pull inflation.* In effect, prices rise to ration a supply of goods too limited to go on selling at constant prices. In an economy completely free from monopoly powers, or other restraint of trade, demand-pull is the only kind of inflation that would occur. The cure would be simple and straight-forward: a reduced money supply. A reduced money supply would soon curtail spending, a recession and unemployment would develop, and the price rise would taper off and stop. A depressed outlook and dismal expectations would eventually result in a falling off of velocity. Individuals and businesses would hold on to their money to help finance spending during the expected difficult times.

Today, both labor and business monopolies wield great market power. Such power often enables special interests to increase the price of their products or services, even when the money supply is being reduced and when total demand is falling. In this event, the resulting inflation is known as *cost-push inflation.* This can occur, for example, if the products or services in question have no substitutes, or if a labor union is willing to see its junior members lose their jobs provided senior ones can obtain significantly higher wage rates.

From 1969 to 1972, cost-push (particularly *wage*-push) inflation was the chief economic problem for the United States and for the world. Its disruptive consequences will be examined in various passages throughout this book. The problem is especially serious because there is no known cure. Tightening the money supply simply brings on recession and unemployment without slowing the price rise. Much of the impact of tight money falls on unoffending sectors of the economy which are not responsible for the cost-push, while those with the legal and market power to push up prices continue to do so. Wage and price controls have generally proved unworkable except in war-time, when people have strong patriotic and emotional incentives to obey them; otherwise, interests with power to override them do so, either by trading in black markets or by openly flouting the law and daring the politicians to risk their displeasure at the next election.

The root cause of cost-push inflation seems to be political, not economic. One weakness of democracy is that democratic governments, even when they know what would be most beneficial for the country, often fail to act because they are likely to offend powerful political pressure groups. Nowhere in the world, for example, through mid-1972, had elected governments taken a determined stand against the wage-push tactics of politically potent labor unions. Furthermore, the unions do not hesitate to "taking the government on": If prolonged strikes in major industries slow down the economy and raise unemployment, politicians hear about it promptly from the voters. When large wage awards are made, employers then increase prices to compensate—or maybe more than enough to compensate, if they, too, enjoy monopoly powers. Monetary authorities then hasten to increase money supply. To avoid economic slowdown and unemployment, they must increase it enough to maintain the former level of output at the new level of prices—all in accordance with $MV = PO$. In effect, this cycle reduces monetary policy to a rubber-stamping of price decisions made by big labor and big business.

Since insufficient power of government over inflation-causing special interests is the root cause of cost-push inflation, cost-push is unlikely to end until governmental powers are increased sufficiently to control such special interests. This, of course, augurs badly for the future of democratic institutions. We should never forget that democracy and freedom assume restraint in the exercise of power by individuals and special interests for a common good. If lust for gain or other advantage overwhelms such restraint, then society as a whole must protect itself by imposing firmer disciplines. Thus cost-push inflation looms as a major test of democracy's workability in the late twentieth century world.

The Cambridge Equation

If we divide both sides of Eq. 3–1 by V, we get

$$M = \frac{P\,O}{V}.$$

If we define $k = \frac{1}{V}$, the equation then reads

$$M = k\,P\,O. \qquad \text{(Eq. 3–2)}$$

This is known as the Cambridge Equation because it was developed by economists at Cambridge University in England. Alternatively, it is called the Cash Balances Equation. Although based on the same identities as the Equation of Exchange, the Cambridge Equation advances our knowledge of monetary behavior by emphasizing what is called, rather paradoxically, people's demand for money. The paradox dissolves if we understand that this demand is for money *to hold*, and not to spend.

The significance of k

Since PO is the national income, k tells what fraction of national income M, the money supply, represents. This focuses our attention on a pivotal consideration: how large is money supply in relation to people's incomes? Or, in different terms, how big are people's cash balances in relation to their incomes?

Let us begin by observing that at any given moment someone must hold each dollar in existence. The total of all such money ownership equals people's total money balances, and the sum of individual balances equals total money supply. But why do people hold money? Why not near-money or goods? Given any actual or expected price level, the demand for money to hold is limited by an individual's choice between holding money and holding other kinds of assets—many of which pay interest (for example, debt securities and savings deposits) or may go up in price (for example, stock and real estate). Therefore, after a certain point, people do prefer to hold near-money or goods, but up to a certain point they feel more comfortable holding money. The reasons why they want to hold a certain amount of money constitute what economists call their demand for money. This demand is very closely linked to k in the Cambridge Equation.

Cash-Holding Motives

The English economist John Maynard Keynes described three reasons why people want to hold cash.

1. *Transactions motive.* To keep enough cash on hand to bridge the intervals between expected payments and anticipated receipts of cash. For example, you are paid $200 every two weeks and, let us suppose, must spend all you make. Then you must stretch each $200 paycheck to last for two weeks. If you begin each bi-weekly period with $200 and end up with nothing, your average cash balance will be very close to $100. This is your *transactions balance.*

2. *Precautionary motive.* To keep money on hand for emergencies, and to prevent a linkage of disasters. Failure to meet an unanticipated expense, no matter how small, causes creditors to lose confidence in your ability to pay. Their pressing for immediate payment may force you into bankruptcy. You may have $200 in reserve to cover doctor bills, car repairs, traffic fines, and so on. This is your *precautionary balance.*

3. *Speculative motive.* To keep cash on hand to take advantage of opportunities. You are still holding in cash the $5,000 you inherited last year from your late Aunt Minerva because you have your eye on two choice city lots which you expect to fall in price during the next several months. This is your *speculative balance.*

All businesses and individuals maintain total cash positions that are really a sum of these three basic motives. The sum of each person's transactions, precautionary, and speculative demands for cash constitutes his total demand for money.

k_a vs. k_d

The significance of k in people's monetary behavior now becomes apparent. If we add together everyone's demand for money, we get $k_d(PO)$. k_d then stands for that fraction of people's total income which they desire to hold in money (currency and demand deposits). But this desired fraction may differ from the actual fraction, which we can designate k_a. If so, then we can expect people to alter their spending behavior in order to align k_a with k_d—that is, to adjust their actual cash holdings to the level desired.

Suppose, for example, that people in general find their actual money balances larger than they think they need. Then they feel "flush" and are willing to spend their surplus money. Total spending then rises. If, however, their actual balances are less than desired, they reduce their spending in order to rebuild their cash holdings. Because it focuses attention on these motives for spending or not spending, the Cash Balances Equation is probably more useful than the Equation of Exchange as a device for explaining monetary behavior and policy.

How Monetary Policy Works

Monetary policy works essentially by making people feel richer or poorer. By changing money supply, it alters people's margin of *spendable funds.* Actually, as we shall see later, monetary policy works mostly through the banks and affects spending by changing the margin of *borrowable funds.* But since a great deal of important spending relies on borrowed money—notably, spending on consumer durables, housing, industrial and commercial construction, and factory plant and equipment—the supply of bank loans strongly influences the economy's final demand for goods and services. People's comparison of their actual with their desired money balances provides the psychological leverage by which changes in spending behavior are induced by money supply changes.

As elementary models, Eq. 3-1 and Eq. 3-2 give a very approximate first idea of how changes in money supply and velocity affect economic behavior. Let us now look at two slightly more complicated models that introduce additional variables into our picture of monetary change.

Income and Asset Circulations

We have seen that not all the economy's money is used to turn over its output of goods and services. People's willingness to store their wealth in near-monies and other financial assets depends on their ability to cash these assets at need. But such assets can be kept liquid only if money is waiting to be exchanged for them. Actually, such money *is* waiting to be exchanged for these assets, at the right price or interest yield: it is stored in people's speculative balances. For these reasons, it is helpful to visualize the total money supply as consisting of two parts: an *income circulation,* devoted to turning over the current output of goods and services and to paying people their money incomes; and an *asset circulation,* devoted to turning over society's supply of existing assets, including financial ones, and keeping them liquid.[4]

Expanded Equations

The above paragraph suggests certain expansions of Eq. 3-1 and Eq. 3-2 that may prove illuminating. For instance, we can rewrite the Cambridge Equation to get

$$M = M_Y + M_A = k_Y P_Y O + k_A P_A A. \tag{Eq. 3-3}$$

[4] This section has been adapted from one of the best—and today, unfortunately, least read—works on finance: John Maynard Keynes, *A Treatise on Money,* 2 vols. (London: MacMillan and Company, Ltd., 1930). See particularly, vol. 1, chapter 15. What Keynes terms the "industrial circulation" we have renamed income circulation. His "financial circulation" is our asset circulation. We believe the new names will be more readily understood by the present generation of students.

in which symbols have the following meanings:

M = total money supply,

M_Y = money tied up in the income circulation,

M_A = money tied up in the asset circulation,

k_Y = M_Y as a proportion of the national income, actually $k_Y = M_Y/PO$,

P_Y = average price level of final goods and services,

O = final output,

k_A = M_A as a proportion of the total value of the economy's financial claims (or investments),

P_A = average price of these claims (bonds, stocks, bills, notes payable, and so forth), and

A = total number of such claims.

We also can rewrite the Equation of Exchange in corresponding fashion to get

$$MV = M_YV_Y + M_AV_A = P_YO + P_AA, \qquad \text{(Eq. 3-4)}$$

wherein most terms are defined as in Eq. 3-3, and, in addition,

V_Y = velocity of the income circulation (income velocity), and

V_A = velocity of the asset circulation.

It also should be evident that

$$M_YV_Y = P_YO,$$

and

$$M_AV_A = P_AA.$$

Money's Twofold Thrust

Eq. 3-1 and Eq. 3-2 illustrate only money's role as a medium of exchange. With Eq. 3-3 and Eq. 3-4, we incorporate money's additional role as a liquidity reserve against the assets in which people store their spendable wealth. The expanded equations therefore offer us a more complete explanation of what happens when money supply eases or tightens. They introduce us formally to money's effects on the prices and yields of financial assets and to the repercussions this has on people's willingness and ability to spend.

Suppose, for example, that money supply falls. People's actual cash balances, on the average, decline below their desired balances, or $k_a < k_d$. What happens? Individuals and businesses first move to cash the near-monies and other financial assets in which their reserve purchasing power is stored. They draw down their savings accounts, cash E-bonds, and sell their stocks. Banks and other financial institutions sell bonds and other investments both to meet cash withdrawals and to raise cash for loans, which now are in avid demand. Broadly, people try to draw down money from the asset circulation to meet the needs of the income circulation.

A Limited Money Supply

There is, however, only so much money available, regardless of how it is shifted around. The liquidity needs of the asset circulation still have to be met: savings institutions still have to attract cash to pay for withdrawals; the Treasury must still raise cash to pay off maturing Treasury bills; and corporations must raise it to pay off obligations falling due. To protect the asset circulation from encroachments of the income circulation, interest rates may rise sharply. Savings institutions raise the rates they pay depositors; the treasury pays higher rates on bills; and corporations pay higher rates on bonds. As more cash-desperate holders dump bills and paper, their prices fall and yields rise.[5]

Eq. 3–3 and Eq. 3–4 show us schematically the anatomy of financial strain. In Eq. 3–3, when M falls uncomfortably low, two things happen. First, the actual level of k_Y drops below its desired level. This puts pressure on O and P_Y. It also spurs people to pull money out of M_A. But if k_A and A stay the same, P_A—the price of financial assets—will fall as money leaves the asset circulation. This means that interest rates and yields on securities rise. Eq. 3–4 shows that when M_Y is squeezed and people are trying to shift money out of M_A, both V_Y and V_A will rise. However, if the squeeze is severe, they are unlikely to rise enough to offset the overall contraction in M, so something else has to give. Ordinarily, this will be O and P_A. This is why the start of a recession is often accompanied not only by a topping out of industrial production but also by a stock market break and credit crunch.

Figure 3–1 illustrates a link between k_a, k_d, money supply *(Ms)*, and total spending, or gross national product (GNP). Slopes of k_a and k_d are positive, reflecting transactions demand for money. M_s reflects the money supply at a given point in time. Suppose individuals think that asset prices will be lower in the near future. There will be an increase in the speculative demand for money: desired money balances will exceed actual balances, or $k_d > k_a$. To build up money balances and avoid the anticipated losses from holding assets while their prices fall, individuals and businesses cash existing near-monies, putting downward pressure on their prices. Resulting high interest rates cause businessmen to cut back investments—a process we examine in chapters 6, 20, and 27—causing GNP to fall from A to B. Individuals reduce their spending on consumer durables and luxuries in general, further contributing to the decline in GNP.

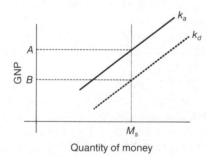

Quantity of money   **Figure 3–1.**

A Surplus of Money

The whole drama is reversed when a surplus of money develops, when $k_a > k_d$. Here, again, the effect is typically divided between the income and asset circulations. As we shall see in subsequent chapters, most new money is created in the banking system and finds its way into circulation by way of bank loans or investments. The part of the additional money that the banks lend to spenders

[5]Since yield is essentially a ratio of interest to price, yield will rise if price falls. One dollar in interest is 5 per cent on a price of $20, but 10 per cent on a price of $10.

goes into M_Y; what they invest by buying bonds and bills goes into M_A. New money going into M_Y acts to increase O, P, or both. Money flowing into M_A works to increase P_A, and so to drive down interest rates.

To Remember

Equation of exchange   Cost-push inflation
Money's two dimensions   Cambridge equation
Income velocity   Cash-holding motives
Demand-pull inflation

Questions

1   Distinguish between the income velocity and the transactions velocity of money. Explain which is higher and why.

2   Using the Equation of Exchange, demonstrate how it might be possible for an inflationary boom to continue even though the central bank was reducing the money supply.

3   Will increased money supply result in increased output or higher prices? Discuss this question with reference to the Equation of Exchange.

4   If the income velocity of money is in a rising trend, should the money supply be increased more rapidly or more slowly than otherwise? Why?

5   Can cost-push inflation continue if the money supply is not expanded? Discuss.

6   Explain, by referring to the Cambridge Equation, how monetary policy works.

7   Discuss the significance of k in the Cambridge Equation.

8   Discuss how the three cash-holding motives might guide the owner of a small business in deciding how much cash to keep in his company's bank account.

9   Distinguish between the income and asset circulations of money. To which circulation would the payment for a second-hand house belong? Why?

10 Explain, through the relation between the income and asset circulations of money, why interest rates on debt securities rise when money becomes tight and difficult to borrow.

4

How Money Is Created

Two statements describe the creation of modern (noncommodity) money. They are:

1. Money originates in a *monetization of debt.* To monetize means "to make money out of."

2. Money originates in a *substitution of promises.* Most money today is the promise of a *bank* to pay. What, precisely, will be paid is rather vague, but this does not seem to affect money's acceptability.

High- and Low-Powered Money

Most U.S. money is a liability of the nation's banks. The bulk of our currency is a liability of the Federal Reserve Banks, our central banking system. Federal Reserve notes of one, two, five, ten, twenty, and higher dollar denominations are issued by the twelve regional banks of the Federal Reserve System. The notes declare on their face that they are "legal tender for all debts public and private," and on their back, "In God we trust." Quite clearly we can only trust God if we do not trust the Federal Reserve, because these notes are not redeemable in any better kind of money and are backed only by U.S. government bonds in the Federal Reserve Banks' vaults.[1]

Demand deposits (which, as "checkbook" money, are the real workhorse of the U.S. money system) are liabilities of the nation's commercial banks. However, the commercial banks' ability to create these liabilities is limited to a certain multiple of *their* deposits in the Federal Reserve Banks. These deposits, called member bank reserves, are—like currency—a liability of the Federal Reserve System. In fact, currency and member bank reserves are exchangeable on a dollar-for-dollar basis by the commercial banks at their district Federal Reserve Banks. When the member banks need more till money, or vault cash, they simply draw on their reserve account at their Federal Reserve Bank, which sends them the currency and reduces their reserve account by the number of dollars shipped.

Thus the volume of Federal Reserve liabilities regulates the size of the nation's money supply. A dollar's worth of Federal Reserve liabilities may take the form of either (1) $1 worth of currency in circulation, or (2) $1 worth of member bank reserves. And because each dollar's worth of member bank reserves can back up approximately $7 worth of deposit money (as you will soon see), these reserves and the currency which is exchangeable for them are often referred to as *high-powered money*. Demand deposits, by contrast, are *low-powered money*.

How the Federal Reserve Creates High-Powered Money

Since both components of high-powered money, currency and member bank reserves, are Federal Reserve liabilities, they must originate in transactions that produce Federal Reserve assets. Look at Table 4–1, a simplified consolidated balance sheet of the Federal Reserve System. Notice particularly two items listed under assets: government securities and discounts. When the Federal Reserve buys U.S. government securities or discounts eligible paper (bank loans to quality customers to finance production and distribution of merchandise), it acquires an asset. Offsetting this asset will be a liability. If the Federal Reserve discounts Treasury bills for a member bank, it will directly credit the member bank's reserve account. If the Federal Reserve buys a government security from an individual, it pays with a check. The seller deposits the check in his commercial bank, receiving a deposit credit to his account or, perhaps, currency. The commercial bank then sends the check to the Federal Reserve receiving either credit to *its* reserve account, or currency.

That is the core of the creation of high-powered money. The Reserve Banks monetize debt when they buy securities to hold as assets and then pay for these assets with liabilities of their own creation, which serve the nation as money. In

---

[1]As of mid-1971, the total U.S. money supply included only about $7.4 billion in Treasury currency and coin. Against this, bank-liability money comprised $54.5 billion in Federal Reserve notes and $175 billion in demand deposits.

Table 4-1. Consolidated Balance Sheet of the Federal Reserve System (simplified),[1] October 27, 1971

Item	Billions of Dollars
Assets	
U.S. Government Securities	67.8
Gold	9.9
Discounts and Advances	2.0
Other Assets[2]	13.3
Total Assets	93.0
Liabilities	
Federal Reserve Notes Outstanding	52.4
Member Bank Reserves	27.2
Other Liabilities[2]	11.7
Total Liabilities 91.3	
Capital	1.7
Total Liabilities and Capital	93.0

[1]More detailed presentations of these and related data are given in Table 9-1.

[2]Other assets and liabilities consist mostly of debits and credits arising out of check clearings between Federal Reserve banks in different districts. The process, not important to understanding money supply, is explained under "Float" in chapter 9.

Source: *Federal Reserve Bulletin*, January 1972.

effect, the Reserve Banks merely substitute their credit (a Federal Reserve IOU) for the Treasury's credit (a Treasury IOU).

T-accounts, or miniature balance sheets, illustrate how various Federal Reserve transactions affect the nation's supply of high-powered money, or currency and member bank reserves. Bookkeeping entries at commercial banks and the Federal Reserve accomplish the credit monetization process. For example:

(a) The Federal Reserve Buys $500 MM in U.S. Government Securities

+ U.S. Government Securities $500 MM	+ Member Bank Reserves $500 MM

(b) The Member Banks Withdraw $200 MM in Currency to Meet the Public's Demand for Hand-to-Hand Money

	− Member Bank Reserves $200 MM
	+ Currency in Circulation $200 MM

(c) The U.S. Sells $50 MM in Gold to France but the Federal Reserve Simultaneously Buys $50 MM in Government Securities

− Gold Certificate Reserve $50 MM	Member Bank Reserves (no change)
+ U.S. Government Securities $50 MM	

Multiple Deposit Expansion

We have said that each dollar of member bank reserves can support approximately $7 of demand deposits, or low-powered money. It is now time to explain why this is so.

The U.S. commercial banking system—and, indeed, every banking system in the world—is a *fractional reserve* banking system. This means both the legal reserves (in the form of member bank reserves) which commercial banks are required to keep and vault cash backing their deposit liabilities are only a fraction of those liabilities. In 1972, the Federal Reserve required all member banks to maintain a reserve ratio that increased from 8 per cent on the first $2 million of demand deposits to 17.5 per cent on those above $400 million. Overall, required reserves averaged about 12 per cent of the banks' demand deposits.

How High-Powered Money Expands: An Example

Let us assume that the Federal Reserve buys a $1,000 Treasury bond from an individual. The Federal Reserve takes the bond and gives the seller a check for $1,000 drawn on itself. The Federal Reserve's accounts read:

Assets		*Liabilities*	
Government securities	$1,000	Checks payable	$1,000

The seller of the bond deposits his check in a commercial bank, Bank Number One, and receives credit in his demand deposit account. The account of Bank Number One reads:

Assets		*Liabilities*	
Due from Federal Reserve	$1,000	Demand deposits	$1,000

Bank Number One now sends the check to the Federal Reserve Bank, which cancels the check and credits Bank Number One's reserve account $1,000. The Federal Reserve's accounts now read:

Assets		*Liabilities*	
Government securities	$1,000	Member bank reserves	$1,000

The accounts of Bank Number One now read:

Assets		*Liabilities*	
Reserves with Federal Reserve	$1,000	Demand deposits	$1,000

Let us now examine the reserve position of Bank Number One. To legally back its $1,000 of demand deposits, it needs reserves of $142.86, or one-seventh of $1,000. The other $857.14 of its $1,000 reserve credit comprises excess, or non-required, reserves. The bank is free to lend or invest these excess reserves for profit, and it *will* lend or invest them, given suitable opportunities, since banks are profit-motivated institutions.

Assume that Bank Number One lends the entire $857.14 to Needy. In so doing it has acquired an asset, Needy's note (IOU) for $857.14. It also has created a new liability, the demand deposit of $857.14 in Needy's checking account. Recall the two statements about money creation at the opening of this chapter. Low-powered money has just originated here in a monetization of debt; the bank has made demand deposit money out of Needy's credit, his personal note. Also, the new money has originated in a substitution of promises. The bank has substituted its promise, a demand deposit, for Needy's promise, his IOU.[2] This transaction illustrates the basic nature of the banking process: the bank creates and issues claims against itself (a demand deposit in this case) and uses this claim to acquire and hold income-producing assets (in this case Needy's IOU, which will produce interest-income for the bank).

You may wonder why, with only a one-seventh reserve requirement, the bank does not lend seven times its $857.14 in excess reserves. But the bank cannot prudently lend more than its excess reserves because borrowers typically use their loans to pay debts. When a borrower writes his check, chances are that the payee will deposit the check in a different bank than the one on which the check is written. In this event, Bank Number One will lose its $857.14 reserve to the other bank when the check is cleared through the Federal Reserve. Therefore, an individual bank cannot lend more than its excess reserves—or invest more either, since the seller of the investment will probably use a different bank as well.

At the moment Bank Number One makes its loan, its accounts will look like this:

Assets		Liabilities	
Reserves with		Demand deposits	$1,857.14
Federal Reserve	$1,000.00		
Loans outstanding	857.14		
Total	$1,857.14		

Now suppose Needy writes a check for $857.14 to his creditor, Dunmore, who banks with Bank Number Two. Dunmore endorses Needy's check and deposits it in Bank Number Two, which increases Dunmore's account for $857.14 and forwards Needy's check on Bank Number One to the Federal Reserve. The Federal Reserve shifts $857.14 from Bank Number One's reserve account to the reserve account of Bank Number Two. It then sends Needy's check back to Bank Number One, which reduces Needy's deposit account for the $857.14 and also subtracts from its reserve account the $857.14 it has just lost to Bank Number Two. At this point, Bank Number One's accounts will read:

Assets		Liabilities	
Reserves with		Demand deposits	$1,000.00
Federal Reserve	$142.86		
Loans outstanding	857.14		
Total	$1,000.00		

---

[2]The bank, a recognized and widely trusted public institution, has substituted its promise (demand deposit) for the promise (personal IOU) of the less widely trusted individual, Needy. In the same way, the Federal Reserve converts government securities (large-denomination, interest-bearing promises of the Treasury) into currency in convenient denominations or into book entries that serve as backing for member-bank deposit money.

Bank Number Two's accounts will show:

Assets		Liabilities	
Reserves with		Demand deposits	$857.14
Federal Reserve	$857.14		

With deposits of $857.14, Bank Number Two will have required reserves of $122.45 and excess reserves of $734.69. The latter it is free to lend or invest.

This is the process that repeats itself as member bank lending (and investing), followed by check clearings, moves a gradually diminishing body of excess reserves through a large number of banks, creating demand deposits in its wake. Table 4–2 traces this process through the first seventeen banks. You will note the regularity with which the figures in most of the columns change. Note also that, for each bank in the series, excess reserves, loans or investments made, and additional deposits created are always the same. Note that the cumulative total (for all banks) of loans and investments is always less, by the original $1,000 of new money, than the total of deposits. Finally, notice in the last column that each additional bank in the series absorbs another chunk of the original $1,000 of new reserves, leaving a continually smaller volume of excess reserves still circulating to create new deposit money.

The Limits of Expansion

The bottom line of Table 4–2 shows the limits toward which the multiple expansion of deposits works. As the first four columns indicate, after migrating through a very large number of banks, the steadily dwindling excess reserves fall to zero so that no new loans or investments can be made, nor deposits created. At that point, however, the last three columns would approach arithmetically predictable limits: (1) Total reserves required by the expansion of demand deposits would approach $1,000—that is, all reserves would finally be absorbed by the multiplication of checkbook money. (2) Total deposits supported by the reserves would approach $7,000. (3) Total loans and investments growing out of the multiple deposit expansion process would approach $6,000.

The Formulae of Monetary Expansion

We are now equipped to formulate some basic relations among money-supply variables. We begin by defining the following symbols:

M = total money supply,
C = the supply of currency,
D = the supply of demand deposits,
R = the supply of member bank reserves (actually Federal Reserve credit, which is capable of adding to *either* member bank reserves *or* currency), and
r = the ratio of required reserves to demand deposits (reserve requirements, or the reserve fraction).

Let us now calculate the limits of money-supply expansion for any given volume of reserve funds, R, assuming a reserve ratio equal to r. Since total money supply is the sum of currency plus demand deposits, we have

$$M = C + D. \qquad\qquad \text{(Eq. 5–1)}$$

Table 4-2. Multiple Deposit Expansion (assuming a 1/7—14.286 per cent—reserve requirement)

Bank No.	This Bank					All Banks		
	Deposit Recd.	Reserve Required	Excess Reserves	Loans or Investments Made	Additional Deposits Created	Total Deposits	Total Loans and Investments	Total Reserves Absorbed
1	$1,000.00	$142.86	$857.14	$857.14	$857.15	$1,857.14	$ 857.14	$265.31
2	857.14	122.45	734.69	734.69	734.69	2,591.83	1,591.83	370.27
3	734.69	104.96	629.73	629.73	629.73	3,221.56	2,221.56	460.23
4	629.73	89.96	539.77	539.77	539.77	3,761.33	2,761.22	537.34
5	539.77	77.11	462.66	462.66	462.66	4,223.99	3,223.99	603.44
6	462.66	66.10	396.56	396.56	396.56	4,620.55	3,620.55	660.09
7	396.56	56.65	339.91	339.91	339.91	4,960.46	3,960.46	708.65
8	339.91	48.56	291.35	291.35	291.35	5,251.81	4,251.81	750.27
9	291.35	41.62	249.73	249.73	249.73	5,501.54	4,501.54	785.95
10	249.73	35.68	214.05	214.05	214.05	5,715.59	4,715.59	816.53
11	214.05	30.58	183.47	183.47	183.47	5,899.06	4,899.06	842.74
12	183.47	26.21	157.26	157.26	157.26	6,056.32	5,056.32	865.21
13	157.26	22.47	134.79	134.79	134.79	6,191.11	5,191.11	884.48
14	134.79	19.27	115.52	115.52	115.52	6,306.63	5,306.63	900.98
15	115.52	16.50	99.02	99.02	99.02	6,405.65	5,405.65	915.12
16	99.02	14.14	84.88	84.88	84.88	6,490.53	5,490.53	927.24
17	84.88	12.12	72.76	72.76	72.76	6,563.29	5,563.29	937.61
Limit	0.00	0.00	0.00	0.00	0.00	7,000.00	6,000.00	1,000.00

What volume of money will reserves equal to R create? First, since currency absorbs reserve funds on a dollar-for-dollar basis, the volume of reserve funds available to create demand deposits will be equal, not to R, but to $R - C$. If multiple deposit expansion based on these funds is carried to the limit, then the volume of demand deposits will be

$$D = \frac{R - C}{r},$$ (Eq. 5–2)

and substituting this value for D into Eq. 5–1, we have, finally

$$M = C + \frac{R - C}{r}.$$ (Eq. 5–3)

An Example

Assume now that the reserve fraction is 14 per cent. The Federal Reserve buys $1,000,000 in Treasury securities. Simultaneously, the public's demand for currency rises by $300,000. By how much can total money supply expand? Eq. 5–3 makes the calculation easy. Since we are calculating additions to money supply, we preface the numerator symbols in Eq. 5–3 with Δ, meaning "change in." We write

$$\Delta M = \Delta C + \frac{\Delta R - \Delta C}{r}.$$

Substituting, we obtain

$$\Delta M = \$300,000 + \frac{\$1,000,000 - \$300,000}{.14},$$

$$= \$300,000 + \frac{\$700,000}{.14},$$

$$= \$5,300,000.$$

As you can see, the public's decision to convert some of the newly added reserve funds into currency constitutes a "leakage" from the multiple expansion process. If there had been no rise in the demand for currency in the above example, the entire expansion could have occurred in checkbook money, and the money supply could have risen by $1,000,000/.14, or $7,142,857.

Time and Savings Deposits

Commercial banks also receive time and savings deposits, which we encountered in the discussion of near-money in chapter 2. Time deposits are usually represented by certificates of deposit (CDs), which are not withdrawable until a definite date but are negotiable, or saleable to another party, when issued in denominations of $100,000 or more. Savings deposits are the familiar passbook accounts, paying interest at fixed dates.

Time and savings deposits are subject to much lower reserve requirements than demand deposits: typically, 3 to 6 per cent. Consequently, when people shift their funds from demand to time or savings deposits, the banks gain lending power. Suppose the Last National's reserve requirements are 17 per cent for demand and 5 per cent for savings deposits. If Moe writes a $1,000 check for deposit in his savings account, the bank at once increases its lending power by $120, which is the difference between the $170 reserve required against Moe's demand deposit and the $50 reserve needed against his savings deposit.

A large flow of checkbook money into savings accounts and CDs expands the banks' ability to make new loans and investments. The gain in lending power may be large enough to offset the additional interest cost the banks incur (since they must pay interest on time and savings deposits). Conversely, a shift of depositor claims out of time and savings deposits back into demand deposits reduces bank lending power by increasing the percentage of reserves that must be held against total deposits. An example will show how shifts in savings and checking deposits affect bank lending powers.

Suppose that the Last National Bank has $1,000,000 in savings deposits and $1,000,000 in checking deposits. With 5 and 17 per cent reserve requirements, respectively, the bank's reserve needs would be $50,000 plus $170,000, or $220,000 in total—an effective overall reserve fraction of 11 per cent. The bank could maintain a theoretical maximum of $1,780,000 in loans and investments, the amount of its excess reserves. If its savings deposits shifted to demand deposits, reserve requirements would rise to $340,000, or 17 per cent. Then the maximum of loans and investments for the bank would fall to $2,000,000 minus $340,000, or $1,660,000. For the banking system, if all banks were at the limit of their reserve ratios with no excess reserves, a shift by the public from savings to demand deposits would force a multiple contraction of loans and investments throughout the banking system. Using the same figures as those for Last National Bank, the theoretical maximum of loans and investments would fall from $1,780,000/.20 to $1,660,000/.20, or by $600,000.

Factors Affecting Money Supply: Reserve Position of the Banks

The bulk of the country's working money supply consists of demand deposits. However, as we have seen, demand deposits can only be erected on a base of reserve funds supplied to commercial banks by the Federal Reserve. Thus the reserve position of commercial banks is the pivot of monetary system.[3]

Measuring Ease or Tightness

The principal measure of ease or tightness in the monetary system is the member banks' standing with respect to the reserves legally required for the volume of demand deposits they are carrying. If a bank's total reserves exceed its required reserves, it has excess reserves and is then in a position to make additional loans

---

[3]Fewer than half of all U.S. banks belong to the Federal Reserve System, but member banks hold the great bulk of bank resources and deposits. Non-member banks' reserve requirements are imposed by state regulatory authorities. Such banks are required to hold either currency, highly liquid investments, or deposits in approved other banks. The ease or tightness in the money-creating abilities of member banks is readily passed along to the non-member banks: non-member banks find they cannot borrow as readily from member banks; they are asked to increase their deposits at member banks which act as approved holders of non-member bank reserves; their liquidity is reduced by the fall in prices of securities as member banks "dump" investments to raise reserve funds. Thus pressure is transmitted throughout the banking system.

or investments. If its total reserves fall short of required reserves, it has a reserve deficiency and is obliged to curtail its credit-granting activities, sell investments, and refuse to make new loans or to renew old ones.

Seldom will member banks collectively have a reserve deficiency. Some banks will have excess reserves because they have not lent or invested to the limit. Their excess reserves may be borrowed by reserve-deficient banks through the *federal funds market,* in which excess reserves are lent daily at interest among the nation's banks. Other banks may cover reserve deficiencies by borrowing at the Federal Reserve discount window, as you will see a few paragraphs on.

If reserve deficiency is a widespread phenomenon among individual banks, the resulting pressure on reserves may produce multiple deposit contraction as banks collectively reduce their loans and investments. That is, if banks generally are short of reserves, and are reluctant to borrow on discounts at the Federal Reserve, they usually try to obtain reserves by liquidating investments, particularly Treasury securities and municipal bonds. The purchaser of these securities writes a check which, in clearing, gives the seller bank additional reserves equal to the price of the securities sold. However, the purchaser's bank loses reserves in the same amount. Thus the pressure of reserve shortage fans out in the banking system.

This pressure in the system will not subside until the banks as a group reduce their loans and investments by a multiple of the reserve deficiency. Suppose, for example, that a certain group of banks has a reserve deficiency of $100 million. If the average reserve requirement of these banks is one-seventh of their deposits, they will remain "under pressure" (in other words, dependent on federal funds purchases or on discounts from the Federal Reserve) until their loans and investments fall by $700 million. Thus ease or tightness in the credit situation—and in interest rate levels—is closely linked to the reserve position of the commercial banks.

Free Reserves

For the banking system as a whole, the most significant indicator of bank credit availability is the *free-reserve position* of the member banks. Free reserves are the difference between excess reserves and borrowed reserves in the banking system. If excess reserves exceed borrowed reserves, the member banks have *net free reserves.* If borrowed reserves exceed excess reserves, the banks have *net borrowed reserves.*

As indicated above, member banks collectively usually have excess reserves. Otherwise, they would be violating reserve requirements. However, it makes a difference whether excess reserves are owned or borrowed. To see why, let us consider the significance of an item we have already noticed in the Federal Reserve System balance sheet (Table 4–1): discounts and advances.

Discounts and Advances

One of the facilities the Federal Reserve offers its member banks is the privilege of obtaining temporary additional reserves to tide them over an interval of reserve deficiency. The vehicle for providing these temporary reserves is a discount or advance by a Reserve Bank to its member bank.[4]

Suppose, for example, that the Last National Bank of Muleshoe has a 12½ per cent reserve requirement, $9,000,000 in demand deposits, and only $1,000,000 in its reserve account at the Federal Reserve. Actual reserves fall $125,000 short of the $1,125,000 ($9,000,000 times .125) reserve requirement. The Last National management, however, has reason to believe the reserve deficiency is only temporary, i.e., that in the next few days the bank will gain enough reserves from other banks (through new deposits and check clearings) to restore balance between the bank's owned reserves and its deposits. Therefore, the bank takes government securities or other eligible paper to the Federal Reserve and pledges them as security for a short-term loan of reserves. Depending on the arrangement, this temporary accommodation is called either a discount or an advance, but for our purpose the distinction is not important. What *is* important is the fact that such borrowed reserves are only an emergency accommodation. Federal Reserve regulations prohibit banks from relying for prolonged intervals on reserves borrowed at the discount window.

Banks' Free Reserve Position

We are now prepared to see why the free reserve position of the member banks is such an important indicator of ease or tightness in the monetary system. Net borrowed reserves leave the member banks in an uncomfortable position; they prefer using new reserves to pay their way out of debt to the Federal Reserve rather than making new loans or investments. By contrast, net free reserves indicate unencumbered lending and investing power in the banks. For these reasons, the free reserve position of the member banks is perhaps the most closely watched of all Federal Reserve System statistics.

The Bank Reserve Equation

How reserve funds are supplied to, and absorbed by, the monetary system is explained by the Bank Reserve Equation. As you will easily see, this equation is actually just a special-purpose rearrangement of the Federal Reserve System balance sheet. It runs:

Sources of reserve funds (gold, government securities held by Federal Reserve Banks, discounts and other loans by the Federal Reserve to member banks, plus Treasury currency)

minus   Factors absorbing reserve funds (chiefly, currency in circulation)
give   Total member bank reserves
less   Required reserves
give   Excess reserves
less   Borrowed reserves
give   Net free (or net borrowed) reserves.

---

[4]The Federal Reserve may refuse discounts to a member bank that abuses the privilege. Funds obtained through discounts are not supposed to be relent or invested for profit at a higher rate than the discount rate of interest which the Federal Reserve charges the borrowing member bank.

Role of Gold

Along with government securities, the Federal Reserve's gold certificate reserve is a major factor in supplying member banks with reserve funds. The certificates are mostly warehouse receipts for gold stored in Fort Knox and elsewhere by the U.S. government. Unlike government securities, however, gold is not a controllable item among factors supplying member bank reserve funds. Additions to and subtractions from the Federal Reserve's gold certificate reserve depend largely on Treasury purchases of newly-mined gold and on the nation's gain or loss of gold in settling its international claims with foreign countries.

Gold no longer plays any role whatever either in making up or backing the domestic money supply. Gold backing requirements for member bank reserve deposits were eliminated by Congress in 1964 and for Federal Reserve currency in 1967. The purpose of gold reserve requirements for member bank reserves and currency was to limit their expansion and so to prevent price inflation. However when this restraint collided with the federal government's desire to print more money—even if it did lead to inflation—the restriction was removed.

Gold today plays a single but vital part in the nation's monetary system. Since only gold has unquestionable, ultimate acceptability in international payments, the U.S. gold stock represents the final reserve buying power of the American nation.

Chapter 11 deals with the nation's balance of international payments. It will suffice here to note that when more dollars are sent abroad by Americans doing business there than are returned to the United States by foreigners doing business here, an excess of dollars winds up in foreign hands. These "refugee" dollars may move into the possession of foreign governments and central banks. Until mid-August 1971, foreign authorities could lawfully demand gold for these dollars at a rate of $35 per ounce.

After 1950, and particularly after 1957, more than half the gold owned by the United States at the end of World War II flowed abroad as foreign authorities cashed in dollars for gold. As gold flowed out, the Federal Reserve's gold certificate reserve declined. How did the Federal Reserve replace the lost gold? It did so by buying more government securities. This prevented gold losses from reducing member bank reserves (or currency) and forcing a multiple contraction of the nation's money supply. T-account (c) on page 36 shows you how.

Although replaceable on the Federal Reserve's books, the gold loss threatened national security. Many materials vital to the country's defense must be imported from overseas. Only the possession of enough gold—the unquestioned international buying power—guarantees access to these strategic resources. So when the U.S. gold reserve fell below $10 billion, in 1971, President Nixon suspended the right of foreign official holders to exchange their dollars for gold.

Summary

We have seen that the Federal Reserve Banks create high-powered money, reserves and currency, by expanding their assets. Some of these assets, such as government securities and discounts, are controllable; the other asset, gold, is not. Commercial banks use reserves, one component of high-powered money, as a base on which to erect a superstructure of low-powered money, demand deposits. Although a single bank will lend or invest an amount equal to only its excess reserves, the total banking system makes loans and investments equal to a multiple of excess reserves.

If commercial banks have a reserve deficiency, they will borrow from the Federal Reserve Banks by discounting government securities or eligible paper. Alternatively, reserve-deficient member banks will borrow excess reserves in the federal funds market. Excess reserves less borrowings and discounts give net free (or borrowed) reserves, the most significant indicator of the banking system's ability to lend and invest.

The financial system's shortage of liquidity, and the resulting scramble for funds, cause interest rates to rise. We can now turn our attention to interest rate calculations and theory.

To Remember

High- and low-powered money   Demand deposits
Multiple deposit expansion   Time deposits
Reserve ratio   Free reserves
Expansion limit   Bank reserve equation

Questions

1   Why does currency in circulation count as high-powered money?

2   Name the components of the public's money supply.

3   Using T-accounts, show what happens to member bank reserves on each of the following transactions.

(a) Federal Reserve sells $500 MM in government securities.
(b) Federal Reserve discounts $1 MM in eligible paper for member bank.
(c) Banks draw down $400 MM in currency from Federal Reserve.

4   Using a reserve requirement of 20 per cent, compute the ultimate theoretical effect of each change in question 3 upon the volume of member bank demand deposits.

5   If, in a system with a reserve requirement of 25 per cent, the central bank buys from commercial banks $10 million in government securities, to what limits may each of the following theoretically expand?

(a) demand deposits,
(b) bank loans and investments,
(c) excess reserves.

6   Given reserve requirements of 20 per cent, what increase in total money supply would be possible if the central bank purchased $20 million in government securities and, *simultaneously,* the demand for currency in circulation rose $12 million?

7   The banks have $20.6 billion in total reserves, $20.2 billion in required reserves, and $0.8 billion in borrowed reserves. What is their free reserve position?

8 If sources of reserve funds total $62 billion, currency in circulation is $41 billion, required reserves are $20 billion, and discounts and advances by the Federal Reserve to the banks are $0.5 billion, what are net free or borrowed reserves?

9 Required reserves against demand deposits are 20 per cent, against time deposits 5 per cent. How much will the Last National Bank's lending power theoretically increase if customers shift $10,000,000 from demand deposits to time deposits?

10 Briefly discuss the present role of gold in the U.S. monetary system.

5

Interest and Discount in Financial Valuation

Fundamental Considerations

Financial studies deal largely with money: money spent or received in various amounts and at different times. Any study of financial alternatives must make a proper evaluation of the money involved in the plans under consideration. Before proceeding further with our study of finance, therefore, it is important to determine the rules which govern the value of money spent or received at different times.

Money and Time

A fundamental characteristic of money forms the basis of the mathematical relations to be developed in this chapter. This characteristic is that money has earning power and, therefore, a borrower must pay for its use. The cost of money can be considered from two standpoints. Money borrowed involves an *explicit* cost in the form of interest demanded by the lender. All funds, including equity, involve an *implicit* cost, known to economists as opportunity cost. Opportunity cost is simply income foregone. It is the highest rate of return the funds could command if they were used in an alternative way.

We begin with the premise that there is a continuous cost for the use of money. It follows that the total cost of the use of money is associated with time and cannot be considered or expressed independently of time. Similar considerations apply to the timing of receipts of money, whether in the form of lump-sum payments or successive installments.

As a simple and familiar illustration, consider an investment of $1,000 which earns at a rate of 7 per cent per year. If the investment is undisturbed and the earnings are reinvested, it will increase with the passage of time. After one year it will amount to $1,070.00; after two years, $1,144.90, and so on, with the accrual of earnings. This multiplication of money with the passage of time can be demonstrated by means of the compound interest formula:

$$(S) = P(1 + i)^n,$$

in which

(S) = future value of the investment,
P = principal, or original investment,
i = annual interest rate or opportunity cost, and
n = number of years.

The sum (S) increases exponentially with time.

Equivalence

A graph of the compound interest function[1] shows that any particular amount of money has a full range, or continuum, of equivalent values at different points in time, although the money itself can have tangible existence and value at one point in time only. Thus to have a precise meaning, an item of money must be identified as to both time and amount.

In order to compare different items or amounts of money in the course of financial studies, it is necessary to express them in terms of a common date, or in an otherwise comparable or equivalent manner. Restating receipts and expenditures on an equivalent basis with respect to time serves an essential purpose in gauging profitability. Results of such purely mathematical calculations are subject, of course, to rationalization and interpretation in the light of various other variables which may change with the passage of time.[2]

---

[1] Since a compound interest function increases at a constant rate, and by increasing absolute amounts, over a succession of periods, the graph of the function will appear on an arithmetically-scaled chart as a curve of continually increasing (positive) slope, and on a semi-logarithmic chart as a straight line of constant (positive) slope.

[2] It should be emphasized that calculations of mathematical equivalence are only the starting point in the analysis of actual financial problems. Financial planning and choices among financial alternatives always involve a variety of factors and constraints, many of which elude financial (or even quantitative) representation and measurement. For example, the financial planner is almost always forced to consider problems of capital availability, the current state of the money and capital markets, demands for so-called non-economic expenditures, and the mutual exclusiveness of different alternatives. In addition, the streams of revenues and expenditures forecast by the planner are themselves subject to major uncertainties involving their magnitude, timing, and even their existence.

Mathematical formulae and tables of factors are available to convert an amount at any date to an equivalent amount at any other date. *Future worth* factors are used to convert an amount at any date to an equivalent amount at any later date. *Present worth* factors, on the other hand, are used to convert an amount at any date to an equivalent amount at any earlier date, not necessarily the present one.

The foregoing considerations apply to a sum of money taken as a single amount at some particular point in time that can be converted to equivalent amounts at other points in time. Another important and useful equivalent form in which an amount of money can be expressed is in *annuity*. This is a series of equal annual amounts over a given number of years, with all of these annual amounts considered as having potential growth into the future at a stated rate of compound interest.

One form of annuity is a series of uniform annual amounts which would accumulate, at a given interest rate, to a single amount at the end of a period of years. For example, $72.38 invested at the end of each year, and earning at the annual rate of 7 per cent, would accumulate to $1,000 at the end of the tenth year. This amount of $1,000 is called the *future worth of an annuity* of $72.38 per year for 10 years at 7 per cent. It is, in fact, the sum of the future worths of the ten $72.38 annual amounts at the given rate.

Annuity factors also can be used to determine the amount of an investment which would be needed to provide withdrawals of $100 per year for 10 years when the investment is earning, for example, 7 per cent. The original amount can be shown to be $702.36, and is called the *present worth of an annuity* of $100 per year for 10 years at 7 per cent.

The evaluation of financial alternatives requires the translation of various amounts of money from one form to another, either as single amounts or as annuities. For example, future annual maintenance charges on a machine can be restated as an equivalent single amount of money at the present time in order to allow comparison with items of capital expense which would be incurred now in alternative plans. To compare or combine money outlays or receipts, they must be expressed in the same terms, as single amounts at a common date, or as annuities over the same period of time.

The following demonstration illustrates how $1,000 at 1-1-70 can be transformed into various alternative amounts without changing its present value, assuming the cost of money to be 7 per cent.

A. $1,000 in spot cash on 1-1-70.
B. $1,967 due in cash on 1-1-80.
C. A $116 annuity for seven years beginning 1-1-63.
D. A single amount of $507 paid 1-1-60.
E. A $186 annuity for seven years beginning 1-1-70.

Compound Interest Tables

The foregoing equivalent amounts of money were computed directly from the compound interest tables in the Appendix. It is not necessary for finance students to understand the mathematics involved in the construction of such interest tables. It is necessary only that a few basic concepts be understood in order to work effectively with interest tables and to use them as a basis for reaching sound conclusions.

Present Worth, Future Worth, and Annuity

You will note that the compound interest tables are always expressed in terms of $1. This is for the sake of convenience: when the value associated with $1 is known, it becomes possible to obtain any desired value merely by multiplication or division. To use the tables, you need understand only three basic concepts.

Present Worth of $1. This is the sum which must be invested immediately at the given rate in order to grow to $1 in the stated period of time. Note that at any positive rate of interest this present worth must always be less than $1.

Future Worth of $1. This is the amount to which $1 will grow at a given rate of compound interest over a stated number of time periods. At any positive rate of interest, this future worth must always exceed $1.

Annuity of $1. Standard annuity tables are based on the assumption that periodic payments of $1 are made at the *end* of each of *n* periods. Originally, the periods were years; hence, the name "annuity" from the Latin *annus,* meaning "year." However, the notion of annuity can be applied to any series of uniform periodic payments, whatever the length of period.

Conversion Factors

Financial problems involving compound interest are solved by converting a given sum of money to its equivalent value at a different point (or, with annuities, at a different set of points) in time. To accomplish this conversion, it is only necessary that you apply to the given sum the proper conversion factor from a compound interest table. There are six conversion factors.

1. *Present Worth to Future Worth.* See Table A–1 in the Appendix. The factors in this table indicate the sum that $1 will grow to at the end of a given number of periods at the stated rate of interest. It is a table of factors for *compounding* sums of money forward in time. The word "present" as here applied does not necessarily denote the current period, but simply an earlier period at which compounding is assumed to begin. Referring to the table of present worth to future worth factors, you will observe that $1 invested for 20 periods at 6 per cent grows to $3.207, but only to $1.48 when invested at 2 per cent.

2. *Future Worth to Present Worth.* See Table A–2. The factors in this table are the reciprocals of those in the preceding table. They indicate what $1 due in the future is worth now, discounted to allow for the futurity of its receipt. Thus, this is a table of factors for *discounting* sums of money backward in time. Referring to Table A–2, you will note that $1 due to be paid in 20 years has a present worth of 67 cents when discounted at 2 per cent; if the rate of discount rises to 6 per cent, the present worth falls to less than 31.9 cents.

3. *Annuity to Future Worth.* See Table A–3. This factor gives the compound sum which will result from the regularly recurring investment of $1 at the given rate for the stated number of periods. More directly, it is a table of factors for converting an annuity of $1 paid for *n* periods into its cumulative future value at the end of the *n* periods. Each $1 installment of the annuity is assumed to accumulate interest from its date of payment. Referring to Table A–3, you will see that the investment of $1 each year for 20 years at compound interest will amount to $24.30 at 2 per cent; but $1 a year invested for 20 years at 6 per cent will increase to $36.78. Actually, if tables showing all annual values are used, annuity to future worth factors can be derived from present worth to future

worth tables. For example, at 6 per cent, the future worth of an annuity of $1 per year for 5 years is $5.637. This figure can be verified through the following summation of present worth to future worth factors.

$1 Annuity installment paid at end of year number	Number of periods to gather interest	Installment plus interest at end of 5 years
1	4	$1.262
2	3	1.191
3	2	1.124
4	1	1.060
5	0	1.000
		$5.637

4. *Future Worth to Annuity.* You may wish to compute what size equal payments must be made into an interest-bearing fund to accumulate a certain sum at the end of n interest periods. This calculation involves the conversion of a future worth to an annuity. Tables of future worth to annuity factors can be obtained by simply inverting the annuity to future worth factors listed in Table A–3. The future worth to annuity ratio is simply the reciprocal of annuity to future worth. Future worth to annuity factors are often referred to as sinking fund factors, since they are the basis on which sinking funds are accumulated.

Suppose, for example, you wish to accumulate through a series of five equal annual deposits (a sinking fund) enough money to replace a machine whose original cost was $1. Assume an interest rate of 6 per cent with annual compounding. The future worth desired is $1. What annuity is needed? The conversion factor is readily derived by taking the reciprocal of the factor annuity to future worth for 5 years at 6 per cent. This is $1/5.637 = .177$. Thus, a deposit of about 18 cents per year for 5 years in a fund compounding at 6 per cent per year will accumulate to $1 at the end of five years.

5. *Annuity to Present Worth.* See Table A–4. This table of factors gives you the present worth of $1 received for a fixed number of years. Referring to Table A–4, you will note that a 20-year annuity of $1 discounted at 6 per cent is $11.470. Given a choice between $11.470 and a 20-year annuity of $1, you would consider each one equal if your investments returned 6 per cent.

Again, if tables showing each year's values are used, present worth to annuity factors can be derived from future worth to present worth tables. For example, at 6 per cent, the present worth of an annuity of $1 per year for 5 years is $4.212. This value can be confirmed by adding together the following future worth to present worth factors.

$1 Annuity installment paid at end of year number	Discounted present worth of installment
1	$ .943
2	.890
3	.840
4	.792
5	.747
	$4.212

6. *Present Worth to Annuity.* These factors tell you how large an annuity can be paid for a given number of years from $1 deposited at the stated rate of interest. Present worth to annuity factors are reciprocals of annuity to present worth factors. Sometimes present worth to annuity factors are termed capital recovery factors, since they indicate how large an annuity payment will be required to repay both principal and interest over the life of a loan or a capital investment.

Suppose, for example, that a businessman invests $1 in an asset or project with a 5-year life yielding a 6 per cent return each year. How much can be withdrawn in equal amounts from the project so that at the end of 5 years no investment remains? You need only determine the factor for converting the asset's present worth ($1) to a 5-year annuity at 6 per cent. This conversion factor is calculated by taking the reciprocal of the annuity to present worth factor for 5 years at 6 per cent. This is $1/4.212 = .2374$. Thus, the businessman can withdraw about 24 cents per year.

Asset Values, Time, and Discounting

The valuation of commercial assets is the present worth of future returns and benefits computed at a discount rate that is appropriate to the uncertainty of the future returns and benefits. The valuation of assets, then, involves (1) an estimate of future returns, (2) the timing of the receipts; and (3) the selection of an appropriate discount rate. In this connection it should be noted that accurate estimates of returns and benefits in remote periods are not always necessary. This is because benefits assignable to remote periods contribute very little to present value.

In solving problems involving the time value of money, always remember the basic concept of *equivalence.* Bear it in mind that essentially your solution simply calls for converting a sum (or annuity) of money at one point in time to its equivalent sum (or annuity) at another point in time. Interest must be taken into account because money has a time value.

Your analysis of problems will be clarified if you plot each problem on a time scale. To do this, simply draw a horizontal line and scale it to show different points of time. See Figure 5–1. Next, plot the amounts given you in the statement of the problem at their appropriate points in time. Then ask yourself to what amounts, and at what points in time, those amounts you have already plotted must be made equivalent. Graphic analysis should always suggest the correct solution to your problem.

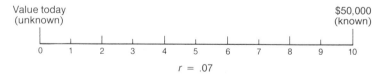

$r = .07$ **Figure 5–1.**

Illustrative Problems

Problem: McWastrel is certain to inherit $50,000 ten years hence. He wishes to sell you this inheritance today. What price can you afford to pay if your opportunity cost is expected to remain at 7 per cent over the next 10 years?

Solution (in steps): (1) Draw and label a time scale depicting the problem. (2) Define your known and unknown. You know the $50,000 must be future worth because it is a single amount, later in time, than your unknown—that is, the value of the inheritance today. This unknown can only be present worth because it is a single amount, earlier in time, than your known. (3) Connect your unknown to your known with the appropriate conversion factor.[3]

$$PW = FW (CF_{\text{fw to pw}})i = .07, n = 10,$$

where

PW = present worth,
FW = future worth,
CF = conversion factor,
i = interest rate or opportunity cost, and
n = number of years.

(4) Substitute numerical values and solve.

$$PW = \$50,000 \ (.508)$$
$$= \$25,400.$$

Not all problems involve the simple application of a single table. Sometimes the flow of benefits is irregular and does not constitute an annuity. In such cases, the proper approach to the problem is to break it down into several problems, perhaps involving more than one table. Here is an example.

Problem: What would be the immediate lump-sum value of an annuity of $3,000 per year for 20 years on a 4 per cent basis if the first payment is to be received 16 years from now?

Solution: From the annuity to present worth factors, Table A–4, we find that the present worth of an annuity of $1 for 20 years at 4 per cent is $13.590. This is multiplied by 3,000, and the result is $40,770. This amount is the cost of a 20-year annuity of $3,000 if purchased one year before the first payment. Remember that all annuity tables are constructed to reflect annual payments, taking place at the end of years. But this is 15 years from now. Next, the problem is to determine how much must be deposited now at 4 per cent in order to have $40,770 in 15 years. This involves the conversion of a future amount to its present worth 15 years earlier, assuming a discount rate of 4 per cent. Therefore, we turn to Table A–2 for factors for converting future worth to present worth. At 4 per cent for 15 years, the conversion factor is 0.555. This means that if 55.5 cents are deposited at 4 per cent compound interest, they will grow to $1 in 15 years. Another way of expressing this is to say that for each $1 of the ultimate price of $40,770, you need pay only 55.5 cents now. The cost of the annuity then is $40,770 times 0.555, or $22,627.

Problem: With a portion of his funds, Jones buys an annuity today for a lump-sum payment of $16,000. The annuity is computed on a 5 per cent basis and runs for 20 years, with the first payment to be received 11 years from now. What will be the annual payment on the annuity?

Answer: $2,194. What steps are involved in the solution?

A routine application of annuity tables involves computing the periodic pay-

---

[3]The authors have found this sort of notation (step 3) useful in solving time-value-of-money problems.

ments required to liquidate a debt, including both principal and interest, in equal annual or periodic payments. Here is an example.

Problem: A corporation has borrowed $480,000 to purchase new equipment. The debt bears 6 per cent interest and is to be retired by equal annual payments over a 10-year period. These equal annual payments are to include both principal and interest. Insurance and taxes are not to be included, since the corporation is required to keep these current in addition to the payments on the debt. What annual payment is required?

Solution: The debt of $480,000 is the present worth of an annuity of the required payments. In effect, the corporation has sold an annuity to the lender, and the annual payment on the annuity is the amount of the payments. Our problem, then, is simply to convert a present worth of $480,000 into a 10-year annuity at 6 per cent. Using the notation we first employed, we find

$$A = PW (CF_{pw \text{ to } a})i = .06, n = 1.$$

We do not have a table of factors for converting present worth to annuity. However, as we have seen above, these factors are simply the reciprocals of annuity to present worth factors in Table A–4. To obtain the factor we need, we find the annuity to present worth factor for 10 years at 6 per cent. This is 7.360. Dividing it into one, we obtain 0.13587. Our solution is

$$A = \$480,000 \times 0.13587.$$

The required annual payment is $65,217.

Problem: A corporation seeks a loan of $80,000 at 6 per cent with 15 annual payments to liquidate both principal and interest. The lender is unwilling to make the loan on the basis of equal payments over the period, since it is considered desirable to reduce the loan more rapidly in its early years. The lender finally agrees to make the loan, provided that payments be $15,000 in each of the first 5 years. The remaining payments are to be equal in amount. What will be the amount of these payments?

Answer: $3,063. What steps are involved in the solution?

Market Rates and Debt Securities

Market rates of interest play key roles in determining prices of marketable debts such as bills and bonds. Prices of these instruments are simply the present values of their future payments discounted at interest rates suitable to the type and quality of obligation.[1] To price bills, bonds, notes, and mortgages, the trader or investor needs to know two facts: (1) the stream of cash payments these instruments have contracted to make, and (2) the appropriate rate of discount.

---

[1]The appropriate discount rate is theoretically the sum of two factors: (1) a "pure" rate of interest, which reflects people's time preference for present money over future money, both being certain of receipt, and (2) an add-on for risk, which reflects the chance that future payments will somehow be impaired. Standard risks include (a) credit risk (also known as business or functional risk), which is the risk of default; (b) money-rate risk, or the chance that a future rise in interest rates will lower the value of debt instruments in general; (c) purchasing-power risk, or the risk that the debt will be repaid in money of reduced buying power; (d) market risk, or the risk that a failure or impairment of the market wherein debts are traded will make them unsaleable or saleable at less than their fair price.

Pricing a Bond

Bonds are issued by corporations, the federal government, and state and local governments in order to borrow long-term funds. Maturities at time of issue ordinarily run from five to thirty-five years.

A bond is a long-term debt obligation which promises two payment streams: (1) its principal (or face) value at maturity, and (2) fixed interest at regular intervals. Bond principal is usually $1,000. Interest is stated as an annual percentage of principal but is ordinarily paid in two semi-annual installments, or coupons, each year. Thus, what market idiom calls a "six per cent bond" would pay 6 per cent of $1,000 to its holder each year: $60 in two $30 coupons six months apart.[5]

Although a bond that pays $30 semi-annually would yield 6 per cent when issued at par ($1,000), its market price may fluctuate above or below this amount. Why? Because a bond, once issued, must meet the competition of new bonds floated.

Suppose, for example, that after our 6 per cent bond had been marketed, new bonds of the same quality are floated paying 8 per cent annually (two $40 coupons per year). To be equally attractive with these new bonds, our 6 per cent bond would have to fall in price sufficiently for its future payments to yield 8 per cent on present value. Eight per cent would be the new *yield to maturity* on this class of bonds. Bonds with less than 8 per cent coupons would sell at a *discount*.

By contrast, suppose that bonds carrying 6 per cent coupons are issued at par to yield 6 per cent. The market yield falls to 4 per cent. Then the 6 per cent bonds would rise in price and sell at a *premium*.

In principle, therefore, the market price of a bond is simply the sum of two components: (1) the present value of the principal ($1,000) discounted to maturity at the *market rate* of interest, and (2) the present value of the annuity formed by the stream of coupon payments—also discounted at the market rate. To calculate a bond's price, you must consider three factors: (1) the dollar amount of the annual coupon payments, (2) the time to maturity of the bond, and (3) the market rate of interest on that class of bonds.

Present worth tables, Tables A–2 and A–4, enable us to calculate bond prices quite readily. To use these tables correctly, however, we must remember that bond coupons are paid semi-annually. Thus, a 10-year, 6 per cent bond paying $60 a year is actually a bond with 20 semi-annual interest coupons, each worth $30. Because bond coupons are paid semi-annually, bond principal is also assumed to compound at semi-annual intervals.[6] Consequently, in using annual interest

---

[5]Bearer bonds, which are transferred by physical delivery, have interest coupons attached to the body of the bond. Each coupon is dated and carries the right to one semi-annual interest payment. A new 30-year bond would have 60 coupons. Registered bonds, which have become common in recent years, do not have coupons, but pay semi-annual interest by check. The issuer must therefore maintain a record or transfer book showing the names of bondholders and the amount of bonds each owns.

[6]All bond tables are constructed on the assumption that both coupons and principal are discounted semi-annually. If you attempt to discount coupons semi-annually and principal annually, your answer will not agree with bond table amounts. Bond men speak idiomatically when they talk of a "three per cent bond selling on a four per cent basis." What they are actually referring to is a bond paying 1½ per cent semi-annual coupons and selling at a yield to maturity of 2 per cent semi-annually.

tables to solve bond problems, two adjustments must be made. (1) The yield to maturity (market rate of interest) quoted for this class of bonds must be divided by two to obtain a semi-annual rate. (2) The years to maturity must be doubled to give the number of semi-annual interest periods.

Subject to these changes, the price of any bond reduces to the following formula:

$$PW = \$1,000 \ (CF_{\text{fw to pw}}) \ + \ C \ (CF_{\text{a to pw}}),$$

where C is the semi-annual coupon in dollars, and all other variables are defined as above.

Problem: What price should be paid for a 10-year bond with a 3 per cent coupon selling on a 4 per cent basis?

Solution: Note first the data of the problem. (1) This bond has 20 semi-annual coupons worth $15 each. (2) There will be 20 semi-annual interest periods to consider. (3) The market rate of interest is 4 per cent per year, equivalent to 2 per cent for each semi-annual period. Therefore, the present value of the $1,000 principal is $1,000 times .673, or $673.00. The present value of the coupon annuity is $15 times 16.351, or $245.27. The sum of these two components is $918.27. This is the theoretical price of the bond.

Now, before reading on, solve this problem: Suppose this 3 per cent bond with a 10-year maturity sells on a 2 per cent basis. What is its theoretical price? Answer: $1,090.69. How is the problem solved?

Pricing a Perpetuity

Perpetuities are financial instruments which promise a perpetual series of equal payments. Preferred stock, non-growth common stock, and British consols, for example, are perpetuities. There is no repayment of their principal because none has a maturity. The mathematics of pricing perpetuities is easy: in conformity with a well-known theorem of elementary algebra—the rule for summing an infinite series of equal values—it is only necessary to divide their periodic payment by the appropriate discount rate.

Problem: Assume all dividends are paid annually in a lump sum at year-end. What price should be paid for a stock that provides $5 in dividends per year in perpetuity if the purchaser is to receive an 8 per cent return on his investment?

Solution: To receive 8 per cent, the buyer must discount all future returns at 8 per cent. Since dividends form a perpetual series of equally spaced payments, the price yielding this return can readily be determined by dividing the $5 annual dividend by 8 per cent. In formula notation,

$$PW = \frac{R}{r},$$

where

R = the dollar amount of the annual payments, and
r = the discount rate expressed as a decimal fraction.

Thus,

$$PW = \frac{\$5}{.08}$$
$$= \$62.50.$$

Now solve this problem: The non-growth common stock of Metatek Industries pays a $3 dividend each year. You require a 10 per cent return from investments of this risk classification. What price will you pay for this stock? *Answer:* $30. How is this problem solved?

To Remember

Equivalence	Conversion factors
Present worth	Time scale
Future worth	Pricing a bond
Annuity	Pricing a perpetuity

Questions

1 Demonstrate how all of the following are equivalent: $1,000 in hand today; $1,967 10 years hence; $258 20 years ago; and an annuity of $243.90 per year for the next 5 years.

2 Convert an annuity of $200 per year for the past 5 years at 9 per cent to its single amount value 5 years from now, assuming that the 9 per cent compounding continues.

3 A manufacturer wishes to deposit equal amounts annually in a fund earning 6 per cent interest to replace a $50,000 machine with a 10-year life. How much must he deposit each year?

4 Ajax, who is 45, wishes to retire at age 65 on an annuity of $10,000 per year for 20 years. If interest remains at 6 per cent over the entire 40 years, and Ajax saves equal amounts each year for 20 years, how much must he begin depositing annually toward the purchase of his annuity at age 65?

5 A 7 per cent coupon bond has 10 years to maturity and sells on a 6 per cent basis. What is the dollar price?

6 What is the price of the bond in question 5 if it sells to yield 10 per cent?

7 What is the price of a 3½ per cent coupon, 8-year bond selling on a 2 per cent basis? An 8 per cent basis?

8 A preferred stock pays $3.50 per year. At what price would it yield 6 per cent?

9 What is true of the price of a bond if the yield to maturity is less than the coupon rate? more than the coupon rate? equal to the coupon rate?

10 Of what two components is the price of a bond the sum?

6

The Theory of Interest

When you borrow money from a bank or other lender, you are expected *to pay* interest. When you deposit money in a savings account or buy a bond, you expect *to be paid* interest. All of us are long accustomed to "money" interest: a payment for the use of borrowed funds. This payment is typically expressed as an annual rate—a ratio of the premium paid for use to the money principal borrowed. Interest, in everyday language, is simply the cost of a loan.

Theories of Interest

Not surprisingly, interest is a subject which has stirred many questions over the centuries. Why is interest paid? Why can it be paid? Is it right to charge interest? What determines the level of interest rates? Why do interest rates change through time? Why do interest rates vary from one kind of loan to another? At various times, each of these questions has proved both difficult to answer and controversial.

Why Interest Is (and Can Be) Paid

The reasons why interest is, and can be, paid can be summarized in two expressions: (1) productivity, and (2) time preference. In economic writings, these two concepts sometimes have other names. Productivity, for example, is also referred to as "opportunity to invest." Time preference is often referred to as "impatience to spend," although sometimes the terms "thrift" and "abstinence" are used.

Productivity means that borrowed money gives a businessman the chance to make enough money using the loan (a) to repay the principal borrowed, (b) to pay a fee to the lender, and (c) to have some profit left for himself. This is what businessmen expect to happen when they borrow money to buy inventory to sell in their stores or to buy machinery or raw materials to make finished goods for resale. The productivity of money used in business provides both the businessman's incentive to borrow and his wherewithal to pay interest to the lender.

Time preference means that people generally prefer to have money now rather than in the future. Interest is, therefore, the rate—or add-on—at which future money is traded for present money. If someone is agreeable to trading $1 today for $1.06 sure of repayment a year from now, the interest rate is 6 per cent per year, and he is receiving 6 cents as a reward for his thriftiness.

Productivity figures mainly in business loans. But time preference affects all loans and is the basis for consumer borrowing. Consumers typically finance their purchases by borrowing in order to enjoy the goods sooner. Mr. Xeonophon could save $15 per month for 30 months to buy his wife a $450 washing machine, but he can hardly be blamed for preferring to buy the washer now "on time" and take Mrs. Xeonophon off the washboard while he repays perhaps $18 per month (counting interest) for 30 months.

Determining Interest Rate Levels: Three Theories

What determines the specific level which interest rates take? Why 6 per cent, for example, instead of 4 or 8 per cent? Let us consider three well-known theories of interest rates. The first, *liquidity preference theory,* is a psychological explanation. The second, *loanable funds theory,* is a market explanation. The third, *classical theory,* is a "real" explanation. Which is valid? All three are, since each explains a different aspect of the interest-determining process.

Liquidity Preference Theory

Liquidity preference theory concentrates on the demand for money (to *hold,* not to spend), which you encountered as *k* in the Cambridge Equation. This theory springs from three basic assumptions. (1) At any time, there is only so much money in the economy. (2) At any given moment, someone must hold each dollar in existence. (3) There are two main alternatives to holding money, however: (a) holding goods, or (b) holding interest-bearing securities or near-money.

Let us ignore, for the moment, the choice between goods and money (which is, after all, ordinary spending) and concentrate on the choice between money and near-money. Each of these has its advantage. Recall that cash has perfect liquidity but pays no return, and near-money pays a return but is less liquid. What, then, determines how each individual will divide his liquid resources between money and near-money? Clearly, the rate of interest is an important factor.

When interest rates are high, the opportunity cost of holding cash is high. Also, the lower market value of near-monies (remember that prices move opposite to yield) suggests that their prices will be rising in the near future. People reduce their cash balances to own more interest-paying near-money. When interest rates are lower, near-money is less attractive and people are willing to hold more cash. Thus, interest rates operate as a "balance wheel," equalizing the desire to hold cash with the desire to hold interest-bearing securities.

Figure 6–1 illustrates graphically how the liquidity preference theory of interest works. The vertical axis measures the interest rates; and the horizontal axis measures money supply. The downsloping curve DD shows, for each level of money supply, what interest rate is necessary to get people to hold exactly that quantity of money. The curve slants down from left to right because—if other factors remain the same—the more plentiful money becomes, the lower the interest rate people are willing to accept.[1] The vertical line MM represents the supply of money actually in existence. Where MM intersects the curve DD (actually the demand curve for money to hold), we find the rate of interest.

Of course, liquidity preference theory is more complex than the bare elements here indicate. A particularly important question is why the demand curve for money,

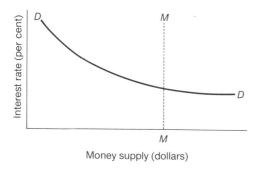

Money supply (dollars)

Figure 6–1.

[1]As money supply increases, money holders are both willing and *compelled* to accept lower interest rates. They are willing to accept lower rates because the marginal utility of money falls as its supply increases. That is, the sacrifice people make in not spending their dollars for immediate consumption drops. They are compelled to accept lower rates because the more urgent borrowers, who would pay higher rates, have already been taken out of the market. To attract new classes of borrowers, lenders must reduce their interest rates. When they reduce interest rates to a figure low enough to make the difference between lending and not lending negligible, then three things happen: (1) further lending ceases, (2) everyone is content to hold what money he has (either owned funds or borrowed funds), and (3) the money market and money supply are in states of equilibrium, i.e., supplies and demands are in balance for (a) money itself, (b) loans, and (c) debt securities.

DD, is in a particular position. Recall that people's demand for money is the sum of their transactions, precautionary, and speculative demands. Behind these demands lie a host of considerations: people's incomes, present and anticipated; their expectations about future price movements; whether or not their housing, autos, and appliances need replacement; the outlook for war, peace, boom, recession, credit conditions, racial troubles, and so on. No system of charts or equations is broad enough to encompass all such factors. Fundamentally, liquidity preference theory of interest is not an operational device for explaining why interest rates are what they are at any time; it is an illustrative device to explain the psychological process by which money supply and other factors affect interest-rate levels. In effect, liquidity preference theory identifies interest as *a reward for parting with liquidity.*

Loanable Funds Theory

In the world's money markets, money is bought (borrowed) and sold (lent) for various periods of time. Like any other commodity, money has a price, and that price is the rate of interest. Price is a market phenomenon. Thus, another approach to the explanation of interest rates deals with the market pricing process. This is the role of the loanable funds theory of interest.

On charts, market price is represented as the point where supply and demand curves intersect. This is how the interest-rate determination process is depicted by loanable funds theory. However, in setting the rate two curves each are needed to represent the supply of, and demand for, money. This is because in actuality supplies of, and demands for, money are each affected by two principal forces.

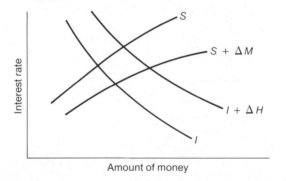

Figure 6-2. Loanable Funds Theory of Interest

Figure 6-2 tells the loanable funds story of interest-rate setting in the money market. First, look at the supply curves for money, which slope upward to the right, showing that the supply of money available for loan rises as interest rates rise. Economists would say that this supply is "interest-elastic." We begin with the curve *S,* which shows (for each level of interest measured on the vertical axis at right) what volume of money savings will be offered in the loan market. But in addition to savings, loanable funds can also be created by pumping up the supply of currency and bank deposits. We label this added source of money

ΔM and add it to the money available from savings. This gives the curve $S + \Delta M$, which represents the total supply of loanable funds. Since added money will bring down the interest rate, this new curve clearly belongs below the curve S.

Now consider the demand curves for money. The basic demand curve I shows the amount of money people will demand at each level of interest for purposes we can broadly describe as investment: to purchase inventories, finance production of goods, or to invest in houses, machinery, automobiles, and the like. But we also have seen that, in addition to money to spend, people also demand money to hold—to satisfy their transactions, precautionary, and speculative motives. To the extent that this "hoarding" demand for money affects borrowing, it is shown as an addition, ΔH, to the demand curve I. This gives you the total demand curve for money $I + \Delta H$. Since the additional demand for money to hold will clearly raise interest rates, the curve $I + \Delta H$ is added *above* demand curve I.

This analysis gives reasons for the rise and fall of interest rates that agree with our common experience. Rates rise if people borrow more money to finance business or consumption needs, or if they hold onto money more tightly in order to stay liquid. Rates also rise if people save less (spend a higher fraction of their incomes), or if a shortage of reserves keeps the banks from creating as much money as before. Conversely, interest rates fall if the economy's rate of investment declines, or if people are "dishoarding" to reduce the size of their cash balances. Interest rates also fall if people's savings increase or if the banking system creates more money to lend. In short, loanable funds theory deals with interest as *the price of money.*

Classical Interest Rate Theory

In contrast to liquidity preference and loanable funds theories, classical interest rate theory does not concern itself with the *monetary rate* of interest. Instead, classical theory is concerned with the *real rate* of interest: it looks at what interest rates would be if all lending and repayment were made in goods instead of money. As such, it is a theory of the supply of, and demand for, economic capital, and not for money. Economic capital (meaning machines, houses, inventories, and the like) takes *time to create,* and is created by what economists call "roundabout production." That means producing output with capital, which lengthens the average production period and makes possible a more efficient technology from use of more specialized tools and division of labor. Since economic capital takes time to create, classical theory is often referred to as a theory of the supply of, and demand for, *waiting.* In this sense, waiting means that the lender must forego the use of his purchasing power and wait while the borrower makes use of it as capital to create some product or service. Thus, classical theory is concerned with the rate of interest as *the price of time.*

Classical interest rate theory brings us near the heart of wealth creation. It shows that waiting is a significant factor in economic progress. When people receive income (purchasing power, or a claim against the stream of wealth), they can either spend it for immediate enjoyment or defer spending. To the extent they save, or defer spending, they release economic resources from having to produce for current needs (consumption); these resources are then available for capital formation, investment in goods, usually durable items, which take time to build and which people will use up in future periods. When this process works smoothly, men and machines not demanded for production of consumer goods are released to produce capital goods. Capital goods, then, are produced through saving. Saving is thus identical to investment—both planned and unplanned by businesses—because what individuals do not consume businesses obviously do not sell.

Figure 6–3 depicts classical interest rate theory. The *real rate of interest* (the rate expressed as the ratio of purchasing power lent to purchasing power repaid) is set by intersection of the curves *S* and *I*. *S* represents the amount of waiting, or abstaining from current consumption, that people are willing to perform at various trade-offs between present and future wealth. *I* represents the amount of waiting which businessmen, homebuyers, and other investors will demand at various real rates of interest. Where the two curves intersect, the real rate of interest is decided.

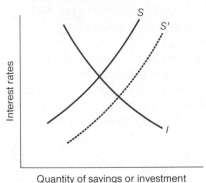

Figure 6–3. Classical Interest Rate Theory

As you can see, classical interest rate theory brings us back fundamentally to our original conception of interest rates as set by (1) time preference, and (2) productivity. The supply curve of waiting, *S*, is actually determined by the interest people demand to persuade them to forego the use of various portions of their wealth. In other words, how long people will wait to enjoy their wealth is determined by the rate at which they are willing to trade present wealth for future wealth. The real rate of interest expresses this rate of trade-off.

Similarly, the demand curve for waiting, *I*, is determined by the productivity of resources (or saved wealth) which are applied, not to producing for current needs, but to the creation of capital goods. The more productive saved resources are when applied to the creation of capital goods, the larger the profits the creators of capital goods can earn. As the productivity of such resources increases, creators of capital goods will bid higher for their use.

There are implications of deviations between real and monetary interest rates. Should the Federal Reserve restrict the money supply so that monetary rates exceed real interest rates, businesses will curtail investment and individuals will save more. The result will be a fall in income, output, and employment. Conversely, if monetary rates are held below real interest rates, spending for investment and consumer goods will increase. The increased money supply finances spending on goods when an insufficient supply of goods is forthcoming, and inflation results.

Deflated vs. Money Rates of Interest

The foregoing theories show that there are actually two kinds of interest rates: (1) money (or "nominal") rates, which are ratios of dollars repaid to dollars borrowed, and (2) deflated rates, which are ratios of *purchasing power* repaid and borrowed. If the price level is changing—and with it the dollar's buying power—deflated and money rates of interest differ. Thus, people who lend or borrow money need to look behind the stated interest rates and see what is happening to the purchasing power lent and repaid. If they do not, they are victims of money illusion.

What effect should price-level inflation or deflation have on interest rates? Let us look at this question from the lender's standpoint. If the change in the price level is not foreseen—and the market rate of interest is not affected by it—the true return to the lender is a compound of the market rate and an add-on figure representing the rate of change of the price level. If the rate of interest is r per cent per year and the change in prices is ΔP per year, the deflated interest rate is $(r - \Delta P)/(1 + \Delta P)$.

If the change in purchasing power is foreseen, creditors will try to correct this divergence by charging a rate of interest that will compensate for the change in prices. If, when prices are rising, the lender wants to receive a certain deflated interest, he can solve the preceding equation for r to find the nominal interest he must charge. For example, if inflation is 4 per cent per year and you want to receive a deflated 3 per cent, then your nominal rate must be $.03 = (r - .04)/(1 + .04)$. Here, r is 7.12 per cent.

Interest Rate Response to Inflation

Do money rates of interest adjust to foreseen inflation rates? There is every indication that they do, and with little delay.[2] Indeed, one of the most dependable relations among economic statistics is the close correlation over the past century between the trend of the general price level and the long-term direction of interest rates.

Figure 6–4 depicts the joint movement of bond yields (long-term interest rates) and the price level since 1865. From 1865 to 1896, prices declined secularly, or in very long-term, cycle-to-cycle movements. Bond yields, despite ups and downs over several business cycles, also trended lower until they reached about 3½ per cent in 1899. Then, at the turn of the century, as prices turned up, so also did interest rates, with bond yields reaching a peak of about 6 per cent in 1920. After World War I, prices turned downward and did not begin rising strongly again until 1946. In this interim, bond yields fell to their lowest historic level, less than 2½ per cent in 1946. Since World War II, inflation has continued and, in the late 1960s, it accelerated. In this same period, bond yields rose almost continuously, reaching a level above 8 per cent in 1970.

This record suggests that, after a while at least, lenders demand compensation

[2]A recent study indicates that past price movements exert a major effect on nominal interest rates, largely manifested within two years. See William P. Yohe and Denis Karnosky, "Interest Rates and Price Level Changes, 1952–1969," Federal Reserve Bank of St. Louis *Bulletin* (December 1969): 18–37.

Figure 6–4. Secular Movement of Bond Yields and Consumer Prices in the United States 1865–1971

for being repaid in depreciated money. It also suggests the fallacy of inflating the money supply in an effort to keep interest rates low, for in the long run this maneuver actually runs interest rates up. At first, additional money may supply banks and others with more loanable funds and, for a time, lenders may cut interest rates. But as the new money gets into circulation, either bringing full employment or encouraging wage-push inflation by labor unions, prices start increasing faster than before. Lenders then increase their interest charges to avoid losses from repayment in debased money.

Interest Rate Structures

To this point, we have spoken of *the* interest rate, as if there were only one. This simplification has helped to show what interest rates essentially are and do. Now we can turn to the real world and deal with the constellation of interest rates that actually exists. To classify actual interest rates most conveniently, we must look at interest-rate structures. By a structure we simply mean rates ordered according to some organizing principle such as time, place, or risk. Four important and illuminating structures are: (1) term, or time to maturity structure, (2) risk, or quality structure, (3) geographical structure, and (4) taxability structure.

Term Structure

A *term structure,* Figure 6–5, depicts interest rates as a function of time to maturity. To hold other factors the same (or to maintain *ceteris paribus,* as economists say) all securities shown in a term structure must be of the same quality. Most term structure studies in this country utilize Treasury securities. Time to maturity is plotted along the horizontal axis. The vertical axis portrays interest rates (security yields).

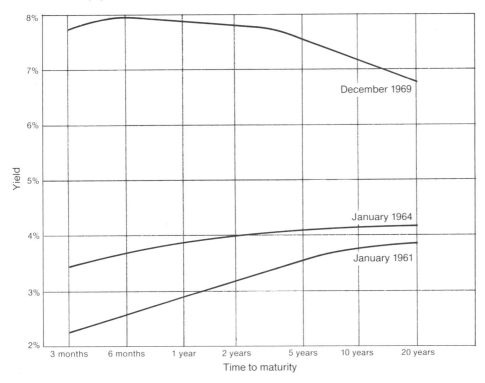

Figure 6–5. Term Structure of Interest Rates on Treasury Securities (Different Dates)

Normally, in the past generation at least, the term structure (sometimes called the yield-to-maturity curve) has sloped upward from left to right, as does the curve depicting the January 1964 term structure. This is because, as we shall see, if interest rates should rise, long-dated securities would incur the largest loss in market price. So, as a premium for greater risk,[3] holders of more distant maturities demand higher rates of interest than holders of short-term paper. This is in agreement with the liquidity preference theory of interest rates. A gracefully upsloping yield curve is typical of times when business activity is normal, as in 1964.

Figure 6–5 shows two other yield curves. The curve for January 1961 is steeply upsloping. This is because 1961 was a recession year and short-term interest rates fell very low. They fell very low because the Federal Reserve created quantities of new money to fight the recession, but since business activity and loan demand were slack, the money had no "safe" place to go but into short-term,

---

[3]Strictly speaking, *uncertainty* is the proper term here. See chapter 1, footnote 4.

high-grade investments. This pushed their prices very high and yields very low. Long-term interest rates (bond yields) fell considerably from their peaks of 1959–60, but since a small change in a yield brings a very large price change for a long-term bond, bond yields do not swing through as wide a range as short-term (bill) yields.

On the other hand, the yield curve for December 1969 is inverted—that is, short-term rates are actually higher than long-term rates. Why? This is because 1969 was a boom year, and three conditions were present. (1) Money was tight. (2) All interest rates were very high. (3) A fall in all interest rates was expected soon. Under these conditions, short-term rates were above long-term ones for two reasons. First, borrowers preferred to bridge the period of high long-term rates with short-term loans, and were willing to pay extra high rates for short-term money. In other words, it is better to pay 10 per cent short-term for a year and then sell bonds at 6 per cent, than to be saddled with 8 per cent for 10 years.[4] Second, lenders had analogous incentives. Lending money at long-term, they "salted it away" at a good return for many years. They could also expect large capital gains if interest rates fell and bond prices rose. Lending at short-term, they might get a high rate for a brief time, but then when interest rates fell and they were repaid, they would have to relend at a much lower rate. Under these circumstances, only very high rates would persuade lenders to lend at short-term.

Quality Structure

Table 6–1 depicts the behavior of the quality structure of corporate bond yields between two recent dates. By *quality structure,* we mean bonds arrayed in order of the estimated reliability of different debtors' credit-worthiness. As you might expect, bond yields always rank in inverse order to their quality. Highest grade bonds yield least, lowest grade, most. This ranking conforms with the fact that, wherever possible, investors charge a risk premium in terms of extra interest when a risk is ascertainable.

However, the size of the risk premium on different bond qualities varies widely, depending on how much confidence investors have in economic and credit conditions. Sometimes, a so-called bad bond looks almost as good as a good one. This is likely to be true in boom-times, when all companies look prosperous and when people are little concerned about a depression. This explains the very small gap between medium- and high-grade bond yields in April 1969, a time of headlong boom. With only .65 points of yield difference between high- and medium-grade bonds, it is evident that investors were not very worried about quality risks.

Now look at the yield spread for August 1970 on Table 6–1. The yield gap between high- and medium-grade bonds has more than doubled. Why? The Penn-Central and other business failures in June and July had shaken investors to their boot-tops. Suddenly they realized that there really was a difference between "gilt-edge" bonds and speculative ones. Money then "rushed for cover": investors dumped doubtful bonds or refused to buy them. The prices of these bonds fell and their yields rose momentously. High-grade bonds were virtually unaffected by the spreading fears because they represented companies with sound financial

---

[4]When bond yields are very high, buyers typically insist that new issues be made non-callable for at least ten years. This restricts an issuer's freedom to refinance his debt at lower cost if interest rates subsequently decline. We discuss callable bonds along with quality ratings in chapter 25.

Table 6-1. Quality Structure of Corporate Bond Yields, Two Recent Dates

Bond Quality Rating	Yield to Maturity (in per cent)	
	April 1969	August 1970
High-grade	6.89	8.13
Medium-grade	7.54	9.44
Spread: Medium minus High	0.65	1.31

Source: Adapted from *Federal Reserve Bulletin,* October 1970, p. A–57.

structures that were earning their interest requirements by comfortably wide margins.[5]

Geographical Structure

The *geographical structure* of interest rates in the United States reveals this rule: interest rates rise from northeast to southwest—that is, moving from Maine to Southern California. This is in part because the older (northeastern) regions generate, on the average, a larger volume of savings than they can utilize. The newer southern and western regions, which are growing more rapidly, generate an excess demand for capital. The magnet of rising interest rates gives money an incentive to move across country—from where it is in surplus to where it is lacking.

Taxability Structure

The *taxability structure* views interest rates on different securities in light of the extent to which returns are subject to federal income tax. The main division here is between tax-exempt (state and municipal) bonds and all other bonds, which are referred to as taxables. Quality for quality, tax-exempt securities almost always carry lower yields than taxables. This is because one needs a higher yield on a taxable security to give him the same after-tax return as he could get from a tax-exempt security.[6]

Patterns of Interest Rate Fluctuation

Like other economic time series, interest rates have three well-defined patterns of fluctuation. The first, the short-period variation, is unimportant, due to small shifts of the daily balance of supply and demand in the loan market. The other two—cyclical and secular movements—are extremely important to businessmen.

Cyclical Movement

In general, interest rates move in concert with the cycle of general business. They rise as business expands, and fall as it contracts. All interest rates, long

---

[5] All bond yields had risen since April 1969 because of very tight money, but high-grade yields had risen only 1.24 percentage points against 1.90 points for medium-grade yields.

[6] Calculations for taxable versus tax-exempt returns on bonds are in chapter 25.

and short, typically reach their peak for the cycle at about the top of a business boom, when money is very tight and many people are trying to borrow it. They reach their bottom at approximately the low point of the recession, when loans of the boom period have largely been paid off, when hardly anyone is borrowing money to expand inventories or plant, and when idle money is accumulating and "looking for some place to go."

Secular Movement

Much less recognized by most businessmen (preoccupied, as they must be, with what is going to happen tomorrow or next week) is the secular, or cycle-to-cycle, movement of interest rates. Such long-term trends, which carry the general level of interest rates significantly higher or lower over a series of business cycles, have already been noted and are depicted in Figure 6–4. Since secular movements in interest rates invariably seem to last two decades or longer, it is worth examining what causes them.

We have already noted that secular trends are closely correlated with price-level shifts—that is, with changes in the purchasing power of money. This association, however, does not prove that inflation and deflation are always, or necessarily, the causes of these long swings in interest rates. Some economists think that inflation and rising interest rates (or deflation and falling ones) are not so much cause and effect as products of a common cause. Not surprisingly, the common cause is usually a combination of productivity and time preference.

Interest rates have risen secularly during superbooms, a succession of business cycles in which booms are very strong and lengthy and recessions are short and shallow. Such superbooms have typically occurred during periods of rapid population growth, exploitation of massive new inventions, opening up of new territories, and war (which is a prolific destroyer of capital and the source of large replacement demands). Such conditions prevailed from 1899 to 1920, and again after 1946. Periods of secularly declining interest have been intervals of so-called rest and digestion, when population grew less rapidly, fewer innovations existed to be exploited, and fewer new territories were being opened to settlement or trade. The 1920s and 1930s were such a time. It also seems true that after people work hard for a generation to accumulate wealth, they need to slow down, and probably even want to. Also, as wealth accumulates, it is sometimes difficult (as it was in England between 1860 and 1899) to find a sufficient number of investment outlets. Thus, as a noted English economist put it, ". . . the history of the interest rate through time appears as the history of the results of a tussle,—a tussle between Fecundity and Invention on the one hand and Affluence and Thrift on the other."[7]

Forecasting Interest Rate Movements

Since interest rates are a cost to borrowers, a source of income to savers, and a regulator of debt-security prices, their shifts are important, eagerly watched, and widely forecast. How are interest rates forecast? In the short run, there are two main methods.

---

[7]D. H. Robertson, *Lectures on Economic Principles* (London: The Staples Press, 1963), vol. 2, p. 87.

Sources and Uses of Funds

Loanable funds theory indicates that interest rates are set by interaction of supplies of, and demands for, money loans. Thus, one way to forecast interest rates is simply to tabulate and total all of the supplies of, and demands for, money loans in prospect for the year ahead. Supplies of money are called sources, demands are called uses, and the result is a table like Table 6-2, which shows expected sources and uses of funds for 1972.

Table 6-2. Expected Sources and Uses of Funds By Economic Sectors, U.S.A., 1972

Item		Billions of Dollars
Sources		
U.S. Government and Agencies		8.0
Federal Reserve System		5.0
Commercial Banks		50.0
Nonbank Financial Institutions		60.0
Foreign		−5.0
Domestic Nonfinancial Sources		42.0
Households	20.0	
Business and Other	22.0	
Total Funds Advanced		160.0
Uses		
U.S. Government (Including Budget Agencies)		27.0
Nonfinancial Business		68.0
Equity	10.0	
Long Debt	40.0	
Short Debt	18.0	
State and Local Governments		20.0
Households		40.0
Mortgage	25.0	
Other	15.0	
Foreign		5.0
Total Funds Raised		160.0

Source: Manufacturers Hanover Trust Company of New York.

Of course, total sources must always equal total uses. How, then, can such a table predict the level of interest rates? The answer is that the finished table does not predict rates; rather, the prediction is made in getting the table to balance. In drawing up such a table you begin by listing all the different sources and uses you foresee for the coming year. Then you total them. If projected sources (supplies) are bigger than projected uses (demands), you can expect interest rates to fall from their present level. If uses exceed sources, you can expect rates to rise. How much will rates rise or fall? It depends on how hard sources or uses— whichever is bigger—have to be squeezed to make one fit the other. You do this by reducing individual items in your list to smaller size. Table 6–3 suggests how Table 6–2 might have been trimmed to fit.

Obviously, the trimming and fitting are a matter of judgment. The fact that an interest rate forecast is supported by an impressive-looking table of figures

Table 6–3. Assumed Worksheet for Deriving Table 6–2 and 1972 Interest Rate Forecast

		Adjustments
SOURCES: (Expected before adjustment)		
U.S. Government and Agencies	$ 8.0	
Federal Reserve System	~~3.0~~	*5.0*
Commercial Banks	~~45.0~~	*50.0*
Nonbank Financial Institutions	~~58.0~~	*60.0*
Foreign	~~−6.0~~	*−5.0*
Domestic Nonfinancial Sources	~~39.0~~	*42.0*
Households	~~$17.0~~ *20.0*	
Business & other	22.0	
TOTAL FUNDS FORESEEN	~~$147.0~~	*160.0*
USES: (Expected before adjustment)		
U.S. Government (including budget agencies)	$27.0	
Nonfinancial Business	~~74.00~~	*68.0*
Equity	~~$12.0~~ *10.0*	
Long debt	~~43.0~~ *40.0*	
Short debt	~~19.0~~ *18.0*	
State and Local Governments	~~21.0~~	*20.0*
Households	~~42.0~~	*40.0*
Mortgage	~~$27.0~~ *25.0*	
Other	15.0	
Foreign	5.0	
TOTAL FUNDS SOUGHT	~~$169.0~~	*160.0*
EXCESS OF USES OVER SOURCES	~~$22.0~~	*0.0*

does not keep it from being anything but "quantified guesswork." That is what most forecasts actually are.

Real Rate and Add-On

Some observers of historic interest trends are convinced that real rates of interest do not change very much. The real rate on bonds, for example, in recent years has remained around 3 per cent. The rest of the *money rate* of interest consists of an add-on for expected inflation or deflation. (Note, that is *expected* inflation or deflation, not the price-level change that actually takes place.) Thus, in the early 1960s, when inflation was expected to (and actually did) average only about 1¼ per cent per year, high-grade corporate bond yields remained around 4¼ per cent. In 1969–70, when inflation leaped to 5½ per cent per year, high-grade corporate yields rose to 8½ per cent. In both instances, the yield was about 3 per cent plus the expected inflation rate.

Long and Short Rates: Cyclical Divergence

In forecasting interest-rate structures, of course, you must remember that short-term interest rates fluctuate a great deal more than long-term rates. Whether short rates are above or below long rates, and how much, depends on the kind of business activity you predict. We have seen that, in an inflationary boom, short rates may well be higher than long rates; in recessions, they may be far below long rates. The best answer to where short rates are going in the year ahead seems to lie in answering this sequence of questions: (1) How much will long rates move up or down next year? (2) What level are short rates starting from as of now? (3) How strongly can business be expected to improve or decline? (4) How much can inflation be expected to accelerate or slow down? The more the answers to these questions suggest a vigorous economy, the more you are entitled to lift your forecast of short rates.

To Remember

Productivity	Term structure of interest rates
Time preference	Quality structure of interest rates
Liquidity preference theory	Cyclical movement
Loanable funds theory	Secular movement
Classical interest-rate theory	Sources and uses
Deflated rate of interest	Real rate and add-on
Money (nominal) rate of interest	

Questions

1 Why *can* a business borrower pay interest? Why *will* a consumer?
2 Liquidity preference theory of interest rates is actually a theory of the demand for money. Why? Is it also a theory of the demand for debt securities? Explain.

3 Discuss the roles of net new money creation and "hoarding or dishoarding" in loanable funds theory.

4 Classical interest-rate theory is a theory of the supply of and demand for waiting, and not for money. Explain.

5 Distinguish between deflated and monetary rates of interest. Which would you prefer to have guaranteed if you were a lender? a borrower?

6 Should bonds contain a "cost of living clause" to assure creditors justice in times of inflation, and debtors justice in times of deflation? Discuss.

7 If you were a lender who needed a real return after taxes of 4 per cent, what interest rate would you have to charge, given 7 per cent inflation?

8 Explain what is going on in the economy when the term structure of interest rates is (1) steeply upsloping, and (2) downsloping.

9 Distinguish between cyclical and secular trends in interest rates.

10 Name and briefly describe the two main methods of interest-rate forecasting.

7

Credit, Securities, and Financial Markets

This chapter examines three closely related subjects: *credit,* which is the life-blood of business; *securities,* which embody credit; and the *financial markets,* wherein securities are traded and priced. A grasp of these terms and their relations should precede chapter 8, which deals with credit control.

Credit: The Five Cs

Few words in the finance vocabulary are more versatile than *credit.* It can mean (1) a loan of money, (2) the right to draw a loan of money, (3) a quality in borrowers which enables them to get a loan of money, or (4) the state of feeling in the financial community that makes loans easy or hard to get. Translated from the Latin *credere,* credit means "he trusts" or "he believes." Clearly, some feeling of trust must lie at the root of credit, no matter which of the above definitions we use.

Whether we are considering the state of credit in the economy or the credit-worthiness of individual borrowers, the "five Cs" of credit are a useful checklist to remember. They are (1) character, (2) capacity, (3) collateral, (4) capital, and (5) conditions. Let us examine their relevance.

Character in a borrower is clearly important to his credit-worthiness. Is the borrower honest, sincere, a man of his word? Does he seriously intend to repay his debts? Is he a sober, hard-working, self-denying person who attends to business and puts first things first? Is he, in a word, responsible? This is the first thing any lender needs to know about a prospective borrower.

Capacity answers the question whether a man is likely to prove capable of repaying a loan. Is he an efficient businessman? Does he have his affairs in good shape, keep neat books, have a firm grip on his business, maintain close control, and make correct decisions? However good a borrower's character or intentions, if he is a slipshod or incompetent manager, his likelihood of repaying a loan is seriously diminished.

Collateral means the assets that a borrower pledges to secure his loan. Not all loans are secured; some borrowers are so obviously strong that no assurance of repayment beyond their bare word is necessary. But as borrowers sink in the scale of credit-worthiness, collateral becomes increasingly important as a guarantee of repayment. Thus, for weaker or less well-known borrowers, the amount, quality, and ready-saleability of the collateral they can pledge becomes crucial. For marginal borrowers, the ability to offer acceptable collateral is often the key to obtaining credit.

Capital refers to the borrower's own stake, or equity, in his enterprise. Such equity is needed (unless collateral is very large in relation to the loan) as a cushion to protect the lender from loss. A businessman borrower is always asked: "How much of your own money have you committed to this proposition?" A borrowing consumer will be asked: "How large a down payment are you prepared to make?" The logic of this requirement should be clear. If the buyer of a $30,000 house must put up $5,000 of his own money before borrowing the other $25,000, the lender is protected in two ways. First, the price of the house must fall to $25,000 before the collateral becomes worth less than the loan. Second, since the borrower has already made a substantial commitment of his own funds, he is less likely to consider defaulting on his loan.

Conditions involve the state of business. These conditions answer such questions as: "What are prospects that loans in general will be repaid without difficulty? Are sales and profits strong? Are people's jobs secure? Are their incomes rising? Are past borrowers meeting their repayment schedules?" If the answers to these questions are yes, credit conditions are good. Loan availability will be high and qualifications for borrowers moderate. But if answers are no, then credit conditions are poor. Loan availability will be low and borrower qualifications more strict.

Kinds of Credit

The kinds of credit can be classified according to their (1) user, (2) time-span, and (3) quality. Each class contains many divisions and sub-divisions, but all types of credit are strongly related. Both borrowers and lenders often have considerable ability to compare the merits of different types of loans and to move from one to another as advantage dictates. These powers of mobility and substitution on both the supply and demand sides of a many-segmented credit market link the various segments together. Thus cost, terms, and availability often show a common trend throughout the entire credit structure. This is particularly true when money is very easy or very tight throughout the economy.

Credit by User

Users of credit fall in three broad categories: businesses, consumers, and governments. Short-term credit to business is advanced by manufacturers, wholesalers, or other suppliers of merchandise ("trade" or "open-book" credit),[1] by commercial banks, commercial credit companies, factors, and buyers of commercial paper. Intermediate-term credit reaches business firms through term-lending by commercial banks, equipment credit (ordinarily supplied by equipment manufacturers), and the purchasers of three-to seven-year notes which corporations may sell in the open market. Long-term credit is provided to businesses by bond-buyers, by insurance companies which buy the long-term IOUs (privately-placed notes) of corporations, and sometimes by mortgage lenders.

Consumer credit is of four main types: (1) residential housing credit, or the familiar home mortgage; (2) installment credit, used largely to finance purchases of automobiles, appliances, and furniture, but increasingly for such other purposes as education, vacation travel, and so on; (3) mercantile credit, familiar as department-store and bank-credit-card charge accounts; and (4) consumer small loans, made for a variety of purposes by many agencies; ranging from banks and "legal-rate" consumer finance companies to loan sharks and the Mafia.

Credit also is extended to governments at all levels. Credit to the federal government is largely embodied in the direct obligations of the United States (such as the Treasury debt) and in the obligations of a growing array of federal agencies, such as the Federal Housing Administration, Bank for Cooperatives, and Tennessee Valley Authority. A large volume of credit also reaches the fifty states and their numerous subdivisions: cities, counties, school districts, sanitary districts, port authorities, and the like. Most longer-term credit to governmental bodies is supplied through purchases of their securities; banks are large buyers of these. Shorter-term credit is supplied to larger governmental bodies through open-market sales of short-dated securities. Very small governmental bodies—too small to sell frequent issues of short-term, open market IOUs to investors—are largely reliant on bank loans for temporary funds.

Credit by Time-Span

The second important classification of credit is according to the length of time for which it is extended. It is customary to distinguish (1) short-term credit, running one year or less, (2) intermediate-term credit, running from one to seven years, and (3) long-term credit.

The chief concern of those extending *short-term credit* is that the borrower have the cash "in sight" to repay the loan, since the interval is too short to permit repayment out of earnings. That is, a borrower at 6 per cent would have to repay

---

[1]Trade credit and its costs are discussed in detail in chapter 21.

106 per cent of the loan in a year's time, and paying all of this amount solely out of profits would require profit of 106 per cent—a highly improbable achievement. Consequently, short-term credit is typically made available only where the borrower satisfies one of three conditions: (1) He has enough income assured over and beyond expenses to meet his repayment obligation. An example would be a $1,000 personal loan for one year to an executive whose secure job clearly paid him a sufficient margin over his family living expenses to enable him to retire the loan in the year ahead. (2) The transaction for which the loan is made is self-liquidating and will itself provide the means of repayment. For instance, a toy merchant may borrow seasonally to enable him to lay in merchandise inventory for his peak business at Christmastime. Sale, at a profit, of the merchandise in which the loan is invested will enable him to pay back the money. (3) The borrower is in position to provide repayment funds by liquidating an excess of current assets over current liabilities.

Short-term loans may call for either lump-sum or installment repayments. They may be made on either a secured or unsecured basis, depending on the lender's assessment of the risks. Short-term loans may be evidenced by private IOUs, as bank borrowings ordinarily are, or by marketable securities, as loans to the U.S. Treasury or federal agencies typically are.

Intermediate-term credit includes such items as commercial bank term loans, equipment financing (extended, for example, by a manufacturer of dental equipment to a dentist-purchaser), and the one- to seven-year notes which are obligations of the U.S. Treasury. The borrower's principal requirement for obtaining intermediate-term credit is income or earnings in the case of a business borrower. This is because intermediate-term credit is usually extended for the purchase of long-lived assets, such as machinery. Term and equipment loans are usually repaid in regular installments over the life of the loan.

Long-term credit is evidenced by bonds, mortgages, and privately placed corporate notes (IOUs). Since long-term credit is almost always used to finance permanent asset requirements, eligibility depends almost totally on a borrower's profits. Over the loan's life, the borrower must appear to be able to generate sufficient earnings from the assets the loan finances (1) to pay periodic interest at the contracted rate, and (2) to repay the loan at maturity. Usually long-term loans, as with intermediate-term loans, are paid off at intervals during their lifetimes.

Two final points should be emphasized about credit for different time periods. (1) Within prudent limits, both lenders and borrowers enjoy considerable freedom in substituting one length of loan for another. We have seen, in the previous chapter, that at times when *all* interest rates seem abnormally high, borrowers will seek to bridge the high-interest interval by substituting short-term loans for long-term. Similarly, when all interest rates appear abnormally low, lenders often substitute short-term lending for the long-term loans ordinarily made. (2) Business and governments have much greater access to intermediate- and long-term credit than do private persons. Most individuals find long-term loans available only to buy a house, and intermediate-term credit only for purchases of consumer durables—autos, appliances, furniture, or house repairs—and then typically only for two or three year intervals.

Credit By Quality

Quality of credit usually means strength of the borrower's promise to repay, and various systems of rating borrowers have been developed. For example,

Standard & Poor's Corporation and Moody's Investor's Service rate corporate and municipal borrowers on their bonds, and Dun & Bradstreet rate business enterprises. Access to credit is strongly affected by credit ratings. Ratings not only determine whether a borrower will get credit, but also decide how large a premium he will have to pay above some risk free rate of interest, whether his loan will have to be secured, how long he can borrow for, and how much he can borrow.

Saving, Credit, and Investment

Credit adds much to the power and flexibility of economic life. It makes possible new cycles of production and consumption, distribution and exchange, by doing two things: (1) It activates idle money, and by so doing (2) it activates idle resources—men, machines, and materials. As we have seen in chapter 4, the extension of credit by commercial banks plays a particularly important part by adding to the nation's money supply. We shall emphasize how credit from commercial banks and other financial intermediaries mobilizes society's savings to finance investment.

Making Possible Capital Accumulation

Suppose the existence of a simple economy consisting only of labor and business. Further, assume the only production cost is labor (Y). If workers spend or consume (C) all of their wages (W) as they receive them, then the wage bill is equal to the total receipts of businesses (TR) and no profit, saving, or investment occurs: $TR = W = C$. Now suppose that labor chooses to save (S) some of its flow of income. Saving, in real terms, simply means "not consuming." The resulting fall in consumption and increase in saving mean that businesses do not sell all their output, as they did previously. With sales down, a particular firm will find that it has merchandise left on its shelves. Its inventory expands. In other words, the firm has *invested (I)* in inventory. Now, we can see these relations:

$$W - C = S,$$
$$Y - C = I.$$

And since

$$Y = C + S,$$

substituting this equation into the one above it gives

$$(C + S) - C = I.$$

Therefore,

$$S = I.$$

The equation $S = I$ is a truism, but a useful one. It tells us that what society does not consume is saved, and what is saved, invested. If the investment is planned or designed by businesses, then the economy will not experience an adverse shock; if unplanned, businessmen will cut back on production and induce unemployment while they try to deplete excess inventories.

We have left businesses in something of a predicament in the model above. Total receipts are less than total expenses, $TR < Y$. How can business meet its expenses and continue production to reap whatever profit it anticipates (assuming the investment was planned)? Here, financial markets and credit come into play.

Businesses must obtain credit to meet their wage bill. They can do so in three ways. (1) They can write IOUs to their employees, who will then use them to save or purchase consumer goods. (2) They can sell securities to laborers. (3) They can sell securities to a bank or other financial intermediary.

The above paragraph emphasizes the fact that saving means an excess of receipts by the public from businesses over payment to businesses $(W - C = S)$ and therefore an increase in the debt of businesses to the public.[2] Financial markets facilitate the necessary flow of credit and permit excess funds S to be put to work I rather than to remain idle, hoarded by the consumer goods sector.

Our model can become more complex and more realistic. We can add a consumer goods sector and a capital goods sector. Firms and industries can buy from each other. In this maze of complex transactions, this key point remains: the extension of credit through the financial system places the savings of society at the disposal of those who use it for productive purposes.

Special Role of Bank Credit

Banks not only mediate credit, or shift already existing money from lenders to borrowers, they can also create money, as we saw in chapter 4. The latter function can have both good and bad results.

Suppose, for example, that uncertainty about the future induces wage earners in the above example to save. In terminology of chapter 3, desired money balances (k_d) exceed actual balances (k_a). If wage earners deposit their savings in the bank, the banking system's assets (reserves) and liabilities (demand deposits) increase. Recall that a single bank can lend an amount equal to the deposit from wage earners less required reserves, an amount equal to excess reserves. The banking system can create money by a *multiple* of its excess reserves. Armed with this created money, optimistic businessmen can now start projects. The economy avoids unemployment because the newly created finance permits businessmen to keep economic resources productive.

Will this credit creation process be inflationary? It depends on whether or not resources are available to use in the new projects or if they must be bid away from other projects. If some industries are dying and freeing economic resources, then businessmen can utilize the now available labor and capital. But if the economy is fully employed, then the new money will only bid up the price level, a point emphasized in the Equation of Exchange in chapter 3.

We have learned that inflation can occur without an expansion of the money supply. If the velocity of money rises, reflecting credit mediation, the activation of idle cash balances—from savers lending to spenders—can put upward pressure on prices. But money creation can accelerate a price increase, changing a leisurely paced inflation to a runaway one.

Of course, if inflation developed, the central bank would be wise to take steps to reduce the money supply to maintain stable prices. It could do this by increasing reserve requirements in such a way as to force the commercial bank to curtail their credit extensions. But often neither central banks nor the politi-

---

[2]This fact is pointed out and supported in Kenneth Boulding, *A Reconstruction of Economics* (New York: Science Editions, Inc., 1962), pp. 246–58, especially pp. 255–58, and in Joan Robinson, *The Accumulation of Capital,* 2nd ed. (New York: Macmillan, St. Martin's Press, 1966), p. 45.

cally minded governments behind them have the courage to do this. So the bank-money mechanism of credit creation, aided and abetted by the reserves "fed" to it by the central bank, has accounted for most of the world's inflationary ills.

Misuse of Credit

Loans and interest are repaid mainly because firms create economic value above the amount of the loan. In addition, borrowers must do nothing to strain their positions in ways that would weaken their repayment capabilities. But we must stress that credit, extended or used unwisely, can endanger economic stability and lead to undesired cycles of boom and bust.

In the real world, credit is often misused. Some credit is obtained through fraud or for fraudulent purposes, and such borrowers do not intend to repay. But much more credit is misused because of borrowers' and lenders' errors of judgment.

Suppose that a business boom is on and the widget business is booming. Ima Promoter decides to consolidate Shaki-Widgets Corporation and Bustable Widgets Company into Giganticus, Inc. The Overboard National Bank lends him money to acquire the two companies' stocks, which are selling at 10 times their price of two years before. A great euphoria grips the country when the deal is made and all stock prices look reasonable. But then the boom ends. A flood of widget imports from Bulgravia destroys the price structure and profits of the widget industry. Giganticus, Inc., is unable to repay its loan to Overboard National, and the bank fails, ruining many of its own depositors[3] and starting a financial panic. This is, in fact, the way all serious depressions in the past have started.

Securities

Securities are documentary titles to wealth. The genus, or family, of securities includes both equity and debt instruments. Equity securities, such as shares of stock, are evidence of ownership interest in private enterprises or property. Debt securities are IOUs which borrowers give lenders as evidence of a loan and of their promise to repay; they are the embodiments of credit transactions. We shall study both kinds of securities in more detail in later chapters, but for the remainder of this chapter we shall be mainly concerned with debt securities and their characteristics.

Marketable vs. Non-Marketable

An IOU to the bank for a $500 auto loan is a security, but it is not a *marketable* security. No organized secondary market exists for the promises to pay of little-known private persons. By contrast, a bank's own promise to pay, for example, $1 million with 6 per cent interest on June 30 (a negotiable time certificate of deposit) *is* a marketable security, because a number of security dealers make a market in this kind of IOU by continually offering to buy them at a certain price (the bid) and resell them at a slightly higher price (the offer). The most marketable

---

[3]Federal Deposit Insurance Corporation protection runs only to $20,000 per account. Large depositors are thus unprotected against bank failures. Their only protection is to remove their money from a shaky bank before it folds.

of all securities are those issued by the U.S. Treasury. Next come those issued by the largest corporations, including banks.

For many purposes, investors prefer marketable securities because they can be disposed of if the holder needs to sell them. Furthermore, their continual quotation in the market place gives them a more or less definite value—as property or as collateral for getting a loan. Finally, since their greater liquidity means less risk for the holder, the issuers of marketable securities can usually obtain their loans at lower rates of interest than can issuers of non-marketable IOUs.

Time to Maturity

The most significant classification of securities is by time to maturity, paralleling our earlier division of credit transactions into short-term, intermediate-term, and long-term. Among Treasury securities, bills are short-term, notes intermediate-term, and bonds long-term. Both Treasury bills and the commercial paper issued by large, well-known corporations are simple, non-interest-bearing IOUs that pay a face amount at maturity. The purchaser receives interest by buying them at a discount in step with the prevailing discount rate for high-grade, short-term securities. Notes of the Treasury and of many corporations are really short-term bonds, maturing in from one to seven years. They bear semi-annual interest coupons (bearer form) or pay interest semi-annually by check (registered form). The principal amount—usually some multiple of $1,000—is paid at maturity on surrender of the note itself. Bonds, which run more than seven years (and often as long as forty years) have much the same appearance as notes and pay interest the same way.

Prices and Their Consequences

We have seen in chapters 5 and 6 that market values of debt securities move opposite to interest rates, and that quality-rating spreads among securities fluctuate according to the state of confidence prevailing in the economy. For these reasons, debt-security markets are closely watched by businessmen seeking a clue to the future moves of business. Rapidly rising yields not only bring falling security prices but also forecast the advent of tight money and a squeeze on businessmen and other borrowers. Falling yields suggest that money is becoming "easier" and more readily available. High or rapidly rising yields are typical of a boom that is becoming unsustainable, while low or falling yields are typical of a recession that is beginning to bottom out.

Security yields are basically a system of signals and incentives for lenders and borrowers of money. But security markets attract speculators as well as investors. Therefore, over short periods of time the direction market yields are taking may not have much significance. However, *sustained* moves that keep the same direction for many months and change prices by appreciable percentages are significant indicators of both the state of money and the state of business.

The Financial Markets

A market is a set of facilities which make it possible to exchange money for goods, or goods for money, on a regular basis. Securities are the goods exchanged in financial markets. In making these exchanges possible, the financial markets play a central part in business and economic life.

Functions of Financial Markets

The financial markets discharge five major functions: (1) shifting funds from suppliers to users, (2) liquifying securities, (3) pricing securities, (4) discounting the future, and (5) allocating funds and economic resources. Let us consider each function briefly.

Shifting Funds

The first task of the financial markets, a task illustrated in the model above; is to gather and mobilize—perhaps from thousands of individuals and separate financial institutions—a large part of the vast sums of money needed each day for the short- and longer-term requirements of business, governmental bodies, and consumers. Banks, other financial institutions, governments, and large business firms must have a dependable, central market where they can (1) bid for money in "wholesale" amounts when they need it, or (2) sell money for various intervals when they have an oversupply of it. The money and capital markets, which will be examined later in this chapter, meet these needs by permitting people with excess money to exchange it for securities, and enabling people who need money to raise it by selling securities. This exchanging of money for *new-issue* securities is the central task of the *primary,* or new issues, securities markets. As we shall see, there is both a primary money and a primary capital market to accomplish these exchanges for short- and long-period money transfers, respectively.

Liquifying Security Holdings

A second function of financial markets is to liquify security holdings. Essential to security buying is the holder's confidence that, if he wants to sell his security, he can do so readily. Thus security-buyers demand marketability, and sometimes liquidity, for their holdings. Supplying these properties is the task of the other main division of the money and capital markets, the *secondary,* or resale, markets. It is mainly because of investors' confidence that their security holdings are readily marketable in secondary markets, at somewhat predictable prices, that they are willing to buy new issues and so provide a continuing flow of funds to the economic system.

Pricing

A third major function—pricing—is shared by both primary and secondary markets. Interest rates, as you know, determine the price of debt securities, and interest rates are set by the supply of, and demand for, money for various time-intervals. It is in the money and capital markets that these supplies and demands converge. That is, the inflow of money into financial markets must always suffice to buy the total volume of new and old securities sold; interest rates and security prices are simply the result of this process. Of course, the relative prices of different securities may shift considerably from day to day. For example, old issues may go up because few are offered; new issues may fall because the supply is large; stocks may be up, bonds down, and bills steady. The different patterns of price and yield movements in these markets are multitudinous, but each has logical explanation rooted in supply-demand factors.

Discounting the Future

The fourth and most elusive function of financial markets is discounting the future. How is this done? It is handled largely through price movements and particularly the trend of prices. Nothing else is as important to most people as money, and foreseen events typically cast long shadows before them as people race to make profits or avoid losses on what they expect to happen. Their actions reflect the speculative demand for money we saw in chapter 3. Thus, in large degree, the economic future is often readable *today* in the money and capital markets. For example, if people expect profits to slide, the stock market falls; if people think money will become scarcer and interest rates will rise, they will race to dump bonds (and avoid capital losses) and acquire bills or cash instead. Because financial markets faithfully mirror peoples' expectations about the future, they are important barometers of business confidence and business forecasting. All top businessmen and financial executives follow the ups and downs of financial markets meticulously, interpreting every twist or turn in hope of "getting a handle" on how business will move in weeks or months ahead.

Allocating Resources

The markets' fifth and final task is to allocate economic resources, a point emphasized in our simple model above. Ostensibly, financial markets allocate money. Parties supplying funds compare the merits of different bids for them; they weigh yield, safety, growth, resaleability, and other qualities which each bidder offers in his securities. Having judged these merits, money suppliers buy some securities and reject others. Long- and short-term funds flow to the successful bidders (including business firms, governmental bodies, and financial institutions) and are denied those groups whose securities are not so attractive.

Behind the allocation of money, something much more fundamental also takes place. Successful bidders use their funds to acquire labor, machinery, raw materials, and other factors of production. By expanding their money resources, they will have enlarged their control of real economic resources. In this way, the money and capital markets guide the economy's all-important allocation of its productive powers.

Financial Markets Classified

Financial markets can be classified in several significant ways. There is the *primary* (new issues) market versus the *secondary* (resale) market. There are *debt* versus *equity* markets. There are *central* financial markets (such as those of New York or London) versus *local* ones (such as Buffalo). There are markets made by *dealers* (who buy and sell for their own "account and risk") and markets manned by *brokers* (who do not themselves take title to the security). And finally, there is the *money market* (for short-term securities, or loans) versus the *capital market* (which deals in long-term loans, equity shares, and the securities evidencing them).

The Money Market

The money market is the central market, or set of facilities, where large amounts of money are lent and borrowed for intervals of less than one year. It is the central "wholesale" market for short-term debt securities, or for the temporary investment of large amounts of short-term funds. It has two key characteristics: (1) The loans (and thus the financial instruments) in which it deals are relatively risk free. (2) Lender-borrower relations are largely impersonal. The money market comprises several major sectors. Let us examine them.

Treasuries

The market for short-term Treasury securities is the largest, broadest, and most important money-market sector. Traded here are Treasury *bills,* or IOUs sold at a discount from face (maturity) value; *certificates,* or interest-bearing obligations with a single interest-coupon paid at maturity; and Treasury bonds and notes within a year or less of maturity. This market has five major participants. (1) The Treasury is, of course, the borrower. (2) Non-financial corporations lend short-term surplus funds in this market. (3) Commercial banks buy and sell short-term Treasuries as secondary reserve instruments. (4) The Federal Reserve buys and sells short-term Treasuries to increase or diminish the reserves of member banks. (5) Dealers, both banks and non-bank houses, maintain a market in short-dated Treasuries by buying and selling for their own account.

Closely linked to the Treasury section of the money market is the market in short-term federal agency obligations. This includes the bills and certificates of the Federal Land Bank, the Bank for Co-Operatives, the Federal Home Loan Bank, The Federal National Mortgage Association, and the Federal Intermediate Credit Banks. While debt of these agencies is not guaranteed by the Treasury, no one expects the Treasury to let their obligations default. Consequently, these securities enjoy almost as high an investment standing and almost as low a yield as Treasury securities of the same maturity. The markets, however, have fewer active participants and choice of maturities is more restricted than in Treasuries.

Commercial Paper

The commercial paper market—the second largest branch of the money market—averaged during 1971 more than $30 billion in outstanding obligations. Commercial paper consists of non-interest-bearing IOUs through which well-known corporations raise short-term funds. Like Treasury bills, they are marketed at a discount. Yields on commercial paper are slightly higher than on Treasury obligations of equal maturity. Issuers typically alter the spread between commercial paper and Treasury bills to attract or repel money. The chief markets for commercial paper are banks outside of money centers (who hold it as part of their secondary reserves) and corporate treasurers, who use it as an interest-earning investment for temporarily surplus funds.

Other Segments

Other major money market segments include negotiable CDs, bankers acceptances, and federal funds.

Negotiable CDs are issued by commercial banks in large denominations and transferrable form primarily to attract corporate deposit balances in competition with Treasury bills and commercial paper. The maximum yield banks can offer on them is regulated by the Reserve Board's Regulation Q, which governs interest on all time deposits. In recent years the volume and competitiveness of negotiable CDs have fluctuated widely with the ups and downs of Regulation Q ceilings.

Bankers acceptances begin as businessmen's promises to pay. They are usually issued to finance imports and exports in foreign trade. They are termed *accepted* when a bank guarantees their payment at maturity. This market is small; the average amount of acceptance credit outstanding does not ordinarily exceed $3 billion. The market is dominated by foreign investors.

The Federal funds market is a market in one-day loans of Federal Reserve member banks' excess reserves to other members with reserve deficiencies. The rate on federal funds may run a percentage point or more above the discount rate and sometimes—when excess reserves are very large—falls below the discount rate. Daily volume in this market typically runs from one billion to several billion dollars.

The money market is important for three main reasons. First, it is the basic influence on the nation's structure of short-term interest rates. Second, it is the focal point—indeed, the injection center—of Federal Reserve monetary and credit policy. Third, its tone and moves have powerful repercussions on the capital market, on businessmen's thinking, and on economic activity in general.

The Capital Market

The capital market includes all agencies concerned with the issuance and trading of long-term securities. These include (1) investment bankers—the "midwives" for new issues of stocks and bonds, and (2) brokers, dealers, and stock exchanges—the key cogs in the secondary markets for bonds and stocks.[4]

Primary Capital Markets

The primary capital markets consist of four major segments. These deal with (1) corporate securities, (2) Federal Government obligations, (3) state and local government securities, and (4) mortgages.[5] Primary capital market transactions are for one of two purposes: (1) sale of net new securities, which adds to the issuer's capital funds; (2) the refunding (refinancing) of outstanding securities about to mature. Prices and yields at which securities can be sold in primary capital markets are closely aligned with prices and yields on similar obligations traded in secondary capital markets. In general, new issues carry slightly lower prices and higher yields to promote prompt sales.

The primary market for corporate securities is described in detail in chapter 29. Since a knowledge of its organization and mechanics is unnecessary at this point, we move on to consider other capital-market sectors.

---

[4]The secondary capital market is discussed in chapters 31 and 32.

Primary Government Market

The capital markets include the market for intermediate and long-term securities of the federal government. The Treasury issues two classes of longer-term securities. Notes have maturities of one to seven years and, like bonds, carry semi-annual interest coupons. Bonds run (at issue time) seven years or longer, though some are callable (or subject to being retired or paid off before maturity at a fixed cash price) anytime within five years of maturity.

The Treasury issues bonds for two purposes: to finance new federal debt and to refund or rollover maturing debt issues. An issue of Treasury securities involves three essential steps: (1) an announcement by the Treasury of the issue and its terms, (2) action by the Federal Reserve as the Treasury's agent in accepting orders and payments, (3) implicit underwriting of the issue both by the Federal Reserve and by the large government security dealers, who are tacitly committed to taking the unsold residue of any issue. During the period immediately preceding a Treasury issue, the Federal Reserve pursues an even-keel policy. It attempts to stabilize bond prices and yields so the capital market will absorb the government issue. The even-keel policy means that Federal Reserve attempts to slow spending must be temporarily halted when the Treasury is floating a new issue.

New Treasury borrowings present some interesting contrasts with refundings. New borrowings have a greater impact than refundings on the capital market; that is, they take more money out, shifting it from the capital market to the Treasury. Refundings generally lead to no net loss of funds because holders merely swap maturing issues for new bonds. However, refundings of maturing securities may shift funds from the capital market to the money market because maturing bonds, having become short-term, are often held by money-market investors who won't exchange them for new long-term issues. To avoid this problem, the Treasury has introduced *advance refundings,* under which holders of bonds maturing in, for example, two years are encouraged to swap them now for new seven-year securities.

State and Local Government Bonds

State and local government bonds, called municipals, fall into two important classes. (1) General obligation bonds are supported by the full taxing authority of a governmental unit. (2) Revenue bonds are supported only by revenues collected from services provided by some public authority not having taxing power: toll roads; bridge, tunnel, and airport authorities, and the like.

The primary market for these issues has several distinctive characteristics. The volume of issues is more sensitive to interest rates than that of corporate bonds. Many states and municipalities have laws setting ceilings on the interest rates they can pay to borrow money; when market rates exceed these ceilings,

---

[3]Every financial market transaction—in either primary or secondary markets—involves the exchange of money for securities, or near-money. So it really doesn't matter whether we think of these markets as markets for money loans of various duration, or, alternatively, as markets for various kinds of securities evidencing these loans. It makes no difference, for example, whether we think of the money market as the market for short-term funds (loans) or for short-dated debt securities.

the borrower is priced out of the market. Secondly, municipals are always sold to underwriters on a competitive bid basis. Sales proceed less rapidly than with corporate bonds; it may take underwriters two or three weeks to dispose completely of an issue once it is taken onto their shelves. Finally, municipals have a rather definitely segmented market. Fully-taxable corporations are large buyers of short-dated municipals, primarily for the tax-exempt interest. Commercial banks are large buyers of both short and intermediate maturities, and casualty companies and trustees also buy intermediate maturities. Wealthy individuals buy most long maturities, particularly when the outlook for common stocks is poor.

Mortgage Market

The primary market for mortgages is entirely a negotiated market, although rates on similar kinds of loans are kept in alignment by force of competition. However, geographical differentials are quite pronounced.

The chief mortgage lenders are savings and loan associations, life insurance companies, mutual savings banks, and commercial banks. Most life insurance company loans are placed through mortgage bankers. These local specialists make mortgage loans and sell the loans to insurance companies, but continue to earn fees by servicing the loans (collecting principal and interest, insurance premiums, and escrow tax payments).

Mortgages are the largest single segment of the capital markets and typically absorb at least one-third of the net annual flow of savings in the United States. They may be resold to two government-backed institutions that function as secondary markets—the Federal National Mortgage Association (now privately owned) and the recently established Government National Mortgage Association. Their task is to buy mortgages when they are in oversupply and their price falls. This is done (1) to keep mortgage yields from rising excessively, and (2) to provide mortgage lenders with new funds. When investors' demand for mortgages overtakes the supply again, these agencies then make a profit selling mortgages out of their inventory on a rising market.

To Remember

Definitions of credit	Discounting the future
Five Cs of credit	Money market
Credit creation	Primary market
Credit mediation	Secondary market
Securities	Capital market
Financial market functions	

Questions

1   Discuss the relations between "conditions" and credit-worthiness.
2   Describe three conditions, at least one of which a short-term borrower must satisfy. Why is it logical for lenders to insist on such conditions?

3 Why do intermediate- and long-term borrowing power typically depend on the borrower's profitability?

4 Discuss ways that credit can make possible new cycles of production and consumption that could not otherwise be undertaken.

5 Discuss the conditions under which credit-creation is, and is not, inflationary. (Hint: recall the Equation of Exchange.)

6 Discuss the changes in the cost of credit to different *quality* borrowers that take place over the business cycle.

7 Why are ups and downs of the securities markets so closely watched by experienced businessmen?

8 Name and briefly describe the five major functions of financial markets.

9 Explain how prices in the securities markets can be said to discount the future.

10 Why are prices in primary and secondary markets closely aligned?

8

Monetary and Fiscal Policy: The Federal Reserve

Objectives of Monetary Policy — Conflicts Among Objectives — The Federal Reserve — Tools of Monetary Management — *Reserve Requirements* — *Discount-Rate Changes* — *Open Market Operations* — *Interest Ceilings on Time Deposits* — *Moral Suasion* — **Selective Tools** — *Stock Market Margins* — *Channels of Influence* — **Technical Guides to Monetary Policy** — **Condition of the Banking System** — *Float* — *Measuring Ease or Strain* — **Fiscal Policy** — *Monetary and Fiscal Policy Contrasted* — *Financing Deficits* — *Retiring Debt Through a Surplus* — *Combining Monetary and Fiscal Policy* — **Monetary Policy: Final Assessment** — *Technical Shortcomings* — *Moral Shortcomings*

There are two devices by which modern free world societies try to steer economic affairs instead of leaving them entirely to chance, free-market, or "automatic" forces.

1. *Monetary policy* is the central bank's effort to regulate the economy by managing the supply, cost, and availability of money and credit.

2. *Fiscal policy* is the government's effort to control the economy through taxation, spending, and management of the public debt.

This chapter deals principally with monetary policy and

its chief instrument, the Federal Reserve System.[1] It deals more briefly with fiscal policy, as it affects the businessman.

Objectives of Monetary Policy

Five main objectives are usually ascribed to monetary policy. The first three are encompassed in the Employment Act of 1946 and apply equally to fiscal policy. The last two are considered the primary domain of monetary policy. The five main objectives are: maximum employment, a stable price level, maximum sustainable economic growth, balance in international payments, and maximum freedom of economic choice. Let us briefly describe each goal.

1. *Maximum employment.* This objective is difficult to define precisely. Statistically, does it mean 3, 4, or 5 per cent of the labor force unemployed? Disagreement is largely over how much unemployment is (1) inevitable—between jobs or from people being overly selective in choosing acceptable jobs, or (2) necessary—to discipline the excessive wage demands that result from "overfull" employment.

2. *A stable price level.* Since inflation and deflation redistribute wealth and affect purchasing power, this objective seeks to keep the general price level steady. Overall price stability would still allow individual prices to move up and down as supply and demand changed for particular goods and services. But again a statistical problem emerges: which of several price indices to stabilize? Should it be the Consumer Price Index? the GNP deflator? or some other?

3. *Maximum sustainable economic growth.* This goal emphasizes the desirability of a rising standard of living and an expanding economy which can create jobs for an increasing population. The word "sustainable" is important, for experience shows that efforts to make the economy grow too fast breed inflation, dislocations, and eventual recessions.

4. *Long-term balance in international payments.* Foreign trade, investment, lending, direct aid, military expenditures, and so on, lead either to our owing foreign countries, or their owing us, a net balance due. These claims must ordinarily be settled in gold or in acceptable foreign monies. Since total loss of gold and foreign-money reserves would leave the United States internationally bankrupt, the country must in the long run balance its international income and outgo.

5. *Preserving maximum economic freedom.* U.S. monetary policy has long aimed at having the central bank create the right *total* amount of money and credit, but letting the market allocate this amount according to the strength of different demands. In this way, the rationing of financial resources by an "all-knowing" or tyrannical government is avoided, and maximum scope is given to individual initiative.

Conflict Among Objectives

Clearly, these objectives are a mixed bag. They are not all compatible, and three notable conflicts have arisen.

---

[1]The authors acknowledge their debt in this chapter to William Tennyson, assistant vice president, French American Banking Corporation, New York City. We borrowed many insights and expressions from his concise and distinctively phrased memorandum of December 23, 1970, written to acquaint his bank's Paris directors with the background of Federal Reserve policies and operations.

Maximum employment versus price stability is one significant conflict. These goals have been at odds since World War II. When money supply has grown fast enough to hold unemployment below 5 per cent, the price-level has increased. When money supply has been restrained enough to slow down inflation, unemployment has increased. In 1970–71, prices zoomed despite high unemployment because monopolistic forces such as big labor and big business could raise *their prices,* forcing the public to spend less on unmonopolized products. President Nixon applied wage and price controls in the summer of 1971, but both theory and experience suggested they would not long succeed unless money supply was held in check. If too much money was created to chase too few goods, prices would inevitably go up—on black markets which would replace legal ones. The root trouble is that if excess money supply is relied on to keep employment full, inflation seems bound to continue.

Balance of payments versus full employment and growth is a second conflict. The standard remedy for international payments exceeding receipts is to cut the growth of money supply and raise interest rates, a process we shall study in chapter 11. However, doing so would enfeeble domestic demand and possibly start a recession. Since our politicians seem to worry more about the next election at home than the dollar's fate abroad, those in power have chosen to continue running deficits. Also, every time a recession strikes, the Federal Reserve and Treasury try to "inflate" the country back to prosperity with cheap money and runaway budgets; this new flood of dollars weakens the U.S. balance of payments.

Maximum employment versus growth is a third conflict. If full employment is impossible without inflation, a further conflict arises between full employment and rapid economic growth. Frequent interludes of monetary restraint needed to prevent runaway prices also slow the pace of economic expansion. This leads to what has been called a "stop and go" economy.

The Federal Reserve

Monetary policy in the United States is decided and carried out by the Board of Governors of the Federal Reserve System, the nation's central bank. The Board is composed of seven members appointed for fourteen-year terms by the President and confirmed by the Senate. Its outstanding feature is its legal independence of both the executive and legislative branches of government in day-to-day operations. Only one member's term expires every two years, and so it would take a President almost two full terms in office to appoint a majority. Furthermore, the Federal Reserve System has its own source of income in its huge portfolio of government securities. Thus, it finds no need to ask Congress for money to carry on its operations. The Board is free to follow its collective conscience, though generally it cooperates with the political administration in power. Like the Supreme Court, it tends in the long run to read the election returns.

Founded in 1913 as a system of twelve district banks, each serving a particular region with its own local problems, the Federal Reserve has long since become a unified system implementing nation-wide policies. But although they have outgrown local autonomy, the district banks and their branches still play important administrative roles locally and serve as listening posts for national policy-making and policy changes.

Tools of Monetary Management

To implement monetary policy, the Federal Reserve relies on a kit of assorted tools. Broadly, these are classed as *general* and *selective* tools. General tools aim at creating or maintaining some given *total amount* of money (or credit) and letting the market mechanism allocate it according to supplies and demands originating in the economy's various sectors. Selective tools are aimed at regulating *particular uses* of money or credit.

The four general instruments of control used by the Federal Reserve are (1) member bank reserve requirements, (2) discount rate changes, (3) open market operations, and (4) interest ceilings on time deposits. The first three instruments operate on the reserve position of the member banks, and constitute the fulcrum of the leverage which Federal Reserve actions can exert on our fractional-reserve money system. Let us examine each of the four general instruments of control.

Reserve Requirements

The most powerful of the Federal Reserve's quantitative controls over money available for lending by the banks is the reserve requirement against member bank deposits. Small changes in member bank reserve requirements can permit huge changes in money supply, a process discussed in chapter 4. The word "permit" in the previous sentence deserves emphasis. The money supply expansion will not take place unless it is generated by loan demand, by investments made by commercial banks on *their* initiative, or by a combination of the two.

It should be stressed that reserve requirements exist only to limit member banks' money-creating and credit-granting activities. Required reserves play no part in bank safety or solvency, since these reserves cannot be paid out or drawn down. To meet withdrawals, banks must rely on their reserves of vault cash and short-term marketable securities, called secondary reserves, plus a properly spaced flow of loan maturities. Since required reserves are only a regulatory device, the Federal Reserve has found it convenient to reduce them occasionally in recent years when there was strong need to expand money and credit. In September 1972, the requirement for all member banks was a ratio that started at 8 per cent on the first $2 million, increasing to 17.5 per cent on over-$400 million.

Discount-Rate Changes

The Federal Reserve's second grip on member banks is through short-term loans to cover temporary deficits in their reserve requirements. By raising the discount rate charged on these loans, the Federal Reserve can raise the cost for the banks to run deficits; by lowering the rate, it can reduce the cost. In this way, the Federal Reserve can either discourage banks from making loans and investments that force them into debt to the Federal Reserve, or—alternatively—encourage such indebtedness and, with it, credit expansion. Discounts are used at the member banks' initiative, but the Federal Reserve decides their cost.

Banks temporarily needing reserves may borrow the excess reserves of other banks on an overnight basis. The rate on these borrowings is called the federal funds rate. When this rate is lower than the discount rate, banks have little incentive to borrow from the Federal Reserve. Conversely, as interest rates at which banks can borrow from each other rise above the discount rate, their incentive to borrow from the Federal Reserve increases. It increases still more as yields rise on Treasury bills and other reserve assets. This is so because it is cheaper for a bank to raise needed funds by borrowing money from the Federal Reserve at, for example, 4 per cent, than to sell a Treasury bill yielding 5 per cent. As profit-motivated enterprises, banks always try to relieve their reserve deficiencies in the cheapest way possible.

However, the Federal Reserve considers discounting to be a privilege, not a right, of member banks, and it will often write a critical letter to the president of a bank which it believes to be borrowing too much and too often. Such warnings are never taken lightly.

Open Market Operations

Reserve requirements are seldom changed; discount rates, infrequently. The Board's real power is felt in the money market. The Federal Reserve sells securities to absorb member bank reserves and buys them to supply reserves. A policy directive is drafted and voted on by the Open Market Committee (composed of the Board of Governors and five Reserve Bank presidents). The manager of the Open Market Account (a vice president of the New York Federal Reserve Bank) then translates this directive into day-to-day decisions to buy and sell specific quantities of securities in the market.

It might seem that speculators could make big money in the government securities market by buying when the Federal Reserve buys and selling when it sells, since the market will move the way the Federal Reserve intends. However, in conducting open market operations, the Federal Reserve covers its tracks quite well. For example, to buy a net of $500 million in securities, it might engage in $5½ billion worth of transactions, of which $2½ billion might be sales transactions. Also, there are a number of dealers in the government securities market, and by using different dealers for different trades, the Federal Reserve effectively conceals its ultimate intentions concerning the market's direction.

The New York securities market is a well-lubricated and instantly responsive channel through which the Board's policy finds its way into the economy. Besides the impact on member bank reserves, open market purchases and sales also bring about prompt and carefully graduated changes in the cost and availability of borrowable money.

Because of their ability to make relatively fine adjustments in bank reserves, open market operations are the most flexible, versatile, and continuously used of all monetary tools. Unlike discounts, this tool is used at the Federal Reserve's initiative.

Interest Ceilings on Time Deposits

The newest active weapon in the Federal Reserve's arsenal is Regulation Q, which regulates the rates of interest that banks can pay on time deposits. (Interest on demand deposits has been outlawed since the early 1930s.) The rate ceilings so set are known as "Q ceilings." If ceilings on CDs are below the yields of other short-term marketable securities, then money will flow into Treasury bills, commercial paper, and the like, and out of time deposits. The banks must either find other sources of funds or cut back their credit-granting (lending and investing) activities. Alternatively, when time deposit ceilings are raised above yields on competing instruments, the banks can again raise loanable funds by selling CDs. Money will be attracted out of idle demand deposits into time deposits, a higher fraction of which may be relent.

The Federal Reserve also can make it easier or more difficult for banks to borrow each other's idle deposits. The chief form this has taken in the United States has been Federal Reserve control of Eurodollar borrowings by U.S. banks, usually from their own foreign branches. Eurodollars are dollars deposited in banks abroad, and U.S. banks borrow these from their foreign branches in the same way a businessman might. Since 1969, the Federal Reserve has regulated inflows and outflows of Eurodollars between U.S. banks and their foreign branches by subjecting Eurodollar borrowings to reserve requirements, i.e., by obliging borrowing banks to deposit a certain percentage of the funds borrowed with their district Reserve bank. This raises the effective rate of interest a U.S. bank must pay to obtain Eurodollars.

Moral Suasion

Moral suasion is often mentioned among the tools of Federal Reserve control. It simply means that the Federal Reserve lets the commercial banks know that it wants them to behave a certain way. Suasion ranges from innocuous statements for public consumption (to which the banks pay no attention)[2] to ferocious brow-beating which terrorizes bankers and brings hasty compliance. Member banks depend on the Federal Reserve's good will for discounts and other accommodations, and they recognize that the Federal Reserve can use its other tools to achieve its objectives if banks do not cooperate voluntarily. So, if seriously intended, moral suasion is another version of the iron fist in the velvet glove.

Selective Tools

The general instruments of Federal Reserve action affect monetary totals (or aggregates), leaving the market mechanism to allocate the credit available. Their effect can be likened to that of a shotgun. At times, however, credit restraint is needed in particular sectors. On these occasions, the Federal Reserve has resorted to selective credit controls; their action can be compared to a sniper's rifle.

During World War II and the Korean War, Congress authorized the Federal Reserve to place special controls on purchases of housing and appliances—goods subject to war-time shortage and panic-buying. These anti-inflationary regulations set minimum down payments and maximum payment periods, thus damping demand by making credit harder to acquire. Such controls expired long ago, but a new crisis could possibly revive them.

---

[2]One should remember Winston Churchill's comment: "I had no idea in those days of the enormous and unquestionably helpful part that humbug plays in the social life of great peoples dwelling in a state of democratic freedom." See Winston Churchill, *A Roving Commission* (New York: Charles Scribner's Sons, 1951), p. 56.

Stock Market Margins

The only selective tool currently in the Federal Reserve's arsenal is the power to prescribe margins, or minimum down payments, for the purchase of securities, particularly common stocks. The theory of this power, vested in the Board since 1934, is the ability to kill speculation without killing prosperity. Margin requirements strongly regulate the flow of credit into the stock market. The Federal Reserve appears to watch both the use of credit to buy stocks and the market level itself. When speculation seems to be getting the upper hand, the Federal Reserve increases margin requirements to 70, 80, and even 100 per cent. High margins usually coincide with bull market peaks, business booms, and accelerating price inflation. When business drifts into recession and stock prices deflate, margins are lowered again, typically to 50 or 60 per cent.

Channels of Influence

Aside from the theoretical effect on people's cash balances,[3] how does monetary policy alter economic activity? Amid considerable debate, there is broad agreement that its effects are felt through three main channels of influence.

1. *Availability of money and credit.* When bank reserves are too small to accommodate the full demand for loans, banks must ration funds. They become more selective in accommodating potential borrowers, reduce loan sizes, and lend for briefer periods. The resulting general shortage of money imposes similar restrictions on non-bank lenders, who find funds harder to acquire. Conversely, plentiful reserves make the banks more willing to lend and less selective. Idle money is then also deposited with non-bank intermediaries, increasing the availability of funds there. This channel of influence acts basically on the supply of loanable funds.

2. *Cost of funds.* When tight reserves create a shortage of money, lenders raise interest rates. This increase in the cost of funds helps reduce borrower demands by pricing marginal borrowers out of the market. But large excess reserves have the opposite effect of lowering interest rates and making borrowing attractive to those who would not have borrowed before. This channel acts primarily on the demand for loanable funds.

3. *Capital-value effects.* Rising interest rates reduce the market price of bonds and mortgages held by banks, insurance companies, and other lenders. Ordinarily, these institutions sell off such investments when they can lend the proceeds at a better return, but they are less anxious to do this when their investments must be sold at a loss. Thus rising interest rates are said to "lock" lenders into their portfolios. Conversely, a fall in interest rates, which raises capital values, makes investment portfolios liquid again and enlarges the supply of funds available for loan. This channel of influence, like the first, affects the supply of loanable funds.

As money tightens, the capital-value effect is strengthened by the forced selling of debt securities. As we have seen, individuals and business firms also use debt securities as stores of value. When tight money makes it difficult for them to obtain loans and brings a slowdown in their own cash inflows, these groups sell their investments to raise cash. Such selling increases the supply of debt securities, pushing their prices down and their yields up.

---

[3]See the subsection, "How Monetary Policy Works," in chapter 3.

Technical Guides to Monetary Policy

It is unlikely that people will ever agree on the objectives of monetary policy. But even if they should, they would still disagree on how to *implement* these objectives. The disagreement centers on the issue of what statistical measures the central bank should use as a guide, to tell it how and when to move. What should central bankers watch? Should they watch interest rates? the *total amount* of money (currency plus demand deposits) in existence? the *rate of increase* in demand deposits plus currency? demand deposits plus currency plus time deposits? the total amount of bank credit outstanding? the total amount of all credit outstanding? the total volume of bank reserves? the readily lendable reserves of the banks? some estimate of "general liquidity" for the whole economy? All these measures have been proposed and discussed, with more heat than light emerging.

In recent years, technical disagreement about monetary policy has become a debate between advocates of a fixed rate of money supply expansion and those who advocate discretion and judgment as the best guides to monetary decisions.

Fixed-rate advocates argue that discretionary management has had such a bad record and has proved so error prone that it is best replaced by putting money supply on a steady expansion of perhaps 4 per cent a year, come what may. They point out that the economy's output of goods and services has grown at about that rate since 1870, so that a 4 per cent increase in money should be non-inflationary in the future. They further argue that a fixed 4 per cent annual increase in the money supply would discourage inflationary booms and wage-push tactics because money to feed them would not be created. Thus, recessions and unemployment—which, since World War II, have resulted primarily from efforts to stop inflation—would be less likely. Tendencies toward recession or slowed growth would be offset by the continuing steady growth of money supply at a predictable rate.

Discretionists counter by arguing that a fixed rate of money expansion ignores changes in velocity,[4] which have upset the economy in the past even when money supply was not changing rapidly. Since people's desire to hold or spend money depends on other factors besides the amount of available money, central banks must take continual note of the changing *demand* for money and alter the *supply* accordingly. The same amount of money might be inflationary under one set of conditions and start a recession under another. Therefore, discretion and judgment must be applied to monetary decisions as to other economic questions.

A few comments on this windy debate seem appropriate. (1) Discretionary monetary policy has had a poor record, but there is no guarantee that the fixed rate "automatic pilot" would be better. (2) Fixed-rate advocates have had their own debate over (a) what rate to fix, and (b) how to measure money. (3) Even if a fixed rate worked, people would not continue to accept it if it led to high unemployment. Monetary policy today is the creature of politics, and if voters are complaining, politicians will change a policy (however right it may be) just to please them. Discretionary policy gives the central bank leeway to take action, whereas a fixed-rate of expansion would suggest to voters that the central bank was indifferent to their hardship. (4) Those who fear inflation are likely to be

---

[4]Table 3–1 shows that over the past twenty-five years the income velocity of money in the United States has approximately doubled.

fixed-rate advocates; those who want full employment, even at the price of inflation, prefer discretion. This suggests that fixed-rate monetary policy offers, at the least, greater promise of price stability. Certainly, over the past generation, discretionary management has proved to be an engine of price inflation.

Condition of the Banking System

To make sound financial decisions, a businessman must know whether money is easy or tight, the direction in which interest rates are moving, and whether financial markets are headed for slack or strain. The point of departure for these judgments is a correct reading of the condition of the country's banking system. Assessment begins with consideration of the Federal Reserve System's balance sheet, a simplified version of which is presented in Table 8–1. Most of the items are probably clear to you, but two call for explanation.

Table 8–1. Combined Balance Sheet of the Reserve Banks, October 27, 1971

Item	Billions of Dollars
Assets	
1. Gold Certificates	9.9
2. Discounts for Member Banks	2.0
3. U.S. Government Securities	67.8
4. Cash Items in Process of Collection	11.2
5. Other Assets	2.1
Total Assets	93.0
Liabilities	
6. Federal Reserve Notes	52.4
7. Deposits	
(a) Member Bank Reserves	27.2
(b) U.S. Treasury	1.7
(c) Foreign	.1
(d) Other	.7
8. Deferred Availability Cash Items	8.6
9. Other Liabilities	.6
Total Liabilities	91.3
Capital	
10. Paid-in Capital	.7
11. Retained Profits	.7
12. Other Capital	.3
Total Capital	1.7
Total Liabilities and Capital	93.0

Source: *Federal Reserve Bulletin,* January 1972.

Float

"Cash items in process of collection" consist of checks written on banks in one Federal Reserve district, credited to the reserve accounts of banks in another Federal Reserve district, but not yet deducted from the reserve account of the payor bank. To offset this reserve increase, a liability—"Deferred availability cash items"—is entered, for the same amount as each in-process-of-collection check. "Deferred availability cash items" is a very brief entry, however; it stays on the books only for the time normally required for the check to clear the payor's district Federal Reserve bank. Then the check is subtracted from the payor's bank's reserves. But weather, slow mail service, clerical mixups, and other causes always delay a certain fraction of collectible checks beyond their deferment periods. Thus "Cash items in process of collection" typically exceeds "Deferred availability cash items" by a billion dollars or more, meaning that the same reserves are being counted twice—at two different Federal Reserve banks. This unintentional and rather unpredictable inflation of member bank reserves is called *float*. It can be troublesome to Federal Reserve officials trying to "fine tune" the money supply.

Measuring Ease or Strain

The Reserve System balance sheet shows the aggregate size of central bank resources backing the nation's money system. But it reveals little about the degree of ease or strain in that system: that is, how abundant or scarce money is relative to the demand for it, how intensively the money supply is being worked, and how much pressure banks are experiencing in trying to meet loan demand and still maintain their required reserves. Among generally accepted measures of the monetary system's condition are (1) interest rates, (2) deposit velocity, and (3) free reserve position of the nation's member banks. Figures relating to each of these indicators are published monthly in the *Federal Reserve Bulletin* and widely followed and interpreted as barometers and forecasts of business conditions.

The *trend*, as well as the level, of these indicators is watched by businessmen, bankers, economists, and others. What happened in any given week to interest rates, velocity, or free reserves may not be significant. Short-run changes in these figures often reflect the Federal Reserve's miscalculations of the consequences of its money-supply moves; they may also stem from temporary influences, such as even-keel policy to facilitate a Treasury borrowing. But persistent changes that predominate in one direction for several weeks almost always indicate one of two possibilities: either the Federal Reserve has embarked on a policy of ease or tightness, or the economy is moving so strongly that the Federal Reserve cannot immediately oppose the underlying trend.

Fiscal Policy

Fiscal policy is concerned with government spending, the way it is financed, and the extent to which it seeks to stimulate or restrain the economy. GNP, the economy's total spending, equals $C + I + G$, where C stands for consumption spending, I for all kinds of real (as distinguished from monetary) investment, and G for government spending. Using the GNP format, you can think of fiscal policy as G, but it also has side effects on C and I.

Fiscal policy affects the economy through three channels: (1) government spending, (2) taxation, and (3) debt management. What government spending and taxation are seems obvious enough. Debt management is the way the Treasury's debt, either new or accumulated, is financed.

Revenues, mostly taxes, minus expenditures equals a deficit if negative, a surplus if positive. Deficits stimulate the economy because the government is putting more dollars back into people's hands than it is taking out of them. A surplus restrains the economy because the government is taking more dollars away from people through taxes than it is adding through spending.

In theory, the Treasury should run a deficit in periods of high unemployment and low inflation, and a surplus in periods of overfull employment and high inflation. History teaches that politicians prefer stimulating to restraining—particularly in election years—so fiscal policy has consisted almost entirely of deficits.[5]

Monetary and Fiscal Policy Contrasted

The role of monetary policy has generally been labeled "permissive." That is, although central banks can create high-powered (and to some extent low-powered) money, they cannot force people to use it, and they cannot assure that the money will be spent in ways that create demand and jobs.

By contrast, fiscal policy directly adds to or subtracts from the economy's stream of spending. We can see this and other important points by considering the equation

$$GNP = C + I + G.$$

Presumably what government takes in taxes, it takes away from either C or I. To the extent that G is financed with taxes, it may simply replace C or I. Only to the extent G is financed either with (1) newly created money, or (2) borrowed money that would otherwise not be spent on C or I, can G be considered an economic stimulant.[6] If there is a surplus, then presumably more dollars are taken away from C and I than are replaced through G.

Financing Deficits

If the Treasury runs a deficit, it must borrow money to cover it. The Treasury borrows money by selling its securities—bills, certificates, notes, and bonds. How much "oomph" a deficit exerts on the cost and availability of loanable funds depends on two conditions: (1) existing level of demand for loanable funds, and (2) how the deficit is financed. Debt management determines how the deficit is financed. There are three ways the Treasury can finance a deficit.

1. The Treasury can sell securities to the non-bank public: individuals, business firms, and non-bank financial intermediaries. When the public buys the placement, existing money is shifted from the public's accounts to the Treasury's.

---

[5]The U.S. Treasury ran deficits in twelve of the thirteen years from 1961 through 1973.

[6]A recent study indicated that government spending financed by taxes or bonds simply crowds out private spending. See Roger W. Spencer and William Yohe, "The 'Crowding Out' of Private Expenditures by Fiscal Policy Actions," Federal Reserve Bank of St. Louis *Review* (October 1970), pp. 12–24.

The banking system maintains the same volume of total and excess reserves, and no new money (demand deposit) is created. Only velocity increases. A near-money is created: the public now holds a government security. Expenditures financed in this way will immediately increase interest rates if the demand for loanable funds is high because the Treasury must outbid borrowers in the private sector of the economy for the existing supply of money. Conversely, expenditures so financed will be less inflationary because the Treasury is crowding out expenditures that would otherwise be made by the private sector.

2. The Treasury can sell securities to commercial banks, who pay for them with excess reserves. Bank reserves decrease, bond holdings increase, and total assets remain the same. The Treasury deposits the funds it receives in the banking system so that the system's assets (reserves) and demand deposits increase. The net results of all of these transactions are for assets to increase by the amount of the bond and liabilities to increase by the amount of the Treasury's demand deposit. Total bank reserves are the same, but excess reserves become required reserves. The amount of near-money (government bond) and money increase. This method of financing a deficit has less of an immediate impact on interest rates than the above method, because the Treasury has not competed with private placements for an existing money supply. The Treasury has used up some of the banking system's ability to lend to other borrowers by absorbing excess reserves. Expenditures so financed are potentially more inflationary because new money is created and Treasury adds to the existing level of spending in the economy rather than crowding it out as when the bonds are sold to the public.

3. The least immediate impact on interest rates occurs when the Treasury sells its placements to the central bank. Here, the Treasury does not compete for loanable funds with the private sector either for the existing money supply or for the excess reserves of the banking system. When the Treasury deposits the proceeds from the bond sale in commercial banks, total assets and demand deposits of the system expand. The asset expansion is in the form of total reserves. Banks can now invest and lend more because excess reserves increase. Interest rates move up less than under the two previous financing methods not only because the Treasury has avoided direct competition with the private sector of the economy, but also because it has enhanced the banking system's ability to lend. Of course, expenditures so financed are potentially the most inflationary of all because of the increase in the money supply that can occur.

Retiring Debt Through a Surplus

When the Treasury runs a surplus it takes more money out of people's pockets through tax collections than it puts back through spending. How much impact on interest rates a surplus exerts depends on what the government does with the surplus. Assuming the demand for loanable funds is high, holding the surplus on deposit at the Federal Reserve will cause interest rates to expand rapidly because banks lose total reserves, excess reserves, and demand deposits when the public writes checks to the Treasury to pay the tax bill. If banks have no excess reserves to begin with, they must cancel loans by a multiple of their reserve loss. That is the same impact that occurs when the Treasury retires bonds held by the Federal

Reserve. The banking system loses demand deposits and reserves when the Treasury pays the Federal Reserve.

Retiring debt held by the public probably has a neutral impact on interest rates.[7] Total reserves, excess reserves, and demand deposits of the banking system remain the same. Only near-money is destroyed (the bond). Finally, retiring debt held by banks has potentially the most favorable impact on interest rates. Banks lose assets (bonds) and liabilities (demand deposits), but total reserves remain constant. Excess reserves increase so the lending and investing power—the power to create money—increases. Banks can acquire the placements of the private sector of the economy, creating demand deposits by a multiple of the excess reserves.

Combining Monetary and Fiscal Policy

Ideally, monetary and fiscal policy should work together, reinforcing or complementing each other. In practice, however, each has proved to be a one-edged tool. Monetary restraint has been effective in choking off booms, but monetary ease has proved to be a feeble business stimulant. Fiscal stimulation has been not only effective but also inviting to apply, since politicians always like to spend money, even when the Federal deficit soars. Fiscal restraint, however, has proved all but impossible to apply (however effective it might really be), because government spending creates vested interests which politicians are hesitant to offend (by cutting off expenditures). So, in the main, fiscal policy is relied on to fight recessions, and monetary policy to do the "dirty work" of killing off inflationary booms.

Frequently, monetary policy is prostituted to help fiscal policy. Politicians in the federal government often want to spend more money but are afraid to raise taxes. So the Federal Reserve quietly prints money by buying bonds directly from the Treasury to cover the deficit. That happened during the Vietnam War, particularly in 1967–68, and led to the inflationary boom of 1969, which had to be attacked with tight money and brought on the recession and rising unemployment of 1970.

Monetary Policy: Final Assessment

In theory, monetary policy is an application of $MV = PO$. M (total money supply) is controlled by the central bank by regulating the quantity of commercial bank reserves and currency (high-powered money) to just the right amount. This in turn keeps O (output) continually at the full-employment level without raising P (price level). Like most ideal models of economic or financial behavior, this one breaks down in practice. Its shortcomings are both technical, related to the process itself, and moral, related to the will of the people who manage it.

---

[7]For simplicity we ignore the differences in consumption propensities between tax payers and creditors repaid, differences that have a bearing on subsequent interest rates. This issue, and similar ones surrounding debt management, we leave to courses in advanced finance.

Technical Shortcomings

In a technical sense, the biggest problem of monetary policy is gauging and forecasting the behavior of velocity. Since total spending is measured by *M* times *V,* rather than by *M* alone, the central bank cannot forecast the consequences of an increase or decrease in money supply unless it can simultaneously predict what velocity will do. This is one reason why the country has had so much inflation. The Federal Reserve usually creates a huge "overhang" or supply of new money during a recession because velocity has slowed down and a great deal of money seems needed to give the economy a shove. Later on, when the next boom begins, the Federal Reserve slows, or even reverses, its additions to money supply, but the velocity of money steps up sharply and thwarts the restraining effort for many months while inflation eats up another chunk of the dollar's buying power. How is velocity accelerated? Banks and other lenders offer higher interest rates for deposits to relend, which activates idle money; and businessmen, consumers, and others get much more mileage out of the existing money supply by reducing their cash balances.

Moral Shortcomings

Of course, the sensible thing would be to not increase money so much in recession years. Then, even with the "stretch" in velocity, there would be less excess money to mop up after the next inflationary boom started. But the Federal Reserve, like most other central banks (and all political administrations since President Eisenhower) has a built-in bias toward inflationary management of money supply; it is always more eager to stimulate than to restrain. The Federal Reserve will begin to expand money at the least suggestion of economic slowdown, but it must see the white of inflation's eyes, so to speak, before it begins to restrain.

Some economists propose to eliminate this surge in velocity through stiffer controls over non-bank lenders. They advocate placing flexible reserve requirements on savings and loan associations, finance companies, issuers of commercial paper, and so on. Fundamentally, however, what seems to be lacking is the will to limit inflation at the price of limiting employment. As long as the public and its elected representatives choose *not* to pay that price, chances are that monetary policy will keep its inflationary bias, regardless of the mechanisms of control added for their cosmetic effect.

To Remember

Monetary policy

Fiscal policy

Objectives of monetary policy

Availability of funds

Cost of funds

Capital-value effect

Tools of monetary policy

Eurodollars

Fixed-rate advocates

Federal funds

Stock market margins

Float

Shortcomings of monetary policy

Questions

1 "Full employment has been the inveterate enemy of price stability." Discuss.

2 "Tight monetary policy shrinks capital values, thereby throttling down economic activity." Explain.

3 "In a fractional reserve system, the reserve position of the member banks is the fulcrum of monetary policy." Explain.

4 Open-market operations are the central bank's most flexible and continuously used tool of monetary policy. Why?

5 "Since 1966, Regulation Q has emerged as a potent weapon of monetary control." Explain.

6 What problems does the employment of selective tools of monetary control raise?

7 Distinguish between "fixed rate" advocates and "discretionists." Which do you think are right? Why?

8 Describe the three ways in which the Treasury can finance a deficit. Which is most inflationary? Why?

9 How does "float" arise in the banking system?

10 How is ease or strain in the nation's credit structure measured? Which barometers are most closely watched?

11 Why is future price stability threatened when the Federal Reserve creates a huge "overhang" of superfluous money to fight a recession?

12 Are technical or moral failures primarily to blame for the shortcomings of monetary policy? Explain.

9

What Commercial Banks Do

Bank Financial Structure: Some Observations — Bank Management: An Overview — *Liability Structure — Asset Structure —* Bank Liabilities — *Demand Deposits — Time Deposits — Other Liabilities (and Sources of Funds) — Bank Capital —* Bank Assets — *Cash Reserves — Loans — Investments —* Bank Earnings — Bank Regulation

---

For four reasons, commercial banks are the nation's most important financial institutions. (1) They hold most of the nation's money supply. (2) They lend money on a vast scale. (3) They are the only lenders that can create money. (4) They play a central part in implementing monetary policy.

Bank Financial Structure: Some Observations

Some salient facts about commercial banks are quickly revealed by a brief look at the items making up their balance sheet. Table 9–1 is an idealized balance sheet which displays, in typical proportions, the main kinds of assets and liabilities a bank holds. Three observations about this balance sheet seem noteworthy.

1. Banks hold relatively little cash, only about 2 per cent in their vaults and tills. How do they stay liquid? It cannot be through the 12 per cent of assets that banks generally maintain

Table 9-1. Balance Sheet of a Typical Commercial Bank, Per Cent Distribution of Major Assets and Liabilities

Item	Per Cent of Total
Assets	
Cash	2
Reserves at FR	16
Secondary Reserves	15
Loans	42
Investments	25
Total	100
Liabilities	
Demand Deposits	50
Time and Savings Deposits	36
Other Liabilities	6
Capital Accounts	8
Total	100

in required reserves, because these are kept on deposit at their reserve banks. Banks therefore depend chiefly for liquidity on their *secondary reserves,* ordinarily about 15 per cent of assets, which consist chiefly of short-term, readily marketable U.S. government securities. Another limited source of liquidity, not shown on the balance sheet, is the privilege of borrowing at the Federal Reserve discount window, and to some degree from other banks.

2. The largest single class of assets is loans. This is because loans are the most profitable way a bank can use its money. Loans (business loans, mortgages, and personal loans) yield banks a higher interest return than do investments. Investments, which consist mainly of marketable securities, have lower yields than loans, but possess the advantage of being more marketable and are thus more liquid and serve as an emergency source of cash. A bank's first-line of reliance for extra cash is either the secondary reserves described above, or the privilege of borrowing at the Federal Reserve, whichever is cheaper. However, a bank's higher-yielding, longer-term investments—ordinarily Treasury and municipal bonds—can also be sold for cash, though sometimes at large losses if interest rates have risen substantially since the banks bought the bonds. Loans, of course, have a definite maturity and are less liquid than investments. A bank tries to keep its loan portfolio reasonably liquid by (a) making a prudent percentage of its loans for short-periods only (typically one year or less), and (b) spacing its loan maturities evenly to assure a steady return of cash.

3. Banks have great financial leverage. That is, they have a very high ratio of borrowed funds to ownership, or equity, funds. Ownership funds consist of common stock; paid-in surplus, which is money paid in by stockholders in excess of the par, or stated, value of their stock; and retained profits, which are profits the bank keeps for expansion instead of paying out in dividends to stockholders.

For the typical bank, these funds, or capital accounts, amount to only about $1 for each $12 raised through customer deposits. Thus, a drop of only about 8 per cent in the value of the bank's assets would deplete its capital and begin eating into depositors' funds. Since a bank also has a fiduciary, or good faith, obligation to its depositors, it must take particular care not to risk their funds through imprudent loans or investments. Its obligation to depositors should always take precedence over its obligation to borrowers—a principle which has long served to distinguish good bankers from bad ones. Since about 50 per cent of the typical bank's liabilities consist of deposits withdrawable on demand, any rumor that a bank is in trouble can quickly produce a ruinous run by fearful depositors, and this can close the bank.[1] A bank must shut its doors if it is unable to pay depositors on demand or to honor at once checks on their accounts. Thus, a bank can fail for lack of cash to meet withdrawals, even though its total assets still exceed its total liabilities.[2]

Bank Management: An Overview

Banking clearly illustrates the financial manager's dilemma, discussed in chapter 1. Banks are run for profit and owned by private stockholders, yet important fiduciary obligations prevent the banker from "wheeling and dealing" as the ordinary businessman is free to do. A bank's pursuit of profit is thus greatly restrained by the need to preserve the assured liquidity that will maintain the bank above suspicion and keep it from failing.

Liability Structure

The central principle of bank management is that the bank must at all times preserve a proper balance between its assets and liabilities.

A bank's liabilities must be paid when due or the bank must close its doors. Thus the character of a bank's liabilities govern the assortment of assets it can safely acquire. This principle does not entirely rule out what has come to be called "liability management": a bank can obtain new flexibility for asset acquisitions by intentionally altering the amount and kind of liabilities it will hold. Banks may, for example, expand their term lending capacity by special attempts to procure more time deposits. But it is nevertheless true that the distribution of assets a bank can prudently hold depends on the nature of its liabilities.

For example, a bank whose deposits are mostly those of individual house-holders on salaries has an inherently stable liability structure; it needs only small secondary reserves and can probably afford to make a substantial percentage of term and real estate loans. On the other hand, a bank whose deposits, both

---

[1]Federal Deposit Insurance has not ended the chance of bank runs. See chapter 7, footnote 3. If, for example, General Electric's treasurer hears that a bank in which his company has $10 million in deposits is in trouble, he has a duty to his stockholders to withdraw the deposit at once. Thus bank runs involving *large* depositors are still a potential danger.

[2]This is a main difference between banks and non-bank financial intermediaries. A bank fails if it is illiquid—if it lacks cash to pay off claims. Non-bank financial intermediaries fail only if insolvent—if total liabilities exceed total assets. A bank failing from illiquidity may, of course, be reorganized and reopened. But confidence in the former management will have vanished, and the bank will almost certainly have to install a new set of officers and directors. Losses, if any, will fall first on stockholders.

demand and time, depend on the continuing prosperity and patronage of a few very large corporations must maintain very large liquidity reserves and lend for much shorter average periods. This is so because if the bank loses one big account, or if one large company decides to withdraw the bulk of its money in order to buy another company, both the cash position and the reserve position of the bank will be badly strained.

Asset Structure

Of particular importance in bank management is the proper balancing of a bank's assets—whether loans or investments—between long- and short-term categories. The more volatile a bank's money sources, the more urgent it is for the bank to maintain liquidity. The eternal temptation and frequent ruin of bankers has been to lend money for very lengthy periods, making their banks too illiquid to withstand unexpected outflows of money.

A long-dead deputy governor of the Bank of England once observed, "Banking is a relatively simple trade. It requires only that the banker be able to distinguish between a bill of exchange and a bill of mortgage."[3] This has been a necessary principle of banking from Adam Smith's time to the present. All the world's great monetary panics have stemmed in some degree from banks' abandonment of their exclusive role as short-term lenders and their excursion into long-term lending, securities underwriting, equity investment, and the like.

Bank Liabilities

Banks obtain funds for loan, investment, or liquidity and required reserves largely by trading liabilities of their own creation for depositor (or other) cash.

Demand Deposits

Demand deposits are claims against a bank, payable in cash, and immediately upon demand, either to a named claimant (the depositor) or to his order (given by check). A bank creates two kinds of deposits. A *primary deposit* arises when someone deposits cash or a check on another bank for credit to his account. The receiving bank thereby gains reserve funds. Under a fractional reserve system, the bank will hold only a fraction of these funds in reserve and lend the rest. When it lends the rest, the bank creates a second kind of deposit, a *derivative deposit*. It is through this creation of derivative deposits that a bank is said to be a money-creating institution.

Although theoretically a bank can lend its excess reserves, a point discussed in chapter 4, in practice no bank could afford to lend down to its last dollar of excess reserves. It would be likely to keep some margin of excess reserves on hand at the Federal Reserve in case the daily check-clearing balance went against it for a while—that is, in case it had to pay out more of its reserves to banks

---

[3]The bill of exchange, a merchant's short-term promise to pay, is here taken as the symbol of a liquid asset, and the bill of mortgage (which is simply a mortgage), as a very long-term liquid asset.

presenting checks on it than it gained in reserves from banks on which it had presented checks. In addition, a bank needs to keep some cash on hand—an alternative to excess reserves—to meet cash claims by its depositors.

Banks operate on the law of large numbers, the premise that only a small fraction of demand deposits will be drawn by cash or check on any given day. Therefore, margins of excess reserves and vault cash are typically small: only 3 or 4 per cent of total assets at most. As a result, any protracted drain on cash or reserves must be met by selling of secondary reserve assets or through emergency borrowings from the Federal Reserve or other banks.

Time Deposits

In contrast to demand deposits, time deposits represent depositor funds on which a bank has the right to withhold repayment for various intervals. Time deposits fall into two main classes: (1) savings accounts (passbook savings), and (2) fixed-period time deposits (typically evidenced by certificates of deposit, or CDs).

Savings deposits ordinarily can be made in any amount. Although passbooks always contain a warning that the bank may require 30 or 60 days notice of withdrawals, banks typically repay savings on demand. However, the interest payable at fixed intervals is forfeited if the depositor withdraws between interest dates, ordinarily the last day of each quarter. Interest rates on passbook savings are lower than those paid on savings and loan share accounts, deposits in mutual savings banks, or by the Treasury's E-bonds.

Time deposits have a definite maturity date, and ordinarily banks will not repay the sums involved prior to maturity. Maturities may run from one month to five years, and CDs have been issued in denominations ranging from $25 to $1 million. Small-denomination CDs are typically non-negotiable and non-marketable; that is, they are not transferable to another person and have no resale market. Large denominations of $100,000 or more *are* negotiable (they can be transferred to another party by endorsement) and they have an active secondary, or resale, market. In fact, yields on the CDs of large, well-known banks are often quoted in the financial sections of newspapers. Interest rates on CDs of all sizes usually rise with their time to maturity, and large-denomination CDs have yields that exceed Treasury bills and compare favorably with those on commercial paper.

As with demand deposits, the Federal Reserve Act of 1913 requires member banks to maintain reserves against time deposits, but time-deposit reserve requirements are typically much lower, averaging only between 3 and 6 per cent. Consequently, banks can relend a much higher fraction of funds raised through time deposits. However, banks must not only pay interest on time deposits; the interest they pay, like the reserves they must carry, is regulated by the Federal Reserve Board (or by state banking authorities for non-member banks).

During the late 1960s, when the Federal Reserve was trying to reduce inflation by limiting the supply of credit, it tried to discourage bank lending by keeping Regulation Q ceilings on negotiable CDs below the rates which Treasury bills and other open-market paper were then paying. This restrained the flow of time deposits into the banks. It forced banks to use other funds to pay off CDs that matured and were not renewed. The emergence of Regulation Q ceilings as a major weapon of credit control raises important questions about how strongly banks should rely on time deposits as a continuous source of funds.[4]

Other Liabilities (and Sources of Funds)

Other bank liabilities are usually minor in size, though sometimes they play important parts in keeping a bank in funds.

Many of these liabilities you are familiar with from chapters 4 and 8. However, a financing method that banks owned by holding companies use should be mentioned. Such banks sometimes borrow large sums by selling their loans to their own holding companies: the holding companies in turn use the underlying credit of the bank they own to sell large volumes of commercial paper in the money market to raise the funds to buy the loans. Legally, banks cannot issue commercial paper (because regulatory authorities class it as a deposit and subject it to reserve requirements), but having the holding company issue it circumvents the law. The resulting flexibility is one reason why, in recent years, many banks have reorganized into holding company systems.

Bank Capital

Equity, or ownership money, typically supplies about 8 per cent of the funds for a bank. It serves chiefly as a cushion for absorbing losses. Recall that banks are expected to maintain capital resources equal to about 8 per cent of deposits. Clearly, if a bank's business is growing, it must either sell more stock from time to time or retain a good part of its profits. Since most banks prefer to grow as much as possible through retained profits, in order to avoid diluting the control enjoyed by existing stockholders, they ordinarily pay out only about 50 per cent of their profits in dividends.

Recently, larger banks have begun to borrow part of their capital through long-term IOUs, as non-financial corporations have long done. Long-term IOUs issued by banks are called *capital notes* and closely resemble corporate bonds. Money raised through capital notes is not risk money as equity is, but it is subordinate to deposits in priority of claim and does not usually have to be paid back for twenty or twenty-five years from date of borrowing. So, like equity, it helps provide a cushion to protect depositors.

Bank Assets

A bank's liabilities show how it *raises* the money it has; its assets show how it *uses* its money either (1) to make money, or (2) to provide reserves. Aside from its banking premises, furniture and equipment, a bank's assets fall in three main classes: (1) cash reserves, (2) loans, (3) investments. Since these assets, and the logic of their proper proportions, were discussed earlier in this chapter, we shall limit this discussion to only a few additional significant details about each class.

---

[4]The unreliability of CDs as a source of bank funds during the 1969–70 period of tight money at least partly accounted for banks' renewed interest in capital-note financing during 1971–72. While interest rates paid on capital notes are typically higher than rates on CDs, the notes are issued for intervals of twenty to twenty-five years. Thus the funds obtained remain dependably with the bank. The characteristics of capital notes are described a few paragraphs below.

Cash Reserves

Banks try to minimize these because they earn nothing. They seek to lend or invest excess reserves and get by with as little vault cash as possible.

Loans

Banks lend money to business firms, to consumers, and to governmental bodies. Further details of bank credit to business will be discussed in chapters 21 and 22, but two broad classes are important to note here.

Commercial loans are for relatively short periods, typically one year or less, and are made chiefly to finance short-term bulges in a firm's inventories or accounts receivable, or to serve as temporary financing for fixed-asset purchases until permanent financing can be arranged. In theory, two observations usually are true of such loans. (1) They finance self-liquidating transactions, i.e., short-term business transactions whose successful outcome will automatically supply funds to repay the loan with interest. (2) The bank funds to make the loans are provided by demand deposits and so should not be lent for long intervals.

Term loans, which have greatly increased in recent years, are made for longer intervals, usually from three to seven years, although the money returns to the bank sooner because loans are repaid in a series of annual or quarterly installments. Funds for term loans are theoretically provided from longer sources, notably time deposits.

Banks make consumer loans for almost every purpose, from meeting doctor bills to financing purchases of automobiles and appliances, but they tend to confine such lending to individuals who are high-grade credit risks. Real estate lending by banks is moderate in amount, highly selective as to risk, and ordinarily for a smaller percentage of appraised value than that for which savings and loan associations or life insurance companies lend.

Investments

Bank investments, as we have seen, fall into two classes. Short-term investments comprise a bank's secondary reserves. Most of them are also highly marketable. Favorite investments for secondary reserve purposes include U.S. Treasury bills, commercial paper, negotiable CDs of other banks, and bankers acceptances. Secondary reserve investments seek liquidity first, then whatever degree of interest return is attainable. A bank's medium- and longer-term investments are made primarily for income and consist almost entirely of U.S. Treasury notes and bonds and tax-exempt municipal bonds. However, the bonds of smaller municipalities are often quite illiquid.[5]

Banks make most of their long-term investments in recession periods when loan demand is abnormally small and the Federal Reserve is practically showering them with reserves to fight the business slowdown. Short-term yields are likely to be quite low at such times. So, to improve their interest returns, the banks "reach out" for longer-dated debt securities.

As we saw in chapter 8, one of the teeth in restrictive monetary policy is the fact that rising interest rates help "lock" banks and other lenders into their

---

[5]On such bonds, the underlying promise to pay interest and principal may be sound, but the bonds, owing to the small size of the issue, lack an organized or ready resale market.

investment portfolios, thus reducing the availability of loanable funds to feed an inflationary boom. Sometimes, however, banks are committed to make loans under lines of credit, which clients have bought and paid for.[6] In such cases, banks may have to dump Treasury and municipal bonds at large losses to meet their commitments. In fact, since 1945, banks have lost more money on their investments than they have on their loans.

Bank Earnings

Most of a bank's earnings consist of interest received from loans and investments, although revenues from trust and collection services, foreign exchange operations, and similar sources sometimes contribute importantly. A bank's two biggest costs are (1) the interest it must pay for money received through time and savings deposits, and (2) operating expenses such as employee wages and salaries. After deducting costs, a bank typically earns only 5/8 to 1 per cent on its total assets. How, then, can a bank make money? The answer is financial leverage.

Since a bank employs about $12 in depositor's funds for each dollar of ownership capital, its overall return on assets makes quite a satisfactory return on equity—from 8 to 13 per cent on the figures just quoted.[7] Moreover, in comparison with most other businesses, bank earnings tend to be quite stable despite the ups and downs of business.

It is often assumed that banks make the most money when interest rates are very high, but this is not necessarily so. Generally, profits are highest when business is good but not booming. In booms, money becomes tight for everyone, including banks; banks then may have to pay almost as much to attract money as they can legally (or at least ethically) earn by lending it. The two factors that most affect bank earnings are (1) volume of loans, and (2) the spread, or difference, between what banks must pay for money and what they can earn by lending or investing it.[8]

Sometimes bank earnings rise during business slowdowns, despite some fall in loan demand, because the banks' cost of money falls much more rapidly than bank interest charges (which are administered prices and so do not respond rapidly to market forces). Then, too, a recession bringing easier money and generally lower interest rates boosts bond prices, so that banks sometimes realize substantial gains on their investment portfolios.

Bank Regulation

Banks are regulated by many state and federal government agencies. Such regulation has two main purposes: (1) to regulate the nation's supply of money and credit, and (2) to keep bankers honest and banks solvent. Banks in the United

---

[6]Chapter 21 explains lines of credit in detail.

[7]Assuming all assets used in generating earnings are reflected on the balance sheet, a simple way to relate the return on equity (ROE) to return on assets (ROA) is: $ROE = ROA(D/E + 1)$, where D is debt and E is equity. Financial leverage is discussed in detail in chapter 17.

[8]The best measure of this spread is ordinarily the gap between the banks' prime lending rate and the interest banks must pay on CDs.

States are regularly inspected; their loans and lending policies are reviewed, their investments are scrutinized, their cash is counted, and a full report is rendered by the examiner-team to both bank managements and heads of the regulatory agency.

Improved bank examination practices, better banker education, deposit insurance, and the "thinning out" of inferior bank managements by thousands of bank failures during the Great Depression reduced the number of bank failures to a trickle during the 1940s and 1950s. By the late 1960s, however, bank failures were rising in both size and number. This rise reflected, at least in part, a lack of regulatory vigilance. Meanwhile, for the first time since the Depression, banks began to make aggressive efforts to have regulatory laws relaxed so that they could branch out into other fields of business, both financial and non-financial.[9] Many banks reorganized into one-bank holding companies, which then owned the bank as well as other enterprises. Regulatory laws were relaxed on many fronts to permit this diversification. Some comments on the possible dangers of these and kindred developments are made at the end of the following chapter.

To Remember

Secondary reserves   Capital notes
Symmetry of assets and liabilities   Commercial loans
Derivative deposits   Term loans
Time deposits

Questions

1 What liquidity needs does a bank have? How does a bank provide for liquidity?
2 Explain why banks have financial leverage.
3 Explain how the composition of a bank's liabilities restricts the assets it is free to acquire.
4 Distinguish between primary and derivative demand deposits at a commercial bank.
5 Name and describe the two main classes of time deposits.
6 To what extent may a member bank rely on discounts for its funds? Explain.
7 Discuss the investment policy of commercial banks. Is it always profitable? Why or why not?
8 "Banks make their biggest earnings when interest rates are highest." True or false? Explain.
9 Why has banking been a growth industry for bank stockholders?
10 What are the two main purposes of bank regulation in the United States?

---

[9]In this regard, the Commission on Financial Structure and Regulation, appointed by the President in December 1971, presented 89 recommendations (called the Hunt Report) for revamping the nation's financial system. The thrust of the report is toward liberalization of the banking structure in the United States. For example, the report suggests phasing out interest rate ceilings on time and savings deposits, granting new powers to thrift institutions so that they can more effectively compete with banks, and so on.

10

Non-Bank Intermediaries: Their Role

In finance, as in other economic activities, it pays to specialize. Financial institutions of all types are specialized links between particular sorts of lenders and borrowers, and between savers of money and users of these savings. The broadest such link is provided by commercial banks. But even these versatile institutions cannot specialize in meeting every kind of financial need. Needs that the banks do not cover, or only partially serve, are the domain of the *non-bank financial intermediaries.*

Specialization in Finance

A century ago, Walter Bagehot, one of the world's most perceptive students of finance, wrote:

Under every system of banking . . . there will always be a class of persons who examine more carefully than busy bankers can the nature of different securities [IOUs]; and who, by attending to only one class, come to be particularly well acquainted with that class. And as these specially qualified dealers can for the most part lend much more than their own capital, they will always be ready to borrow largely from bankers and others, and to deposit the securities which they know to be as good as a pledge for that loan. They thus act as intermediaries between the borrowing public and the less qualified capitalist [saver]; knowing better than the ordinary capitalist which loans are better and which are worse, they borrow from him, and gain a profit by charging to the public more than they pay to him.[1]

Though Bagehot's language sounds quaint and old-fashioned, he states precisely the main points of *financial intermediation.* The intermediary institution acts as a middleman between a certain class of savers, who provide funds, and a certain class of borrowers, who wish to use these funds. What enables the intermediary to "gain a profit" by charging the borrower a higher rate of interest than it pays the saver? It is, as Bagehot notes, the expertise with which the intermediary can judge the credit-worthiness of a particular class of borrowers. Financial intermediaries are always highly specialized in the kind of lending they perform.

Linking Particular Classes of Lenders and Borrowers

Probably the easiest way to classify—and, at the same time, to under-stand—non-bank intermediaries is to ask four basic questions about each kind of intermediary. (1) What sort of borrowers does it serve? (2) From what class of savers does it raise money? (3) What kind of services does it offer its borrowers? (4) What type of liability (near-money or other financial claim) does it use to attract the funds of savers?

Using savings and loan associations as an example, we can see how each sort of intermediary succeeds by working out answers to these four questions. (1) Each specializes in meeting the needs of a particular kind of borrowers. Savings and loan associations aim particularly at making mortgage loans to buyers of one- to four-family dwelling units. (2) Each type of intermediary solicits the savings of a particular class of investors. Savings and loan associations chiefly attract the funds of small savers, mobilizing them into the relatively large sums needed to finance dwelling-unit purchases. (3) Each intermediary develops expertise in handling particular kinds of loans so that it can make them more cheaply, more efficiently, and more safely than its rivals can. Savings and loan associations have a particular expertise in making conventional home loans, which are mortgage loans that are not insured or guaranteed by the federal government. The associations can gauge risks accurately, they know the law and paperwork, and have the personnel and organization to process and service these loans at minimum cost. (4) Each intermediary must design an appealing form of financial claim to attract funds. Savings and loan associations typically offer the saver a passbook share account which pays a higher rate of interest than a savings deposit in a commercial bank.

---

[1]Walter Bagehot, *Lombard Street, A Description of the Money Market,* with an introduction by Frank C. Genovese (Homewood, Ill.: R. D. Irwin, 1962), p. 137.

Structure of Savings Institutions

Since each type of financial intermediary makes its own kinds of loans and taps its own source of savings, it will present a unique pattern of assets and liabilities. Most of its assets will be represented by the principal type of loans it makes. For savings and loan associations, for example, the principal asset is conventional mortgages on one- to four-family housing units. Most of its liabilities will comprise the financial claim it uses to attract savers' funds. The main liability of savings and loan associations are the share accounts of savers.

An intermediary's principal kind of asset will provide most of its interest earnings or other income. But it also must maintain some liquidity reserves, consisting of cash and short-term, readily-marketable securities. These are used to meet an excess of cash withdrawals over cash deposits. How large these reserves must be, and how they are divided between cash and interest-bearing securities, depends on the expected pattern, or probability distribution, of deposits and withdrawals. Since these flows ordinarily obey the law of large numbers, they tend to fall in a statistically predictable pattern.[2]

Suppose, for example, that the daily pattern of net deposits or withdrawals for a savings and loan association is normally distributed with a standard deviation of $10,000. Since about 95 per cent of a normal frequency distribution lies within plus and minus two standard deviations of the mean, 95 per cent of the time the net deposits or withdrawals on any given day will fall within a $40,000 range, or a positive $20,000 or negative $20,000. Only 5 times in 100 will they exceed these amounts. The management must consider the liquidity needs to protect the association against a 2½ per cent probability of net withdrawals in excess of $20,000. Of course, management would also have to consider the likelihood of runs—days of successive net withdrawals or net deposits—but these usually occur in predictable patterns during certain seasons of the year.

Patterns of deposit and withdrawal vary, of course, from one institution to another, and managements must always remain alert to possible long-term changes in their cash flow patterns. Such changes could result from population shifts, changes in an area's economy, emergence or disappearance of competing institutions, and so forth. The needed volume of liquidity reserves also depends on the intermediary's ability to borrow from other sources, such as commercial banks and government agencies. In 1969, savings and loan associations held an average of 1.5 per cent of their assets in cash and 5.3 per cent in the form of government securities. They also had (and utilized) large borrowing privileges at the Federal Home Loan Banks, as noted a few paragraphs hence.

Since an intermediary's principal liability consists of the financial claim it creates to attract deposits or other funds, it is necessary for this liability to surpass money in its attractiveness as a store of value. Almost all intermediary liabilities take the form of interest-bearing near-monies. They may be represented by passbook accounts, savings certificates, or—in the case of life insurance—a policy promising conditional benefits and having a certain cash value. In general, the returns paid by intermediary liabilities increase as they become less liquid and higher in risk.

---

[2]The law of large numbers is discussed in chapter 2, footnote 6.

Savings and Loan Associations

Probably the best known of non-bank financial intermediaries are the savings and loan associations. Originally organized to make mortgage loans to their own members, they have increasingly emphasized their role as savings institutions catering to small investors.

Savings and loan associations may have either state or federal incorporation charters. They may be either mutual institutions, owned and controlled by their "depositor"-shareholders, or business corporations owned by stockholders, as commercial banks are. The quotation marks around the word "depositor" are significant. One who places money in a savings and loan account is technically not a depositor. A depositor is one who has the legal status of a creditor. The savings and loan "depositor" is not a creditor, but rather an owner of shares in the association. When he withdraws money, he is technically not withdrawing a deposit. Instead, the association "repurchases" his shares.

Over the past three decades, savings and loan associations have almost always been both able and willing to pay off their shareholders on demand. This has given savings share accounts their present near-money status. Since share accounts typically pay higher interest rates than do savings accounts in commercial banks, the public has shown an increasing preference for savings and loan shares over savings deposits. However, unlike banks, savings associations in most states have no legal obligation to provide withdrawals if they lack the cash. Instead, they can simply file shareholders' "repurchase requests" in a waiting list, and pay them off at such time as money becomes available.

The foregoing point involves an interesting and basic distinction in financial terminology: the distinction between *insolvency* and *illiquidity*. A business or financial institution is insolvent if its liabilities exceed its assets—that is, if it owes creditors a sum greater than its properties would bring when sold, taking due time and care. If it merely lacks the cash to pay off creditors whose claims have come due, but still has total assets worth more than its total liabilities, it is merely illiquid. This distinction is important with respect to federal insurance of savings and loan share accounts.

Share accounts in federally insured associations are usually insured to $20,000 by the Federal Savings and Loan Insurance Corporation (FSLIC). But this insurance only protects the shareholder against association insolvency. Illiquidity in a savings and loan association is not classed as failure for insurance purposes. In this respect, the FSLIC differs from the Federal Deposit Insurance Corporation (FDIC), which insures savings accounts in commercial banks. If the savings account is not paid off at the end of the legal withdrawal-notice interval (normally 60 days), the FDIC declares the bank "failed," and pays off depositors in full, up to the $20,000 limit. Savings and loan shareholders enjoy no such protection, and during the 1930s they often had to wait months or years to retrieve their money.

Borrowing Short and Lending Long

One weakness of savings and loan associations is that they violate a major— perhaps *the* major—rule of sound financial management: they borrow short and lend long. That is, they obtain money on the understanding (implicit, not legally binding) that the shareholder can withdraw it on demand. Yet they relend that money for very long intervals in using it to make mortgage loans. This leads to an imbalance and lack of symmetry between their assets and liabilities. Their liabilities are—or so the public has been persuaded—demand liabilities. Yet their assets are largely frozen in mortgage loans for very long periods. Only three sources of funds are regularly available to meet withdrawal demands from shareholders: (1) inflows of money from new share purchases, (2) monthly interest and principal payments from mortgage debtors, and (3) the association's own liquidity reserves.

Somewhat easing the precarious financial imbalance of the associations is their ability to borrow from the Federal Home Loan Bank System (FHLB), which functions as a kind of Federal Reserve for savings and loan associations. This federal agency often raises funds to relend to the associations by selling its own securities (IOUs) in the open market.

Savings and loan associations have followed aggressive lending policies, preferring to be "loaned to limit" at practically all times. In the years when interest rates remained relatively stable, these tactics caused no problems. But the rapid rise in interest rates after 1965 subjected them to a new hazard, which won the formidable name of disintermediation.

Disintermediation

Disintermediation occurs when people withdraw their money from deposit-type financial intermediaries in order to buy higher-yielding marketable securities. If savings and loan associations, for example, are paying 4¾ per cent and U.S. Government Treasury notes are yielding 8 per cent, the small saver can make $32.50 more per year on each $1,000 invested by switching his funds. In 1966 and 1969 record numbers of savings and loan shareholders made just this switch. The disintermediation almost broke the associations, for the following reasons.

When yields on marketable securities rise, savings and loan associations cannot afford to make competitive increases in the interest rates they pay their shareholders. Most of their loans date from past years when interest rates were lower, and their average interest earning on mortgages responds only slowly to the rise in rates at which new loans are being made. To cover operating costs, associations require at least 1½ percentage points of difference between the average rate earned on their mortgage loans and the rate they pay on savings share accounts. For savings and loan associations to offer share-account rates at levels competitive with Treasury bills, commercial paper, and corporate bonds in high-interest periods would involve ruinous losses. In 1969, for example, savings and loan associations were severely squeezed paying average interest of 4.78 per cent on share accounts against an average yield of 6.35 per cent on assets. By contrast, yields on marketable securities were in the 8 to 9 per cent region.

In 1969–70, when wholesale disintermediation threatened to collapse savings and loan associations the Nixon administration hastily applied two remedies. First, associations were permitted to expand tremendously their borrowings from the Federal Home Loan Bank System. During 1970, almost 10 per cent of the total liabilities of the nation's associations were to the FHLB.[3] Second, the government began confining Treasury bills and U.S. agency notes to relatively large denominations—$10,000 or more—making them too expensive for the average savings and loan depositor to buy.[4] Late in 1970, the associations also obtained at least temporary relief through a sharp drop in all market rates of interest that finally reduced Treasury-bill and other open market yields to levels roughly competitive with those paid by savings and loan share accounts.

The asset-liability structure of the savings and loan industry is shown in Table 10–1, the combined balance sheet of all savings and loan associations. Its dominant features are those discussed earlier in this chapter: relatively small liquidity reserves

Table 10–1. Condensed Statement of Condition of All Savings and Loan Associations as of December 31, 1969

Item	Millions of Dollars	Per Cent of Total
Assets		
Cash on Hand and in Banks	2,441	1.5
U.S. Government Securities	8,553	5.3
Conventional Loans	124,646	76.9
Veterans Administration Loans	7,653	4.7
Federal Housing Administration Loans	7,910	4.9
Federal Home Loan Bank Stock	1,478	0.9
Real Estate Owned	780	0.5
All Other Assets	8,701	5.4
Total Assets	162,162	100.0
Liabilities and Reserves		
Savings Balances	135,489	83.6
FHLB Advances & Other Borrowed Money	9,754	6.0
Loans in Process	2,454	1.5
All Other Liabilities	3,239	2.0
General and Unallocated Reserves	11,226	6.9
Total Liabilities and Reserves	162,162	100.0

Notes: Percentages may not add to totals due to rounding; 1969 was chosen because it shows the associations under their maximum financial strain of the past generation.

Sources: Federal Home Loan Bank Board, *Combined Financial Statements, 1970;* United States Savings & Loan League, *Savings and Loan Fact Book, 1971.*

---

[3]FHLB efforts to aid the associations in 1969–70 resulted for a while in a vicious circle of disintermediation. The FHLB sold notes paying, for example, 7 per cent. Savings and loan shareholders withdrew funds to buy these juicier yields. This reduced association cash reserves again, requiring the FHLB to sell still more notes to raise more "help" money for the associations, which caused still more disintermediation.

[4]In effect, this condemned the small saver to accept an inferior return while subsidizing the residential housing market. Meanwhile, wealthy people and financial institutions got 7 or 8 per cent on large-denomination investments in marketable securities.

(cash and U.S. government securities); very large holdings of mortgages (conventional, Veterans Administration and Federal Housing Administration loans); huge liabilities in the form of share accounts (savings balances); and substantial liabilities to the FHLB and other "emergency" lenders.

Mutual Savings Banks

Similar in structure and function to savings and loan associations are the mutual savings banks, found in seventeen of the fifty states. Only three states—New York, Massachusetts, and Connecticut—account for three-fourths of their numbers and four-fifths of their assets. Historically, mutual savings banks have emphasized their role as savings institutions, and they compiled an enviable safety record during the Great Depression. Though technically *mutual* institutions run by vote of their depositors, mutual savings banks are actually controlled by self-perpetuating boards of trustees, typically well-to-do persons interested in promoting the welfare of small savers.

About 90 per cent of the typical mutual savings bank's liabilities consists of legal-debt deposits, payable on 30 to 60 days notice, although in practice on demand. Great stability of deposits has precluded the need for large liquidity reserves, and so less than 2 per cent of assets are typically held in cash. About three-fourths of total assets consists of real estate mortgages. Another 15 per cent consists of government and corporate securities; these are primarily bonds with distant maturities and substantial yields. Interest payments to depositors are generally competitive with those paid by savings and loan associations.

Other Deposit-Type Intermediaries

Credit unions are mutual thrift institutions serving the members of some common-interest group such as a church or lodge, or the employees of a business firm. Chartered by either state or federal government, they provide both a savings outlet and low-cost loans to members. Loans made are typically to finance purchases of automobiles, household appliances, vacations, and so forth, and to keep members out of the clutches of loan sharks.

Practically all of a credit union's liabilities consist of savings shares, which are not legally deposits. Earnings after expenses are ordinarily paid out in dividends to shareholders, typically at annual intervals. Loans to members comprise about 85 per cent of assets; to assist liquidity, most remaining assets are held in cash and government securities.

Credit unions have enjoyed popularity and rapid growth since World War II, and have paid higher rates to savers than savings and loan associations or mutual savings banks. But since most of their loans are made to people with a common occupational or geographic tie, their operation is less diversified and considerably riskier.

Other kinds of intermediaries engaged in consumer or real estate lending sometimes accept (and even advertise for) small-saver accounts, but their collective role in the economy is not important. Often offering above-average rates of interest, they are seldom subject to effective regulation, and are best avoided by all but the most knowledgeable savers.

Intermediation vs. Money-Creation

Having described deposit-type financial intermediaries, it remains to point out a basic distinction between them and commercial banks. This distinction is between money-creation (the exclusive function of the commercial banks) and financial intermediation (a function shared by non-bank intermediaries).

You have seen in chapter 4 how commercial banks create demand-deposit money through lending and investing excess reserves. Non-bank intermediaries have no such abilities. They can lend only the currency or demand deposits which are transferred to them by the public.

Suppose, for example, that Howard W. Campbell, Jr., has a $1,000 checking account at the Whattatown State Bank, as shown in Figure 10–1, step 1. He decides to take advantage of the high interest offered by the Friendly Savings and Loan Association. Campbell makes a "deposit" at the savings and loan by writing a check on his account at the Whattatown State Bank. For simplicity, assume that Friendly Savings and Loan keeps its checking account at the same bank as Campbell. What happens? As we see in step 2, the savings and loan enters $1,000 in Campbell's passbook (share) and sends the check to the bank. The bank switches $1,000 from Campbell's demand deposit to the association's. No new money has been created, but near-money has been. Campbell's $1,000 passbook

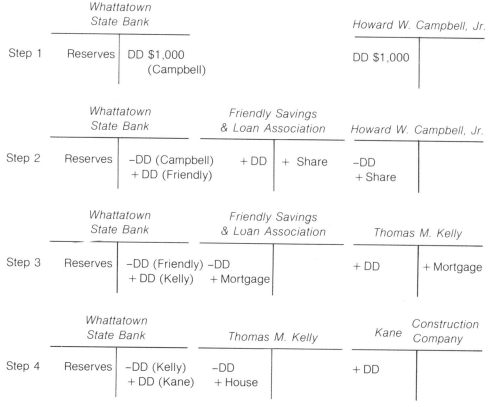

Figure 10–1.

entry—to him an asset, to the association a liability—is erected on the $1,000 money base.

Now visualize the Friendly Savings and Loan lending the $1,000 to Thomas M. Kelly to finance part of a house purchase. The association will trade its $1,000 demand deposit for Kelly's mortgage note, and the bank will transfer the $1,000 to his account. These transactions are illustrated in step 3. Now another financial claim—the mortgage—has been created, but still no new money. When Kelly uses the $1,000 deposit to pay the builder, Kane Construction Company, there is still in existence only the same $1,000 in demand deposits. This final transaction is shown in step 4.

If you total the changes in demand deposits (DD) in steps 2 through 4, they would all cancel out. The banking system is left with the same amount of reserves and deposits. What has changed? The volume of financial claims—of credit or near-money—has changed. Two financial claims and a real asset (the house) have come into being through the saving and loan association's intermediating, its activating idle money balances. The velocity of money has increased.

Figure 10–1 emphasizes the chief role of non-bank intermediaries: they accelerate the lending and relending of otherwise idle money balances, thus giving the nation's money supply better mileage to the dollar. Their chief inducement for activating money is, as we have seen, the offer of interest to those who lend money to them.

Insurance Companies

The nation's huge insurance industry, although primarily a provider of protective services to policy-holders, is also a major financial intermediary. Funds provided by premium payments are invested in a wide range of securities and debt-type obligations, thereby furnishing financing to many sectors of the economy.

Life insurance companies have the largest total assets of any financial institutions except for commercial banks. They raise funds by selling policies on which the insureds paid fixed-amount premiums over a series of months or years. Except for term insurance, which is protection alone, all life insurance contracts involve a combination of protection and savings elements. Policies with savings features range from ordinary life to limited life insurance and endowment policies on which cash values and insurance reserves (the savings element) build up quite rapidly.

Chartered by the fifty states, life insurance firms are of two kinds: (1) mutual companies, which are largest and hold about 60 per cent of life insurance in force, and (2) stockholder-owned companies, which are more numerous, but smaller. Since the Great Depression, regulation of the industry appears to be satisfactory; with failures infrequent, life insurance has proved a secure and reliable form of saving, but inflation has rapidly reduced the purchasing-power value of this savings element.

Life insurance companies can lend out practically all of their funds since, for two reasons, their liquidity needs are small. (1) Reliable mortality tables enable them to predict with great accuracy what volume of death benefits will have to be paid out in any coming year. (2) A continuous inflow of contractual premium payments keeps them well supplied with cash. Thus, most of their assets (investments) consist of long-term corporate bonds and real estate mortgages—highest-yielding classes of debt securities—and small but increasing amounts of common stock. Stock investments have developed as a result of growing policy-holder dissatisfaction over savings losses resulting from inflation. To meet rising demands for inflation-resistant forms of insurance-savings, companies have begun offering variable annuities, and soon will be offering "variable life insurance," wherein benefits and cash values are backed by common-stock investments.[5]

Fire and casualty insurance companies are also important financial intermediaries. They are not savings institutions, but in the course of insuring property against damage, they collect premiums in advance and invest the proceeds for intervals ranging up to three years, almost entirely in fixed-income securities such as bonds and notes.

Other Savings Institutions

A few other kinds of savings institutions which handle large volumes of funds and play important parts in the financial system should be mentioned.

Pension funds are built up through employer and employee contributions to provide employees of business firms and government bodies with retirement income. Since continuous cash inflows more than meet liquidity needs, these funds are almost entirely invested in stocks and bonds.

Investment companies sell stock to the public and purchase securities of other corporations with the proceeds. The investment company stockholder owns a small slice of a diversified security portfolio which is professionally managed. The investment company may aim at safety, long-term capital growth, successful speculation, income, or some combination of these objectives, concentrating its investment in bonds, conservative stocks, or fast-fluctuating stocks as appropriate.

Investment companies are of two kinds. *Open-end companies,* or mutual funds, stand ready continually to sell new shares or repurchase old ones on the basis of the current value of the fund's own securities portfolio. Funds ordinarily sell new shares at the prevailing net asset value of existing shares plus an 8 to 10 per cent "load," or sales fee; they redeem shares at asset value. *Closed-end investment companies* have a fixed amount of stock outstanding, which is bought and sold on the same basis as other marketable stocks: whatever people think the company is worth. Prices per share are related—but seldom conform precisely—to what a proportionate slice of the underlying security portfolio should sell for.

Personal trusts relieve individuals of responsibility for managing their funds and are administered by bank trust departments to meet the needs of individual beneficiaries. Testamentary trusts are often set up under a will to care for (and invest) the funds left a decedent's widow or heirs.

Trend Toward Diversification

Fluctuations in earning power and value for different kinds of assets owned by financial intermediaries bring continual changes in the public's distribution of its savings. Disintermediation of the savings and loan associations and insurance

---

[5]In recent years many life companies have also acquired or started mutual-fund investment company subsidiaries. If a prospect tells the insurance agent that he's worried about inflation eating up his savings, the agent can suggest that he buy term life insurance and invest the difference in the mutual fund.

companies during the inflation of the late 1960s illustrates the hazards which a non-diversified intermediary may face. Other financial institutions dependent on a narrow base of business have suffered in recent years; investment banking houses, for example, encountered starvation diets in the early 1960s when new stock and bond flotations fell.

To insulate themselves from misfortunes connected with a single financial market, financial institutions, like non-financial corporations, are diversifying and/or merging. We discuss mergers in detail in chapter 30, but note here that for financial institutions mergers broaden the base of their business and lessen its sensitivity to fluctuations or evolutionary changes in particular lines of finance. Investment bankers are merging with brokers, insurance companies are acquiring mutual funds, savings and loan associations are striving to become more like banks. Almost every kind of financial intermediary seems headed toward becoming a "department store" of finance: a one-stop center where clients can satisfy all their financial needs, be they interest-bearing savings, stock market investment, life insurance, mortgage financing, or credit-card charge accounts.

A widely used route to diversification in the financial community is through formation of holding companies, corporations that acquire other firms by buying up their stock. By acquiring diversified enterprises, holding companies can offer multiple-line financial services under the control of a single management. While this evolution may add to the public's convenience in meeting its financial needs, it also opens the way to major hazards and abuses. A similar merger trend in the late 1920s contributed heavily to the financial ruin that followed 1929. Eliminating the arms-length relationship between financial institutions and borrowers removes the objectivity necessary to make accurate decisions. A financial institution may be tempted to lend funds on grounds other than likely profit. The institution may be induced to reach out for a riskier investment because the need for funds springs from another division of the same holding company. The present structure of the financial system emphasizing specialization has evolved over centuries to satisfy our industrial society's needs. The burden of proof that department stores of finance will serve those needs more efficiently than the present system of specialization lies on those who support the department store approach.

To Remember

Specialization	Disintermediation
Financial intermediaries	Kinds of intermediaries
Insolvency	Holding company
Illiquidity	

Questions

1 Why do specialized financial intermediaries exist? What distinctive capabilities must an intermediary offer its customers?

2 Discuss the liquidity needs of different kinds of intermediaries.

3 How do savings and loan associations violate a central rule of sound finance? Why do they?

4 Explain why shareholders of a savings and loan association that cannot pay off its "deposits" are not necessarily entitled to government insurance payments on their accounts. What major distinction in financial terms is involved here?

5 How do non-bank intermediaries affect money supply? What feature of money do they affect?

6 Distinguish between open-end and closed-end investment companies.

7 Why are financial institutions now seeking to diversify?

11

When Money Goes International

So long as American deals with American on the home scene business is done in dollars. No problem of different currencies arises. When, however, an American deals with a foreigner, problems of foreign exchange and foreign exchange rates typically emerge. Suppose, for example, that a U.S. importer buys Scotch whiskey from a British seller. Ordinarily, the seller will want payment in his own currency, the pound sterling. To make this payment, the American buyer will have to exchange his dollars for pounds. Even if the British seller initially accepts payment in dollars, he will very likely sell them to his bank in order to obtain his home currency.

Foreign Exchange Rates

The prices at which dollars are sold for other currencies, or vice versa, are called *foreign exchange rates.* Foreign exchange means foreign monies, and foreign exchange *rates* are simply the prices of foreign currencies in terms of one's own. On December 21, 1971, for example, selected foreign currencies had the following dollar prices:

Pound (Great Britain)	$2.5547
Franc (France)	.1920
Deutschemark (West Germany)	.3073
Yen (Japan)	.00319

Like all other prices, foreign exchange rates are primarily set by forces of supply and demand. However, the supply-demand framework which sets the world's foreign exchange rates is quite complicated, since there are more than 100 recognized national monies, each of which can be exchanged for any other. The number of resulting cross rates is quite large: among just 40 major currencies, some 780 cross rates are possible.[1] More will be said about this complexity in chapter 34 but for present purposes we can view exchange-rate determination in a simplified setting.

International Payments

At first glance, international payments seem bewildering in their variety. Consider the United States' position. We sell goods and services abroad (exports) for which foreigners must pay us. We buy goods and services from foreigners (imports) for which we must pay them. American businessmen and individuals make investments abroad. American banks and financial institutions lend money in foreign countries. Foreigners also make investments and loans in this country. American tourists spend money travelling abroad just as foreigners spend money traveling here. The U.S. government spends prolifically abroad for defense, war, and foreign aid. Americans pay interest on money lent them by foreigners, and foreigners pay interest on loans from Americans. This list of transactions could be prolonged considerably. Furthermore, in U.S. dealings with the entire world, a very large number of currencies is involved.

Despite this complexity, all transactions can be classed under two headings. One set of these transactions creates a demand for foreign currencies, or alternatively, a supply of dollars. This is true of (1) U.S. imports of foreign goods and services, (2) American loans or investments abroad, (3) American tourists' expenditures foreign countries, and (4) U.S. government spending, lending, or aid grants in other countries. Each such transaction requires Americans to sell dollars to get foreign monies (in which to make payments), or provides dollars to foreigners which *they* can be expected to sell for their own national currencies. Fundamentally, these transactions produce a *supply of dollars*.

Similarly, the opposite set of transactions creates a supply of foreign currencies or, alternatively, a demand for dollars. This is true of (1) U.S. exports of goods and services, (2) foreign lending or investing in the United States, (3) foreign tourists' expenditures here, and (4) spending or lending by foreign governments in the United States. Fundamentally, each of these transactions produces a *demand for dollars*.

---

[1] Algebraically, the number of different combinations of forty items, taken two at a time, is $\dfrac{40 \times 39}{1 \times 2}$.

Dollars Supplied and Demanded

Why do we emphasize the first class of transactions as creating a *supply* of dollars, and the second, a *demand* for dollars? This simplification enables us to treat all foreign monies alike and thus to ignore (for present purposes) the very large number of different foreign exchange rates. The counterpart of the demand for foreign monies as a whole is the supply of dollars. The counterpart of the supply of foreign monies as a whole is the demand for dollars. These facts enable us to ignore the myriad of cross rates and to look at the exchange-rate determining mechanism in terms of dollars alone.

Considering now the supply of, and demand for, dollars, we can readily perceive why the dollar rises or falls against foreign currencies. If this country's international transactions are generating a larger demand for dollars than supply, the dollar will rise in the world's currency markets and prices of foreign exchange will fall. If the supply of dollars is greater than the demand for dollars, then the dollar's value will fall and the price of foreign exchange will rise.

Another way to look at the exchange rate-making process is to visualize business and other transactions as leading to inflows or outflows of dollars. If Americans pay for foreign goods, lend or invest funds abroad, or travel in foreign countries, dollars must pass from U.S. to foreign hands: such transactions therefore produce *dollar outflows.* Conversely, U.S. sales to foreigners, foreign loans or investments in the United States, foreigners' paying interest or dividends to Americans, and so forth, mean either that foreigners must buy dollars to make such payments, or that Americans will receive foreign money and sell it for dollars; these transactions thus will produce *dollar inflows.* If dollar inflows exceed dollar outflows, then the demand for dollars exceeds the supply. In that case, the dollar will rise against foreign currencies. If dollar outflows exceed dollar inflows, the dollar will fall and the dollar price of other currencies will rise.

Significance of Exchange Rate Changes

Fluctuations of exchange rates have great economic importance because they reflect changes in buying power of the monies involved. If, for example, the dollar strengthens, or rises, against the pound, Americans will be able to buy more British goods for each dollar spent in England. On the other hand, since each pound will then buy fewer dollars, Britishers are likely to reduce their purchases from Americans. Thus, a rise in the dollar is a mixed blessing. A fall in the dollar, similarly, brings mixed results. If the dollar price of the pound rises, then Britishers will be able to buy more U.S. goods with each pound, but American buyers' dollars will not go so far in Britain. Clearly, changes in the foreign value of a nation's money spill over into the domestic market for goods and services; they affect the supply of, and demand for, imports and exports. This in turn alters expenditures, incomes, living standards, and employment in the countries involved.

Nations often face difficult choices with respect to exchange-rate policy. For example, if a nation keeps the value of its money high in terms of other currencies, then its citizens will enjoy high purchasing power abroad. By being able to import foreign goods at low prices in terms of domestic money, they can raise their living standards. However, high value for a nation's currency in the foreign exchange markets also makes its goods and services more costly to foreigners. This circumstance can bring a fall in a nation's exports and lead to a decline in its output and employment.

During the 1930s, many nations intentionally depreciated, or cheapened, their money on the foreign exchange markets through a policy of deliberate price change. By cheapening their goods in terms of foreign currencies, these nations sought to expand their exports at the expense of other countries—a policy which won the opprobrious name of "beggaring one's neighbor."

Limits on Rate Fluctuations

Today, the rules of the international monetary game prohibit the beggaring of one's neighbors through deliberate exchange-rate depreciation. These rules also help to stimulate confidence: people will be more willing to trade and invest internationally if they are reasonably sure what foreign monies will be worth when transactions are settled.[2] So under the International Monetary Fund Agreement, which most free-world countries signed in 1946, nations are pledged to keep exchange rate moves within definite "bands," 2¼ per cent on either side of a declared "par," or stated, value of their currencies. Under IMF rules, the par value of a currency is ordinarily defined as so many dollars and/or cents.[3] Only the U.S. dollar, which serves as the standard for all other currencies, is defined in terms of gold content. In effect, this puts the free world on a "dollar standard."

A Ceiling and a Floor

The IMF 2¼ per cent rule sets a ceiling and a floor to fluctuation of each country's currency unit in the world's foreign exchange markets. For example, take the pound: par $2.6057. The 2¼ per cent fluctuation limit sets a ceiling of approximately $2.66 and a floor of approximately $2.55. The Bank of England is pledged to contain the pound's dollar price within these limits. How? It does so by buying and selling, if need be, other monies.

Suppose the pound is sinking toward its floor. It can only be sinking because too many pounds are being sold, and too few bought, in the currency markets, perhaps reflecting excessive British imports. But when the pound reaches $2.55—or even before, if less drop is desired—the Bank of England must intervene and begin *buying* pounds. What does the Bank buy pounds with? The answer is other—and, at the moment at least, more desirable—currencies.

International Reserves

The Bank of England, like all other central banks, maintains an international reserve consisting of dollars and other "hard," or widely-acceptable, currencies. In fact, a nation must have enough international reserves to support its own

---

[2]The 1930s were marked by international financial chaos, competitive exchange-rate deprecia-tion, and falling world trade. After World War II, the International Monetary Fund (IMF) was set up to bring greater order to the international financial system and, particularly, more stability to exchange rates.

[3]After World War II, currencies' par values were defined as so many dollars (instead of so much gold, as in former generations) for two main reasons: (1) the Great Depression had swept away the gold standard, and (2) the dollar stood unquestioned as the world's leading currency because of America's dominant economic power.

currency at its floor or it is internationally bankrupt. In 1967, when the Bank of England seemed likely to run out of international reserves in trying to support the pound at a par of $2.80, it abandoned the hopeless struggle and devalued the pound to a new par of $2.40.[4]

Just as a central bank must use its foreign exchange reserves to support its own currency at its floor, so it must supply its currency (thereby buying and accumulating foreign currencies) when the home currency reaches its ceiling. Currencies go to their ceilings when they are very much in demand either for making purchases or because currency speculators think their par values may be raised. This happened repeatedly with the West German mark after 1960: to keep the mark from rising through its ceiling, the Bundesbank, the West German central bank, had to supply enormous quantities of its own currency in exchange for the foreign currencies people wanted to trade for marks. In the process, the Bundesbank accumulated very large foreign exchange reserves. But in the process it also had to supply foreigners with German purchasing power; when this came back to Germany and was spent, it drove up the price level. So, to choke off the demand for marks and the inflation it was causing, the Bundesbank three times revalued, or up-valued, its currency unit. By making marks more expensive for foreigners, it cooled—for a while, at least—the demand for them and for German goods.

But from 1960 through 1971, high productivity and exports at bargain prices gave West Germany an almost continuously favorable balance of payments. The country thus enjoyed a strong foreign exchange reserve position and large demands for its currency. Currency speculators gambled that the currency would eventually be revalued, and the mark typically sold near its IMF ceiling.

U.S. Reserves: A Special Case

While most nations, since 1945, have maintained the bulk of their international reserves in the form of foreign currencies, the U.S. reserve has consisted chiefly of gold. Until August 1971, foreign governments and central banks (though not private foreigners) had the right of converting unwanted dollars into gold at a price of $35 per ounce. Of course, not all deficit dollars were cashed for gold; foreigners added many of them to their cash balances (in either U.S. banks or in foreign banks as Eurodollars) or lent them at interest in U.S. or foreign money markets. But *unwanted* dollars eventually wound up in foreign central banks because foreigners insisted on exchanging them for their home currencies.

After 1960, the Federal Reserve encouraged foreign central banks to invest their dollars in the U.S. money market by trying to keep short-term interest rates here above levels in foreign money centers.[5] But these and other expedients were

---

[4]This was the pound's par until the United States devalued the dollar in December 1971. Our 7.89 per cent devaluation raised the pound's par 8.57 per cent to $2.6057.

[5]This was part of the goal of Operation Twist, a strategy devised by the Federal Reserve in 1961. The idea was to keep short-term interest rates up to assist the balance of payments, while pushing long-term rates down to stimulate the domestic economy. It worked this way: when the Federal Reserve bought Treasury securities to add to bank reserves, it bought Treasury bonds (to help bring long-term rates down); and when it sold Treasury securities to knock out bank reserves, it sold Treasury bills (to push their rates up). Operation Twist is generally regarded to have been a failure.

partly fruitless, and by August 1971, nearly $17 billion in U.S. gold had been drawn down. The nation's gold reserve dwindled from more than $26 billion in 1951 to less than $10 billion.

At this point, President Nixon suspended the dollar's gold convertibility. For three and a half months, the dollar floated, or sold at whatever price supply-demand forces set, on the world exchange markets while other currencies, dancing in disorder around the floating dollar, generally rose. Then, in early December 1971, the world's ten major trading nations tentatively agreed to a new set of parities based on a 7.89 per cent devaluation of the dollar. The devaluation was effected by declaring that the dollar was now worth 1/38 ounce of gold instead of 1/35 ounce, as it had been since 1934. However, the dollar at the new rate was not convertible into gold, so the agreement still left much unsettled.

Table 11–1. U.S. Balance of Payments Summary, 1971 First Half Data Annualized

Item		Billions of Dollars
I. Current Account Transactions		
Merchandise Trade Balance		– 1.5
Exports	$43.5	
Imports	45.0	
Military Transactions		– 2.7
Travel and Transportation		– 2.1
Investment Income		7.8
Other Services (Net)		0.8
Balance on Goods and Services		2.2
Remittances and Pensions		– 1.4
U.S. Government Grants (Excluding Military)		– 1.8
Balance on Current Account		– 1.0
II. Capital Account Transactions		
U.S. Government Capital Flows		– 2.6
Private Long-term Capital		– 5.3
Balance on Current Account		
and Long-term Capital		– 8.9
III. Items for Final Balance		
A. Liquidity Basis		
Non-liquid *Short-term* Private Capital (Net)		– 1.7
Loans from IMF (SDRs)		– 0.7
Errors and Omissions		– 6.7
Net Liquidity Balance		–16.6
B. Official Settlements Basis		
Increase in Liquid Liabilities to Foreign Official Agencies		
Less Increase in Holdings of Short-term Dollar Obligations		
by Private Foreigners		– 5.9
Official Settlements Balance		–22.5

Source: Derived from *Federal Reserve Bulletin*, October 1971, p. A–13. Some headings condensed and simplified.

The Balance of Payments

Whether U.S. dollars flow abroad or not is reflected in the nation's balance of international payments. To understand clearly what the balance of payments is, we need only remember what has already been pointed out: all international transactions—imports, exports, investments, loans, interest payments, government grants, CIA hush-money, and so on—result either in dollars flowing into the country or dollars flowing out. Our balance of payments is simply the algebraic sum of these dollar inflows (+) and outflows (–).

The balance of payments can be computed and displayed in various ways, many confusing. Table 11–1 shows the U.S. balance of payments for the first half of 1971 as reported in the *Federal Reserve Bulletin* and annualized, or doubled to represent a year's data. This table summarizes the nation's international payments in three main categories. The first consists of *current account* transactions: imports, exports, military and travel spending, investment income (interest and dividend payments both ways), services (such as shipping and insurance), and remittances and pension payments. The second category comprises *capital account* transactions: government spending, lending, or grants abroad; investments made abroad by U.S. business firms and private citizens, and investments made in the U.S. by foreigners. The resulting total, Balance on Current Account and Long-Term Capital, is sometimes called the basic balance, since it can be argued that this reflects the stable, independently motivated, and long-run factors underlying the nation's balance of payments. However, other transactions—particularly short-term shifts of capital, or people's flight from the dollar into foreign currencies when the dollar is weak—also enter into the actual balance. The third category of the payments report includes these other transactions and indicates how they have been paid for. The presumption is that these transactions are not independently motivated but are induced by governments to correct a basic imbalance.

You will notice that Table 11–1 shows the balance of payments for the first half of 1971 on two different bases. The *liquidity basis* adds to the balance on current and capital account the net change in *total* foreign holdings of liquid dollar assets—currency, demand deposits in U.S. banks, and U.S.-issued IOUs maturing in less than one year—plus or minus the change in U.S. international reserve assets (gold and foreign exchange reserves).[6] This change is measured by totalling three items: (1) flows of non-liquid, *short-term* private capital, (2) U.S. use of its Special Drawing Rights at the IMF (draws count as a minus), and (3) a large volume of unrecorded transactions.[7]

The *official settlements basis* (also called the Official Reserves Transactions

---

[6]To the extent that foreigners settle their debts by paying foreign monies to Americans, these payments offset dollar outflows. When an American businessman receives yen, marks, or other hard foreign currencies, and exchanges them for dollars at his bank, the bank is likely to trade them to the Federal Reserve for reserve account credit in dollars. At this point, the foreign currency winds up in U.S. international reserves. Since it can be sold at any time to redeem dollars that have gone abroad, it counts as a (+) item in the balance of payments.

[7]Special Drawing Rights (SDRs) are a kind of "paper" reserve money created in limited amounts by the IMF for deficit countries to use in paying surplus countries. To some extent, SDRs are supplementing gold and hard currencies as a means of settling deficits, though not all nations will accept them. Unrecorded flows include currency smugglings, Mafia funds moving to Switzerland, currency payments in the dope traffic, etc.

Balance) does not count the change in *private* holdings of dollars and short-term dollar debts abroad; it considers only the change occurring in the dollar and short-term dollar-debt holdings of foreign governments and central banks, plus or minus the change in U.S. international reserve assets.

Thus the nation's balance of payments can be, and is, reported on two different bases (with still others possible). Since the balance of payments has important political implications, as well as economic and financial ones, successive administrations in Washington have typically emphasized whichever balance of payments figure has put them in the best light.

The Balance of Payments and Monetary Policy

There is a strong relation between the nation's balance of international payments and its monetary policy. Ideally, the long-range goal would be to have neither a net inflow nor net outflow of dollars, but rather a fluctuating series of small surpluses and deficits that would wind up offsetting each other. Monetary policy has a well-defined theoretical part to play in such a result.

Deficits in the basic balance are likely to occur when domestic prices and incomes are inflating and when interest rates at home are too low. Foreign goods are comparatively cheaper, so Americans buy them. American goods become more expensive, so foreigners *don't* buy them. Americans have surplus income to spend, and some of it is spent abroad on goods which the domestic economy does not produce. Finally, if American interest rates are below world interest rates, foreigners eagerly borrow here, which leads to further dollar outflows.

The remedy for this situation is tighter money and increased interest rates. This will reduce the inflation of prices and incomes and make money more expensive to borrow, both for natives and foreigners. Tighter money at home will reduce business activity, lowering upward pressures on prices and reducing incomes and employment to more sustainable levels. Higher interest rates will reinforce this effect in three ways. (1) At home, it will make businessmen less willing to borrow to finance further activity. (2) It will make foreigners reluctant to borrow in U.S. money and capital markets. (3) It will act as a magnet for dollars, encouraging American investors to buy U.S. debt securities (instead of foreign ones), and also encourage foreign investment in U.S. securities. Foreigners will not only be encouraged to lend their dollars back to the United States (a dollar inflow) instead of cashing them for gold or other currencies: if the interest spread between U.S. and foreign yields is large enough, foreigners may even be persuaded to sell foreign monies in order to obtain dollars to invest in attractive U.S. yields.

Interest Rate Policy: Two Effects

Tight money as a corrective for balance of payments deficits can be said to work in two stages. That is, it has both a short-run (first-aid) effect, and a long-run (more permanent) one. The short-run effect works through the ability of high interest rates in a deficit country to attract speculative money balances. An old saying in pre-World War I Britain reflects this: ''A seven per cent Bank [of England] rate will bring gold from the North Pole.'' Thus if the United States is suffering a deficit, the dollar outflows can be cancelled—and even reversed—if a very high interest rate here draws in dollars from England, France, Germany,

Japan, and Switzerland. Of course, this effect is only temporary because such speculative money flows are typically invested only for short periods, in securities like three-month Treasury bills. But temporarily, such inflows do strengthen the dollar on the foreign exchange markets and eliminate net dollar outflow.

With the time thus gained, more permanent remedies are generated by tight money's influence on the home economy. A slowdown occurs in business investment, consumer demand, sales, incomes, employment, and prices. In short, a recession takes place. A halt to rising prices enhances the appeal of domestic versus foreign goods; with less income to spend, people reduce their imports; businessmen, shorn of a booming domestic market, work harder to make sales abroad. Furthermore, so long as bond yields stay high and stock prices low, U.S. money and capital markets remain uninviting to foreigners wishing to raise funds. Thus, the basic tendency toward an excess of dollar outflows is overturned and a new trend toward net dollar inflows is set up.

Opposite monetary policies would, of course, be used to combat a persistent surplus (though our nation has not had one in years and would probably rejoice rather than worry should one occur). In theory, money would loosen and interest rates would decline. There would be a short-run effect of speculative capital flowing out, repelled by low interest rates, and a longer-run effect of economic expansion and rising prices resulting from cheap money. These consequences would remove the surplus by converting it into a deficit. Then, when the deficit became serious, the monetary gears would be reversed again.

Double-Headed Trouble

Monetary policy might be able to correct an imbalance in the basic accounts if the balance of payments were the only problem facing official money managers. If the balance of payments deficit were combined with a boom at home, tight money would be a good remedy for both, just as a surplus coexisting with a recession would make easy money an across-the-board solution. But suppose that a deficit coincides with a recession. In that case, the trouble is double-headed. Tight money would help to correct the deficit but would aggravate the recession. Similarly, easy money would reduce a surplus but would feed a simultaneous inflationary boom. What can the government do to solve a two-headed problem of this sort?

One proposal is to let monetary and fiscal policy work together for different purposes. Assume that a deficit is accompanied by a recession. Then use *tight monetary policy* to fight the deficit, and *expansive fiscal policy* (tax cuts plus big government spending and borrowing) to fight the recession. If a surplus is accompanied by an inflation, use easy money (low interest rates) to fight the surplus and restrictive fiscal policy to combat the inflation. The problem with these proposals is that monetary policy may overwhelm fiscal policy, leaving the problems unsolved. Thus, tight money may induce a recession so that a deficit returns, and easy money may feed inflation so that a surplus returns.

What to do about balance of payments deficits generally, and the U.S. deficit in particular, are today unsolved problems.[8] The Federal Reserve and Treasury

---

[8]Devaluation is not a *solution;* rather, it is a formal recognition of losses already suffered. If the fundamental causes of deficit—chiefly, persistent inflation—are not removed, further devaluations will prove necessary.

will no doubt continue to try to reduce the deficit, or at least keep it from getting hopelessly out of hand. But the impact of international finance on the domestic financial system has been—to put it charitably—erratic.

Direct Controls

Whenever monetary and fiscal policies fail or are slow to correct a basic imbalance, governments turn to direct controls on international trade and finance. One such United States attempt at direct controls occurred with enactment of the *interest equalization tax* in 1964. Although originally intended to be temporary, it is still in effect. This tax is designed to discourage American purchases of foreign securities, and contains restrictive guidelines on lending abroad by U.S. financial institutions and on investment abroad by U.S. business firms by taxing these financial flows.

In recent years, with domestic inflation rates beginning to rise faster than those abroad, the U.S. balance of trade has become much less favorable. Leaders of U.S. industries which have been particularly hard hit by foreign competition have complained bitterly about it and have demanded tariffs and other trade barriers to protect their high-cost operations. However, using direct controls to protect inefficient U.S. production of steel, shoes, and textiles would almost certainly result in widespread loss of U.S. sales abroad for efficiently-produced items such as electrical machinery and foodstuffs. It would also set an example of protectionism that could readily drive other countries into retaliation, halt the growth of world trade, and possibly even bring on world-wide depression.

Direct controls are a final, even desperation, method used by a nation to correct an imbalance in its international payments. When used as a temporary measure to permit corrective monetary and fiscal policies to take hold, direct controls serve a constructive purpose. But when direct controls become permanent and are used instead of monetary and fiscal policies, they foster protectionism and retaliatory controls which jeopardize world stability and peace.

To Remember

Foreign exchange	"Floating" dollar
Exchange rates	Balance of payments
Dollar inflows and outflows	Liquidity basis
Ceiling and floor	Official settlements basis
International reserves	Direct controls
Convertibility	

Questions

1 Define: foreign exchange, foreign exchange rate.
2 Explain how this nation's balance of payments with all other countries can be reduced to one simple basis.

3 Is it better for a nation's money to appreciate or depreciate in the foreign exchange markets? Discuss.

4 Explain how an IMF member-nation keeps its currency from going through either the ceiling or the floor. What sets the limits to fluctuation of a member-nation's currency?

5 Explain what action a foreign central bank would take to keep its currency from going through the ceiling vis-à-vis the dollar, given that the dollar is inconvertible. Is this a handicap to that country in administering its own monetary policy?

6 What constitute a nation's international reserves? Why has the dollar been an exception to the rule that deficit countries must pay out their reserves?

7 What is the U.S. balance of payments? What are its main divisions? On what bases can it be measured?

8 What is the proper monetary policy for a country with a balance of payments deficit? In what two steps do interest rates counteract a deficit?

9 What monetary-fiscal policy combination has been proposed for a country suffering a simultaneous deficit and recession? surplus and boom?

10 What prompts the spirit of protectionism? Is it a sound policy? Explain.

12

The Financial System: A Final View

The previous chapters have examined many of the separate parts and processes of the financial system. In this chapter, we shall combine these elements into a unified picture and look at the system itself, and its operation as a whole. In so doing, we shall draw together some separate threads and loose ends, which you may feel have been left dangling.

Definition of System

We have called the network of financial institutions and activities in our economy a financial *system.* A good starting point for our overview of the financial apparatus is to ask what the term *system* implies, applied to finance or anything else. A system is a set of interrelated parts working together to achieve some purpose. We can visualize many kinds of systems—the human body, the automobile, human societies, ant colonies, electric power companies—but all systems appear to have in common seven essential properties: (1) an objective, (2) parts, (3) an environment, (4) resources, (5) constraints, (6) communication facilities, (7) control or management.[1]

Let us first examine briefly each of these terms. The *objective* is the purpose the system fulfills. *Parts* are the separate organs or components from which the system is built. The *environment* consists of the surrounding circumstances to which it must adjust. Its *resources* are the powers and flexibilities it can exert. The *constraints* are the limitations on what it can do. Its *communication facilities* comprise the means by which information is transmitted between the control center, or management, and the separate parts; such information may involve the condition of the parts, problems that are arising, and the adjustments that need to be made. Finally, every system has some means of management or *control* to govern the separate parts, harmonize their teamwork, order adjustments, and keep the organism as a whole functioning to achieve its objective.

Financial System: Elements in Review

Let us now analyze the financial system according to the above format.

Objective

The objective of the financial system—in a capitalistic, business economy—is to supply funds to the various sectors and activities of the economy in ways that promote the fullest possible utilization of resources without the destabilizing consequences of price-level changes or unnecessary interference with individual decisions. Clearly, this statement suggests the five goals of monetary policy discussed in chapter 8: (1) maximum employment, (2) stable price level, (3) maximum sustainable growth, (4) satisfactory balance of international payments, (5) maximum scope for individual freedom and decision-making.

Two further points need emphasis. First, the U.S. financial system itself is, in large degree, merely a phase, or sub-system, of the world financial system. Second, the U.S. financial system is composed of a great many sub-systems which, through their own subordinate objectives, contribute to effective operation of the main system. For example, the banking system, money market, and stock market are clearly sub-systems of the financial system itself.

The overall system objective implies many subordinate objectives for effective functioning of the sub-systems. For example, the banking sub-system must receive a fair return, or profit, in order to fulfill its function in the system. No whole can function well without healthy parts. Any appraisal of how well the total financial system is doing must therefore include close inquiry into how well each of its sub-systems, or separate sectors, is faring. Problems of sectoral need and performance always underlie questions about the effectiveness of the system as a whole, just as soundness in each of a man's organs is prerequisite to his total health and efficiency.

---

[1]In the authors' opinion, systems theory is the greatest intellectual advance of the twentieth century. Many books on systems are available. A good, readable elementary book is C. West Churchman, *The Systems Approach* (New York: Dell Publishing Company, Delta paperback, 1968).

Parts

We have already looked separately at the main parts of the financial system: the institutions and people who compose it. Important among these are (1) the central bank, which creates reserves for the banking system; (2) the commercial banks, which create working-money through their loans and investments; (3) the non-bank intermediaries, which assist in the transfer of funds from savers to spenders and investors; (4) the money and capital markets, which link savers and users of funds through the sale and resale of securities; (5) the foreign exchange markets, which exchange and price one nation's money against another's; (6) the Treasury, whose fiscal and debt-management policies importantly affect the stability and direction of the system, and (7) the most important of all, the multifarious suppliers and users of funds who rely on the financial system for support of their economic activities: consumers, business firms, governments, and foreign businessmen and financial authorities. Parts, like sub-systems, must be kept in healthy repair if the system is to function effectively.

Environment

The financial system is a sub-system (and almost certainly, not the most important one) of the economic system as a whole. Therefore, the immediate environment of the financial system is the total economic system—including its goals, institutions, phases, parts, and activities. Broader environments include (1) the American social system as a whole, (2) the civilized world, and (3) the planet earth, including all of its human and natural resources. Among these vast, complex, interlocking systems, almost everything that happens in one part is likely to have some ultimate effect on the rest.

Consider, for example, how interest rates have been affected since the 1930s by changing attitudes toward debt and deficits, and by a growing tolerance of inflation. Notice how the stock market tumbles on each new "war scare" (or how, for that matter, stocks with an interest in the military-industrial complex tumble on a "peace scare").

This brief list suggests the ways that economic factors, social attitudes, political events, and nature's bounty affect the operation of the financial system. In other words, it suggests that the mechanism of finance, its institutions and practices, are inevitably shaped by broader influences. Thus, to become wise in the ways of finance, one must be a broad student of economics, history, social trends, government, and geography—not to mention more specialized disciplines such as geology, anthropology, and meteorology, which contribute to a still fuller understanding of the way the world and civilization evolve.

Resources

Since finance is a service industry, and money itself is manufactured virtually out of thin air, the most important resources of the financial system are largely intangible. They consist not of bricks and mortar, but of such intangibles as sound attitudes, self-discipline, efficient institutions, expertise, sound business practices, honesty, and effective organization within the financial system as a whole. No stream can rise higher than its source; and no financial system can prove effective if people are generally dishonest, sloppy in their work, or poorly organized in their efforts.

One chief resource has always distinguished the American financial system: its inventiveness. A teacher of finance has said that, "Wherever a financial need exists, a financial institution will develop to meet it."[2] In the past, this continual ability of American financial managers to adapt to new conditions, and increase efficiency through new financial processes, has been a major force for progress in the American economy. Without development of the American investment banking apparatus in the nineteenth century, for example, mobilization of the immense amounts of capital needed to build the nation's railroads, utility plants, and giant factories would probably not have been possible. Without the introduction, in the 1930s, of the amortized home mortgage, the present system of low-down-payment home ownership with predictably manageable future payments would not have been possible. Necessity may be the mother of invention, but, in the world of finance, invention has been the spear-point of progress.

Constraints

No system functions indefinitely without running into a net of constraints, or limitations, and the financial system is no exception. Many constraints on the financial system arise from the fact that no matter how much dollar flows are increased, real economic factors—employment, output, and wealth—set absolute limits to performance. Thus, doubling U.S. money supply overnight would not make everyone twice as wealthy; it would merely launch a disastrous inflation, because output would not have doubled overnight. No matter how much a company invested in plant improvements, it would not increase its earnings unless the improvements increased efficiency and output.

Other constraints are essentially financial. In any financial operation, liabilities cannot exceed assets, or ownership interest vanishes. Borrowing power cannot exceed the earning power out of which debts will have to be repaid.

Communication Facilities

In the human body, the nervous system relays information. If we overeat, nerve-endings in our belly complain. We "adjust" to the difficulty by taking an antacid or abstaining from more eating. The financial system, like the human body, contains a built-in set of signals and incentives to keep it on the right track. Of course, in the financial system, the main *incentive* is the profit motive. By this standard people and institutions typically adjust their financial activities and resources. The *signals* include a vast network of interest rates, security prices and yields, stock market indicators, financial reports, balance sheets, flow-of-funds statements, news stories in the *Wall Street Journal,* company profit forecasts, economic opinions, and the like; the list is practically endless.

Much of the skill of financial management—and other executive functions—consists of being able to scan each day's financial news and separate what is of longer-range significance and of basic import from what is superficial and

---

[2]One of the co-authors is indebted for this principle to his former teacher and long esteemed friend, Dr. Ernest W. Walker.

transitory. Perhaps basic trends in the stock and money markets are the most widely followed (or at least, sought for) indicators. Great skill in reading the financial signals is needed if one is to become a successful financial executive, investor, or speculator; considerable skill is needed by the head of any business, even a small one. However, the art of forecasting the financial future is extremely challenging and difficult, and even after a lifetime of practice those with the most aptitude and most successful records are still often wrong.

Management and Control

In machines and simpler animal bodies, controls are almost automatic, based on mechanical governors, instincts, or reflex actions. In higher animals and other complex systems, controls are both automatic and voluntary.

In human bodies, a pin-prick brings an instant, automatic response. One jerks away without thinking. But a decision to buy one particular block of stock or another involves a deliberate and often prolonged process of choice.

In both the financial system and its sub-systems, too, many adjustments are virtually automatic: they are built into the structures of financial markets, money flows, security prices, and so on. If, for example, the Federal Reserve tightens money supply, the reduced availability of money is promptly signalled by a rise in interest rates. The various suppliers and users of funds respond to this signal: some spend less and lend more, others borrow less and spend less. Thus supply and demand soon move into a new balance more or less automatically. Similarly, if too much investment in plant and equipment takes place, profits fall because companies have excess capacity; in response, stock prices tumble, and less money flows into equity investment and thus into industrial expansion.

Other adjustments are both more deliberate and more centralized. Such adjustments are needed, particularly, when automatic mechanisms break down or are not permitted to operate. In the late 1920s, for example, uncontrolled speculation in stocks brought financial disaster and so paved the way for legislated controls over the stock market in the early 1930s. In recent years, high interest rates on bonds have drawn money from mortgage investment, where interest ceilings (some statutory, and some based on what people are willing and able to pay) have kept mortgage yields from rising in step with bond yields. What adjustment should be made? Should supplies of money for bond issues be rationed to make more available for housing? Should interest ceilings on FHA mortgages, savings and loan shares, and so forth, be abolished in order to draw more funds into mortgages? Should the federal government subsidize mortgage payments at the expense of all taxpayers? The continuing effectiveness of the financial system and, along with it, the U.S. economy and social order, depends on the wisdom with which such issues are resolved.

Managing the financial system is obviously a highly complex task. Complexity arises both in the numbers who share in management and in the intricacy of its problems.

A host of authorities make important decisions at different levels in the system. These range from members of Congress and managers of the Federal Reserve at the top, through the heads of the stock exchanges and important banks, down to minor officials in local savings associations and small loan companies. Each decision, however small or obscure, throws some weight on the final scale.

Many problems arising in the system are not clearly or immediately soluble. The financial machinery, though flexible and adaptable, is far from perfect; kinks, blockages, and—sometimes—major maladjustments develop. Resolving such problems is never easy because conflicting interests are always involved. If, for example, defense expenditures are contributing heavily to the federal deficit and augmenting inflationary pressures, what should be done? Should defense spending be reduced at the risk of weakening military might and creating unemployment? Should taxes be increased at the risk of having the party in power voted out? Or should those on fixed incomes continue to be subjected to the hidden tax of inflation? Resolving such thorny problems involves difficult decisions and compromises which rarely please everyone, since their solution almost invariably raises the old question: "Whose ox will be gored?"

Financial Indicators

Money is the lubricant of economic activity. For that reason, supplies of and demands for money precede and accompany almost everything that happens in the economy. Chapter 2 noted that money flows and real flows are distinct but inseparable sides of the same process. Because money flows are easier to follow, businessmen, investors, and others usually take their cues from them.

Money Rates and Stock Prices

Two financial indicators, interest rates and stock prices, surpass all others in the extent to which they are followed and interpreted. Interest rates measure, fundamentally, the availability of capital (money capital immediately, but behind that, real capital); while stock prices signify the expected course of business earnings.

Since borrowers pay interest and repay principal *out of earnings,* it is clear that the combination of rising interest rates and falling stock prices suggests trouble ahead. Traditionally, this combination has warned businessmen, bankers, investors, and even consumers to pull in their economic horns. Conversely, rising stock prices (a sign that speculators see rising profits) accompanied by low and stable interest rates constitute an encouraging environment for business expansion, safe loans, and promising investment.

In following interest rates, one sometimes spots divergent moves in short- and long-term rates—in money market yields versus bond yields. Short rates are more volatile and erratic than long rates; they are more inclined to impulsive, nervous, frequently meaningless moves. Over several months, however, the money market and bond market are likely to move in the same direction. Traditionally, money rates have led the way, but not always: general rises in interest rates in 1967 and 1971 were led upward by bond yields. But if either group of yields moves strongly, the other is bound to follow. Yield spreads between different kinds of debt securities, both short- and long-term, vary appreciably over the years, largely reflecting changes in supplies of, and demands for, particular issuers' obligations.

The variable price trends that different stocks and industry groups pursue in the stock market, particularly from cycle to cycle, often reveal clearly the fortunes and outlook of companies and industries. If a company or industry enjoys healthy earnings growth, its stock should rise at least from one business cycle to the next. (Within cycles, of course, it can be expected to fluctuate.) But when the course is downward over successive cycles, the signs are ominous. Properly interpreted, these signs can warn investors, and even lenders, what industries to avoid. The difficulties experienced by steel companies from 1960 through the early 1970s, and the increasingly shaky position of the utilities from 1965 through 1971, were clearly forecast by the action of stock prices in these industries during the 1960s, especially after 1965. The long-term decline in prices signified a deliberate, collective judgment by investors to pull out of them.

Signals and Incentives

Responses to signals given by the financial system powerfully affect the strength and direction of economic activity. Particularly important are security price movements, since most of the nation's private wealth is stored in securities. Rising security prices make people feel richer, and more willing to spend, lend, and invest; falling security prices make them feel poorer, and less willing. By definition, rising interest rates mean lower bond prices; in effect, they almost always bring, after a time, lower stock prices.[3] This is as it should be. Rising interest rates signify a tendency toward excess demand and price inflation in the economy, and such trends need to be arrested, or at least controlled, if serious maladjustments are to be avoided. Thus, rising interest rates are a powerful incentive to people to make the kind of adjustment the economy requires. By contrast, falling and/or very low interest rates suggest that the economy is under-employed and that real resources are running to waste. Here, the effect of low interest in raising the prices of debt instruments and stocks is also beneficial.[4] It makes investors feel richer and gives banks and other lending institutions profits on their security portfolios, thus increasing their willingness to lend. Both influences promote spending and the employment of idle men and machines, thus moving the economy in the right direction.

Naturally, each observer of the financial markets watches particularly those quotations that affect him most immediately. The head of a sales finance company will be most concerned with "quotes" on commercial paper, a city manager with municipal bond prices, a corporate treasurer probably with the trend of the corporate bond market. Since, however, all interest rates move more or less together, whatever happens in any sector of the financial markets is likely ultimately to affect all others.

Persistent Problems

A catalog of the system's persistent problems would begin with *inflation*. Certainly it would include *sectoral disparities,* such as the unequal access to funds of different economic sectors, or the differing degrees of harshness with which

---

[3]The inverse relation between interest rates and stock prices has been empirically examined in Michael W. Keran, "Expectations, Money, and the Stock Market," Federal Reserve Bank of St. Louis *Review* (January 1971): 16–31. See especially pp. 17, 20.

[4]The tendency for stocks to begin rising in the early stages of recession has been notable since 1958. Some authorities have even said that the stock markets since that time have been characterized by "knee-jerk" reactions to easy or tight money. Most bull markets since that date have begun when money became easy and ended when money became uncomfortably tight.

tight money afflicts various sectors. The chance of *perverse reactions* is a perennial problem: for example, money supply is expanded to reduce interest rates; instead, it increases them. *Lags* between the time that changes in policy are made and the time they bring results frequently produce doubts about their effectiveness, and sometimes lead to the mistaken abandonment of sound courses.

Inflation has already received ample discussion; the basic dilemma, always, is how to kill inflation without killing prosperity, people's jobs, or the party in power. The other three problem-areas raise new issues.

Discrimination

The problem of sectoral disparities surfaces when tight money is applied to slow the rate of inflation. The usual argument is that high interest rates and reduced loan availabilities *discriminate* against certain sectors and activities by choking them badly while leaving others free to "wheel and deal." In particular, it is argued that tight money hurts small business, while leaving big business untouched; it restricts the flow of funds into the mortgage and municipal bond markets while permitting corporations and big speculative borrowers to bid whatever rate they need to attract money. The housing and local government issue will be discussed a few paragraphs hence, but a few words about the alleged discrimination against small business can be said here.

Tight money usually does hit small- and medium-size companies first, since they are typically less liquid in the first place. But its consequences are soon transmitted to larger firms in (1) a slow-down in orders from smaller firms, and (2) a rise in the volume of trade credit which big firms must now extend to their hard-pressed small customers to keep their business.[5] Thus, big firms soon feel the pinch.

The lack of liquidity in smaller firms is typically the result of inferior management and one reason why most small businesses do not grow large. Thus, on analysis, the contention that tight money hurts small business simply dissolves into the basic point that small business is usually less efficient or less innovative than big business, and hence less profitable. Given this basic premise, small business is bound to be hurt more than big business, not only by tight money, but also by recessions, wars, race riots, or any other difficulties—simply because it has less inherent strength to withstand the dislocations.

Perverse Reactions

The financial system is said to react perversely when it moves against a "nudge" from its managers instead of with it. *Perverse* is economic jargon for *unexpected.*

Actually, most perverse reactions are quite logical; thus the term "perverse" is either misapplied, or perhaps intended to divert inquiry from the real reason: the manager's failure to understand the system he is trying to control. For example, conventional economic wisdom has taught that expanding the money supply leads to lower interest rates. That, however, is not always the case. A recent example of such a perverse reaction occurred in the first six months of 1971. Interest

---

[5]Trade credit is discussed in detail in chapter 21.

rates rose on all maturities while the money supply increased at a 12 per cent annual rate.[6] The investing public—aware from the past seven years' experience that a flood of new money would inevitably lead to more inflation, stiffer borrowing requirements, and higher interest rates—had finally become conditioned to the familiar pattern and knew what to do. It rushed to borrow or sell its security holdings before interest rates went up, and in so doing actually pushed them up. This was not a perverse reaction. It was simply evidence that borrowers no longer trusted the Federal Reserve to manage money in a way that would keep prices and interest rates from rising, a reaction the Federal Reserve did not count on.

Lags

Akin to perverse reactions are lags, or time-gaps between policy action by the money managers and any noticeable effect. Monetary policy itself usually operates with a pronounced lag, both in stimulating the economy out of a recession and in choking off an inflationary boom.

For example, one study has indicated the following lag structure for the period 1955–69:

> . . . Monetary actions generally affect total spending with a two- to three-quarter lag. A change in the rate of growth of total spending is accompanied by a simultaneous change in the rate of growth of output, and it is not until three quarters later that the response of prices builds to 70 per cent of the total. The response of prices to a change in total spending is yet slower when there are anticipations of a high rate of inflation.[7]

Lagged responses are not surprising. Take the case of a boom. The first response to tighter money (meaning less of it, and higher interest) is not necessarily less spending by businessmen and consumers, but a running down of their stored liquidity reserves.[8] Businessmen sell off their stocks and bonds to raise working capital; banks dump Treasury bills; commercial paper is not resold, but matures; consumers draw on their savings deposits. And, if inflationary expectations are strongly embedded, liquidity may be run down a long way before any slowdown in spending occurs. In fact, spending may accelerate; people may liquidate financial assets and borrow at rising rates of interest because they are afraid that everything will cost even more next year.

With lags, as with perverse reactions, faulty monetary policy is often to blame. If people had confidence that the government and Federal Reserve seriously intended to stop inflation, there would be no perverse reactions and few lags. But in 1969, 1970, and 1971, people had good reason to suppose that authorities were no more determined to halt inflation then than they were in 1966, 1967, and 1968, when they talked and acted in much the same way but didn't take the necessary measures.

---

[6]We direct your attention to a perceptive and readable article covering interest rates, the money supply, and inflation: Denis Karnosky, "The Significance of Recent Interest Rate Movements," Federal Reserve Bank of St. Louis *Review* (August 1971): 2–7.

[7]See Leonall C. Andersen and Keith M. Carlson, "A Monetarist Model for Economic Stabilization," Federal Reserve Bank of St. Louis *Review* (April 1970): 15.

[8]For a timely warning about this, see George A. Christy, "Three Risks of 'Ample' Liquidity," *The Commercial and Financial Chronicle* (New York), May 7, 1964.

The System's Adjustment

Much of the financial system's adjustment takes place almost automatically through interest rate changes which help balance demands for funds against available supplies. Another seemingly automatic adjustment occurs through funds-rationing by lenders, who raise credit standards when funds are scarce and lower them when funds are abundant, thus widening or narrowing what Keynes called "the fringe of unsatisfied borrowers."[9] Similarly, as already pointed out, rising and falling interest rates greatly affect liquidity and expectations through their impact on capital values.

Occasionally, however, strains develop in the system which are great enough to require its top management—the central bank—to take action: typically, to relieve a painful shortage of money or to restrain an inflationary and heady excess. Thus, monetary policy is the *balance wheel* of the financial system. But if erratic or erroneous monetary measures are pursued, the financial system comes to resemble a machine that has lost its governor. The serious credit crunch of late 1969 and early 1970 was undoubtedly abetted by Federal Reserve monetary measures taken in early 1967 and in mid-1968; on both occasions, money supply was expanded with reckless misjudgment.

Price inflation, consistent balance of payments deficits, and interest rates which are so high that they prevent local governments from borrowing, are all feverish symptoms of monetary sickness. Such symptoms have become almost chronic in the U.S. financial system in recent years. These disorders result, as we have said, from too much money chasing too few goods, and suggest that our government and central bank have continually taken the path of least resistance: increasing the money supply, rather than increasing taxes, to pay for increased government spending.

Sectoral vs. Aggregate Adjustment

Even if *total* demands for and supplies of funds are in satisfactory balance, it is important that supplies and demands in particular economic sectors also be in balance. Distress occurs if, as happened in 1969, the corporate sector receives excess supplies of funds at the expense of the mortgage or municipal bond market. Interest rate ceilings and other rigid impediments to the free flow of funds contribute, of course, to such unwelcome results. Often the rigidities themselves arise out of efforts to keep interest rates artificially low.

Left to themselves, disparities in availability of financial resources to different economic sectors and activities would probably iron themselves out through adjustments in relative prices, particularly interest rates. The removal of artificial interest ceilings on home mortgages and municipal bonds, for example, in 1969 would have permitted these sectors to bid successfully against corporations for their share of funds. Sectoral imbalances are usually traceable to faulty overall policies of the government and central bank, rather than to any inherent mechanics of the financial system.

---

[9]See John Maynard Keynes, *A Treatise on Money* (London: Macmillan & Company, Ltd., 1930), vol. 2, pp. 364–65.

The Basic Problem

The basic problem in the financial system is political, and not economic. The underlying issue posed by inflation, sectoral imbalances, and other financial difficulties is really the question of whether or not democratic political processes have become incapable of coping with today's monetary problems and, behind them, the economic rivalries of different classes and pressure groups. This is the essential problem Winston Churchill noted in *Thoughts and Adventures,* in 1932:

> We see our race doubtful of its mission and no longer confident about its principles, infirm of purpose, drifting to and fro with the tides and currents of a deeply disturbed ocean. The compass has been damaged. The charts are out of date. The crew have to take it in turns to be captain; and every captain before every movement of the helm has to take a ballot not only of the crew, but of an ever-increasing number of passengers.[10]

The foregoing quotation brings us back to our initial statement that the financial system must be viewed merely as a sub-system of many other systems —economic, political, social, and philosophical—all of which incorporate conflicting views. It is naive to think that finance, or any other business activity, can be viewed in complete or even substantial detachment, divorced from the rest of social life. Everything that shapes and motivates people—their politics, personal disciplines, character traits, physical health, worries about the future, knowledge of the past—affects their financial behavior in some way, and thus shapes the structure and functioning of their financial system.

The fact that the financial system is only one part of a broader system implies that the former has little influence over the latter. That is by no means the case in the short run, as the previous eleven chapters indicate. But for the long run, some evidence exists that monetary policy—and fiscal policy—has little influence on the total system. As a study by the Federal Reserve Bank of St. Louis noted,

> A change in the rate of monetary expansion influences only nominal magnitudes in the long run. . . . Real magnitudes, notably output and employment, are unaffected. . . . Growth [in output] is determined by growth in the economy's productive potential, which depends on growth of natural resources, capital stock, labor force, and productivity.[11]

It is to a system constituted, regulated, and behaving like the one described in the past twelve chapters that a businessman must go frequently to find funds to finance his enterprise and profit-making activity. This introduction to its nature and behavior should be of some help in understanding what now follows: the account of how the businessman should manage money in his own firm.

---

[10]Winston S. Churchill, *Thoughts and Adventures* (London: Oldhams Press Ltd., 1949), p. 183.
[11]Andersen and Carlson, pp. 8–9.

To Remember

Properties of a system   Sectoral disparities
Financial indicators   Perverse reactions
Signals and incentives   Lags

Questions

1   Explain how the financial system meets the definition of a system.

2   Discuss the environment of the financial system.

3   Distinguish between automatic and deliberate adjustments in the financial system.

4   What are the most significant financial indicators? What does each one tell you?

5   What importance attaches to security price movements? Are they signals? incentives? both? Why?

6   Does tight money discriminate against small business? Explain.

7   Are perverse reactions really perverse? Explain.

8   Are sectoral imbalances in supplies of funds a sign of faulty mechanics in the monetary system? Explain.

9   In what ways is price inflation related to political considerations?

10 Is the inflation problem related to weaknesses in democratic society? Explain. What solutions can you propose for the control of inflation?

2

The Financing of Business Firms

13

The Three A's
of Financial Management

The Changing Role of Financial Management — Anticipating Financial Needs — *Anticipation in the Large Firm* — *Considering Lags and Growth* — *Interlocking Forecasts* — Acquiring Financial Resources — *When to Acquire Funds* — *Where to Acquire Funds* — *How to Acquire Funds* — Allocating Funds in the Business — *The Marginal Principle* — *Key Ratios* — *Equalizing Cost of Capital and Return* — The Three A's in Review

Every business, however small, has a financial manager. Someone has to make the key decisions concerning money. He may be a vice president, treasurer, or controller, or he may be a harassed proprietor or partner who wears three other managerial hats. He may even be (heaven help the business where he is!) one of the clerks or other subordinates. But, whoever he is, the financial manager is always there because *his function* is always there. Someone has to handle the "three A's" of financial management.

Why three A's? Reduced to its essential elements, financial management involves three inescapable tasks—and each begins with the letter *A*. The financial manager must:

1. Anticipate financial needs.
2. Acquire financial resources.
3. Allocate funds in the business.

If the financial manager handles each of these tasks well, his firm is on the road to good financial health.

The Changing Role of Financial Management

Before looking at the three A's in detail, let us view financial management in perspective and appraise its place in the business scheme.

Effective management of financial matters is indispensable to every firm. Without it, assets and capital soon leak away. But good financial management alone cannot guarantee that a business will succeed. It cannot make up for a decision to enter the wrong industry; it cannot atone for poor management of sales, costs, or personnel. Financial management is thus a necessary condition of business success, but not a sufficient one.

Records kept through the years by Dun & Bradstreet highlight the importance of effective financial management. These records show that financial failure is always present at the corporate death. Lack of capital ranks just below lack of experience as a principal explanation for the thousands of business failures occurring each year. Unwise extensions of credit, improper inventory policies, and excessive investment in fixed assets also are proximate causes of failure which are at least partly financial in character. What the records do not reveal, however, is the way that the role of financial management itself has changed in recent years.

A generation ago, business students ordinarily took a dry course called "Corporation Finance." More often than not, it described fifty-seven or so varieties of stocks and bonds, and revealed which kinds big corporations should issue when they needed long-term capital (which, in those days—the 1930s—was rarely).

Today, business students study "Financial Management"—the dynamic, evolving art of making *day-to-day* financial decisions in a business of any size. The old conception of finance as treasureship has broadened to include the new, equally meaningful approach of controllership.[1] The treasurer is an officer who keeps track of money and raises it when necessary from the banks or through security issues. The controller's duties extend to the planning, analysis, and improvement of every phase of a company's operations capable of being measured with a financial yardstick. The controller's growing role reflects an aggressive new doctrine: profits don't just happen—they must be planned in advance. Profits are the result of more than hard work, and more even than foresight. They are the product of ambition and determination in the men who manage a business—a determination that, far from having to react passively to its environment, the successful firm can reach out and, in many ways, bend the environment to its own will.

The treasurer's job also has grown bigger and more challenging. Thirty years ago, aside from infrequent episodes of external financing, the treasurer was regarded as a passive custodian of company funds. Today, he is still a custodian, but no longer passive. With the big rise in interest rates since 1951, he has become responsible for investing his firm's short-term surplus funds in order to bring

---

[1] Treasurer and controller functions are detailed in chapter 19.

maximum interest return. In an era of stop-and-go monetary policy, recurring credit crunches, and inflation-battered stock markets, he stays on the jump, keeping close touch with bankers, brokers, stockholders—and everyone else in the business of lending or investing money. Most of all, he is watchdog of the firm's financial environment. It is his responsibility to give timely warning of tighter, more costly money; to pick the cheapest and most reasonable lenders; and to devise new tactics for raising money when it is needed.

Anticipating Financial Needs

How does one anticipate financial needs? By forecasting *expected events* in his business and noting their *financial implications*. Every event that leads, immediately or later, to cash entering or leaving the business should be forecast. For example, this is what Tac Luferac, alert owner of a neighborhood toy store, expects to happen in his business during October:

1. He estimates his total sales for the month at $4,500, based on sales for the past three years. He forecasts cash sales at $3,800 and credit sales at $700.
2. He has receivables of $900 on the books at the end of September. Experience tells him he will collect about $700 of these accounts during October.
3. He expects a refund of $50 from Moe Jenkins Company for a damaged shipment he returned last month.
4. He will take a salary of $500 for the month. His shop assistant's salary will be $350.
5. His utility bills will run about as follows: gas, $45; electricity, $30; and water, $10.
6. He will order $12,000 worth of merchandise (mostly for Christmas). He expects to pay $3,500 of the total cost in cash during October to take advantage of discounts.
7. He has accounts payable of $8,500. He expects to pay $7,500 of these during October.
8. A new display case, installed last month, must be paid for; the bill is $500.
9. The insurance on his plate glass window, and fire insurance on his premises, are coming due. That will be another $250.
10. The washroom plumbing needs fixing. Allow $50 for that.

Luferac's bank balance in late September was $9,082. He writes each item down as he thinks of it; that way, important events are less likely to be overlooked. He tries to think of anything else that might be important, and then simply summarizes the events in a list of cash inflows and outflows, as follows:

Cash Inflows

Cash sales	$3,800
Collections	700
Refund	50
Total	$4,550

Cash Outflows

Salaries	$ 850
Utilities	85
Payments for merchandise	11,000
Display case	500
Insurance premiums	250
Plumbing repairs	50
Total	$12,735

This shows Luferac that his cash outflow in October will exceed his cash inflow by more than $8,000. It looks as if he will have less than $1,000 left in the bank at the end of the month.

Luferac will make similar forecasts of his cash flows for each month. His expected cash position will be compared with his desired cash balance to determine whether he needs to borrow money. If he has a surplus of cash, he must decide what to do with it until he needs it in the business.

Of course, this rudimentary financial forecast is the kind the proprietor-owner of a very small business can figure out for himself in a few minutes of careful thinking. If he is able to think of all receipts and expenditures, this simple cash-flow summary is quite adequate as a basis for anticipating financial needs.

Anticipation in the Large Firm

In a larger business, a financial forecast expands into an impressive array of documents. It would include the following items.

A *cash budget,* which is essentially the cash-flow statement given above, covers several months in the same detail as October is presented for Luferac.

A *pro forma income statement* summarizes sales, other income, costs, taxes, and net income for the period.

A *pro forma balance sheet* shows how assets, liabilities, and proprietorship will look at the end of the forecast period.

A statement of *sources and uses of funds* shows where the funds to operate the business will come from and how they will be absorbed during the period.

In a large company, the cash budget itself is based on a series of other forecasts: a sales budget, collections budget, wages and salary budget, purchases budget, and capital budget. The capital budget includes expenditures for fixed assets.

Considering Lags and Growth

Often, items which are bought or sold in one period result in cash flows in another. Luferac's cash budget illustrates this. His display case was installed in September, but he pays for it in October. He seems to pay for most of his inventory of toys about thirty days after it is delivered. On the other hand, some of his sales are credit sales; he does not collect the cash on these sales until a month or so later. The financial needs of an enterprise are strongly shaped by lags such as these.

Lags between flows of assets and flows of money are particularly crucial when a company is just getting started. Almost any business faces a period of several months—or even years—before cumulative cash inflows equal cumulative cash outflows. This is especially true of a new company that sells on credit and ties up a large part of its starting capital in customer receivables. Unless the owners painstakingly forecast their cash needs and make sure funds will be available, even a highly profitable new business may fail for lack of cash with which to pay its bills.

Growth presents another problem. As a successful firm expands its sales volume, it must sooner or later add more plant, equipment, and facilities, and enlarge its ability to carry inventory and receivables. These needs for long-term financing must be carefully anticipated. Sometimes a company can satisfy its expanding capital needs from internal sources, depreciation flows and retained profits. But if internal flows are relied on for expansion capital, then the management must carefully avoid distributing too much of the profit in dividends or payments to partners. If external financing—stocks and bonds—must be relied on, then plans for selling these securities must be made well ahead of time.

Interlocking Forecasts

The previous section suggests that, in a well-run firm of any size, financial requirements are not forecast merely for the next few months. A financial manager must make the most detailed forecast of financial requirements for the months immediately ahead. But he also needs to forecast, in a more general way, financial needs a year from now, two years hence, five years in the future.

The well-armed financial manager always has within easy reach a comprehensive set of _interlocking forecasts_ of his company's financial needs, tied to the long-term profit and growth plan decided on by top management. Detailed forecasts over the next three months or the next year prepare the financial manager for the months ahead—when funds will be short or abundant, when he will need to borrow money, or when he will have money to invest on a short-term basis. More general forecasts over the next one to five, or even ten, years will warn him of the time, down the line, when the company will have to float new issues of stocks or bonds or, alternatively, of the time when cash flows will become large enough to begin or increase dividends to owners.

Acquiring Financial Resources

Acquiring financial resources implies knowing when, where, and how to procure the funds a business needs. It involves keeping in touch with providers of funds, making timely requests, and backing requests with convincing facts and figures.

When to Acquire Funds

Funds should be acquired before a firm's need for them becomes embarrassing. Needy borrowers usually get rough treatment. The mere fact they have waited so long before approaching the lender is itself evidence of poor management. On the other hand, a timely request for funds, supported by a detailed forecast of operations and financial needs, indicates that management has a firm grip on the business and invites a lender's confidence and favor.

Advance notice of financial needs also eases the lender's problem and makes him more receptive. It is usually easier for a banker to commit himself to lending money two months from now than to provide the money on ten minutes' notice. Also, advance checking of sources of funds may prevent a later cash crisis; if the regular lender cannot assure funds, there is still time to try elsewhere.

Where to Acquire Funds

Where a financial manager goes to get money depends on how long he needs the funds and on what basis he is able to raise them. At the outset, therefore, he must ask himself two questions: (1) Do I need long- or short-term funds? (2) How strong is my position as a borrower?

Access to sources of finance and the terms on which they can be obtained will depend on the size and strength of a business. For a small, weak business, suppliers' credit may be the only source of short-term funds available. Unless the firm's credit standing is first class, bank loans will have to be secured by pledges of receivables, inventories, or securities. Long-term funds are a special problem for the small business, particularly if it is growing rapidly. Term loans are available only if a banker is convinced that the borrower can meet a stiff schedule of amortization payments. Investment bankers will handle stock and bond issues only after a firm has grown large enough and profitable enough to excite public interest; even then, flotation costs will be very high until new securities are sold in multi-million-dollar batches. For most smaller firms, the only reliable source of long-term funds for growth is retained earnings. This means that partners or stockholders must reconcile themselves to a Spartan existence until the firm has attained substantial size.

In choosing a lender, the financial manager should consider three other questions: (1) How do his charges compare with those of other lenders? (2) How stable and reliable will the lender be in meeting my future needs? (3) Is he capable of giving me valuable advice along with the loan?

How to Acquire Funds

What evidence can the firm give of its ability to repay borrowed funds? The firm's credit rating will usually determine whether it gets the money or not. Trade creditors are impressed by records of prompt payment and by settlement of past-due accounts on the dates promised. Bankers like evidence of orderly, efficient management and financial awareness. A manager impresses his banker when he supports his request for funds with a recent balance sheet and income statement (certified by a public accountant), and a careful, detailed projection of cash income and outgo over the period of the requested loan. Many investment bankers like an aura of youth and vigor in management, and an impressive record of earnings growth; these are features they can dramatize to an investing public that is hungry for glamour stocks and "young" growth companies. If the firm is retaining profits instead of paying them out, it is important that stockholders understand so that the maximum sustainable market price of the stock can be attained. Stockholders should be kept aware of the company's progress and dividends to come.

Above all, it is worth remembering that financial institutions are run by human beings, and that many benefits are obtained by favor as well as merit. Thus a financial manager should maintain close, friendly relations with a banker, and perhaps use the bank's other services: its trust department, personal loans, safety deposit vault, and so forth. He might also take newcomers and employees to the bank to discuss opening accounts. It is worthwhile for him to find out what services the finance companies can offer if he does not already know. Finally, he might try to get acquainted with other suppliers of corporate finance and let them know his plans for building the business. In short, the financial manager must become known and respected in financial circles before his firm needs help.

Allocating Funds in the Business

Allocating funds in a business involves the assignment of assets into profitability and liquidity classes. Profitability in the narrow sense means maximum earnings, in the broader sense, maximum sustainable market price of the firm's common stock. Liquidity means closeness to money. We shall look at these two elements of funds allocation in chapter 17 when we discuss the financial manager's dilemma.

The financial manager must steer a prudent course between overfinancing the business and underfinancing it. Squeezing funds to the last dollar may boost profitability, but doing so runs the risk that the firm will lack resources to meet unexpected emergencies or opportunities. An abundance of financial resources will keep the business liquid (and thus safe), but profitability will fall because highly liquid assets generally yield a low return.

The Marginal Principle

The allocation task of financial management concerns itself with the left-hand, or asset, side of the balance sheet. Investing in each asset helps a firm operate more smoothly and efficiently. But in adding to each sort of asset, a point is reached where additions become less and less profitable, particularly if some other kind of asset needs the investment more urgently. Here, then, is the problem of allocation.

In allocating the total available capital, the financial manager should not overemphasize one sort of asset and slight another. For instance, he must guard against sinking so much capital in a building that he cannot pay his bills on time. He should not invest so heavily in machinery that he cannot afford to offer customers the credit terms important to making sales. He must not become so loaded with inventories that he cannot find cash to replace worn-out delivery trucks.

How can a financial manager preserve a proper balance among various assets? He can use what is known as the *marginal principle* to aid in the allocation of funds. This involves making sure that the last, or marginal, dollar invested in each kind of assets has the same usefulness to the business as the last one invested in every other kind of asset.[2]

Key Ratios

Key financial ratios offer guideposts for balancing investment among various kinds of assets. The ratios compare different items on the balance sheet and income statement with each other. Each ratio is designed to tell a financial manager

---

[2]The marginal principle is discussed in detail in chapter 26; as it applies to capital budgeting, in chapter 27; as it applies to granting trade credit, chapter 28.

something specific about how effectively a particular asset is contributing to his firm.

Collectively, the ratios measure four factors:

1. Asset *activity*. (How fast do inventories, receivables, or working capital turn over?)
2. Asset *profitability*. (What is the percent return on total assets, fixed assets, owners' investment?)
3. Asset *liquidity*. (What part of total assets consists of cash or quickly cashable assets?)
4. *Leverage*. (What part of current, fixed, or total assets is financed with borrowed funds rather than owner investment?)

If the financial manager knows what ratios are about right for his line of business, then he can appraise investment in each kind of asset from the standpoint of its activity, profitability, liquidity, and leverage. He can thus see whether a commitment in a particular asset is too small for safety, about right, or too large for efficiency.

Ratios vary widely from one line of business to another. A list of standard ratios based on a particular line of business is needed. This can ordinarily be obtained from a trade association, nearest Small Business Administration office, or Dun & Bradstreet's useful booklet, *Key Business Ratios: Cost of Doing Business in 125 Lines.*[3]

Ratios, of course, have their limitations. They are a screening device, not a final answer to how a business should utilize its financial resources. One or more ratios may be badly out of line with the average of an industry, but special circumstances in a company (such as different sales categories or a different class of customers) may more than justify the deviation. In the final analysis, ratios, like other management tools, are subject to the judgment and discretion of the manager who applies them.

Equalizing Cost of Capital and Return

Finally, you should note—and only note, at this point—an abstract principle that summarizes the theoretical foundation of business financial policy: A firm should carry its business activities to the point where its marginal (or "last chunk of") return just equals the cost of its marginal (or "last added") increment of capital. In so doing, a firm will accomplish two central purposes: (1) correctly decide what its total investment (and volume of assets) should be, and (2) make the maximum profit open to it.

Roughly, at least, a firm accomplishes these purposes when it keeps its key ratios near the top for its industry.

Three A's in Review

In this overview, we have necessarily missed many important phases of financial management: capital budgeting, capital structure, cash management, and

---

[3]Also available: R. Sanzo, *Ratio Analysis for the Small Business*, Small Business Management Series, no. 20 (Washington, D.C.: U.S. Government Printing Office, 1957).

other significant subjects will be described later. Our aim was to give you, at this point, the kind of introduction to the main tasks and viewpoint of financial management that a student, management specialist in a field other than finance, or small business owner needs to put in proper perspective the detailed descriptions ahead.

As you have seen, the core of financial management in any firm can be summed up in three operations:

1. Anticipating financial needs.
2. Acquiring financial resources.
3. Allocating funds in the business.

For each operation, we can now set down a corresponding rule. In order, they are:

1. Forecasting cash inflows and outflows.
2. Keeping in touch with sources of funds.
3. Applying key ratios to the business.

If you keep in mind the three A's and their corresponding rules, you may be surprised at the ease with which you can comprehend and master the detailed presentation of financial management that follows this introductory chapter.

To Remember

The "three A's"	Interlocking forecasts
Financial management's new look	Profit versus liquidity
Cash budget	The marginal principle
Financial forecast	

Questions

1. Why does every business need a financial manager?
2. Discuss the expanded roles of the controller and treasurer in modern financial management.
3. Describe how a small businessman can anticipate his financial needs.
4. What documents comprise the complete financial forecast of a large business enterprise?
5. Does the growth of a business impose special financial problems? What are they? How can they be met?
6. Explain the nature and use of interlocking forecasts.
7. What principles and rules should the financial manager follow in acquiring financial resources from outside lenders?
8. What does proper allocation of funds in a business mean? How can a financial manager help assure himself that he is properly allocating funds?
9. What four properties of a business do key ratios measure? Define them.
10. What principle summarizes the theoretical foundation of business financial policy?

14

Forms of Enterprise and Business Taxes

Forms of Business Enterprise — *Proprietorships and Partnerships* — *Corporations* — *Selecting the Form* — **Tax Management in the Corporation** — *Splitting the Corporation* — *Loss Carry-Back and Carry-Forward* — **Capital Gains and Losses** — *Rates* — *Depreciable Assets* — *Dividend Income*

The financial manager's job is shaped by the legal form of business enterprise he manages. The form of enterprise also decides the taxes to which his company is subject and the rates it will pay. Thus it is logical and convenient to consider these two topics together.

Forms of Business Enterprise

Businesses exist in various sizes, shapes, and forms. Although sizes and shapes vary indefinitely, the important forms number only three: proprietorship, partnership, and corporation. Each form is distinct so far as legal and tax status are concerned, but their financial management has much in common.

A *proprietorship* is a business owned by a single individual. Although size of firm is not the sole determinant, a proprietorship is usually a small firm managed by the owner. A *partnership* is owned by two or more individuals who have entered into an agreement; no legal documentation of the agreement is necessary. A *corporation,* on the other hand, is an agreement between the state and the several persons forming the business, and legal documentation of the agreement is needed.

Proprietorships and Partnerships

While proprietorships and partnerships are distinct, these two forms are similar enough to be discussed together. When a business begins, it usually takes one of these forms because they are easy to establish. All that is necessary is to begin operation and conform with state laws. The ease and low cost of organization are major attractions of these forms.

Table 14-1 shows the number, total receipts, and net profits for each form of business for selected years from 1939 through 1967. Proprietorships, which have stabilized at around nine million, are by far the most numerous form. Partnerships, whose numbers have actually declined between 1960 and 1967, are in third place with respect to both number and receipts. In 1967, partnerships and proprietorships comprised 87 per cent of the total number of firms, and obtained 17 per cent of total business receipts.

If partnerships and proprietorships are the usual forms new businesses take, does Table 14-1 suggest that a large percentage of firms existing in 1967 were just beginning? No. For many kinds of business, the proprietorship or partnership form may be suitable through a firm's entire life. Also, some enterprises in the past were required to operate either as a partnership or proprietorship. Physicians' practices, for example, were subject to such a requirement, and most doctors have continued to practice this way even though the law has changed.

Proprietorships and partnerships have other distinguishing characteristics, which can be classed under the following headings.

Freedom and unanimity of action. Usually the owner or owners of the firm also manage it. Thus, there is little likelihood of a disharmony of interest between owner and manager occurring. Decisions can be made quickly and agreement reached with a minimum of effort (providing the owners of a partnership agree on management matters).

In operating the firm, this unity of ownership and management facilitates financial decision-making. A decision made by the manager obviously is consistent with the owner's objectives, and vice versa. For example, the decision to borrow money, and so increase the firm's financial risk, can be made by management with full knowledge of how the owners feel about such a move. This may not be the case in a corporation, however, where management sometimes has to make such a decision without knowing the owners' wishes.

Taxation. For small businesses, definite tax advantages may be associated with the proprietorship or partnership form. Taxes are not levied against a person in his role as a proprietor or partner. The income of the business is considered the personal income of the owners, and each owner is taxed at his own personal rate on his share of the firm's profits. The firm itself pays no tax. Such an arrangement is beneficial to the owners, so long as they are withdrawing the earnings from the firm, because only one tax is paid. However, if owners want to leave earnings in the firm to finance accumulation of more assets, the personal income form of taxation may prove costly. If the owner is in an extremely high tax bracket—

Table 14–1. Proprietorships, Partnerships, and Corporations—Number, Receipts, and Profit: 1939 to 1967

(Number in thousands; money figures in billions of dollars.)

Item	1939	1945	1950	1955	1960	1963	1964	1965	1966	1967
Total, Number	1,793	6,737	(NA)	(NA)	11,172	11,383	11,489	11,416	11,479	11,566
Receipts	171	382	(NA)	(NA)	1,095	1,264	1,350	1,469	1,594	1,666
Net Profit (Less Loss)	11	40	(NA)	(NA)	73	87	96	111	121	119
Proprietorships, Number	1,052	5,689	6,865	8,239	9,090	9,136	9,193	9,078	9,087	9,126
Business Receipts	24	79	(NA)	139	171	182	189	199	207	211
Net Profit (Less Loss)	2	12	15	18	21	24	26	28	30	30
Partnerships, Number	271	627	(NA)	(NA)	941	924	922	914	923	906
Total Receipts	15	47	(NA)	(NA)	74	73	75	75	80	80
Net Profit (Less Loss)	2	7	(NA)	(NA)	8	9	9	10	10	11
Corporations, Number	470	421	629	807	1,141	1,323	1,374	1,424	1,469	1,531
Total Receipts[1]	133	255	458	642	849	1,009	1,087	1,195	1,306	1,375
Net Profit (Less Loss)[2]	7	21	43	47	44	54	62	74	81	78

NA   Not available.

[1] Gross taxable receipts before deduction of cost of goods sold, cost of operations, and net loss from sales of property other than capital assets. Includes nontaxable interest; excludes all other nontaxable income.

[2] Beginning 1963, includes constructive taxable income from related foreign corporations.

Source: Derived from *Statistical Abstract of the United States 1971*, U.S. Dept. of Commerce, Bureau of the Census, Washington, D.C., p. 459.

for example, 60 per cent—then for every dollar of before-tax earnings the firm generates, it can reinvest only forty cents.

Table 14–2 shows a tax-rate schedule on income of married individuals filing separate returns. A proprietor or partner would be taxed at these rates, or comparable ones on a joint return, even though the funds are plowed back into the firm. Recognizing that such an approach weakens a firm's ability to finance new assets, the Internal Revenue Service (IRS) permits a proprietorship or small partnership to be taxed as a corporation if management desires. However, once made, this decision cannot be changed: the firm will always be taxed as a corporation.

Income. In *The Wealth of Nations,* published in 1776, Adam Smith noted that the return falling to proprietors consists not only of profit, a reward for risk-taking, but also of "wages of superintendance," or a salary for managing the enterprise. This distinction, unfortunately, is not recognized by the IRS. So far as the IRS is concerned, proprietorships and partnerships must not treat owners as employees. This means that salaries to owners are not tax deductible expenses. It also means that these business forms cannot provide fringe benefits, such as insurance plans, retirement plans, and stock options, to owner-employees and deduct these benefits for tax purposes. Taxes must be paid by the owner immediately. In contrast, corporations may deduct these contributions before figuring their taxes and so pay less tax. Even though a partnership or proprietorship may choose to be taxed as a corporation, under the option mentioned above, contributions to manager-owners of the proprietorship or partnership for fringe benefits cannot be treated as tax deductible expenses.

Due to certain tax regulations, income may be greater for a proprietorship or partnership over its life than for a similar corporation. Firms during their early

Table 14–2. Married Individuals Filing Separate Returns; Estates and Trusts

Taxable Income	Tax on Column 1	% on Excess	Taxable Income	Tax on Column 1	% on Excess
$	$	14	$ 22,000	$ 7,030	50
500	70	15	26,000	9,030	53
1,000	145	16	32,000	12,210	55
1,500	225	17	38,000	15,510	58
2,000	310	19	44,000	18,990	60
4,000	690	22	50,000	22,590	62
6,000	1,130	25	60,000	28,790	64
8,000	1,630	28	70,000	35,190	66
10,000	2,190	32	80,000	41,790	68
12,000	2,830	36	90,000	48,590	69
14,000	3,550	39	100,000	55,490	70
16,000	4,330	42	150,000	90,490	70
18,000	5,170	45	200,000	125,490	70
20,000	6,070	48			

Source: *Understanding Taxes,* Teaching Taxes Program, Department of the Treasury, Internal Revenue Service, 1972 General Edition, p. 22.

years typically lose money; rare is the firm that enters business and makes a profit from the start. According to IRS rule, losses may be applied against earnings in other years to recoup taxes. All businesses can carry any loss back three years, and forward five, to apply against earnings and so receive a *tax shelter,* or benefit. However, a new corporation can carry a loss only forward into the future because it did not exist before it was chartered by the state. A proprietorship or partnership can apply the loss against the preceding three years of income received by the owner(s), even though the income of the previous three years was not generated by this particular firm. Since money has time value, obtaining an immediate refund from the IRS of taxes paid in the past is of greater value than having to wait until some future date to get the money back. For proprietors and partners, this advantage can have the consequence of reducing tax payments and, hence, increasing income during the early years of an enterprise.

Other characteristics. Other characteristics of proprietorships and partnerships do not apply directly to financial management, but deserve mention. First, proprietors and partners have unlimited personal liability. Creditors have a claim on the income and assets of not only the firm, but also of the individual in the event of financial difficulties on the part of the firm. Second, there is a problem of transferability of ownership. A proprietor may have trouble finding someone who wants to acquire his firm. If a partner wants to sell his interest in the firm, he must find someone acceptable to the remaining partner(s). A partner can transfer his interest in the firm to someone else only with the consent of the other partners. Hence, his ability to liquidate his position, to convert the assets to cash, is restricted. Third, these forms do not have perpetual life; they cease to exist upon the death, withdrawal, bankruptcy, or retirement of one of the principals.

Corporations

In the twentieth century the corporate form has dominated business enterprise. Table 14–1 reveals that although corporations are numerically in a minority, by all other measures they prevail.

Why has the corporate form risen to such an important place in American business enterprise? To a great extent, the answer lies in the realm of finance: corporations are able to tap more efficiently large sums of money to finance growth. But this benefit is not without disadvantages, as the following discussion of corporation characteristics will show. These characteristics can be discussed under the following headings.

Expansion. A corporation can enlarge its assets by tapping many sources of funds ordinarily unavailable to other forms of enterprise. This ability stems from three defining characteristics of the corporate form. (1) *Limited liability.* Holders of the shares of stock are the legal owners of a corporation, and each shareholder is liable only to the extent of his original investment. Should the corporation fail, creditors cannot press their claims on the corporation against the shareholders as individuals. (2) *Transferability.* Any shareholder can sell any portion of his ownership to anyone willing to buy it. No approval from the other owners (shareholders) is needed. (3) *Perpetual life.* The corporation is chartered by the state and thus becomes a separate entity, an artificial being with an existence apart from its natural owners. It is a being whose life has no legal limit, for, with few exceptions, charters are granted in perpetuity.

The advantages of the corporation for marshalling large-scale finance are evident. An individual is more willing to invest his savings in a corporation because he knows that managerial miscues cannot result in additional claims against his personal assets and income. He is more willing to invest because he believes he can convert his portion of ownership into money without undue delay. Finally, he will invest because he believes his offspring and kin will be able to profit from ownership even though something might happen to him. All of these factors make the supply of funds to the corporation cheaper and more abundant than to the proprietorship or partnership.

Taxation. An important characteristic of the corporation is that it must pay taxes in its own behalf. After all, it is a separate entity from its shareholders, and hence, like them, it must pay an income tax. All earnings of the firm are subject to federal income taxes, and, where applicable, to state income taxes.

Federal income tax takes roughly 50 per cent of a large corporation's before-tax earnings. The rate breaks down into a normal tax plus a surcharge. In 1972, the normal tax rate was 22 per cent on all income, and the surcharge was 26 per cent on income over $25,000, which brought the rate to 48 per cent on all income above $25,000. A corporation earning income of $60,000 would compute its tax liability as follows:

$$.22 \times \$25,000 = \$\ 5,500$$
$$.48 \times \underline{\ \ 35,000} = \underline{\ \ 16,800}$$
$$\ \ \ \ \ \ \ \ \ \ \$60,000 \ \ \ \ \$22,300$$

The average tax rate is approximately 37 per cent ($22,300/$60,000).

An advantage to the corporation over other forms of business can be seen in comparing the corporate tax rate on $60,000 earnings with the personal rate in Table 14–2. If Hiram Scarum, who is in the 64 per cent marginal, or incremental, tax bracket, wanted to leave his proprietorship earnings in the firm to finance expansion, he could reinvest only $31,210 ($60,000 less his $28,790 tax bill). The above corporation, however, could reinvest $37,700 ($60,000 – $22,300)—clearly an advantage. Of course, a corporation would be a disadvantage to Scarum if he wished to withdraw the funds and spend them personally. Dividends paid to any shareholder are subject to personal income tax, in addition to the corporate tax. In the above example, if the corporation paid Scarum a dividend of $37,700 (the total amount of earnings after taxes), he would pay personal income tax of .60 × 37,700 = $22,620. He could then spend only $15,080, far less than the $24,000 he would have had under the proprietorship-partnership form of business.

Corporations are subject to other taxes. An incorporation tax must be paid when the charter is granted by the state. This tax is usually based on the amount of authorized stock. In addition, annual franchise taxes, levied by states, are often imposed. Finally, the United States Treasury can impose an excessive accumulation tax on corporations that it believes to be accumulating earnings in order to help shareholders avoid paying taxes on dividends. If no dividends are paid, the Treasury receives no taxes from this potential source. Up to $100,000 of retained earnings is exempt from this tax, no questions asked. Retentions above this amount are subject to the tax (which averages about 35 per cent), if the Treasury Department can prove the accumulation is undertaken to avoid personal taxation.[1]

Conflict. Some economists have pointed to the separation of ownership and management in the corporation as a source of financial conflict. Where management is a professional elite with only a small financial stake in the firm, there is a possibility that the personal objectives of the managers might be out of harmony with those of the shareholders.

For example, if the management seeks rapid expansion for the corporation, it may proceed recklessly, borrowing a large proportion of funds. Shareholders, on the other hand, may prefer safety to growth and abhor the use of debt. Or, to conserve funds for corporate purposes, management may prefer to pay no dividends, whereas shareholders may desire and need dividends. Or, management may feel some social concern for the environment, for example, and perhaps divert funds for use in clearing a contaminated river. Shareholders, on the other hand, may prefer higher earnings and dividends to such use of earnings. Hence, management may pursue financial policies unacceptable to owners.

In such cases, owners then have three options. They can tacitly agree with management's policy, hold their stock, and adjust their objectives to conform with those of management. Or, they can sell their stock to someone whose objectives conform with those of management. Or, finally, they can replace the directors at the next shareholders' meeting (assuming they have enough support from other shareholders) and have the new directors fire the managers. The important point to notice is that the possibility for such a conflict does exist within a corporation.

A corporation has other important characteristics, but the preceding ones have been emphasized because of their bearing on financial policy.

Selecting the Form

In describing the characteristics and advantages of proprietorships, partnerships, and corporations, the previous sections offer implicit suggestions for selecting the form of a business. Two additional points should be considered in selecting the form. First, legal fees and a time delay must be incurred when beginning a corporation. These may be unacceptable to someone entering business. Second, the aspect of limited liability for a small corporation may be more apparent than real. Often, the officers of a small corporation are forced to sign personally for any loans the corporation receives, so that creditors will have recourse against individuals if the corporation defaults on repayment.

Selecting the form of business may involve timing. A logical sequence of forms for a business to follow over its life might be this one. It begins as a proprietorship, with one man serving as owner and manager. He performs all of the managerial functions—finance, production, personnel, and marketing. His own finance, personality, and ability are hopefully enough to make him successful. As the firm grows and funds are needed in excess of what he can provide, he brings in a partner. Probably the partner is able to assume some of the managerial responsibilities.

---

[1] Burden of proof that accumulation is excessive lies upon the IRS. A company is considered innocent until proved guilty. Ordinarily, it is easy for publicly-held companies to justify their retained earnings. Questions rarely arise so long as management files a statement with the IRS that earnings are being used for such things as growth, debt retirement, or precautionary cash.

Finally, if the business continues successfully, the partners may decide that doing all jobs themselves, and relying on their own limited finance, is too large a burden and a limitation. The partnership becomes a corporation. Now, professional managers enter the picture. The firm can sell new common stock and obtain equity financing from sources other than earnings retention or the partners. Debt financing also becomes easier to acquire, due to enlargement of the equity base which provides the foundation for borrowing.

Tax Management in the Corporation

A business begins life only once and changes form infrequently, but taxes are an ever-recurring matter. Tax management is a vital function of financial management. A business rarely makes a transaction for the tax savings alone, but whenever possible it should seek to reduce its tax bill. The realistic businessman views taxes as a cost of doing business; and, like other costs, they deserve to be minimized. This suggests that a firm should (a) pay the lowest total tax, and (2) delay payment as long as legally allowable.

Splitting the Corporation

We have seen that corporate income taxes consist of two parts, a normal tax rate of 22 per cent on all income, plus a surtax of 26 per cent on income above $25,000. This amounts to a 22 per cent rate on income up to $25,000 and 48 per cent on income above $25,000.

The large jump in taxes at $25,000 has made it profitable for corporations to split themselves into several separate companies to reduce the taxable income of each below $25,000. This maneuver is known as divisionalization. In the example above, if the firm had divided itself into three separate corporations for tax purposes, its tax burden would have been:

$$
\begin{array}{llll}
.22 \times \$25,000 & = & \$5,500 \\
.22 \times 25,000 & = & 5,500 \\
.22 \times \underline{10,000} & = & \underline{2,200} \\
\$60,000 & & \$13,200
\end{array}
$$

The new combination would then have paid only a 22 per cent ($13,200/$60,000) average tax rate.

This source of tax advantage is disappearing. The Tax Reform Act of 1969 eliminates all tax advantages from divisionalization by 1975. After that, only one firm in such a group will be taxed at the 22 per cent base rate; all others must pay the 48 per cent rate.

Corporations must pay their taxes in the year they are incurred. A company is required to estimate its earnings for the coming year and calculate its estimated tax. It then pays 25 per cent of the estimate in each quarter of the year.

Loss Carry-Back and Carry-Forward

Many companies have widely fluctuating sales and earnings. For example, brokerage firms live and die according to sales volume on the stock exchanges.[2]

---

[2]The relation between sales volume and earnings is explained by operating leverage. Leverage is discussed in chapter 17.

When no one is buying, these firms lose money; when the market is strong and volume is high, the firms generate huge earnings. To attract capital into industries where uncertainties are large, i.e., earnings unstable, the Treasury permits businesses to normalize their earnings and so alter their tax burden. That is, if a firm loses money in any one year, it can apply this loss against previous or later profits, thereby reducing the fluctuation in its after-tax earnings. If the loss is carried back against a previous year's earnings, the latest year's loss is applied against taxes paid in the earlier year, and the Treasury will rebate the amount of the overpayment.

Specifically, a loss in any year can be carried back three years and forward five years. The loss must be carried to the earliest year (three years back), applied to the limit of earnings in that year, then applied in the next year to the limit, and so on. Where losses are incurred in two successive years, the first year's loss still can be applied only to five succeeding years, even though one of those is a loss, too.

Suppose that Mervin Zinch, Snitch, Brenner and Deem, Inc., has a loss before taxes of $27 million in 1973. Its earnings and taxes before 1973 are depicted in Table 14–3. It can apply its 1973 loss against the previous three years earnings and receive an immediate rebate of $10,750,000. Since Mervin Zinch had used up $21.5 million of its total $27 million loss, it would have $5.5 million left to carry forward and reduce taxes on future earnings.

This privilege of allocating a loss to past profitable periods gave impetus to the merger mania of the late 1960s. When firms were unable to obtain desperately needed funds from any other source, they could merge with another firm (even one without cash) which had suffered large losses, and obtain funds from the Treasury through an acquired tax-loss carry-back. The merger was often on a stock-for-stock or bonds-for-stock basis, so the acquiring firm needed no cash to finance the corporate wedding.

Capital Gains and Losses

The above discussion applies to ordinary income, meaning income generated through normal operation of the business. Taxation of capital gains and losses is handled differently. A *capital gain* is profit received from the sale of an asset outside the normal operation of a business. This means the assets sold are not inventory. For a manufacturing concern, securities, land, and separable divisions of the company are examples.

Rates

The tax rate a firm pays on a capital gain depends on whether the gain is short- or long-term. Short-term capital gains and losses occur when the asset disposed of has been held less than six months. These gains and losses are treated as ordinary income and added to or subtracted from the company's before-tax income from normal operations.

Long-term capital gains and losses occur on the disposal of assets held

Table 14-3. Mervin Zinch, Snitch, Brenner and Deem, Inc., Income Statement

	1969	1970	1971	1972	1973
Stated					
Earnings Before Taxes	$8,000,000	$7,500,000	$4,000,000	$10,000,000	($27,000,000)
Less: Taxes*	4,000,000	3,750,000	2,000,000	5,000,000	–0–
Earnings After Taxes	$4,000,000	$3,750,000	$2,000,000	$ 5,000,000	($27,000,000)
Adjusted					
Earnings Before Taxes	$8,000,000	$7,500,000	$4,000,000	$10,000,000	
Less: Loss Carry Back	–0–	7,500,000	4,000,000	10,000,000	
Adjusted Earnings Before Taxes	$8,000,000	–0–	–0–	–0–	
Taxes	4,000,000	–0–	–0–	–0–	
Taxes Paid	$4,000,000	$3,750,000	$2,000,000	$ 5,000,000	
Rebate	–0–	$3,750,000	$2,000,000	$ 5,000,000	

*For simplicity, we assume a tax rate of 50%. In fact, of course, the tax would be 22% of the first $25,000 and 48% of the amount above $25,000.

six months or longer. Such income receives special tax treatment. Long-term capital *gains* are subject to a maximum tax rate of 30 per cent, if ordinary income is above $25,000, or a minimum of 22 per cent, if ordinary income is below $25,000. If a firm earning $85,000 before taxes incurs a $20,000 long-term capital gain, its total taxes will be:

```
.22 × $25,000  = $ 5,500
.48 ×   60,000  =  28,800
.30 ×   20,000  =   6,000
      $105,000      $40,300
```

Long-term capital *losses* can be applied only against long-term capital gains. A loss must first be carried back three years and applied to the earliest year, then forward five years, just as with ordinary profits and losses. If a firm buys securities for $100,000 in 1973 and sells them eight months later for $20,000, it would have an $80,000 long-term capital loss. This loss would be carried back and applied against the following capital gains:

	1970	1971	1972	1973
Gain	$45,000	$30,000	$15,000	($80,000)
Tax (30%)	13,500	9,000	4,500	
Rebate	$13,500	$ 9,000	$ 1,500	
Loss to carry forward	$35,000	$ 5,000	–0–	

The $80,000 loss would first be applied against the $45,000 gain in 1970, reducing it to zero. Since the tax on zero is zero and the company paid $13,500, the Treasury would return the $13,500 to the firm. Now, the firm still has $35,000 ($80,000 – $45,000) to use. It applies $30,000 of the loss to 1971, receiving a $9,000 rebate. Finally, it has $5,000 of the loss to apply in 1972, bringing the taxable gain in 1972 to an adjusted $10,000. The tax on $10,000 is $3,000, assuming normal operating income is above $25,000. Since the firm paid $4,500, the Treasury would rebate $1,500 to the firm. There is no loss left to carry forward.

Depreciable Assets

When a firm disposes of fixed assets, profit or loss often occurs. Here, the rule is that any *gain* will be divided between ordinary income and capital gain; any *loss* will be considered an ordinary operating loss.

How is the gain distributed between ordinary and capital components? Gain up to the total amount of accumulated depreciation is ordinary; the excess, capital. Hence, ordinary gain is taxed at 48 per cent and the excess at 30 per cent (assuming the firm is in the 48 per cent bracket). Take an example. Fatback Datawhack five years ago purchased a card sorter for $100,000 which had an anticipated life of ten years. It sells the sorter at the end of five years to acquire a more efficient one. If it receives $60,000 for the sorter, its tax obligation will be calculated as follows:

Original value	$100,000
Less: accumulated depreciation	50,000
Book value	$ 50,000
Market value	$ 60,000
Less: book value	50,000
Gain	$ 10,000
Less: tax	.48
	$ 4,800

Since the $10,000 gain is less than the amount of accumulated depreciation, it is taxed at the ordinary rate. Why? The firm has been *overstating* depreciation. It has written the asset down further than it should have, given the present market value thus *understating* its past taxes. Because the past taxes so understated were at the ordinary rate, the IRS insists that this gain be taxed at the ordinary income rate.

A capital gain on a depreciable asset can arise *only* when the selling price exceeds the original value of the asset, for only then can the gain exceed the amount of accumulated depreciation. In the above example, if Datawhack had sold the sorter for $120,000, its tax burden would have been calculated as follows:

Original value	$100,000
Less: accumulated depreciation	50,000
Book value	$ 50,000
Market value	$120,000
Less: book value	50,000
Gain	$ 70,000

Since Datawhack sold the sorter for $120,000 and it originally cost $100,000, the firm has a $20,000 capital gain. The remainder of the total $70,000 gain is taxed at the ordinary rate. Thus its tax burden is:

Gain	$ 70,000	
Less: excess of market over original value	20,000	
Normal gain	$ 50,000	
Tax	50,000 × .48 =	$24,000
	20,000 × .30 =	6,000
	$70,000	$30,000

The $30,000 tax represents an average of 43 per cent ($30,000/$70,000).

If disposal of the asset leads to a loss, the loss applies to ordinary income because the firm has been understating depreciation and overpaying taxes. A loss on sale of a depreciable asset can be deducted in full from operating income.

Dividend Income

When a corporation receives dividend income from another domestic corporation it is permitted to shield 85 per cent of this income from taxation, paying ordinary income tax on only 15 per cent of the gross amount. On $100 worth of dividends, a corporation in the 48 per cent marginal tax bracket would pay only .48 × $15, or $7.20. This provision of the tax law explains why fully taxable corporations often buy preferred stock instead of bonds or bills as long- or short-term investments. Although price fluctuations and other risks on preferreds may be greater, after-tax income is also enlarged.

To Remember

Perpetual life

Transferable ownership

Limited liability

Normal tax

Surcharge

Tax-loss carry-back and carry-forward

Capital gain

Tax shelter

Excessive accumulation

Questions

1. Two college friends plan to open a sporting goods store. They ask you to help them decide whether or not to incorporate the store. What are some primary factors you would consider in advising them?

2. Finster Dingbat last year earned taxable income of $19,640. He and Mrs. Dingbat file separate returns, each claiming half the income. How much income tax do the Dingbats pay? What are their marginal and average tax brackets?

3. Howard Cayse Myth last year had taxable earnings of $27,000 in his pinball and pool hall pub. As a proprietor, he pays taxes using the form for married persons filing separate returns, so he claims the full $27,000.
   (a) If Myth operated his business as a corporation and paid himself a salary of $17,000, how much *total* taxes would be paid by the firm and by Myth?
   (b) How much taxes are paid as a propriertorship?
   (c) How much is reinvested under (1) the corporate form, and (2) the proprietorship form, assuming Myth spends $7,810 on personal consumption?

4. "The fact that corporations have limited liability is important to owners of small firms. When a corporation borrows from a bank, the shareholders do not experience so much uneasiness and uncertainty as they would if the firm were a partnership."
   (a) What is meant by limited liability?
   (b) How is the limited liability advantage often negated when a small corporation borrows money?

5. Before 1964, corporations paid income tax in the year following that in which the income was generated. The Internal Revenue Act of 1964 required them to change to a quarterly, pay-as-you-go basis. What do you think the financial implications were for corporations, and the economy, between 1964 and 1966?

6. Achilles Ludlum, a West Coast mining firm, earned—*after* taxes—$300,000 in each of the past four years (1969–72). This year (1973) it suffers a staggering loss due to strikes, failure of customers to pay their bills, and management's misjudgment of the market. Show the tax rebate attributable to each of the past four years, and the loss left to carry forward, assuming the following losses in 1973. For ease of calculation assume a 40 per cent corporate tax rate.
   (a) $700,000.
   (b) $2,600,000.
   (c) $1,000,000, and 1972 showed a loss of $600,000, but 1969–71 had the same earnings as (a).

7. Explain why the IRS taxes the gain on a depreciable asset at the ordinary rate when the gain is less than accumulated depreciation.

15

Financial Reports and What They Tell You

What Financial Reports Contain — The Balance Sheet — *The Balance Sheet Layout — Assets — Fixed Assets — Liabilities — Stockholders' Equity* — The Income Statement — Accumulated Retained Earnings Statement — Sources and Applications of Funds Statement — Financial Statements: Further Aspects — *Footnotes — Independent Audits — Reliability — Usefulness*

What Financial Reports Contain

The financial manager looks at his company from within. Creditors and investors study it from without. But either way, the starting point is usually a company's financial reports. These reports summarize where a company stands financially and how well it is making money for its owners. Financial reports can never tell the whole story about a company's position and prospects, but they contain much illuminating information and can be analyzed to reveal still more. The four most important documents in a financial report are (1) the balance sheet, (2) the income statement, (3) the statement of retained earnings, and (4) the sources and applications of funds statement.

The Balance Sheet

In understanding balance sheets, it is important to remember that a corporation, legally, is an "artificial" person, separate and distinct from the persons (or financial institutions) who own it. A corporation in turn is legally separate from the property it owns. Properties owned by the corporation, whether tangible or intangible, are assets. All of the corporation's assets are owned by the corporation itself, but against the *total value* of these assets are ranked the claims of various "outsider" interests. Claims of creditors, to whom the corporation is indebted for money or goods, are liabilities. These claims have priority over the remainder or residual claims of owners; their claims are called *net worth*, or equity.

Balance Sheet Layout

Table 15–1 is a sample balance sheet. It is typical of the kind issued by a medium-size manufacturing company, neither the simplest that could be issued nor the most complicated.

A balance sheet is a financial photograph of a company at a given instant of time, typically the close of business on a particular day. It is divided into two parts: above, assets are shown; below, liabilities and owners' net worth. The Assets column lists all goods and property owned by the company, including its claims against others that are still to be collected. The Liabilities column lists all debts the company owes: these are creditors' claims against the assets. Stockholders' equity, which measures *their* interest in the company, is simply a remainder: an equity in the assets after creditors' claims are subtracted. In fact, the basic accounting equation runs:

Assets minus Liabilities = Net Worth = Stockholders' Equity.

So for Sample Manufacturing Company:

Total assets	$9,700,000
Less: liabilities	5,200,000
Stockholders' equity	$4,500,000

Assets

The first group on the asset part of the balance sheet is *Current Assets.* It includes cash and those other assets which, in the normal course of business, will be turned into cash within the coming year.

Cash consists of currency and coin in the till (petty cash) and money on deposit at the bank.

Marketable securities comprise temporary investments of excess or idle cash which is not needed immediately. Since such funds may be required on short notice, they are ordinarily invested in readily marketable, short-term securities subject to minimum price fluctuation. U.S. Treasury bills, commercial bank CDs, and commerical paper are ideal for this purpose, though corporate treasurers greedy for income or market profits sometimes take larger risks by investing in stocks or bonds. The usual practice is to show marketable securities at cost, with a parenthetic note of market value. For example:

Marketable securities, at cost $1,550,000
    (Market value $1,570,000)

Table 15–1. Sample Manufacturing Company, Inc., and Consolidated Subsidiaries, Balance Sheet, December 31, 19____

Item		Amount
Assets		
Current Assets		
Cash		$ 950,000
Marketable Securities, at Cost		
(Market Value $1,570,000)		1,550,000
Accounts Receivable	$2,100,000	
Less: Provision for Bad Debts	100,000	2,000,000
Inventories		1,500,000
Total Current Assets		$6,000,000
Investment in Unconsolidated Subsidiaries		300,000
Property, Plant, and Equipment		
Land	$ 150,000	
Buildings	3,800,000	
Machinery	950,000	
Office Equipment	100,000	
	$5,000,000	
Less: Accumulated Depreciation	1,800,000	
Net Property, Plant, and Equipment		3,200,000
Prepaid Expenses and Deferred Charges		100,000
Goodwill, Patents, Trademarks		100,000
Total Assets		$9,700,000
Liabilities and Stockholders' Equity		
Current Liabilities		
Accounts Payable	$1,000,000	
Notes Payable	850,000	
Accrued Expenses Payable	330,000	
Federal Income Tax Payable	320,000	
Total Current Liabilities		$2,500,000
Long-term Liabilities		
First Mortgage Bonds, 7% Interest, Due 1982		2,700,000
Total Liabilities		$5,200,000
Stockholders' Equity		
Capital Stock		
Preferred Stock, 8% Cumulative, $50 Par Value Each; Authorized, Issued, and Outstanding 12,000 Shares	$ 600,000	
Common Stock, No Par Value; Stated Value $5 Each; Authorized, Issued, and Outstanding 300,000 Shares	$1,500,000	
Paid-in Capital in Excess of Par	700,000	
Accumulated Retained Earnings	1,700,000	
Total Stockholders' Equity		$4,500,000
Total Liabilities and Stockholders' Equity		$9,700,000

Accounts receivable is the amount not yet collected from customers to whom goods were shipped prior to payment. The total amount due from customers as shown on Sample's balance sheet is $2,100,000. However, experience indicates that some customers fail to pay their bills. Therefore, in order to state accounts receivable at the figure likely to be collected, the total amount is reduced by a provision for bad debts. The net balance of $2,000,000 is thus shown as the asset value for balance sheet purposes:

Accounts receivable	$2,100,000
Less: provision for bad debts	100,000
Net accounts receivable	$2,000,000

Inventories are composed of three components: raw materials, partly finished goods in process of manufacture, and finished goods ready for shipment to customers. The generally accepted basis of valuing inventories is cost or market value, whichever is *lower*. This gives a conservative figure for balance sheet purposes: cost, if the value is equal to or greater than cost; market, if, as a consequence of deterioration, obsolescence, or decline in market price, less than cost can be realized on selling the inventory. Three of the total current assets items—cash, receivables, and inventories—comprise a firm's *circulating capital*. These assets move in a continual cycle: cash becomes inventories through manufacturing or purchase; inventories are converted into receivables through credit sales; receivables come back to cash through collections.

Investment in unconsolidated subsidiaries is the cost to Sample Manufacturing Company of the capital stock it owns in another company. The word *subsidiary* signifies that Sample (the parent) owns more than 50 per cent of the subsidiary's outstanding shares.[1]

Fixed Assets

The next item, *Property, Plant and Equipment,* is often referred to as *fixed assets.* It includes land, buildings, machinery, equipment, furniture, trucks, autos, and other durable items. These items (1) are used to manufacture, warehouse, or transport products, and (2) are not intended for resale.

The generally approved method of valuing fixed assets is cost minus depreciation accumulated to date of the balance sheet.

Depreciation, in the economic sense, represents decline in the useful value of a fixed asset. This loss of value is due to wear and tear from use, passage of time, or action of elements. Obsolescence because of new inventions or more advanced techniques may also reduce fixed asset values. In the accounting sense, depreciation means the spreading of fixed assets' cost over their useful lives.

Our sample balance sheet shows a figure for *accumulated depreciation.* This is the total amount of depreciation accumulated for buildings, machinery, and office furniture. Land is not subject to depreciation, and its balance sheet value remains unchanged from year to year.

---

[1]When a parent owns 80 per cent or more of a subsidiary's stock, then a *consolidated* balance sheet may be issued. This combines all assets and liabilities of the two companies as if they were a single entity.

The next figure, *Net Property, Plant, and Equipment,* is the valuation for balance sheet purposes of the company's investment in fixed assets. It consists of the *cost* of the various kinds of fixed assets, diminished by the depreciation accumulated to date:

Land		$ 150,000
Buildings	$3,800,000	
Machinery	950,000	
Office equipment	100,000	
	$4,850,000	
Less: accumulated depreciation	1,800,000	3,050,000
Net Property, Plant, and Equipment		$3,200,000

As you can see, land has been separated from the depreciable assets.

It must be emphasized that the net value of fixed assets shown on the balance sheet is not intended to reflect either *market value* at present or *replacement cost* in the future. Nor does balance sheet depreciation claim to correspond closely with the rate at which the value or usefulness of assets actually declines. Depreciation is simply a device for distributing the cost of a fixed asset over its useful life. For sake of clarity and consistency, depreciation (the using up of fixed assets) is recorded *as if* the dollar's value remains fixed. If inflation raises the cost of fixed-asset replacement, management should recognize that some profits will be needed to replace fixed assets. Fewer dividend increases—and sometimes even dividend cuts or omissions—will be required to permit companies to retain a higher fraction of their earnings.

The term depreciation applies to allocating the cost of man-made durable assets. Two other analogous terms occur in financial accounting: depletion and amortization. *Depletion* recognizes a firm's using up of some natural resource: a deposit of oil, coal, clay, gravel, and the like. In a similar sense, *amortization* accounts for the loss of value in a patent, leasehold, franchise, or some other intangible right owned by a company.

The next entry on the balance sheet, *Prepaid Expenses and Deferred Charges,* represents the unexpired portion of costs paid in advance. A *prepaid expense* would be, for example, two year's remaining value of a three-year fire insurance premium paid at the start of the year now ended. An example of a *deferred charge* would be $300,000 spent last year to promote a new product's sale over the next several years.

These assets have three characteristics in common. (1) A cash cost or outlay has already been paid, but part of the benefit will be reaped in future years. (2) The value paid for but not yet enjoyed is recognized by entering an asset on the balance sheet. (3) The remaining cost of this asset will be allocated to the future years in which the benefits are enjoyed. This is done by writing off the remaining cost of the prepaid or deferred item against the revenues of future years.[2]

The final asset shown on Sample Manufacturing Company's balance sheet, *Goodwill, Patents, Trademarks,* consists of intangibles, assets having value without physical existence. *Goodwill* often represents the difference between the cost of acquired assets and the value at which they are taken onto a company's books. Suppose, for example, that Sample Manufacturing Company paid $500,000 to acquire Green Giant Goofball in a merger. If Green Giant's plant, equipment, inventories, cash, and other physical assets were taken onto the books at $300,000, the remaining $200,000 of the purchase price might be accounted for as goodwill. The lower the value is at which a company carries intangibles, the stronger the indication of conservative accounting practices. Very conservative companies often carry patents at a value of $1.

Liabilities

The liability part of the balance sheet shows the claims against the corporation's assets—their size and, roughly, their order of precedence.

Current liabilities are typically shown first. They include all debts that fall due within the coming year. *Accounts payable* are amounts the company owes its suppliers and other business creditors. Most of these represent open-account purchases of goods for which the company has thirty, sixty, or ninety days to pay. *Notes payable* are money owed banks and other lenders and evidenced by written promissory notes. *Accrued expenses* include a variety of sums which are owed but unpaid on the date of the balance sheet: salaries and wages of employees, interest on borrowed funds, pensions, attorney fees, and the like. *Federal income tax payable* is usually stated separately from other accrued items. Finally, *total current liabilities* are the total of items listed in this classification.

Long-term liabilities include all debts on which the principal falls due more than one year after date of the report. Our sample balance sheet lists only one long-term liability: 7 per cent first mortgage bonds, due in 1982. These bonds are formal IOUs under which the company promises to repay the borrowed principal in 1982 and to pay interest meanwhile at 7 per cent annually.[3]

Stockholders' Equity

Stockholders' equity comprises the total of ownership claims in the corporation. For legal, accounting, or financial purposes, it can be separated in various ways. Since our viewpoint is financial, we shall consider equity under two main headings: (1) preferred stock, and (2) common stockholders' equity, or *net worth.*

---

[2]This can be stated differently. Prepayments and deferrals are a means of recognizing a difference *in timing* between making a cash outlay and charging the cost (for profit and loss purposes) against revenues. Initially, cash is traded for another asset—the prepaid expense or deferred charge; this asset is then written off against the revenues of the future periods in which the benefits of the outlay are enjoyed.

[3]Bonds are described in greater detail in chapter 25. Interest is usually paid semi-annually. The words *first mortgage* mean that the company's promise to pay is reinforced by the bondholders' claim or lien on certain specifically pledged assets. If the company cannot pay interest or principal in cash as promised, these assets may be sold and the proceeds used to satisfy the debt.

which includes (a) common stock, (b) capital (paid-in) surplus, and (c) retained earnings.

Both preferred and common stock are evidenced by stock certificates, issued by the corporation to its shareholders.

Preferred stock is a limited kind of ownership, entitled to dividend payments at a fixed rate before anything is paid on common shares. It also is paid off ahead of the common if the corporation is liquidated. The designation of *8 per cent cumulative, $50 par value* means that each preferred share is entitled to .08 × $50 = $4 in dividends annually, before any dividends are paid on the common. *Cumulative* means that any dividend payments on the preferred missed must be made up before any dividends can be declared on the common.

Common stockholders' equity, as noted above, includes the last three items on the liabilities part of the balance sheet. The *book value,* or *net asset value,* per common share consists of the sum of common stock, capital surplus, and retained earnings divided by the number of shares outstanding. For Sample Manufacturing Company, book value per common share is equal to $1,500,000 plus $700,000 plus $1,700,000, all divided by 300,000, or $13.

Common stock, as it appears on the books, is simply a par, or stated, value arbitrarily assigned to the common shares. This figure may or may not represent, or closely resemble, what the original stockholders paid for their interest in the company.

Paid-in capital in excess of par is the amount paid in by common stockholders in excess of the par value of their shares. Apparently, Sample Manufacturing Company stockholders paid a total of $2,200,000 for the 300,000 common shares outstanding. A total of $1,500,000—300,000 times $5—represents the *par value* of their holdings. The other $700,000 comprises the *capital* (or *paid-in*) surplus.

Retained earnings (sometimes called earned surplus) consist of the profits of past years that have been plowed back into the company instead of being paid out in dividends to stockholders. Sample Manufacturing Company has now accumulated $1,700,000 in retained earnings. Retained earnings are used by companies to expand their assets.

The Income Statement

Sometimes called the profit and loss statement, the *income statement* summarizes a firm's operating results for a past period, typically one year. It matches amounts received from sales of goods and other items with all costs incurred in operating the company over the period. The result is a net profit or net loss for the period. Thus, while the balance sheet is a *stock* concept like a "still" photograph, the income statement is a *flow* like a moving picture; the final frame in this movie is the balance sheet.

Let us now review the income statement of Sample Manufacturing Company, Table 15–2.

The first item, *Net Sales,* represents the money received by the company from its customers for goods or services sold.[4] Net means that allowance has

---

[4] In railroads, utilities, airlines, and other government regulated industries, this item is usually called *operating revenues.*

Table 15-2. Sample Manufacturing Company, Inc., and Consolidated Subsidiaries, Income Statement, Year 19____

Item		Amount
Net Sales		$6,500,000
Cost of Sales and Operating Expenses		
Cost of Goods Sold	$4,400,000	
Depreciation	900,000	
Selling and Administrative Expenses	500,000	5,800,000
Operating Profit		$ 700,000
Other Income		
Dividends and Interest		110,000
Total Income		$ 810,000
Less: Interest on Bonds		189,000
Profit before Provision for Federal Income Tax		$ 621,000
Provision for Federal Income Tax		266,000
Net Profit for the Year		$ 355,000

been made for goods returned, discounts taken by customers for prompt payment, and the likelihood that some accounts are uncollectible.

Cost of Sales and Operating Expenses, the first subtraction made in determining profit, includes three components. (1) *Cost of goods sold* covers cash payments made or debts incurred in the operating period for raw materials, direct labor, and factory overhead items such as supervision, rent, electricity, supplies, maintenance, and repairs. (2) *Depreciation* is the allowance made each year for loss of value in long-lived assets (plant, equipment, and machinery) used in production. (3) *Selling and administrative expenses* comprise salesmen's salaries and commissions, advertising, promotion, travel, and entertainment outlays (selling expenses); and executive salaries, office payroll, and office expenses (administrative expenses).

Operating profit is computed by subtracting cost of sales and operating expenses from net sales. Operating profit divided by net sales gives a very important measure of financial results: the *operating margin.* For Sample Manufacturing Company, the operating margin is $700,000 ÷ $6,500,000, or 10.8 per cent. Dividing cost of sales plus operating expenses by net sales gives us the *operating ratio,* the complement of the operating margin. The operating ratio for Sample is 100 per cent minus 10.8 per cent, or 89.2 per cent. The same result can be obtained from $5,800,000 divided by $6,500,000.[5]

Other income comes from sources outside the company's main product or service. For Sample Manufacturing Company, it consists of dividends and interest on stocks and bonds the company owns. Beginning in 1972, other income will show the profit or loss of ventures in which the company owns 20 per cent or more of the subsidiary's common stock. For example, if Sample Manufacturing Company owns 30 per cent of Amitonics United and Amitonics had a $10,000

---

[5]Operating ratios are most widely used in analyzing the financial results of regulated companies. These ratios are discussed in detail in chapter 16.

loss in 1972, Sample would show a $3,000 decrease in other income. Other income is added to operating profit to get *total income.*

Interest expense is the return paid to suppliers of debt capital (in this case, bondholders) for the use of their money. It is sometimes referred to as a *fixed charge,* since it must be paid whether the company is making money or not. Other fixed charges, not owed by Sample Manufacturing Company, would include payments which a company is required to make to retain use of leased or rented property.

Tax laws treat interest as a cost of doing business, so interest is deductible from total income in arriving at the entry *Profit before Provision for Federal Income Tax.*

Provision for Federal Income Tax is the last "minus" factor to be subtracted in arriving at net profit or earnings for the year.

Net profit or earnings represents what a company has left after meeting all costs of a year's operations. It is the amount technically available to pay dividends on the preferred and common stock and to use in the business. Net earnings not paid out in dividends are shown as *retained earnings.*

Two points of caution with respect to net earnings need to be made. First, the net earnings of any single year are a much less reliable index to a company's *earning power* than its earnings averaged over several years. A single year may be one of extreme business boom or recession, and hence unrepresentative. The trend as well as the level of earnings is also important. Second, accounting procedures such as income statements and balance sheets account only for the ebb and flow of dollars, and not real values. Where price-level inflation produces significant differences in current-dollar and constant-dollar or deflated values of assets, debts, asset-replacement costs, and so on, reported net earnings may have little bearing on the volume of dividends a company can actually afford to pay.

Accumulated Retained Earnings Statement

An *accumulated retained earnings statement* (sometimes called a statement of earned surplus) summarizes the change in retained earnings from the figure shown on the previous year's balance sheet. As the statement for Sample Manufacturing Company (Table 15–3) illustrates, the structure is simple and straightforward:

> Previous retained earnings
> + Net income for year past
> − Dividends paid
> = New balance of retained earnings.

Sources and Applications of Funds Statement

A *sources and applications of funds statement* shows why and how working capital has increased or decreased from one balance sheet date to another.[6]

---

[6]Funds may be defined otherwise than as working capital, but the working capital definition is most common. Other definitions (such as cash, cash and equivalents, or total current assets) are not considered in this introductory account.

Table 15–3. Accumulated Retained Earnings Statement, Year 19____

Item		Amount
Balance January 1		$1,513,000
Add: Net Profit for Year		355,000
Total		$1,868,000
Less: Dividends Paid		
On Preferred Stock	$ 48,000	
On Common Stock	120,000	168,000
Balance December 31		$1,700,000

Working capital means current assets financed from long-term or equity sources. Unlike current assets raised from short-term sources, working capital does not disappear when current liabilities are paid off. It is important because it represents the volume of current assets that will dependably stay with a company. A company's financial strength or weakness is in large degree reflected in its working capital position. Since working capital changes from year to year, it is important for the financial manager to know two things about it: (1) whether it is increasing or decreasing (he can tell this by looking at previous balance sheets), and (2) *why* it is increasing or decreasing.

Derivation of a sources and applications of funds statement calls for scrutiny of both the most recent balance sheet and last year's balance sheet, the income statement, the statement of retained earnings, and sometimes other sources. By examining these documents, an accountant can determine where working capital came from or was lost during the year. Briefly, the following can be classified as *sources* and *uses* of working capital.

Sources	*Uses*
1. Net profit for the year.	1. Net loss for year.
2. Depreciation or other capital consumption allowance.	2. Dividend payments.
3. Sale of fixed assets.	3. Purchase of fixed assets.
4. New equity or long-term debt financing.	4. Retirement or repurchase of stock or long-term debt.

More rigorously, changes in working capital are explained by changes in balance sheet items other than current assets and liabilities. Sources are increases in long-term liabilities (including equity) and decreases in fixed assets. Uses are increases in fixed assets and reductions of long-term liabilities.

The Sources and Applications of Funds Statement for Sample Manufacturing Company, Table 15–4, conforms to the above description.

Financial Statements: Further Aspects

A few additional aspects of financial statements should be mentioned. These are (1) footnotes, (2) independent audits, (3) reliability, and (4) usefulness.

Table 15–4. Sample Manufacturing Company, Inc., and Consolidated Subsidiaries, Sources and Applications of Funds, Year 19____

Item		Amount
Sources of Funds		
Net Profit for Year		$ 355,000
Add: Back Depreciation		900,000
Total Source of Funds		$1,255,000
Applications as Follows		
Purchase of New Plant and Equipment	$675,000 .	
Redemption of Long-term Debt	150,000	
Payment of Dividends	168,000	$ 993,000
Balance Remaining Added to		
Working Capital		$ 262,000

Footnotes

Financial reports of many companies contain this statement: "The accompanying footnotes are an integral part of the financial statements." Although footnotes are usually printed in small, hard-to-read type, they call for careful reading. Financial reports are, after all, condensed summaries, and important explanatory matter not readily abbreviated must be, and often is, presented in footnotes. In addition, unfavorable or embarrassing items which a management is required to disclose but wishes to play down are often buried in footnotes. Thus, the corporate outsider—investor, banker, or supplier—neglects footnotes at his peril.

Independent Audits

"Certified" financial statements have been audited by outside accountants. The certificate from the accountants is printed in the report. It ordinarily declares that (1) the statements have been prepared in conformity with "generally accepted accounting principles," and on a basis consistent with previous statements, and (2) the auditing steps taken in the process of verification were in accordance with approved practice.

The American Institute of Certified Public Accountants is responsible for adopting auditing procedures and for broad policy with respect to accounting principles. Outsiders are thus generally entitled to place somewhat more reliance on audited financial reports than on unaudited ones. Firms seeking to borrow money and investor-owned companies reporting to their stockholders are required to submit audited financial reports.

Reliability

In recent years, many companies have played a game which might be called "get the earnings up": the object is to show large profits (whether earned or not) in order to raise the price at which their stock sells in the stock market.

A high or rising stock price will (1) make a company's stock more valuable to use in buying other companies, (2) enhance the value of stock-purchase options held by the company's executives, and (3) enable the company to finance itself more cheaply by bringing in more money for each new share sold. Consequently, much "imagination," to be charitable, has gone into the preparation of financial reports. The investing public—and even bankers—have become increasingly skeptical of so-called generally accepted accounting principles that seem to stretch like rubber, or even taffy, when the aim is to produce higher reported earnings.

One difficulty is that the accounting profession itself cannot agree on what accounting principles ought to be.[7] Accountants rightly argue that no one way of reckoning profits, assets, liabilities, revenues, costs, and so on, would fit every company in every situation. Therefore, some flexibility in interpretating each company's position and performance is genuinely needed. But variations in accounting practice have gone far beyond this degree of necessity. Accounting firms often appear to have been intimidated by the corporate managements that hired them. Management has said, in effect, to its CPAs, "Show it our way or we'll fire you and hire some other CPA firm that will show what we want." Instead of presenting a united front in support of sound practice, the accounting profession has apparently permitted itself to be divided and conquered by some of its less scrupulous clients.

Usefulness

The usefulness and reliability of financial reports is different for those inside the corporation and those outside. The outsider—unless he is a banker, some other powerful lender, or a government regulator—can rarely demand a company's full financial story. He must rest content with the condensed summary of financial history and position reflected in the audited reports made public. He can rarely look behind the published figures to see how they were derived. The insider, being one of the company's managers, directors, or controlling stockholders need not—indeed, should not and must not—rest with the bare financial summary. He must go behind the figures and look at the subsidiary accounts, at how important transactions were entered on the books, and at the host of "adjustments" made in the books themselves in the process of preparing the financial statements.

As we shall see in the next few chapters, the highly detailed financial reports available to a company's management aid that management in three main activities: analysis, planning, and control. (1) Financial analysis reveals both the extent of a company's financial resources and the ability with which management is using them. Specifically, financial analysis discloses where a company stands with respect to profitability, liquidity, leverage, and the efficient use of its assets. (2) Financial reports provide the framework within which business planning takes place. All plans call for resources (inputs) and results (outputs). These must be both financed and measured with money. Typically, corporate plans are embodied in budgets for which dollars serve as a common denominator of resources applied and results

---

[7]Accounting principles are outlined in various numbered opinions of the Accounting Principles Board of the American Institute of Certified Public Accountants. Regulations and directives of the Securities and Exchange Commission also exercise considerable influence on the accounting practices of publicly-owned companies.

expected. (3) Financial reports are the key to the effective control of business enterprise. Results stated in money terms are compared with budgeted (intended) performance, and deviations and exceptions noted. This review paves the way for rewarding good performance and penalizing poor performance, for corrective action, and for subsequent stages of planning.

To Remember

Circulating capital	Amortization
Fixed assets	Intangibles
Depreciation	Operating ratio
Replacement cost	Fixed charge
Depletion	Sources and applications of funds

Questions

1. What are the four most important documents in a financial report and what does each tell you about a company?
2. Distinguish between balance sheet and income statement. Describe the purpose and content of each document.
3. How are inventories valued conservatively for balance-sheet purposes?
4. Distinguish between fixed assets and circulating capital.
5. Distinguish between depreciation, depletion, and amortization.
6. What are prepaid expenses and deferred charges? On which side of the balance sheet do they occur? What becomes of them as time passes?
7. What are the components of stockholders' equity? What purposes does equity serve in a business enterprise?
8. Does a company's income statement reveal its earning power? Discuss.
9. What comprises a firm's working capital? Defining funds as working capital, list the principal sources and applications of funds.
10. Discuss the usefulness of footnotes in financial analysis.

16

Profitability and Turnover

Ratio Analysis — *Uses* — *Sources* — **Profit and Risk** — **Profitability Measures** — *Gross Profit Margin* — *Gross Operating Margin* — *Net Operating Margin* — *Sales Margin* — *Earning Power* — *Return on Equity* — **Turnover** — *Receivables Turnover* — *Inventory Turnover* — **Return on Assets**

We come now to measurement of a firm's financial position and performance. There are two primary measures: *profitability* and *liquidity*. These terms will be defined more precisely later, but they answer, respectively, the two all-important questions: How much is a business making for its owners? How able is it to pay its bills? In addition, and as important supports to profitability and liquidity, are two other criteria: *turnover* and *leverage*. Like the first two measures, these also answer important questions about the business. Turnover tells how effectively the assets of the enterprise are being utilized. Leverage describes how rapidly profits change in relation to changes in sales.

In this chapter, we shall see how firms measure their profitability and turnover. In the following chapter, we shall see how they measure their liquidity and leverage.

Ratio Analysis

A firm's business performance can be measured by the use of ratios. Ratios involving figures from the income statement, the balance sheet, or both, may reveal much about a company's financial position to its management, shareholders and creditors.

Uses

A ratio is simply the quotient of two numbers. By itself, it is almost meaningless. For a financial ratio to have meaning, it must be interpreted against some standard. There are two main ways to analyze a ratio. The first is *time series analysis,* which involves seeing how the ratio has behaved across time. By observing its variation, the manager can gain perspective on the firm's performance and see what direction it is headed in. The second is *cross-sectional analysis.* Here, the manager, creditor, or shareholder observes how the firm is performing at a single point in time relative either to other firms in the industry or to some other generally accepted industry standard.

Ratio analysis usually proceeds on the assumption that the industry average is a suitable yardstick of performance for individual firms in that industry. The financial community is generally conservative and often insists that an enterprise achieve industry-average performance if it is to have access to finance on acceptable terms from either banks or long-term capital suppliers. Shareholders may avoid buying new common stock issues and even vote to replace management if the industry standards of performance are not achieved by their firm. All in all, a harsh fate may await managers whose ratios fall significantly short of industry averages.

Sources

Where does a financial manager discover the average for his industry? The most accessible source is *Dun's Review and Modern Industry,* published annually by Dun & Bradstreet.[1] This publication contains a number of significant ratios for each of the nation's leading industries. For each ratio in each industry, it shows the twenty-fifth percentile, median, and seventy-fifth percentile of the firms in that industry.[2] A manager can calculate the ratios for his own firm, then compare them with these industry norms. An additional source of information for the canny manager is the annual financial reports of his competition. Many firms own stock in their competitors so that they can receive the income statement, balance sheet, and other information that must be sent to shareholders.

Profit and Risk

Before looking at profit ratios, we need to recall that accountants and economists define *profit* in different ways. For the accountant—and businessman—profit is synonymous with owners' earnings: it is found by subtracting all costs (including interest charges) from the total revenue accruing to the firm during the operating period.

The economist views profit differently. To him, it is a differential return, a

---

[1]For other sources, see the subsection, "Key Ratios," in chapter 13.

[2]The twenty-fifth percentile is the ratio 25 per cent of the way up from the bottom, with all ratios ranked in descending order. The median is the middle ratio, with 50 per cent above and below. The seventy-fifth percentile is three-fourths of the way up.

special reward for risk-bearing[3] or for being cleverer or more enterprising than one's competitors. But if this is so, and if this risk premium is separated from accounting profit, what does the economist call what is left? He calls it *interest*, for, in classical economics, interest is the share of the product going to capital, just as wages are the share going to labor. Very often, too, as the economist will point out, in the case of small, owner-operated businesses, much of what an owner may call his profit is actually an unrecognized salary for his work as manager.

The economist's distinction is fruitful, for it reminds us that accounting profit lumps together two very different sorts of returns. First, there is a basic return on the owners' money, equal to the opportunity rate they could earn by investing in virtually riskless instruments such as Treasury bills or high-grade bonds. If the owners do not earn *at least* that much, they would do better to shut down their business and become mere investors in Treasury bills. Second, there is true economic profit: a reward for risk-bearing, or what is much the same thing, a reward for superior ability to take, manage, or outguess the risks.[4] For these reasons, we can write a firm's *rate* of profit as

$$k = i_p + r,$$ (Eq. 16-1)

where

k = rate of profit,
i_p = pure (or riskless) rate of return to capital, and
r = risk premium for the particular firm.

Profitability Measures

Profitability is to profit as a rate is to an amount. Profit is the figure at the bottom of the income statement—what is left for shareholders after all charges have been paid. Profit is a dollar amount; profitability is a ratio. Because it is a ratio, profitability is a more meaningful measure. It can be used as a standard of performance regardless of a firm's size. For example, to know that one firm made after-tax profits last year of $50,000 while another made $100,000 is not very meaningful. However, to know that the first firm used assets of $500,000, and the second, $1,000,000, tells us that the difference in profit is not really significant, but comes from the difference in available assets.

We will use the financial data for the Sample Manufacturing Company, presented in chapter 15, to illustrate each ratio.

The significance of all profitability ratios lies in indicating the percent costs can rise and prices fall (assuming no change in quantity produced) to eliminate profit. Why the concern with no change in quantity? Why not say simply sales revenue and be done with it? The reason is that changes in sales volume affect production, and changes in production affect costs. A full elaboration must await

---

[3]For true "risk" to exist, the probabilities of the various outcomes—making it big, losing a little, losing it all—would have to be known. Recall that risk refers to a situation in which the probability distribution of outcomes can be calculated, as in a spin of a roulette wheel. Otherwise, the matter adds up to uncertainty, which is another name for ignorance.

[4]We examine two ways of coping with uncertainty surrounding capital budgeting in chapter 27.

chapter 17, in which we discuss operating leverage. It will suffice to note here that a decrease in variable costs accompanies a fall in production. With a fall in production, total costs fall, and this fall cushions the impact that a fall in sales revenue would otherwise have on earnings.

Gross Profit Margin

This ratio is measured by deducting cost of goods sold from sales and putting the difference over sales:

Sales	$6,500,000
Less: cost of goods	4,400,000
Gross profit	$2,100,000

Gross profit/sales = $2,100,000/$6,500,000 = 32.3%.

The gross profit margin tells management the ability of sales to generate earnings before any other costs of business are met. Its financial significance is this: the ratio indicates the percentage that selling prices can fall, or costs can increase, to eliminate gross profit. Prices can fall 32.3 per cent and, if quantity sold remains constant, sales revenue will fall 32.3 per cent. This percentage decline will reduce revenue $2,100,000 to $4,400,000. After meeting its direct costs to produce goods, no earnings remain. Cost-wise, $6,500,000 is 147.7 per cent of $4,400,000 (or $6.5 million ÷ $4.4 million), so a 47.7 per cent increase in cost of goods sold will make this amount equal to sales revenue. After meeting these costs, nothing remains.

Gross Operating Margin

This ratio goes a step further than the gross profit margin and considers the firm's ability to cover administrative and selling costs associated with doing business. It is calculated like this:

Gross profit	$2,100,000
Less: selling and administrative expenses	500,000
Gross operating profit	$1,600,000

Gross operating margin = Gross operating profit/Sales
= $1,600,000/$6,500,000 = 24.6%

Since the gross profit margin is 32.3 per cent and the gross operating margin 24.6 per cent, the difference of 7.7 per cent is the ratio of selling and administrative expenses to sales.

As with the gross profit margin, the gross operating margin tells the financial manager about the impact of price decreases and cost increases on profit. Here, if prices fall 24.6 per cent Sample Company would have nothing left over after paying its cost of goods sold, selling, and administrative expenses. Gross operating profit would be zero. On the other hand, if selling and administrative expenses increase 320 per cent ($2,100,000/$500,000 = 4.20; 4.20 − 1.0 = 3.20) gross operating profit would be eliminated.

Net Operating Margin

This ratio takes one more forward step in examining a firm's profitability. For Sample Company it is

Gross operating profit	$1,600,000
Less: depreciation	900,000
Net operating profit	$ 700,000

Net operating profit/Sales = $700,000/$6,500,000 = 10.8%.

This ratio tells Sample Company's management that sales prices can fall 10.8 per cent before net operating profit is wiped out. Conversely, depreciation can increase 78 per cent to accomplish the same result.

Sales Margin

This measure may be computed using profit before taxes or after taxes. It makes little difference so long as the person using the ratio is aware which relation is being used. Using the before-tax measure, Sample has a sales margin of

Profit before taxes/Sales = $621,000/$6,500,000
= 9.5%.

If prices and sales revenue fall 9.5 per cent (to $6,155,000), then profit before (and after) taxes will be wiped out. Or, if total expenses increase ($6,500,000/$5,879,000) − 1.0 = 10.5, or 10.5 per cent, the result will be the same: no profit before or after taxes. Sample Company will be meeting expenses, including the interest it pays to finance assets, but will have nothing left to pay taxes or shareholders.

What is the sales margin after taxes? Obviously, to find this ratio we need to know profit after taxes. We can find profit after taxes by looking at the income statement, or by a calculation. Here is the relation between profit before and after taxes:

$$K_{bt} (1 - t) = K_{at},$$ (Eq. 16-2)

or

$$K_{bt} = K_{at}/(1 - t),$$ (Eq. 16-3)

where

K_{bt} = profit before taxes,
K_{at} = profit after taxes, and
t = average tax rate (42 per cent for Sample Company).

The sales margin after taxes is

$355,000/$6,500,000 = 5.4%,
9.5%(1−.42) = 5.4%.

You cannot use the after-tax margin to say what percentage sales can fall before eliminating profit after taxes. You *can* use the before-tax margin. For this reason, the sales margin before taxes is more meaningful.

Earning Power

Perhaps the best measure of profitability is earning power. Indeed, this is the specific ratio which most people have in mind whenever they use the term profitability. It is calculated by dividing total claims (or assets) into earnings before interest and taxes (EBIT).[5] For Sample Company, earning power is

EBIT/Total claims = $810,000/$9,700,000
                  = 8.3%.

The advantage in using this measure to represent profitability is that it shows management's ability to use the firm's assets to generate earnings on its invested capital. Earning power is a measure that can show all investors, both creditors and shareholders, how effectively management is using each dollar they provided. Here, Sample is using each dollar of assets to generate 8.3 per cent.

Investors can use this measure of profitability to help decide whether to leave their money in the firm, withdraw it, or invest more. If better (higher) earning power is being generated by another firm, they may prefer to withdraw their money from the first and invest it in the second, assuming, of course, that the risk does not increase proportionately more than the return.

Return on Equity

This type of ratio tells how much management is earning on funds contributed by stockholders after all expenses, including interest, have been met. Return may be computed for total equity (common and preferred stockholder funds combined) or, as is more commonly the case, for common stockholder equity only.

For Sample, return on total equity is

Net profit after taxes/Total stockholders' equity = $355,000/$4,500,000 = 7.9%.

If return on common shareholders' equity is desired, then the preferred dividend must be deducted from earnings. Since Sample has outstanding $600,000 in 8 per cent preferred, the preferred dividend is $600,000 × .08, or $48,000. This leaves a net profit available to common stock of $307,000. Thus, return on common equity is

Net profit for common/Common equity = $307,000/$3,900,000 = 7.9%.

Identity of the two rates of return results from the coincidental fact that the dividend rate on the preferred, 8 per cent, almost exactly matched the return on total equity.

Three other ratios deserve mention in connection with return on equity. First, *earnings per common share* is simply net profit for common divided by the number of common shares outstanding. For Sample, earnings per common share are $307,000/300,000 = $1.02. Similarly, we can compute *dividends per common share*. For Sample, they are $120,000/300,000 = $.40. Finally, the *payout rate* is the percentage of the earnings available to common paid out in common dividends. Sample's payout rate is $120,000/$307,000, or about 39 per cent.

---

[5]This way of measuring earning power is superior to using the ratio of profit after taxes to total claims, as some might be tempted to do. Using total income (EBIT) shows earning power *independent* of the financing mix. Profit after taxes is affected by the financing mix because interest, which reflects the use of debt by the firm, and taxes are deducted.

Turnover

Turnover ratios, as we have said, measure the effectiveness with which different assets are being utilized in the business. Specifically, turnover means the number of times an asset flows through the firm and into sales. A record dealer, for instance, may stock 100 albums by the Carpenters and sell 500 albums in a month's time, ending the month with 100 albums. In this case, he has turned his inventory over five times (500/100). Any turnover ratio has sales in the numerator and some asset in the denominator. The asset is whatever is turning over.

Receivables Turnover

This ratio is simply annual sales divided by accounts receivable. Where all sales are not on trade credit, the numerator should be adjusted to include only sales made on credit. For Sample the ratio is

Sales/Net receivables = $6,500,000/$2,000,000 = 3.25.

This ratio indicates that receivables turned over 3.25 times during the year.

A related ratio is the average collection period (ACP), sometimes called number of days' sales in accounts receivable. Since Sample is turning over its accounts receivable 3.25 times in a year, it takes, on the average, 360 days/3.25 = 110 days to collect its accounts receivable. If Sample made no more sales, it would presumably take 110 days for the last sale to flow through accounts receivable and become cash. A more direct way to measure the average collection period is to divide accounts receivable by daily sales, using a 360-day year for ease of calculation. Thus, for Sample,

ACP = Net receivables/(Sales ÷ 360) = $2,000,000/$18,058 = 110 days.

The ACP is an important ratio because it indicates to management (1) the quality of its receivables, (2) the wisdom of its credit-granting policies, and (3) the effectiveness of its collection policy. A low turnover ratio (long collection period) suggests that the firm's customers may be having trouble generating enough cash to pay their bills. Furthermore, if the ACP is a great deal longer than the payment terms granted on credit sales, or if it greatly exceeds the industry average, it may suggest that the credit department is granting credit too liberally. For example, if Sample requires payment in 60 days (the industry average), the 110-day ACP may mean that the credit manager is not screening applications rigorously enough, or that the firm's collection policy lacks vigor.

Inventory Turnover

Another ratio resembling receivables turnover is the inventory turnover ratio. Inventory and sales figures are not exactly comparable because inventories are recorded on a cost basis while sales are reported at selling prices. To correct for this discrepancy, rather than using sales we base our ratio on cost of goods sold. Hence, for Sample, the ratio is

Cost of goods sold/Inventories = $4,400,000/$1,500,000 = 2.93.

Sample is turning over its inventory 2.93 times, or, stated differently, Sample sold and resold its inventory nearly three times last year.

If inventory tends to fluctuate widely, it is wise to take an average inventory size into consideration. This can be done by taking the highest and lowest levels in a year, totalling them, and dividing by 2.

Return on Assets

We shall now see how profitability and turnover ratios can usefully be combined to analyze a company's financial performance. Let us begin by looking at one measure of return on investment: a company's return on assets (ROA), its ratio of net profit after taxes/total assets.[6] Starting with the identity

$$\frac{\text{Net profit after taxes}}{\text{Total assets}} = \frac{\text{Net profit after taxes}}{\text{Total assets}},$$

we multiply both numerator and denominator of our left hand member by sales:

$$\frac{\text{Net profit after taxes}}{\text{Total assets}} \times \frac{\text{Sales}}{\text{Sales}} = \frac{\text{Net profit after taxes}}{\text{Total assets}}.$$

While we have not changed the truth of our equation, we can now rewrite it in a more meaningful, expanded form:

$$\frac{\text{Net profit after taxes}}{\text{Sales}} \times \frac{\text{Sales}}{\text{Total assets}} = \frac{\text{Net profit after taxes}}{\text{Total assets}}, \qquad \text{(Eq. 16–4)}$$

or,

$$\text{Sales margin} \times \text{Asset turnover} = \text{Return on assets}.$$

This breakdown shows that a firm's return on investment depends on two factors: its profit margin, or what per cent of each sales dollar is kept as profit; and its turnover, or how many times per year each dollar's worth of assets is turned over in sales. If a company's profit margin is 3 per cent and it turns its investment over four times annually, its return on investment is .03 times 4, or 12 per cent.

Combinations of profit margin and turnover vary widely among different industries. For example, a retail grocery chain will have a very low profit margin and a very high turnover, and an oil refiner will have a much higher profit margin, but lower turnover. Yet competitive pressures toward equal returns on capital suggest that both firms will have similar returns on total investment. This is borne out by comparison of the three companies shown in Table 16–1. The slight differences in return on investment (ROA) in part illustrate the different risk premiums among the three industries in accordance with Eq. 16–1.

Analyzing a company's ROA into sales margin and asset turnover components is usually referred to as the DuPont method because that company's finance division developed and refined this device as a managerial tool. Both sales margin and asset turnover can in turn be factored into further components. This subdivision is illustrated in Figure 16–1.

The DuPont method shows the factors into which a company's financial results can be successfully broken down. It thus provides a framework for asking

---

[6]This use of ROA is discussed in *Return on Capital As a Guide To Managerial Decisions*, Research Report No. 35 (New York: National Association of Accountants, 1959).

Table 16-1. Companies with Similar Returns on Investment

Company	Profit Margin (% of sales)	Turnover (sales/capital)	Return on Investment (in per cent)
Texaco, Inc.	16.5	0.82	13.6
Safeway Stores	1.8	7.11	12.8
Campbell Soup	7.3	1.74	12.7

Source: Standard & Poor's Corporation.

meaningful questions about these results. Consider, for example, Sample Company. Substituting in Eq. 16-4, we have

$$\frac{\$355,000}{\$6,500,000} \times \frac{\$6,500,000}{\$9,700,000} = \frac{\$355,000}{\$9,700,000}$$

$$.054 \times .669 = .037.$$

Although the firm is earning, after interest and taxes, 5.4 per cent on its total sales, sales are flowing through assets at a suspiciously slow pace, .669 times in a year. The result is an ROA less than the sales margin. Why? Are insufficient

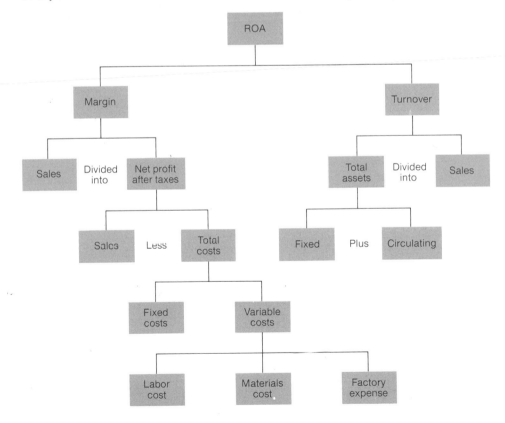

Figure 16-1. DuPont Method of Return on Assets

sales being generated for the volume of assets? Or is the company's asset invest-ment too large for the sales volume that can fairly be expected? If so, is the company carrying too large an investment in fixed assets, in circulating assets, or in both? Industry-average ratios should offer the company's financial manager tentative answers to these questions.

Similarly, too low a sales margin can raise significant questions: Is sales volume too low to absorb fixed costs adequately? (If so, fire the sales manager.) Is the spread between prices and costs too low? Are we getting an insufficient price for our product? Or is it costing too much to manufacture our product? (Fire the vice-president in charge of manufacturing.) What accounts for the high costs? Materials waste? Inefficient labor? Machine breakdowns? The list of mean-ingful questions suggested by the DuPont method of analysis can explore all aspects of a company's operation and investment.

To Remember

Time-series analysis	Turnover
Cross-sectional analysis	Average collection period
Risk-bearing differential	DuPont method

Questions

1 "The problem with the firm," states a financial analysis of Zeus, Incorporated, "is its remarkably low sales margin for 1972. We do not advise purchase of this stock because of these ratios." What else should the analyst consider, besides other ratios, before passing judgment?

2 Do you agree with the assertion that financial institutions' reliance on industry averages to determine credit-worthiness before lending restricts managerial inventiveness and creativity?

3 John Kramer is considering beginning a professional tennis tour, a venture requiring an initial investment of $80,000. Kramer, basically a risk averter, asks you to advise him. He says it looks as though he can obtain a return of 7 per cent. If the return on Treasury bills is 6 per cent, what would you tell him about his implicit, or estimated, reward for risk taking?

4 How do you explain the fact that, for Sample Company, it takes a 32.3 per cent decline in sales revenue to eliminate gross profit, but only a 9.5 per cent decline to eliminate profit before taxes?

5 The Velaco Company has income statement and balance sheet variables as follows:

Income Statement Variables

Depreciation	$ 1,000
Cost of goods sold	4,000
Sales revenue	10,000
Interest expense	600
Selling and administrative expenses	2,000
Taxes (40 per cent)	—

Balance Sheet Variables

Long-term debt	$ 8,000
Accounts receivable	3,000
Accounts payable	2,000
Shareholders' equity	8,000
Fixed assets	9,000
Inventory	5,000
Cash	1,000
	$36,000

(a) Complete the income statement and balance sheet for Velaco Company.
(b) Calculate and interpret:
  (1) gross operating margin,   ―――――――
  (2) net operating margin,   ―――――――
  (3) sales margin,   ―――――――
  (4) earning power,   ―――――――
  (5) return on equity.   ―――――――
(c) Velaco has 5,000 shares of common outstanding and paid dividends of $1,000. Calculate:
  (1) earnings per share,   ―――――――
  (2) payout rate,   ―――――――
  (3) dividends per share.   ―――――――

6 Joe Fojtasek, credit manager for a small textile representative, brags to his superior, the treasurer, that the average collection is eighteen days. He beams, "No doubt this performance warrants a nice bonus."

(a) How many days' sales are in accounts receivable?
(b) What is the firm's receivables turnover?
(c) The firm grants terms requiring its customers to pay in thirty days. In deciding whether or not to give the credit manager a bonus, you and the treasurer evaluate the performance relative to
  (1) quality of receivables,
  (2) wisdom of credit-granting policies,
  (3) effectiveness of collection policy.

7 Calculate and comment on the following ratios for the Velaco Company in question 5 above:

(a) average collection period,   ―――――――
(b) turnover of accounts receivable,   ―――――――
(c) inventory turnover.   ―――――――

8 Contrast earning power and ROA. What is the major difference between the two?

9 The Beall Company has an ROA of 15 per cent. It has $1,000 in sales and turns its assets over five times a year.

(a) What is Beall Company's sales margin?
(b) What are its total assets?
(c) What is its profit after taxes?

17

Leverage and Liquidity

Leverage — *Operating Leverage* — *Degree of Operating Leverage* — *Break-Even Analysis* — *Financial Leverage* — *Debt-Equity Ratio* — *Debt Ratio* — *Times Interest Earned* — *Consequences of Financial Leverage* — *Degree of Financial Leverage* — *Operating and Financial Leverage: Their Relation* — Liquidity — *Static Measures of Liquidity* — *Current Ratio* — *Working Capital* — *Quick Ratio* — *Dynamic Liquidity* — *Cash Flow Forecast* — Financial Manager's Dilemma

Leverage

Leverage means the tendency for profits to change at a faster rate than sales. Two kinds of leverage concern the financial manager. *Operating leverage* is the tendency for profits to change at a faster rate than sales because of the presence of fixed costs in the firm's cost structure. The more fixed costs a firm employs in its production process, the greater its degree of operating leverage will be. *Financial leverage* is the tendency for profits to change at a faster rate than sales because of the presence of fixed-cost elements in the firm's financial structure. The greater a firm's ratio of debt and preferred stock to common stock equity is, the larger its financial leverage will be.

Operating Leverage

A firm's costs can be divided into fixed costs and variable costs. Fixed costs include such costs as salaries, depreciation, and rental expenses. They do not vary as output varies. Variable costs include wages, utilities, and raw materials. As output increases, variable costs increase. Fixed costs are always with the financial manager, even when the plant is closed for holidays, vacations, or strikes. Variable costs are with him only when the plant is operating.

A firm generally assumes greater fixed costs in order to lessen its variable costs, a process economists call "increasing capital intensity." For example, Ford Motor Company has automated its production line, and has thus increased the fixed cost of depreciation; it has done this in part to replace labor, and so to reduce variable costs.

Because changes in sales are generally governed by economic conditions and competition, operating leverage is said to increase the _business risk_ of the firm. In other words, a small downturn in business activity and the associated sales decline can be magnified by fixed costs into a large downturn in earnings, even a large loss.

How operating leverage multiplies changes in sales into proportionately larger changes in earnings is illustrated below. Suppose Matrix Corporation has fixed costs of $300,000. Variable costs are $2.00 per unit sold and the selling price per unit is $4.00. When sales are 200,000 units, the income statement looks like this:

Sales (200,000 @ $4)		$800,000	
Variable costs	$400,000		
Fixed costs	300,000		
		700,000	
Earnings before interest and taxes		$100,000	(Sales level 1)

However, when sales decline 20,000 units to 180,000 units, the income statement looks like this:

Sales (180,000 @ $4)		$720,000	
Variable costs	$360,000		
Fixed costs	300,000		
		660,000	
Earnings before interest and taxes		$ 60,000	(Sales level 2)

A 10 per cent decline in sales ($800,000 – $720,000 ÷ $800,000) has dropped earnings before interest and taxes (EBIT) by 40 per cent ($100,000 – $60,000 ÷ $100,000).

Finally, if sales fall to 150,000 units, we have:

Sales (150,000 @ $4)		$600,000	
Variable costs	$300,000		
Fixed costs	300,000		
		600,000	
Earnings before interest and taxes		— 0 —	(Sales level 3)

From its original level of $800,000, sales fell 25 per cent and EBIT fell 100 per cent. If the company had lower fixed costs, the impact on earnings of this drop in sales would have been less drastic.

Degree of Operating Leverage

How can we measure the extent of a company's operating leverage? Remembering that the symbol Δ means "change in," let us define the following:

% Δ EBIT = per cent change in earnings before interest and taxes, and
% Δ Q   = per cent change in quantity produced and sold.

Since operating leverage is the change in earnings resulting from a change in sales volume, but without regard to financial structure, a good measure of operating leverage is the ratio

$$\frac{\% \Delta EBIT}{\% \Delta Q},$$

or the per cent change in quantity sold divided into the resulting per cent change in earnings before interest and taxes. Let us call this ratio the *degree of operating leverage*.[1]

Thus if, at a certain level of output, a firm's unit sales rose from 1,000 to 1,050 (5 per cent), and earnings before interest and taxes increased from $5,000 to $6,000 (20 per cent), the degree of operating leverage would be

$$\frac{20\%}{5\%}, \text{ or } 4.$$

In interpreting degrees of leverage, one point is important. When the degree of leverage is 1, a firm's sales and earnings change at the same rate. Degree 1 thus signifies no leverage. If leverage is present, the degree must be greater than 1.

Break-Even Analysis

The relation between fixed costs, variable costs, and sales level is illustrated by break-even analysis. *Break-even analysis* calculates the sales volume a firm needs to just cover its sum of fixed and variable costs. It can be figured in either unit sales or dollar sales.

The level of unit sales at which total costs equal total revenue can be arrived at in this way. Total revenue equals price (P) times quantity (Q). Total costs are equal to the sum of fixed costs (FC) and variable cost per unit (V) times units produced (Q). If we solve for Q, we will have the number of sales Matrix Corporation must attain to cover all its operating costs:

$$TR = TC$$
$$P \times Q = FC + VQ$$
$$(P \times Q) - (V \times Q) = FC$$
$$Q(P - V) = FC$$
$$Q = FC/(P - V).$$

(Eq. 17-1)

----

[1] It is important to emphasize that degrees of leverage as calculated here exist only at the level of output for which they are calculated. If you have much mathematical background, you will recognize that what we call degrees of leverage are rough substitutes for mathematical derivatives. You will also recognize that unless the relations on which leverage is based are linear, the derivatives will change over the range of the function.

Thus, the break-even point in *unit sales* is found by dividing fixed costs by price per unit minus variable cost per unit.

To find the break-even point in *dollars* of sales, we use the variable cost ratio: price per unit less variable cost per unit, all divided by price. Sometimes called the contribution margin, this ratio measures the percentage of each dollar that is left to contribute to fixed costs after meeting variable costs. For Matrix, the variable cost ratio *(VR)* is ($4 − $2)/$4 = .50. The specific formula for finding the break-even point in dollars *(S)* is

$$S = FC \div VR.$$

For Matrix, the dollar break-even point is

$$\$300,000 \div .5 = \$600,000.$$

Figure 17–1 visualizes these relations.

$\dfrac{\text{fix cost}}{\text{c.m ratio}} = \$ \text{ break even}$

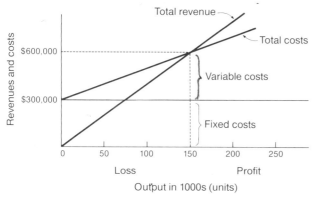

Figure 17–1. The Break-Even Point

By calculating the break-even point, managers can see what balance of sales and costs will be required to make a profit. Suppose that Matrix's sales are projected at 140,000 units, resulting in a loss of $20,000. The company must then consider means of eliminating, or at least reducing, this projected loss. Should price be changed? Should less advertising (a variable cost) be budgeted? Should the firm sell some of its plant and equipment, thereby reducing depreciation expense (a fixed cost)? Management would discuss these and other alternatives.

We must recognize, of course, that break-even analysis is not so simple as this textbook example suggests. In actuality, costs are difficult to gauge in advance, a shifting sales mix may contain many products, and production may outrun sales, building up inventory. These and other circumstances make break-even analysis certainly a less-than-exact science. Nevertheless, it sheds significant light on the way profits or losses arise. Like many other calculations and forecasts an alert businessman will make, it helps him understand the tendencies working in his business—even when the exact figures are wide of the mark.

Financial Leverage

Financial leverage arises from use of fixed-cost financing, ordinarily debt, though for many applications preferred stock also contributes toward the degree of financial leverage. In this introductory treatment, we shall deal only with debt's role in leverage, although the extent to which either debt or preferred stock is used has much to do with the return management earns on common stock equity. The extent also affects the stability and assurance of this return.

Three ratios of financial leverage deserve particular attention: (1) the debt-equity ratio, (2) the debt ratio, and (3) the times-interest-earned ratio.

Debt-Equity Ratio

The most widely used measure of financial leverage is the debt-equity ratio. This ratio is simply the dollar amount of total debt divided by the total dollar amount of shareholders' equity. For Sample Company (see chapter 15), the ratio is:

$$\text{Debt-Equity ratio} = \text{Debt}/\text{Equity}$$
$$= \$5,200,000/\$4,500,000 = 1.15.$$

The debt-equity ratio is important to management, creditors, and shareholders because it indicates the firm's financial risk. As the debt-equity ratio rises, financial risk increases. The greater this ratio is, the greater the chance will be that if the company encounters financial difficulty (1) shareholders will be wiped out, and (2) creditors will lose money. Let us see why this is so.

When there is no debt in the financial structure, assets must fall in value by 100 per cent before the claim of the shareholders is completely wiped out, as you see in Figure 17–2. But as the debt-equity ratio increases, assets need fall by a smaller and smaller percentage to annihilate the shareholders' claim and begin eating into the claims of creditors. When the debt-equity ratio is 1:1, assets need fall only 50 per cent before the shareholders' stake disappears and creditors are exposed to loss. When the debt-equity ratio is 2:1, assets need fall only 33 per cent. This tendency, as the debt-equity ratio rises, for an increasingly small drop in total-assets value to wipe out stockholders' equity is called the *principle of increasing shareholders' risk*.

Debt Ratio

The debt ratio indicates the percentage contribution of creditors to the firm. It is measured by dividing total debt by total assets. For Sample Company, the debt ratio is:

$$\text{Debt ratio} = \text{Total debt}/\text{Total assets}$$
$$= \$5,200,000/\$9,700,000 = .53.$$

The debt ratio is interpreted in the same way as the debt-equity ratio. Indeed, the two ratios are related. Notice that the greater the debt ratio is, the greater the debt-equity ratio will be. And since total assets are equal to debt plus equity, from any debt ratio we can obtain the debt-equity ratio. Consider, for example, a company with a debt ratio *(D)* of 40 per cent. First, we would calculate the proportion of assets contributed by shareholders:

$$TA = D + E$$
$$1.0 = .40 + E$$
$$.60 = E.$$

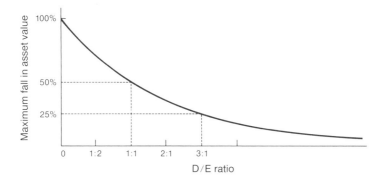

Figure 17–2. Decline in Assets, *D/E* Ratio, and Elimination of Shareholders' Claim

Shareholders have contributed 60 per cent of the value of total assets. Now, we can solve for the debt-equity ratio using the proportion each component is of total assets (we do not need to know the dollar values to do this):

$$D = .40, \quad E = .60, \quad D/E = .40/.60 = .67.$$

Times Interest Earned

This ratio consists of a firm's total income (earnings before interest and taxes) divided by the annual interest charge. It thus indicates the margin of safety with which interest requirements are being earned. For Sample Company, bond interest was earned $810,000/$189,000, or 4.29 times. This means that the company's income before interest and taxes could shrink to 1/4.29 of its present level, or by about 77 per cent, before interest charges would not be earned.

Two points about times interest earned need to be stressed. First, the figure divided by interest charges is always earnings *before* taxes, never earnings after taxes. This is because interest payments are tax-deductible expenses and so have priority on company earning power. Second, if the company has fixed rental or lease obligations on buildings or equipment necessary to its continued operations, then these rentals or lease payments should be included with bond interest in the divisor of the ratio. Such rental obligations are as imperative for a company to meet as its interest requirement. Modified to include these and any fixed financial obligations, the ratio is termed "times fixed charges earned."

Consequences of Financial Leverage

Financial leverage means that any change in a company's earning power will be reflected in a proportionately greater change in its return on equity. The fundamental relation is between earning power (earnings before interest and taxes divided by total assets) and the rate of interest. Whenever earning power exceeds the cost of borrowed capital, leverage is favorable. When leverage is favorable, the higher the debt-equity ratio is, the higher the *return* on equity will be. Conversely, when earning power is less than the cost of borrowed capital, leverage is unfavorable. When leverage is unfavorable, the higher the debt-equity ratio is, the greater the *loss* on equity will be. Finally, whenever earning power is equal to the cost of borrowed capital, leverage is neutral. Whatever the level of the debt-equity ratio, the return on equity will be the same.

The income statements in Table 17–1 illustrate the working of financial leverage. The two firms are similar in all respects except financial structure. Firm A has $300 in debt and $200 in equity, a debt-equity ratio of 1.5. Firm B has $100 in debt and $400 in equity, a debt-equity ratio of .25. The point to notice is that both loss and gain on equity vary directly with the debt-equity ratio. In Case 1, where financial leverage is favorable (earning power is higher than interest rate), A enjoys a far higher return on equity than B. Although A's earnings after taxes are smaller than B's, A's earnings are distributed over a much smaller equity, so the percentage return is proportionately higher. In Case 2, where financial leverage is neutral, per cent return on equity is the same for both firms, despite

Table 17–1. Impact of Financial Leverage

	Capital Structures		
	Firm A: $300 debt $200 equity	*Firm B:* $100 debt $400 equity	
Case 1: Leverage Favorable: $i = 6\%$, EBIT/TA = 20%			
	Firm A		*Firm B*
EBIT	$ 100		$ 100
Less: Interest (.06 x $300)	18	(.06 x $100)	6
EBT	$ 82		$ 94
Less: Taxes (50%)	41		47
Earnings After Taxes	$ 41		$ 47
ROE: $41/$200 =	20.5%	ROE: $47/$400 =	11.7%
Case 2: Leverage Neutral: $i = 6\%$, EBIT/TA = 6%			
	Firm A		*Firm B*
EBIT	$ 30		$ 30
Less: Interest (.06 x $300)	18	(.06 x $100)	6
EBT	$ 12		$ 24
Less: Taxes (50%)	6		12
Earnings After Taxes	$ 6		$ 12
ROE: $6/$200 =	3%	ROE: $12/$400 =	3%
Case 3: Leverage Unfavorable: $i = 6\%$, EBIT/TA = 2%			
	Firm A		*Firm B*
EBIT	$ 10		$ 10
Less: Interest (.06 x $300)	18	(.06 x $100)	6
EBT	($ –8)		$ 4
Less: Taxes (50%)	–0–		2
Earnings After Taxes	($ –8)		$ 2
ROE: ($8)/$200 =	–4%	ROE: $2/$400 =	0.5%

their difference in capital structure. Finally, in Case 3, where earning power is lower than the interest rate, A's larger interest charges result in a large loss before taxes. B, with a moderate interest expense, manages to eke out a small profit on its equity.

Financial leverage boils down to this: So long as you can invest borrowed money in an asset which yields a return greater than the interest you pay, you should borrow the money and invest it. Generally speaking, if you can borrow money at 3 per cent and invest it at 5 per cent, you make a net gain of two percentage points.[2] Your absolute gain will increase as your debt-equity ratio becomes higher. Of course, when the investment yields only 2 per cent and you must pay 3 per cent, the opposite occurs.

Degree of Financial Leverage

Like operating leverage, financial leverage can be measured in degrees. We define

$$\% \Delta EAT = \text{per cent change in earnings after taxes.}$$

Since financial leverage is the change in equity earnings stemming from changes in earnings before interest and taxes, a good measure of financial leverage is the ratio

$$\frac{\% \Delta EAT}{\% \Delta EBIT},$$

or the per cent change in earnings before interest and taxes divided into the resulting change in earnings after tax. We call this ratio the *degree of financial leverage.*

If, at a certain point, a company's earnings before interest and taxes rose from \$5,000 to \$6,000 (20 per cent) and earnings on common equity increased from \$3,000 to \$4,200 (40 per cent), the degree of financial leverage would be

$$\frac{40\%}{20\%}, \text{ or 2.}$$

Operating and Financial Leverage: Their Relation

Let us now note how operating and financial leverage, at any level of a firm's output, interact to determine total leverage. We have already defined *degrees* of operating and financial leverage. Now it is clear that if we multiply

$$\frac{\% \Delta EBIT}{\% \Delta Q} \times \frac{\% \Delta EAT}{\% \Delta EBIT},$$

$\% \Delta EBIT$ in the left numerator and right denominator cancel out, and we are left with

$$\frac{\% \Delta EBIT}{\% \Delta Q} \times \frac{\% \Delta EAT}{\% \Delta EBIT} = \frac{\% \Delta EAT}{\% \Delta Q}.$$

---

[2]This illustration of financial leverage also illustrates the importance of observing the statistician's carefully-drawn distinction between "per cent gain" and "percentage points of gain." In our example, you would gain two percentage points at all debt-equity ratios. But the per cent gain on your equity would rise rapidly as your debt-equity ratio increased.

But % Δ EAT/% Δ Q is the definition of total leverage. Consequently, it is true that at any given level of a firm's operation

$$\text{Degree of operating leverage} \times \text{Degree of financial leverage} = \text{Degree of total leverage.}$$

In our previous examples, where the firm has operating leverage of degree 4 and financial leverage of degree 2, its degree of total leverage is 2 $\times$ 4 = 8. What this signifies is that operating and financial leverage "gang up" to widen the swings in after-tax earnings that result from any change in sales. Consequently, other things being equal, the more operating leverage a firm has, the less financial leverage it can afford. But other things are not necessarily equal. An important third consideration is the stability of sales revenue. The more stable sales are, the higher degree of financial leverage a firm can undertake for any degree of operating leverage. Operating leverage is largely determined by production technology, and management must usually accept operating leverage as a given factor. Thus, electric light and power companies have very great operating leverage because a huge proportion of their costs are fixed costs, but final sales are so stable that they also can afford to finance about two-thirds of their capital needs with bonds and preferred stock. By contrast, producers of specialty steels (a highly cyclical industry) have such unstable sales revenues accompanying large operating leverage that it is doubtful whether they should issue bonds at all. Thus, *sales stability* is the link between operating leverage and the degree of financial leverage advisable.[3]

Liquidity

Liquidity is the "moneyness" of an asset. That is, the more easily an asset can be converted into cash, the more liquid it is. The less loss incurred in converting the asset into cash, the more liquid the asset is. For example, merchandise inventory is more liquid than a building because it is easier to convert merchandise into cash than to sell a building.

Static Measures of Liquidity

An analyst or manager can calculate static measures of liquidity from a firm's balance sheet. These ratios—current, working capital, and quick—are static because they fail to include the firm's financial environment. For example, a low ratio may be acceptable when money is easy, but unacceptable when money is tight.

Current Ratio

The current ratio consists of current assets divided by current liabilities. For Sample Company, the ratio is

Current ratio = Current assets/Current liabilities
= $6,000,000/$2,500,000 = 2.4.

The current ratio is the most widely used measure of business liquidity. It indicates

---

[3]Sales stability of course includes stability of both unit sales and selling prices.

the extent to which the claims of short-term creditors, i.e., the most pressing claims a firm has, can be met by assets in a period roughly corresponding to the maturity of the claims, one year or less.

Working Capital

Working capital represents the volume of current assets financed from long-term sources. It is that part of a firm's current assets that will *stay with* the firm. Current assets financed by current liabilities will vanish within the year, when the current liabilities are paid. These current liabilities may or may not be renewable. But there is no renewal problem with working capital.

For Sample Company, $2,500,000 of its $6,000,000 in current assets are financed from short-term sources. The remainder, $3,500,000 financed from long-term or equity sources, comprises its working capital.

Quick Ratio

The current ratio includes an asset which requires the firm's operations to continue in order to convert it into cash. This asset is inventories. The quick ratio, or acid test, removes this least liquid of current assets to indicate how liquid the firm would be if operations were to halt abruptly—for example, should a fire destroy all the firm's real assets.[1]

For Sample Company, the quick ratio is:

Quick ratio = (Current assets – Inventories) / Current liabilities
= ($6,000,000 – $1,500,000) / $2,500,000 = 1.8.

As with all ratios, the quick ratio needs to be compared with other firms in the industry (cross-sectional analysis) and with previous years' levels (time series analysis) to provide a meaningful measure of liquidity.

Dynamic Liquidity

Dynamic liquidity refers to an asset's liquidity with reference to the business environment. The above static measures of liquidity do not give a complete picture of a firm's liquidity. The financial manager should recognize that liquidity is a property of his firm that varies through time according to (1) the *business cycle*, (2) the rate of *technological change,* and (3) the *sophistication of financial management.* A given liquidity ratio can have varying implications for a firm's liquidity, according to those three dynamic conditions.

Why does a firm's liquidity vary over the *business cycle?* It does so primarily for three reasons. First, the availability of credit varies over the cycle. During the early stages of business recovery, banks have sufficient reserves and are anxious to make loans to businesses. A firm may rely on bank loans to finance plant and equipment, pulling down its current ratio, but because the bank has sufficient reserves, it can renew the short-term loan. Therefore, although the current ratio is low, the firm is more liquid than the simple ratio implies.

However, later in the business cycle, when banks find themselves short of

---

[1]Real assets are non-paper assets. Monetary assets are all paper assets, or all assets above inventories on a firm's balance sheet.

reserves due to restrictive monetary policy, the firm may be unable to renew its loan. Many firms may find themselves in this situation. A large volume of financing may then be forced into other markets as firms scramble for liquidity. Companies will have to sell bonds, liquidate other assets, or even merge with firms that can provide them with finance.

Second, the market value of assets varies over the business cycle. This is particularly true of the debt-type financial instruments in which both companies and lending institutions typically store their reserve buying power. As interest rates rise higher during a boom, the market price of these fixed-income securities declines far below the price at which they were bought in times of easy money. The threat of large financial losses makes lenders unwilling (and even unable) to liquidate these investments. Other assets become harder to sell or to borrow money on because money is tight and businessmen are reducing their purchases. In short, all assets become less liquid at such times, so any static ratio based on balance sheet numbers is likely to overstate liquidity.

Finally, the credit-worthiness of a firm's receivables varies over a business cycle. When times are bouyant and earnings are high, customers can pay their liabilities readily. Hence, the accounts receivable among a firm's current assets appear financially sound. But when the economy begins to turn down, customers find it increasingly difficult to meet their current obligations. They resort to putting off payments as long as possible, running well past the due date, which is usually thirty days. In other words, customer firms make their suppliers finance them. The accounts receivable of the suppliers become financially weak. Hence, the quality of the current ratio can vary because the soundness of the accounts receivable component varies.

Marketability and prices of assets may reflect *technological developments.* The securities a firm holds may be virtually valueless if they represent investments in companies that produce outdated equipment. By the same token, inventories consisting of products which have been replaced due to advances in technology are obviously illiquid. Ask someone who owns a four-track tape player how much he can get for it and you will see how onrushing technology creates illiquidity in its wake. The industry now produces only eight-track tapes, so the four-track player is almost worthless.

Improvements in *financial management* can make dynamic liquidity much better than static measures imply. The sophisticated manager has learned ways to minimize the volume of current assets so that his firm can generate the same earnings from a smaller asset base, thus increasing the rate of return on assets. Also, he may establish a line of credit with a bank which permits him to economize the volume of cash he must keep on hand, again leading to a lower current ratio but without any deterioration of dynamic liquidity.[5]

Cash Flow Forecast

The current and quick ratios are what we call stock measures of liquidity; they measure one stock against another, for example, current assets against current liabilities. While such measures indicate liquidity, they do not embody it. Actual

---

[5]A line of credit is a guaranteed loan to a firm which the firm can draw on at any time at a predetermined interest rate. The subject is discussed in some detail in chapter 21.

liquidity comes only when cash is available to pay bills at the precise instant of need. If a firm could always raise cash at the exact instant it needed to pay its bills, a current ratio of 1:1 would be quite adequate.

In addition to stock measures of liquidity, we can use *cash flow measures*. They show how well inflows of cash (either past or expected) match outflows. An example of a flow measure is Mr. Luferac's cash flow forecast illustrated in chapter 13.

Financial Manager's Dilemma

A dilemma is a perplexing predicament. It is a necessary choice between alternatives, each having undesirable qualities. For the financial manager, as you have seen, a dilemma exists in his choice between profitability and liquidity.

Profitability is desirable, but to take advantage of profitable opportunities the financial manager must move assets *down* the balance sheet into less liquid forms. For example, to exploit an expanding market, the firm will increase its inventory by pulling down cash, a procedure which reduces liquidity and increases profitability.

Liquidity is desirable, but to increase liquidity the financial manager must move assets *up* the balance sheet into less profitable forms. For example, the manager may choose to keep proceeds from the sale of inventory in cash rather than to reinvest them in new inventory. Since cash earns no return, the firm will be increasing its liquidity at the expense of profitability.

Figure 17–3 illustrates the general relation between liquidity and profitability. As profitability increases, liquidity decreases. And as liquidity increases, profitability decreases.

The financial manager's dilemma is not unique to corporation finance. Each of us is faced with the choice between liquidity and profitability in his personal finance, too. How one structures his portfolio, or list of asset holdings, reflects the priorities he assigns to the two alternatives.

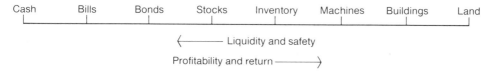

Figure 17–3. The Financial Manager's Dilemma

To Remember

Business risk	Degree of financial leverage
Break-even point	Current ratio
Degree of operating leverage	Working capital
Principle of increasing shareholders' risk	Financial manager's dilemma
Times interest earned	Dynamic liquidity

Questions

1. Vinson Associates, a regional distributor of slushy drink dispensers, has fixed costs of $20,000. Dispensers sell for $400 each. Variable costs, consisting primarily of sales commissions, are 20 per cent of the selling price ($80 per unit).

   (a) What is the variable cost ratio for Vinson?
   (b) What is the break-even point for Vinson? (Use the variable cost ratio.) How do you interpret the fact that the break-even point in units involves a fraction of a unit?

2. One of the items in fixed costs is depreciation, a non-cash expense. How does the presence of depreciation affect the cash break-even point, i.e., the sales volume that must be reached to enable the firm to pay its cash operating expenses from operating revenues?

3. Cnossus, International, has a debt-equity ratio of 0.5.

   (a) What is the debt ratio?
   (b) In a forced liquidation, by what percentage can Cnossus' assets fall in value before creditors begin losing any of their invested capital? (Remember, shareholders' equity absorbs any initial loss.)

4. Zephyr Industries is covering its interest and other fixed financial expenses four times. By what percentage can EBIT fall before Zephyr fails to meet all of these expenses?

5. The Hesiod Company and Theojony, Inc., are similar in all respects save two: Hesiod has a debt-equity ratio of 3, Theojony, 1. The number of shares outstanding differs, but the book values per share (shareholders' equity/number of shares) are similar: $10. Net operating income (EBIT) is $200 for both firms, representing a 20 per cent gross return on their $1,000 in assets. Assume a 40 per cent tax rate.

   (a) Interest expense is 6 per cent. Is leverage favorable? Calculate earnings after taxes, return on equity (ROE), and price per share for each firm, assuming a P/E multiple (ratio of market price per share of common to earnings per share) of 20.
   (b) Interest expense is 10 per cent. Is leverage favorable? Calculate ROE and price per share for each firm at a P/E multiple of 20.
   (c) What principle do questions (a) and (b) illustrate?

6. Ajax Consolidated has a degree of operating leverage of 3, and a degree of financial leverage of 3.

   (a) What do these two measures imply for Ajax's business and financial risks?
   (b) If Ajax experiences a 5 per cent increase in sales from last year, by what percentage will EBIT increase? If interest was covered three times last year, what is it this year?
   (c) What is its percentage increase in EAT? If the tax rate is 40 per cent, what is the percentage increase in earnings after taxes?
   (d) What is the degree of total leverage for Ajax? Show your answer arithmetically and explain verbally.

7. Why are the current and quick ratios and working capital measures of *static* liquidity as opposed to dynamic liquidity?

8 Some people contend that liquidity is subjective: what one person might consider a liquid asset or ratio, another may not. Can you think of reasons that might support such a contention?

9 Look at question 5 in chapter 16. Calculate:
   (a) current ratio,
   (b) quick ratio,
   (c) working capital.

18

Fixed and Circulating Capital: Depreciation

What Capital Is — *Real vs. Financial Capital* — *Fluid vs. Sunk Capital* — *Fixed vs. Circulating Capital* — What Depreciation Is — *Depreciation Methods* — *Straight-line* — *Double-Declining Balance* — *Sum of the Years' Digits* — *Depreciable Life: Its Importance* — *Depreciation and Working Capital* — *Tax Shield* — Selecting the Depreciation Method — *Accelerated Depreciation* — *Two Sets of Books* — Relation Between Fixed and Circulating Capital

What Capital Is

Like other versatile terms, *capital* has many meanings and involves numerous distinctions. One may speak of real or financial capital, fluid or sunk capital, fixed or circulating capital. Each meaning is important in its domain and requires at least brief definition and discussion here.

Real vs. Financial Capital

Real capital is the economist's generic name for tangible, man-made objects that cooperate in the productive process. This factor of production includes machines, buildings, vehicles, and tools, plus inventories of finished goods, goods in process, and raw materials. Real capital always consists of tangible things.

By contrast, financial capital (sometimes referred to as

money capital) comprises money and financial instruments devoted immediately or ultimately to the production of goods and services. Financial capital is represented by stocks, bonds, bills, mortgages, and securities issued by business and other economic units. Bank loans, lendable money waiting in banks, and cash in corporate treasuries or bank accounts also constitute financial capital.

Fluid vs. Sunk Capital

Some capital—for example, a corporation's proceeds from a recent bond issue—is in the form of cash. Some may be embodied in short-term, normally liquid assets such as inventories or accounts receivable. Capital in this state is described as fluid, which is merely a synonym for liquid. By contrast, a company may spend $500 million to open a new mine in Chile, or to build a steel plant at Muleshoe, Texas, using a revolutionary production process. The capital represented by these investments is sunk; that is, it is irretrievably committed to a particular location or specialized use. To the extent that capital so invested cannot be extricated, its value depends solely on its earning power. If earning power is large or respectable, its sunk character may entail little or no disadvantage. But if its earning power becomes small or vanishes, sunk capital may shrivel in value or become entirely worthless. A zero value would hold, for instance, for a useless machine whose removal cost exceeded its salvage value, or for a confiscated copper mine in Chile against which the Chilean government had levied fines larger than the compensation offered U.S. owners.

Fixed vs. Circulating Capital

A final distinction is between fixed capital, embodied in long-lived assets (buildings, machinery, and—in most tabulations—land), and circulating capital, which is equivalent to current assets (cash, receivables, and inventories). It is with the characteristics of capital so divided that this chapter is concerned. Let us examine briefly this distinction.

To make sales, a firm must have circulating capital. This is capital that circulates, or revolves, indefinitely in the cycle: cash to inventory to receivables, and back to cash. It begins when cash is used to acquire inventory, either through purchase or through manufacturing. Through credit sales inventory is then transformed into receivables. Finally, accounts receivable are collected, returning capital to cash. The flow is depicted in Figure 18–1.

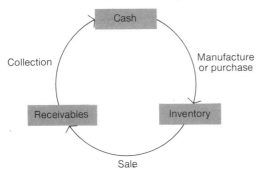

Figure 18–1. Cash Cycle

How rapid is this flow? It varies widely from one industry to another. The more rapidly circulating capital turns over—the faster it flows through its cycle, the more quickly it returns to cash—the more liquid this part of a firm's investment will be.[1]

Whereas the cash-to-cash cycle is typically short for circulating capital (almost always less than a year), it is ordinarily a number of years for fixed capital. Fixed assets may, of course, be returned to cash by being sold (for example, one company sells a machine or building to another), but such resales are not contemplated in the normal course of business by going concerns. Ordinarily, a firm must continue using its fixed assets to generate its product or service. For a going concern, therefore, the only way fixed assets normally return to cash is through the slow process of *cash flow*, which is a combination of depreciation and after-tax profits. Since most businesses buy and sell on a credit basis, cash flow is often referred to as working capital generated from operations. This term indicates that operations can contribute to working capital, changing either circulating capital (for example, an increase in accounts receivable) or current liabilities (for example, an increase in accounts payable). The cash-flow equation is

Cash flow = Profit after taxes + Depreciation.   (Eq. 18–1)

What Depreciation Is

To generate sales, a firm incurs costs. Some costs—wages, materials, supplies, and taxes—involve immediate cash payments. These are called out-of-pocket costs. However, one cost incurred in operating the firm does not involve an immediate corresponding cash outlay. That cost is depreciation, which is the "cost" of fixed assets.

The cash outlay, or expenditure, on fixed assets is made at the time they are acquired. However, it would not be right to charge the entire cost of a fixed asset to the operating period in which the company happened to buy it. After all, the asset will last a number of years and will contribute to the firm's production in each year. If management charged the entire outlay on a fixed asset against the year of purchase, two distortions would result. In the first year, costs would be overstated and profit understated. In subsequent years, costs would be understated and profit overstated.

The *matching* principle in accounting says that revenues and the costs required to produce them should be matched as closely as possible. Thus, it is logical to distribute, or allocate, the cash outlay for fixed assets over the whole sequence of operating periods during which they are gradually used up. This is the role of depreciation.[2]

Depreciation Methods

Although depreciation reflects the matching and allocation principles, management has some latitude over exactly how the allocation will be accomplished.

[1]Circulating capital is discussed in detail in chapter 28.

[2]See chapter 15 for a brief discussion of the similar roles of depletion and amortization in the cases of wasting and intangible assets, respectively.

For many purposes, it is free to select the depreciation method it deems most appropriate. The three most widely used methods are (1) straight-line, (2) double-declining balance, and (3) sum of the years' digits.

To illustrate each method, we can use the following example. A firm purchases a machine that requires a $20,500 outlay and is estimated to last five years; that is, it will generate revenues for five years. Management also anticipates a *salvage value* of $500 for the machine at the end of the five year period. In other words, $500 is the price expected to prevail when the asset is sold or junked. Management knows it should match the revenues with the cost incurred in generating these revenues, so it will use a five-year life over which to allocate the machine's cost.

Straight-line

Straight-line depreciation allocates the original outlay, less the salvage value, equally to each year of asset life. For this machine, *depreciable value* is $20,500 − $500 = $20,000. Since the machine will last five years, depreciation per year is $20,000/5 years = $4,000. Each year, management will allocate $4,000 of the machine's original cost to that year's expenses.

Double-Declining Balance

The double-declining balance method is more sophisticated than the straight-line one. It requires the application of a constant rate of depreciation each year to the remaining depreciable value of the asset. This rate may equal twice the straight-line rate. In our example, straight-line depreciation per year is at a rate of $4,000/$20,000 = 20 per cent. Under the double-declining balance method, depreciation would be two times 20 per cent, or 40 per cent, and the company's first-year charge to depreciation would be .40 times 20,000 = $8,000. The remaining depreciable value is:

Original depreciable value	$20,000
Less: depreciation	− 8,000
Equals: remaining depreciable value	$12,000

The company can then apply the double rate to this remaining value, making next year's depreciation .40 times $12,000 = $4,800. This time the depreciable value would be reduced to $7,200, and the company can continue to apply the .40 rate of depreciation in the third and subsequent years.

The Internal Revenue Service permits a company to shift from the double-declining balance method to the straight-line method at any time. If this were not possible, the asset could never be fully depreciated. Management will shift to straight-line depreciation as soon as this method yields larger depreciation installments than the double-declining balance method; by so doing, earnings before taxes are reduced and taxes lessened. Table 18–1 shows that, in our example, the switch is made in the fourth year. Straight-line depreciation in the fourth and fifth years will be $4,320/2, or $2,160 per year. That is more than the amounts of the double-declining balance method, $1,628 and $1,076, respectively.

Table 18–1. Depreciation Methods Contrasted

Year	Straight-line	D D B	Sum of Years' Digits
1	$4,000	$8,000	$6,667
2	4,000	4,800	5,333
3	4,000	2,880	4,000
4	4,000	2,160*	2,667
5	4,000	2,160*	1,333
	$20,000	$20,000	$20,000

*In years 4 and 5, straight-line method is used.

Sum of the Years' Digits

The sum of the years' digits method is an accelerated method of depreciation which calculates annual depreciation by using a ratio. The ratio consists of the following:

1. Denominator: the sum of the years' digits. It *remains constant.* In our example of five-year life, the sum is 1 + 2 + 3 + 4 + 5 = 15.
2. Numerator: for each year, it is the number of years left in the asset's life. That is, you begin with the *last* year in the numerator and progress to the first year.

For our asset, the depreciable ratios each year will be 5/15, 4/15, 3/15, 2/15, and 1/15. Each ratio is applied successively to the full $20,000 depreciable cost of the machine: 5/15 times $20,000 = $6,666, 4/15 times $20,000 = $5,333, and so on.

Table 18–1 compares the annual depreciation amounts calculated by each method.

Depreciable Life: Its Importance

The speed with which cash is recovered from fixed assets depends not only on depreciation method but also on the assumed life of the asset. Under U.S. tax laws, asset-life for depreciation purposes may differ considerably from physical asset-life. The regulations are too complex to discuss here, but it should suffice to point out that if the asset illustrated in Table 18–1 were accorded a four-year life instead of five, straight-line depreciation would rise to $5,000 per year and the asset's cost would be recovered a whole year sooner. Cash recoveries with the other depreciation methods would have been similarly accelerated.

Depreciation and Working Capital

Depreciation flows increase a firm's working capital through their impact on tax outlays. To illustrate this, let us look at Frizbee International Corporation, shown below, with 1973 sales of $150,000, and costs and profits as shown. The depreciation charge reflects management's estimate of the deterioration of plant and equipment during the year.

Frizbee International
Income Statement, 1973

Sales		$150,000
Less:		
Labor	$35,000	
Interest	5,000	
Depreciation	25,000	$ 65,000
Earnings before taxes		$ 85,000
Less: taxes (50%)		42,500
Earnings after taxes		$ 42,500

First, look at the impact of depreciation on working capital where there is *no* corporate income tax. How has Frizbee's working capital been affected?

Transactions increasing working capital (increases in current assets):

Sales	$150,000

Transactions reducing working capital (decreases in current assets, increases in current liabilities):

Labor	$35,000	
Interest	5,000	40,000
	Net Increase	110,000

Working capital generated from operations (cash flow) was $110,000 in 1973.

What would happen to cash flow if depreciation were doubled, say because Frizbee's management turns to the double-declining balance depreciation method? In our no-tax world, working capital generated from operations stays the same. From Eq. 18–1, except using profit before rather than after taxes, cash flow when depreciation is $25,000 equals

$85,000 + $25,000 = $110,000.

When depreciation is $50,000, cash flow becomes

$60,000 + $50,000 = $110,000.

Tax Shield

In the real world, taxes do indeed exist. Depreciation is a tax-deductible expense that furnishes a firm with a *tax shield*. That is, it shields a portion of a firm's receipts from taxation, thereby making the firm's outlay for income tax less than it otherwise would be. In the example above, where depreciation is $25,000 and the tax rate 50 per cent, Frizbee International was able to recover $25,000 of sales revenue free of tax liability. This, plus $42,500 in after-tax profits brought a $67,500 increase in the firm's working and circulating capital.

What if no depreciation deduction had been available? The earnings statement would then have run:

Sales		$150,000
Less:		
Labor	$35,000	
Interest	5,000	$ 40,000
Earnings before taxes		$110,000
Less: taxes (50%)		55,000
Earnings after taxes		$ 55,000

Working capital would have been affected in this way:

Transactions increasing working capital:		
Sales		$150,000
Transactions reducing working capital:		
Labor	$35,000	
Interest	5,000	
Taxes	55,000	95,000
	Net Increase	$55,000

Working capital would have increased $55,000, or, by the cash flow method, profit after taxes plus depreciation = $55,000 + 0 = $55,000. What is the difference between the two?

Cash flow with depreciation of $25,000		$67,500
Cash flow with depreciation of	–0–	55,000
	Difference	$12,500

This difference is equal to, and arises from, the increased outlay for income taxes that would have been incurred if the company had lacked the tax shield furnished by depreciation: $55,000 – $42,500 = $12,500. Thus, depreciation adds to a company's available funds by reducing its income tax expense. You might also note that the difference between the two cash flows is 50 per cent of the total difference between the two depreciation expenses. A depreciation allowance of $35,000 would have provided $17,500 more in cash flow than zero depreciation, or $5,000 more than the $25,000 allowance actually used.

In general, the difference between cash flows can be found by using the formula $t \times \Delta D$, where t is the firm's marginal tax bracket and ΔD is the difference in depreciation. The formula, of course, can also be used to see what the impact is on any single firm when it changes its depreciation method.

Selecting the Depreciation Method

Since several depreciation methods are available, which one should management select? The general rule is this: Select the one that will maximize near-year cash flows by delaying payment of taxes the longest.

Accelerated Depreciation

Accelerated methods of depreciation ordinarily permit companies to defer payment of taxes until some distant date. Both declining balance and sum of the years' digits depreciation take large chunks out of income before taxes early in the asset's life, and so reduce taxes.

Since accelerated methods take less out of income before taxes late in the asset's life, taxes then are greater than under the straight-line method. But since total taxes paid over an asset's life are the same for all methods, the advantage lies with the accelerated methods which defer taxes the longest and thus maximize cash flows in the early years of an asset's life. Management can use the funds thus provided until it must pay taxes. Accelerated depreciation is often said to constitute a "tax-free loan from the Treasury," and its advantage boils down to the familiar concept, time value of money.

Figure 18–2 compares the depreciation flows provided by straight-line and sum of the years' digits methods, using the amounts from our $20,500 outlay above.[3]

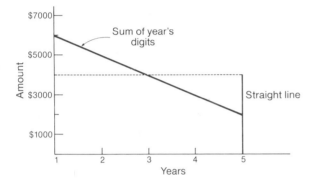

Figure 18–2. Straight-line vs. Sum of the Years' Digits

Two Sets of Books

For stockholders, management wants to "put its best foot forward" and show high earnings. For the Internal Revenue Service, it wants to show minimum earnings. Can it do both? Yes, a firm can keep two sets of books, one for the IRS and one for shareholders. It is part of a game managements often play which might be called "get the stock price up"—a very important game to play when management is anxious to cash out its stock purchase options at high prices.

To shareholders, management will show straight-line depreciation. It will report earnings before taxes as determined under straight-line depreciation. But it will then show the taxes actually paid under accelerated depreciation. Let us see how this way of reporting earnings "gets them up."

Suppose that in the first year on Table 18–1, earnings before depreciation and taxes are $8,000. The double-declining balance method yields depreciation expense of $8,000 and reduces the firm's taxes to zero. Straight-line depreciation

---

[3]You may want to try your hand at calculating cash flow for the $20,500 example. Since earnings before depreciation and taxes were $8,000 per year, the reduced taxes associated with the accelerated methods provided a higher cash flow in the early years. For example, in the first year, assuming a 50 per cent tax rate, the cash flows for the straight-line, double-declining balance, and sum of the years' digits are, respectively, $6,000, $8,000, and $7,333.

is $4,000 and carries with it $2,000 in taxes. Calculated incomes under the two methods will look like this:

	Straight-line	DDB
Earnings before depreciation and taxes	$8,000	$8,000
Less: depreciation	4,000	8,000
Earnings before taxes	$4,000	–0–
Less: taxes (50%)	2,000	–0–
Earnings after taxes	$2,000	–0–

What will shareholders see? They will see the best of both worlds: the mixture of the two methods producing the largest earnings: straight-line depreciation, but taxes based on double-declining balance depreciation.

Earnings before depreciation and taxes	$8,000
Less: depreciation (straight-line)	4,000
Earnings before taxes	$4,000
Less: taxes (DDB)	–0–
Earnings after taxes	$4,000

Not all the $4,000 belongs to the shareholders; $2,000 are taxes that must be paid in the future. But the fact that only $2,000 comprise earnings in any real sense of the word is lost to sight because the future tax liability is buried in footnotes or in accounting-statement complexities which investors do not understand—and rarely worry about anyway unless the stock price falls.

An alternative way to use straight-line depreciation in shareholder reporting and accelerated depreciation for tax purposes is to present, in the annual statement, earnings calculated like those in the straight-line one above. Since the firm pays no taxes, its assets are then $2,000 more than the income statement indicates they should be. On the balance sheet, a liability, "Deferred Taxes Payable," of $2,000 is recorded.[1]

Though many would consider these kinds of deceptions unethical, they are not illegal. Where used, they are presented as being "in accordance with generally accepted accounting principles." As you have seen, the difficulty lies in the fact that, to deal with the great variety of business backgrounds encountered, accounting principles must necessarily contain flexibility, or stretch. Unfortunately, this stretch is sometimes exploited in questionable ways for doubtful purposes.

Relation Between Fixed and Circulating Capital

Although different in their life cycles, fixed and circulating capital are closely linked in the business enterprise. There are three reasons for this linkage: (1) their joint role in production, (2) the tendency of circulating capital to disappear into fixed assets, and (3) the offsetting tendency of the cash flows generated by fixed assets to replenish circulating capital.

The first link involves the fact that most projects a firm undertakes call for

---

[1] See, for example, Walter Meigs and Charles Johnson, *Accounting*, 2nd ed. (New York: Mc-Graw-Hill Book Company, 1967), pp. 892–93.

increases in both fixed and circulating capital. The manufacture and sale of a new product may require not only a new building and new machinery, but also added inventories of raw materials and finished items, plus a rise in accounts receivables to support credit sales of the new product.

A second link is the persistent tendency for circulating capital to disappear into fixed assets. By definition, circulating capital frequently returns to cash. A financial manager, pressed for money to pay for an expansion in fixed assets, is strongly tempted to preempt cash from the circulating cycle to make his payments. This tactic, as we shall see, is a frequent cause of later financial difficulties for firms unwise or unfortunate enough to resort to it. By shifting funds from the relatively liquid circulating capital cycle and investing them in slow-moving fixed assets, a company may seriously undermine its liquidity. This is one reason why companies which have just completed ambitious expansion programs sometimes are unable to pay their bills.

Finally, as we have noted, fixed assets generate cash flows consisting of depreciation allowances and after-tax profits. While depreciation is ultimately destined to replace fixed assets, in the short run it may be, and often is, used to expand circulating capital—as a company grows, or as inflation increases its circulating capital requirement.

To Remember

Fixed capital

Cash cycle

Fixed and circulating
  capital links

Matching and allocation
  principles

Depreciation methods

Switchover point

Tax shield

Advantage of accelerated
  depreciation

Questions

1   What is the relation between fixed and sunk capital? Is fixed capital a component of sunk capital, or vice versa?

②   Why is "working capital generated from operations" a more accurate term than "cash flow" for firms that make sales and purchases on trade credit?

③   Splacknuck, Inc., purchased a glumdalclitch for $800. It will have a four-year life. Assume the corporate tax rate is 40 per cent.

   (a) What happens to the current ratio and working capital when the fixed asset is acquired?   *decrease   exchange CA cash for f.A.*
   (b) In year 1, Splacknuck has zero sales and earns nothing. What is cash flow this year? What is cash flow if the glumdalclitch has a $300 salvage value?
   (c) Now assume the original conditions. Calculate depreciation per year using the
      (1) sum of the years' digits method,
      (2) double-declining balance method.

4   M. B. Drapier, Inc., has a milling machine that originally cost $60,000. It will generate ten years of benefits for the Drapier company. These gross benefits (EBIT plus depreciation) will be $8,000 per year. The tax rate is 40 per cent. M. B. Drapier, president of the firm, wants to use straight-line depreciation. You, as a new assistant to the controller, are directed by the controller to write a one-paragraph report to show the superiority of accelerated depreciation. Do it.

5   The Satyr Company has assets of $50,000 with a five-year life. This year the firm had EBIT plus depreciation of $25,000. Satyr's management has some stock options to exercise this year (year 1 in the assets' lives). Show how the income statement might look, using straight-line depreciation but double-declining balance to compute its taxes (40 per cent rate). What would after-tax earnings be, using only straight-line? With a P/E multiple of 30, what does the difference mean in terms of market price of the common stock?

6   Stock brokers emphasize cash flows per share often to the exclusion of earnings per share. What are some reasons for their doing this, and why is it misleading?

19

Financial Planning and Control: An Overview

Planning — *Forecasting Sales* — *Forecasting Asset Needs* — *Forecasting Financial Needs* — Suitability — *Long and Short-Term Needs* — Violating Suitability: The Dangers — *Losing Liquidity* — *Losing Profitability* — *Availability and Cost* — Control — *Profit Centers and Responsibility* — Reports — *Accountability* — *The Exception Principle* — Treasurer and Controller Functions

---

As emphasized in chapter 13, modern business planning is *profit-planning,* and a profit plan always requires an accompanying financial plan. But plans are fruitless without effective controls to see that they are implemented. Thus planning and control are readily identified as major responsibilities of the financial manager.

Planning involves setting goals, identifying resource needs, forecasting events that lie beyond a firm's control, and establishing a scheme of action that harmonizes both with these events and with the firm's purposes.

Control involves the use of budgets to state a company's plans in detail. Results are then measured against budgeted objectives to see how the company's performance has conformed with objectives. Finally, purposeful action is taken to correct deviations and deficiencies.

Planning

Necessarily, the financial manager is largely absorbed in day-to-day problems. But his handling of these problems will be orderly and effective only if it fits within an overall plan. This plan may be nebulous and inexact, suiting managers who prefer great flexibility, or concrete and specific, suiting those who emphasize detailed planning. But its main outlines and requirements should be clear to the manager as he works from day to day.

A plan begins with an objective and purpose. A businessman may set his 1974 goal as a 20 per cent sales gain and a 25 per cent increase in after-tax profits. But however ambitious, one's objective must always be attainable. Judging the feasibility of an objective depends on a correct forecast of two factors: (1) the resources needed to reach the objective, and (2) the business and other conditions that will prevail over the term of the plan.

Forecasting Sales

The foundation of the financial plan is a sales forecast. Businessmen have found that there is a fairly stable relation, at least in the long run, among sales, assets, and financial needs. This stability exists because a company's sales are equal to its output, and its output is governed by its volume of assets. Assets, in turn, must be financed.

A firm's sales forecast should be based on the successive consideration of three factors: (1) economic prospects, (2) expected size of total market, and (3) market share attainable by the firm. We briefly review each of these in turn.

1. *Economic prospects.* Economic conditions affect some businesses more than others. Management of a company producing consumer durable goods, such as refrigerators and televisions, would be highly attentive to the course of personal income over the next year because sales of consumer durables are keenly sensitive to income changes. In contrast, a grocery chain management might be less concerned because its sales are relatively unresponsive to fluctuations in income. But most firms will probably pay considerable attention to anticipated moves of the economy as a first step in forecasting their sales volume.

2. *Size of total market.* Estimates of the future size of the total market are usually based on growth rate of the present market. If a market has been growing at 10 per cent per year, management simply assumes that it will grow 10 per cent next year. Only when specific factors indicate otherwise are executives likely to anticipate a change of trend. Such mechanistic projections of past trends are called *extrapolations.*

3. *Market share.* Forecasting the firm's share of the expected total market calls for judging how aggressive and successful the firm will be relative to its competitors. Will the firm increase or reduce its advertising budget? Will the firm's competitors begin lowering prices in an attempt to lure customers away? These policies and many more will affect the firm's market share, and only management can guess their total effect. If management believes that all competitors in the market (including itself) will not change their marketing strategies, then it can assume that it will maintain its share of the market.

Forecasting Asset Needs

Having forecast the expected sales level, a company's next step is to translate this figure into asset requirements. One widely used approach for forecasting asset needs is the _per cent of sales method._ Here the financial manager calculates what percentage of sales each asset normally comprises, and then projects this ratio into the future against expected sales. (For reasons soon to be discussed, he also calculates all claims as a percentage of sales.)

An example will clarify this procedure. In 1971, the McClusky Company had a profit margin after taxes of 2 per cent (the ratio of earnings after taxes to sales). Sales were $200,000. Table 19–1 presents the year-end balance sheet. The ratio of each asset to the year's sales is also shown, calculated by the financial manager. (Be sure you can explain why the per cent column does not total 1.0.)

Note two key facts: (1) For every $1 of sales, there are 37.5 cents worth of assets. (2) For every $1 _increase_ in sales, assets can be presumed to increase 37.5 cents.

Table 19–1. Balance Sheet Showing Assets as Per Cent of Sales, McClusky Corporation, 1971

Assets	Dollar Amount	Per Cent	Claims	Dollar Amount	Per Cent
Cash	4,000	.020	Accounts Payable	10,000	.050
Securities	2,000	.010	Taxes Payable	4,000	.020
Accounts Receivable	8,000	.040	Bonds	28,000	.140
Inventory	11,000	.055	Common Stock	14,000	.070
Fixed Assets	50,000	.250	Retained Earnings	19,000	.095
	75,000	.375		75,000	.375

Obviously, judgment and foresight must be used in projecting per cent of sales ratios. Changes may overturn formerly stable relations. Better control may reduce inventories as a per cent of sales. At the same time, fixed assets may rise as a per cent of sales because computers have been acquired to control the inventories. Fixed assets, like factory buildings or large machines, must obviously grow in "lumps." After major expansions, the ratio of fixed assets to sales tends to fall for a time (as sales "grow up" to capacity), then to rise when the next "lump" of capacity is added. Financially, this process reflects managers' reluctance to commit funds to fixed assets until they are confident an increase in sales will be _permanent._

Now suppose that McClusky's 1972 sales are projected at $220,000, up $20,000. Then, at the end of 1972, McClusky's total assets will be .375 times $220,000 = $82,500. Necessarily, its total claims will be the same. Both assets and sources of finance will increase from $75,000 to $82,500.

Forecasting Financial Needs

Once assets, or _uses_ of finance, have been forecast, the next step is to select the _sources_ of finance. Some sources of finance are _automatic;_ that is, they tend to rise in step with the growth of sales. These include accounts and taxes payable and retained earnings. The financial manager calculates them next. He then subtracts his automatic sources from the increase in his asset requirements. The remainder comprises his non-automatic financial needs, or his discretionary sources of funds. We can illustrate by returning to McClusky.

The company needs some $7,500 in new sources. However, Table 19-2 indicates that $5,800 can be expected from automatic sources. Some $1,400 will be supplied by the expected rise in accounts and taxes payable. These amounts are percentages of the *rise* in sales, not total sales for the year. In addition, Mc-Clusky's profit margin (2 per cent of total sales) can be expected to provide $220,000 times .02 = $4,400 of retained earnings. Altogether, these automatic sources can be expected to furnish $5,800 of the $7,500 increase in funds required. The remaining $1,700 must come from non-automatic sources.

Suitability

On what basis should the financial manager of the McClusky Company decide the source of the $1,700? His most important yardstick is *suitability*. Recall that suitability means financing permanent asset requirements from long-term or equity sources, and temporary asset needs from short-term sources. It is a principle of symmetry, or time-balancing, between sources and uses of funds. The consideration of suitability raises two issues. (1) What actually constitute long- and short-term uses of funds? (2) What dangers do companies incur by violating suitability?

Long- and Short-Term Needs

Clearly, the growth of a company's fixed assets imposes a permanent financing need. These assets are long-lived, essential to operation of the enterprise, and quite illiquid. Therefore, they should be financed from long-term or equity sources so that no renewal of their financing will become necessary.

Fixed assets, however, do not represent a firm's only requirement for permanent financing. Although current assets are short-lived and liquid, their level can

Table 19-2. "Automatic" Financing Sources, McClusky Corporation, 1972

Source	Per Cent of Increase in Sales	Per Cent of Sales	Dollar Amount Provided
Accounts Payable	.05	—	1,000
Taxes Payable	.02	—	400
Bonds	—	—	
Common Stock	—	—	
Retained Earnings	—	.02	4,400
Total			5,800

never fall to zero. Even at the lowest point of the sales year or business cycle, some inventory and receivables are still needed. Moreover, no firm can afford to run completely out of cash. Thus, at the lowest point of any firm's activity, an *irreducible minimum* of current assets (circulating capital) must remain in the business. And since it must remain, it, like fixed assets, should be financed from dependable long-term or equity sources.

On the other hand, a substantial part of a company's current-asset needs is temporary. Inventories and receivables have large bulges at seasonal peaks or during business booms; they shrink back again at seasonal low points or during recessions. This fluctuating component of current asset needs should not be financed from long-term sources. The need for funds is temporary, and the business will minimize the investment on which earnings are required if it raises these funds from sources which permit their retirement when the need is past.

Figure 19-1 illustrates the principle of suitability, operating through time. It shows a firm's fixed assets growing by "lumps," its *permanent* current assets requirement rising steadily as the enterprise itself grows. Both these types of assets should be financed from permanent sources. The wavy line above permanent current-assets requirements shows the firm's *fluctuating needs* for current assets. Because these needs occasionally fall to zero, they should be met from temporary sources.

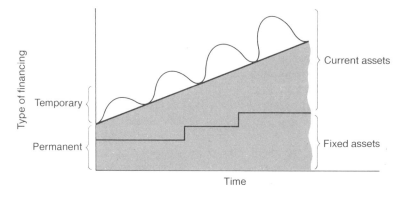

Figure 19-1. Temporary and Permanent Uses and Sources

Violating Suitability: The Dangers

A second major point about suitability is that observing it helps the financial manager maintain his two most important goals: liquidity and profitability for his firm. Conversely, violations of suitability expose a company to illiquidity on one side and low profitability on the other. Let us now see what mistakes the financial manager must avoid in selecting discretionary, or non-automatic, sources of finance.

Losing Liquidity

Suppose a firm buys a piece of capital equipment, perhaps a turret lathe with five-year life, and finances the purchase with a one-year note for $75,000 at the bank. The company's liquidity immediately suffers in two ways. First, its liquidity *ratios* (current, quick, and working capital) decline. Its borrowing power and credit-worthiness are thus undermined. Second, cash has been sunk in a fixed asset, yet the cash itself is due for repayment within one year. Of course, the lathe may throw off $15,000 or more in depreciation during the year, but that would still leave $60,000 or so of the loan to be renewed at year end.

With good luck, the company may get the bank to renew the loan, though the banker will be violating the key principle of sound banking by supplying his depositors' short-term funds for a long-term purpose. But suppose the bank is unwilling or unable to renew the loan. Then the borrower will be forced to pay it off. How? Where will he raise the money? If he cannot find another lender, and cannot raise cash from his other assets, he will be forced to default on his loan and likely to announce bankruptcy. This is often the penalty for those who "borrow short and invest long."

Losing Profitability

An opposite mistake regarding suitability can impair a company's profitability. This mistake consists of financing temporary needs from permanent sources; for example, selling new stock or a 25-year bond to finance a seasonal rise in inventory. To be sure, such financing will improve a firm's liquidity. Current assets (inventories) rise with no corresponding climb in short-term liabilities. But while current ratio and working capital both increase, profitability falls. It falls because, while the earning power of the newly acquired funds lasts only part of the year (the time when it is gainfully invested in inventories), the investment on which the company must earn a return is permanently enlarged. A look at the DuPont formula explained in chapter 16 will show you that when new investment in a company can be made to earn a return only part of the year, the ROA is bound to fall.

Stated differently, once the peak inventory season passes, the funds will sit around as idle cash or as low-earning temporary investments. But interest payments on the bonds, or dividends on the stock, by which the funds were raised, will continue. By contrast, if the temporary rise in inventory had been met from short-term sources, the money could have been repaid to the lender when no longer needed. The company's assets would shrink with repayment.

One other consideration arises. Long-term funds ordinarily cost more than short-term funds. A six-month loan may cost 6 per cent, but a ten-year one, 9 per cent. Again, management should seek to avoid the more expensive long-term sources of funds if it is borrowing for a short-term purpose.

Availability and Cost

In addition to suitability, availability and cost of finance play unavoidable parts in deciding what non-automatic financing sources to tap. If using a long-term source is suitable, but no long-term sources of finance are available or the cost seems exorbitant, management has no choice but to violate the principle of suitability.

Planning—looking ahead—is the only way to protect a business from unavailable or prohibitively costly funds. If its managers foresee what the company's financial requirement will be, they can often acquire the funds in advance of need, thereby ensuring their availability or acceptable cost.

Planning is based on a forecast of sales, and combines the decision concerning what assets to acquire with the decision about how the assets will be financed. So constituted, it serves as a managerial framework to optimize choices and minimize the chance of a crisis. A well planned financial program cannot *guarantee* the absence of crises—a shortage of cash may still develop from lost sales due to a wildcat strike, for example—but it does ensure that damage from such mishaps will be minimized.

Control

A profit plan is a reasonably precise statement of the steps and resources by which a company's goals for present and future years will be achieved. But to keep operations and performance aligned with this plan, effective control is indispensable. Because the guiding framework of the plan—profit—is financial, the basis of control is also financial: the "money" yardstick (return on investment, or ROA) is the chief measure of managerial performance.

How is the ROA criterion applied? Chapter 16 suggests the answer. If return on investment is the product of profit margin times investment turnover, then the key to financial control lies in various relations centered in the DuPont method. How adequate is the profit margin—the spread between price and cost? Are enough sales being generated for the investment? How effective is the utilization of various assets—cash, inventory, receivables, fixed assets—as measured by their turnover? Are manufacturing costs too high? Is the company getting too low a price for its product? Is sufficient order volume per sales call being generated? Is telephone expense too high in relation to business volume? This list of questions could be amplified almost endlessly, but each would relate in some way to one of four main criteria of the company's operating and financial performance: profitability, turnover, liquidity, and leverage.

Profit Centers and Responsibility

Modern methods of financial control typically reflect two features of company organization: (1) division of a company into profit centers, and (2) pushing profit responsibility as far down into management ranks as possible.

Profit centers mean the division of a company's total investment into parts and assigning each part to a given manager along with the responsibility to earn a satisfactory return on the investment so allotted. For example, a $20 million company may divide its investment into eight sections. It might allocate $3 million of its investment to the manager of Division C, requiring him to earn 12 per cent after taxes ($360,000) in the coming year. Managers with profit center responsibility typically enjoy wide authority and discretion over the specific steps through which they attain their earnings goals.

Pushing profit responsibility down into management ranks means that each higher manager delegates, as far as possible, a certain part of his overall profit responsibility to his subordinates. For example, the manager of Division C may allocate to each of his three product-managers $1 million of the $3 million investment for which he is himself responsible. Each product-manager would then be held responsible for earning 12 per cent ($120,000) on the investment committed to his charge. In this way, even subordinate managers receive direct responsibility for generating profit on the firm's investment; their compensation is likely to depend heavily on their ability to meet their earnings targets.

Companies may employ either fixed or variable budgets. A fixed budget is rigidly based on a given sales forecast and makes no allowances for deviations beyond a manager's control. Variable budgets, by contrast, gear expected results to different levels of activity. If, for example, a company's sales volume was less than expected, the vice president in charge of manufacturing would be allowed a higher cost per unit of output since there would be fewer units to absorb his plant overhead.

Reports

Operating managers commit themselves to profit goals through budgets, which are accounting-type blueprints of intended performance. The financial manager must then measure each manager's performance with respect to his own budget, and report his degree of success or failure to the manager himself and to his superiors. A company's accounting system, if properly designed and administered, provides an immense range of information about every manager's performance. In preparing his operations control reports, the financial manager's chief problem is to select those data that are (1) relevant to measuring a given manager's performance, and (2) understandable to those for whom they are intended.

How can the financial manager make his reports relevant and effective? He can do so by following the two principles of *accountability* and *exception.*

Accountability

Reports going to a particular manager should generally include only those matters for which that manager is accountable. A district sales manager, for example, might be measured each month on such matters as unit sales volume, prices obtained, sales mix, sales salary expense, travel expense, telephone expense, average revenue per salesman, average revenue per sales call, and so on. His performance on each criterion would be measured against his planned operations for the period—against his sales and expense budgets.

The Exception Principle

The exception principle is an instance of the familiar saying, "The squeaky wheel should get the grease." The focus of reports organized on this principle is on deviations from set standards or from planned (budgeted) performance. Large variances from planned results are red-flagged to the lower-level manager directly responsible, and only these exceptions to his satisfactory performance are brought to the attention of higher management. A man's superior thus wastes no time reviewing those aspects of his performance that are "in line." The subordinate's remedial action or follow-up on red-flagged items is reported to, and checked by, his boss.

In the example above, the district sales manager might have met or surpassed all but two of his budgeted goals: his salary expense was above, and his average revenue per sales call below, budgeted levels. His division manager would ask him to explain why. The explanation might be that, owing to promotions and retirements, his district had several new salesmen on the job who were not yet fully productive. This explanation might be entirely acceptable, but at least higher management would have investigated what could have been a symptom of more serious trouble.

Treasurer and Controller Functions

Who handles the functions of financial planning and control? In smaller firms, it is usually one man, often the president or owner. The larger the firm is, the more likely that these functions will be divided between a treasurer and a controller.

Chapter 13 introduced you to the broad roles of these two officials. Table 19–3 presents a more detailed view. As you can see, the *controller function* is

Table 19–3. Controller and Treasurer Functions

Controller	Treasurer
Planning for Control To establish, coordinate and administer, as part of management, a plan for the control of operations. This plan would provide, to the extent required in the business, profit planning, programs for capital investing and for financing, sales forecasts, and expense budgets.	*Provision of Finance* To establish and execute programs for the provision of the finance required by the business, including negotiating its procurement and maintaining the required financial arrangements.
Reporting and Interpreting To compare actual performance with operating plans and standards, and to report and interpret the results of operations to all levels of management and to the owners of the business. To consult with all management about the financial implications of its actions.	*Investor Relations* To establish and maintain an adequate market for the company's securities and to maintain adequate contact with the investment community.
Tax Administration To establish and administer tax policies and procedures.	*Short-term Financing* To maintain adequate sources for the company's current borrowings from the money market.
Government Reporting To supervise or coordinate the preparation of reports to government agencies.	*Banking and Custody* To maintain banking arrangements, to receive, have custody of and disburse the company's monies and securities and to be responsible for the financial aspects of real estate transactions.
Protection of Assets To assure protection of business assets through internal control, internal auditing and assuring proper insurance coverage.	*Credits and Collections* To direct the granting of credit and the collection of accounts due the company.
Economic Appraisal To appraise economic and social forces and government influences, and to interpret their effect upon the business.	*Investments* To invest the company's funds as required and to establish and coordinate policies for investment in pension and other similar trusts.
	Insurance To provide insurance coverage as may be required.

Source: Reprinted by permission from *Financial Executive*, October 1968, p. 22.

concerned primarily with selecting appropriate assets, measuring operations, and presenting results in a form meaningful and useful to management. To a great extent it is an internal function. The *treasurer function* is, broadly speaking, concerned with identifying the best sources of finance to utilize in the business and timing the acquisition of funds. It is to a great extent externally oriented. Another way of looking at these functions is this: The controller function concentrates on the asset side of the balance sheet, while the treasurer function concentrates on the claims side.

To Remember

Treasurer and controller functions   Investment lumps
Planning vs. forecasting   Automatic sources
Extrapolation   Exception principle
Suitability   Permanent current assets
Per cent of sales method

Questions

1   The well-known economist, George Katona, noted, "During the past ten years executives in charge of engineering and marketing have usually made the decisions about adding or not adding to capacity, and about the rate of expansion. Having done so, they 'instructed' the executives in charge of finance to provide the necessary funds." [*Business Looks at Banks* (Ann Arbor: University of Michigan Press, 1957), p. 141.] Evaluate this statement with respect to its implications regarding (a) lack of coordination of plans, and (b) suitability.

2   Classify the following duties as controller or treasurer:

   (a) Concern with the cost and availability of finance.
   (b) Determining ways to minimize the firm's tax burden.
   (c) Supervising trade credit and collections.
   (d) Capital budgeting.
   (e) Maintenance of working capital and investment of excessive funds.
   (f) Economic forecast.
   (g) Sales forecast and per cent of sales method of determining asset needs.
   (h) Insuring sound relations with shareholders.
   (i) Managing the accounting division.
   (j) Determining the proper level of cash and controlling its level.

3   Bokonon Amalgamated, a producer of pleasure pies, is making its sales forecast. Bokonon has 15 per cent of the current market for pleasure pies. The market is expected to grow 6 per cent next year.

   (a) By what percentage should Bokonon's sales expand next year?
   (b) What are some factors that might affect Bokonon's share of the market, and thus its growth rate?

4   Boko-Maru, Incorporated, has the following balance sheet this year:

Cash	$ 500	Accounts payable	$ 200
Securities	500	Taxes payable	400
Accounts receivable	1,000	Bonds	2,400
Inventory	2,000	Shareholders' equity	2,000
Fixed assets	1,000		
	$5,000		$5,000

Salaries too [handwritten]

Sales this year are $10,000. The marketing division forecasts a sales increase next year of 30 per cent because Boko-Maru is establishing new relations abroad.

(a) What is the new level of sales? *13,000* [handwritten]
(b) By what percentage will assets expand? *$\frac{1500}{5000} = 130$* [handwritten]
(c) By what percentage must financial sources expand? *$\frac{1500}{5000} = .30$* [handwritten]
? (d) What will be the dollar value of sources and uses next year? *$1500 source or funding* [handwritten]
(e) How much new financing will be generated by the automatic sources? *180* [handwritten]
(f) Boko-Maru has a 5 per cent sales margin. How much finance is generated from the internal automatic source? From non-automatic sources?

5   Explain clearly the impact on liquidity and profitability of failing to follow the principle of suitability. Use the ROA equation in your answer.

6   Is accountability simply another way of looking at the exception principle? Explain.

7   Economists refer to the "principle of acceleration." This principle relates the volume of investment to the volume of output or income, expressed quantitively like this:

$$I = f(Y).$$

Investment equals some function of output or income.

(a) Do you see a close relation between this principle and the per cent of sales forecasting method? Explain.
(b) What do you think the existence of excess or idle capacity might do to the accuracy of the per cent of sales forecasting method?

[handwritten notes]

S1

e. $\frac{600}{10,000} = .06$ *S2* *A/P, taxs. .06 × 3000 = 180*

650

$30

Automatic

Internal

f   13,000 × .05 = profit

650 = profit

1500

830

Need to acquire 670

sell stock
sell bonds
use mortgage
loans from a bank

20

Cost of Capital and Other Topics

Having forecast financial requirements and gauged the suitability of different sources, management must act to procure the funds. Major considerations here are (1) cost, (2) availability, and (3) timing. In approaching the funds-raising decision, however, we should first note how sources are classified and the extent to which corporate business has been using each class.

Sources of Funds: Classified

Companies raise funds from both internal and external sources. *Internal sources* are chiefly depreciation and retained earnings, though minor amounts may be raised from two others: a rise in accrued income taxes, and the running down of current assets, particularly cash and temporary investments. *External sources* divide into long- and short-term funds. Long-term funds arise from the sale of new securities (stocks and bonds), mortgage loans, and term loans from commercial banks. Short-term funds are provided principally by bank loans, loans from non-bank lenders (finance companies, factors, commercial paper sales, and the like) and from increased trade credit (accounts payable).

Internal sources derive from company operations. They comprise what we called in chapter 18 cash flow. To some extent, cash flow is automatic, although depreciation involves a choice of method, and retained earnings depend on decisions about dividend payments. External sources, however, must be selected. Management must decide whether funds sought shall be debt or equity, and if debt, whether short- or long-term.

Recent Use of Sources

Table 20–1 shows sources of funds for U.S. non-financial corporations over the years 1966–72. It suggests four significant points. First, internal sources greatly predominate, with depreciation the largest single source; it now more than doubles retained earnings, which is the next largest source. Second, the proportion of external funds fluctuates with their availability, the state of business, and the adequacy of internal sources. Third, the proportion of common stock financing has risen sharply in recent years, reflecting companies' efforts to reduce debt ratios from the dangerous levels reached at the end of the 1960s. Finally, years of tight money—1966 and 1969—show greatly increased reliance on short-term sources.

Table 20–1. Sources of Funds, Nonfinancial Corporations (billions of current dollars)

	1966	1969	1970	1972 (estimated)
Internal Sources				
Undistributed Profits	$24.7	$15.8	$12.3	$24.0
Depreciation	38.2	49.2	53.8	66.2
Tax Liability	0.2	−1.9	−3.3	—
Other Sources	−1.8	−5.5	−4.5	−4.0
External Sources				
Long-term Funds				
Stocks and Bonds	11.4	15.5	26.1	25.0
Mortgages	4.2	4.8	5.3	8.5
Term Bank Loans	2.6	5.8	2.1	2.5
Short-term Funds				
Open Market Paper	1.0	2.7	2.6	1.4
Bank Loans	5.3	5.2	−0.1	6.0
Other	8.1	6.9	5.2	3.4
Total	$93.9	$98.5	$99.5	$133.0

Source: *The Investment Outlook For 1972.* Bankers Trust Company, New York, Table 26.

The Cost of Capital

Funds have both a market cost and an opportunity cost. Their *market cost* is the return that must be paid to obtain them. Their *opportunity cost* is the minimum return they should earn when invested in the business. Their true cost is whichever of the two is higher.

Measuring a company's cost of funds, however, is complicated by an additional consideration. A firm's capital structure—the long-term elements of the right-hand side of its balance sheet—is actually a composite whole. True, it consists of different kinds of debt and equity, but the proportions in which these are joined together are very important. In particular, the debt-equity mix and the relative shares of long- and short-term financing must be acceptable to the investors who put up the funds. In a sense, therefore, to speak of a company's cost of *debt* capital or *common stock* capital, as if either were totally separate from the other, creates an artificial and unreal picture. As we shall see, a company's capital actually consists of composite slices made up of debt and equity in some fairly precise proportion. Thus, attempts to attach costs to particular *ingredients* of capital structure are not only artificial, but also likely to involve a famous fallacy in logic, the *fallacy of division*.[1]

Nevertheless, we must learn how to compute the costs of different kinds of funds. The cost of each slice of a company's capital can only be figured as a weighted average of the costs of the different kinds of securities comprising it, and the cost of each kind of security—bonds, preferred stock, common stock equity—is arrived at in a different way.

Before illustrating these calculations, one other point is important. The cost of capital is logically figured, not on the basis of what it cost to sell securities at the time they were issued, but on what it would cost the company to sell these securities today. *Present* market prices and yields measure what the money raised by securities is worth now: what interest, dividends, or other returns these securities must pay to be acceptable to *present* investors. This, of course, is an application of the opportunity cost principle discussed above.

Debt

The cost of debt capital is determined by three factors, two clearly measurable, the third usually less so. These three factors are (1) the yield to maturity at which a company's bonds are now selling, (2) the cost-reducing influence of income tax, and (3) the non-interest dimensions of cost.

Bonds' yield to maturity is the same as the coupon yield only if the bonds are selling at par. Most bonds sell on the market above or below par, depending on whether the yield to maturity investors currently require is higher or lower than the coupon rate the bonds carry. The yield to maturity of a marketable bond can be figured approximately by use of the following formula:

$$Y = \frac{C + \dfrac{(\$1{,}000 - P)}{N}}{\dfrac{P + \$1{,}000}{2}}, \qquad \text{(Eq. 20-1)}$$

---

[1] Division is the fallacy of asserting of things separately what is only true of them collectively.

where

    C = annual coupon interest paid by the bond,
    P = bond's market price,
    N = number of years to maturity, and
    Y = approximate yield to maturity.

Consider, for example, a bond paying 4¾ per cent ($47.50 per year), due in ten years, and selling at $820. Its approximate yield to maturity will be

$$Y = \frac{\$47.50 + \dfrac{\$1{,}000 - \$820}{10}}{\dfrac{\$820 + \$1{,}000}{2}} = \frac{\$47.50 + \$18}{\$910} = 7.2\%.$$

Obviously, if the bond is selling at a premium, i.e., for more than $1,000, the yield to maturity will be *less* than the coupon yield.

However, this yield on a company's bonds is only the starting point for figuring the cost of long-term debt. This is because yield to maturity is expressed in before-tax dollars. Since interest is a tax-deductible expense, its cost in *after-tax dollars* is substantially reduced. The following example illustrates the point. Two companies, A and B, both have earnings before interest and taxes of $100. However, company A is financed with $1,000 in common stock, while B is financed with $1,000 worth of 10 per cent bonds. Returns to suppliers of capital are paid as below.

	A	B
Net before interest and taxes	$100	$100
Interest	—	$100
Net before tax	$100	—
Income tax at 50%	$50	—
Net for stockholders	$50	—

The example shows that $1 of income before interest and taxes will pay $1 of interest. But because $100 in before-tax earnings pays only $50 to stockholders, we can say that it takes $2 of pre-tax earnings to supply $1 of earnings on equity. For this reason, a 50 per cent corporate income tax rate is said to cut the cost of interest in half.

More generally, it is true that

$$k_d = (1 - t)\, r, \tag{Eq. 20-2}$$

where

    k_d = after-tax cost of borrowed capital,
    t = firm's marginal income tax rate, and
    r = rate of interest paid on the debt.

For example, a firm in the 40 per cent tax bracket paying a 7 per cent rate of interest would have an after-tax cost of debt of 4.2 per cent: $(1 - .4) \times 7$ per cent. Since costs of *equity capital* are always expressed in after-tax dollars, debt costs are usually reduced to this same basis so that all costs of capital can be compared.

Finally, debt costs may include large "non-interest" dimensions. A sinking fund attached to a bond issue to retire much of it before maturity may double or triple its final cost. This is so because, in addition to interest on the bonds, the issue is also chargeable with the cost of the retained earnings that will be used to retire the issue. Since retained earnings are equity their cost will be based on the cost of equity, which, as we shall see, typically far exceeds the cost of debt. A conversion privilege (the holder's right to convert a bond into common stock) also raises the cost of a bond issue through an eventual dilution of stockholders' equity. Lastly, bond indentures and other lending agreements often include burdensome restrictions on management's freedom to act. These restrictions are intended to safeguard creditor rights. Their cost can rarely be assessed in dollars-and-cents terms. But their cost is *felt* when a company is forced to maintain a certain current ratio, to limit or omit dividends, or to submit officer promotions to the trustee of a bond issue.

Preferred Stock

The cost of preferred stock is simply the dividend rate the company must pay on its preferred shares. In the absence of sinking funds, convertibility, or other special features, it is simply

$$k_p = \frac{D}{P}, \qquad \text{(Eq. 20–3)}$$

where

k_p = cost of preferred,
D = annual dividend in dollars, and
P = current market price per share in dollars.

The ratio D/P tells a company what yield will be required to attract investors to its preferred shares. Note that P is *current* market price, and not the price at which shares may originally have been issued. For example, Brownout Power & Light $4.50 preferred may originally have been sold at $100 per share. But if the present price is $60, the present cost to the company of preferred stock is $4.50/$60, or 7½ per cent.

Common Stock Equity

What common stock equity costs a firm is a complicated issue on which experts disagree. Common sense suggests that one measure might be the ratio of net earnings per common share to stock price. Earnings are what the stockholder gets from the company, and the stock price shows what he will pay for these earnings. This ratio, written E/P, is called the *earnings yield* of the stock.

However, the price a company can obtain for its stock depends on what multiple of earnings a prospective shareholder is willing to pay for it. From *his* standpoint, his return comes in two separate streams: a dividend stream and a capital-gains stream. The dividend stream consists of the future dividends the shareholder expects to be paid. The capital-gains stream is the increase in market price which he expects to realize while holding the stock. If we make the simplifying assumption that the stock's price, earnings, and dividends per share will all grow across time at the same rate, we can write a formula for the shareholder's expected rate of return:

$$k_{se} = (D/P) + g, \qquad \text{(Eq. 20–4)}$$

where

> k_{se} = rate of return to common shareholders,
> D = present dividend in dollars,
> P = market price per share, and
> g = annual growth rate of earnings and dividend.

If management is shrewd or fortunate, it will be investing in assets that yield a very high return so that earnings and dividends may be increasing rapidly. Suppose Global Corporation is earning 20 per cent on stockholders' book equity of $50 per share, paying an annual dividend of $5 per share, and retaining the other $5 of annual earnings. This retention rate will permit equity, earnings, and dividend—all three—to grow at a 10 per cent annual rate. In these circumstances, Global's common shares could easily sell at $200, four times book value and twenty times annual earnings, a P/E multiple of 20. At this price, the stockholder's expected return would be

$$k_{se} = (D/P) + g = \$5/\$200 + .10 = 12.5\%.$$

Is this 12.5 per cent the cost of equity capital to the firm? In a sense it is, and in a sense it isn't. Since the firm can sell new shares for $200 on a promise of earning $10, it might seem that the cost of equity capital is only $10/$200, or 5 per cent, our E/P ratio. However, management can only obtain the $200 per share price so long as earnings and dividend per share continue to grow at 10 per cent annually. What does this growth depend on? It depends on continuation of the unusually high *rate of return on equity*, which is 20 per cent.[2] If this return on equity (ROE) should fall, the stock's price can be expected to decline.

The authors believe that ROE is the most useful and truest measure of a company's cost of equity capital. For reasons beyond the scope of this text, it may not be the only measure. But we believe it serves the purpose more effectively and more logically than any other.

What minimum return should a firm's projects earn on new equity funds invested in them? A firm's present ROE is a plausible yardstick. It is this ROE which enables common shares to sell at their present price by making possible the earnings-, dividend-, and growth-rates that have attracted existing shareholders. If the firm began investing equity funds in projects at a lower rate of return than this ROE, the ROE would become diluted and it would fall. Along with it, the price of the firm's shares would fall, and more shares would have to be sold to raise a given volume of equity funds.[3]

The cost of capital, as chapter 26 will show, is of central importance when expressed as *opportunity cost*. For the business enterprise, this means the cut-off, or "hurdle," rate which a company's investment proposals *must earn* to be financially acceptable. This brings us to the heart of the cost of capital definition. It is the rate of return that must be earned on invested funds to maximize the

---

[2] Investing the $5 retained to yield 20 per cent will lead to total earnings of .20 ($55) = $11, a 10 per cent increase. If the dividend grows 10 per cent, the payout rate remains 50 per cent, the dividend is $5.50. The stock price grows 10 per cent to $220. In this way, k_{se} remains constant at 12.5 per cent, and the common shareholders are satisfied.

[3] Advanced texts usually note that external equity, that raised in a new flotation of common, is more expensive, i.e., necessitates a higher hurdle rate, than internal equity by the shareholders' personal tax rate, brokerage fees, and flotation costs. We leave this topic to future courses in finance.

sustainable market price of the firm's common stock. A high and increasing stock price makes stockholders satisfied, and satisfied stockholders permit management to reward itself with healthy stock options, bonuses, salaries, and other fringe benefits.

Weighted Cost of Capital: An Example

Now we can pull all the costs together and figure what average return the claimants as a whole require. In the following example, we compute a *weighted average cost of capital,* one in which the cost of each kind of capital is weighted according to its percentage share in the firm's capital structure.

Global Corporation has the following capital structure:

Assets	Claims	
	Bonds (7% coupon)	$200,000
	Preferred (10%)	50,000
	Equity	150,000
$400,000		$400,00

The yield to maturity of the bonds at their present market price is approximately 6.5 per cent. The preferred stock pays a $10 dividend and is selling for $100. The return on common stock equity is 20 per cent; the tax rate is 50 per cent.

We construct a table with the following headings and fill in the spaces.

(1) Type	(2) Amount	(3) Cost (rounded)	(4) % Total	(5) Weighted Share
Bonds	$200,000	.032	.50	.016
Preferred	50,000	.10	.12	.012
Equity	150,000	.20	.38	.076
	$400,000		1.00	.104

The yield on the bonds is 6.5 per cent. But since interest is tax-deductible, the net cost is reduced by the firm's tax rate. Thus, using Eq. 20–2, k_d = 0.65 times .50 = .0325. The cost of preferred, as Eq. 20–3 indicates, is the dividend divided by the market price of the stock, or 10 per cent. The cost of common stock equity is equal to ROE, or 20 per cent. The percent-of-total column is simply the proportion of total capital each component constitutes. Bonds are $200,000/$400,000, or 50 per cent; common stock equity is $150,000/$400,000, or 38 per cent; and preferred is $50,000/$400,000, or 12 per cent.

We now multiply column (3) by column (4) to obtain the weighted cost of each component in the capital structure. Finally, we total these figures to obtain k_a, the weighted average cost of capital, 10.4 per cent.

This 10.4 per cent, then, represents the cost of each "slice" of capital consisting of 50 per cent of debt, 12 per cent of preferred stock, and 38 per cent of common stock equity. You should now see why one commits a fallacy of division by speaking of separate costs for the different kinds of capital: clearly, these separate costs depend on the specific proportions in which the different kinds of capital are brought together. If, for example, the percentage of debt rose to

60 per cent, it is most unlikely that the bond yield would remain as low as 6.5 per cent. Bond buyers would claim that the company was over-leveraged, they would pay less for its bonds, and its cost of debt capital would rise. Likewise, the cost of equity would increase. Management would have to select investments yielding a higher return to reward shareholders for incurring the increased financial risk associated with greater financial leverage. Otherwise, shareholders would most likely sell their common and acquire a stock more suited to their risk attitude.

Minimizing Cost of Capital

As already noted, companies aim at maintaining through time a capital structure acceptable to investors. By so doing, they can minimize their cost of capital. Figure 20–1 illustrates how changes in a firm's debt-equity ratio affect its cost of capital. As you can see, k_a, the cost of capital, is saucer-shaped, minimal over a good space, indicating that investors find a certain *range* of leverage acceptable for the average company. Outside this range—the bottom of the saucer—the cost of capital rises on either side. Too much leverage makes bonds more costly to issue. Too little leverage makes the stock unattractive and unduly lowers its price.

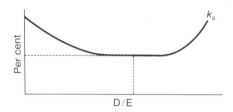

Figure 20–1. Leverage and
Cost of Capital

Figure 20–1 also suggests a theoretical reason why management will want to minimize its cost of capital. The market value of the firm is theoretically equal to the present value of the firm's future earnings, just as the value of any asset is equal to the present value of its future receipts. For the value of the firm, earnings are discounted at the firm's cost of capital. We can say that

$$V = E/k_a,$$

(Eq. 20–5)

where

   V = market value of the firm,
   E = future earnings of the firm, and
   k_a = average cost of capital.

As with any other present value computation, the lower the discount (or capitalization) rate applied, the higher will be the present value of the foreseen earnings stream. Minimizing the cost of capital will maximize V, the value of the firm. If the financial manager can enlarge V by changing the debt-equity ratio, he should do so.

Availability

The availability of different kinds of funds often plays an overriding part in a firm's decision to use debt or equity, and *what kind* of debt or equity. Ordinarily, retained earnings are the most readily available of all sources, so these funds can be thought of as standing first in line. Access to the bond market is restricted to fairly large companies, and so small- and medium-size enterprises find this source unavailable. The same is true of the stock markets, though in less degree. Consequently, small- and medium-size firms are typically forced to restrict their long-term financing to retained earnings. Their primary sources of other funds are trade credit (an automatic source) and bank loans.

Availability sometimes bears no relation to cost. Although the prime rate of interest (the cost of bank loans to their most secure borrowers) may be 4 per cent, very weak firms may be unable to obtain bank credit at any price. Furthermore, although the rate on high-grade, long-term bonds may be 7 per cent, shaky firms may be unable to sell new bonds even at 12 per cent. In these circumstances, credit is said to be rationed; the supply of funds is restricted not by cost (interest charges), but by other means. Lenders simply refuse to lend or require impossibly restrictive conditions from borrowers. This rationing occurs primarily because the economy's overall demand for funds exceeds the supply available from savings and other sources. Lenders are thus able to pick and choose. Since notions of usury restrain lenders from charging borrowers what the market will bear, they simply raise interest rates as high as they dare and skim off the "cream" of the prospective borrowers.

Timing

Sound financial policy involves not only a wise selection of sources but also effective timing in the acquisition of funds. Availability and cost of finance fluctuate widely over the business cycle, reflecting changes in security-market prices and in supplies of, and demands for, loanable funds. The key to effective timing is correct forecasting, and this in turn depends upon an understanding of how business cycles behave and how interest rates and stock prices typically move over the cycle. Experience is important here in providing a businessman with a "feel" for what is coming next. These questions will be discussed more fully in chapter 33, but a brief introduction to the main ideas will be offered here.

Both cost and availability of debt funds typically move counter to the need for them. Bond yields are lowest, and new bond issues easiest to sell, in times of recession—when money is easy, when few businesses need more funds, and when bond flotations are relatively infrequent. Yields are highest, and new bonds hardest to sell, near the peak of a boom—when money is tight, when many companies are trying to raise funds for expansion, and when the bond market new issues calendar is jammed.

Timing possibilities are better with respect to equity funds. Along with profits, retained earnings are likely to rise and fall with the business cycle, thus moving in step with needs. Stock prices typically rise with business expansion, and though they usually begin declining ahead of business, companies can typically obtain their best prices for stock near the peak of prosperity.

The far-sighted financial manager will remember these patterns, and take advantage of them. He will avoid times of "standing room only" in the bond markets. He will sell bonds early in the expansion stage to fund his permanent capital needs, and will negotiate ample lines of credit with his banks to meet his temporary financing needs. Then, as prosperity heads into the boom and stock prices near a peak, he will sell additional common stock. By selling stock at this time, he will (1) obtain a high price per share, and (2) assure his company of entering the next recession with a comfortably low debt-equity ratio. As business tops out and begins the slide into recession, the equity funds he has raised enable him to repay most of his bank loans and so reduce interest charges.

Further Considerations

Besides suitability, cost, availability, and timing, still other considerations affect a company's selection of capital sources. Conspicuous among these are the need to preserve maneuverability, expectations about future tax rates and inflation, and present stockholders' desire to maintain voting control of the corporation. A final consideration is the risk attitude of management and stockholders, sometimes called the "eat well or sleep well" dilemma.

Maneuverability

A firm's ability to choose its source of finance, debt or equity, long- or short-term, at its own discretion, is termed *maneuverability*. Maneuverability is the direct result of management's adherence to a financial structure that is acceptable to the financial community—bankers, long-term creditors, and stockholders. Maneuverability is compromised when the financial structure diverges from some norm, usually the industry average. For example, when the debt-equity ratio is too high, the firm has difficulty in selling more debt; investment bankers may label its bonds "unacceptable" and insist that the company sell stock instead.

A firm possessing maneuverability can temporarily substitute one form of financing for another. If the stock market is depressed, and a fair price for its stock unobtainable, the company may sell bonds now and float common stock later on. If the bond market is depressed (and interest rates are high), it may defer bonds in favor of stock. If both stock and bond markets are down, it may be able to substitute short-term financing (commercial paper or bank loans) and await the time when capital markets recover.

Other Factors

Inflation puts a premium on debt because borrowers expect to repay lenders in cheaper money. The tax deductibility of interest reinforces companies' bias toward debt, and this bias increases as tax rates increase. The wishes of present owners to maintain control may force them to rely excessively on debt. Selling more common stock may give outside interests unwelcome voting power. Finally, the risk attitude of both management and stockholders is influential. If these parties prefer to run large risks to make large profits ("eat well"), the company will utilize leverage and finance heavily from debt sources. If, instead, they prefer to avoid worry over possible ruinous losses ("sleep well"), they will finance conservatively from equity sources.

To Remember

Cost of capital	Availability
Cost of equity	Timing
Weighted average cost of capital	Maneuverability

Questions

1 Examine the formula for the net burden of interest expense, k_d.

    (a) The interest rate is 10 per cent. What is the net burden if the tax rate is 30 per cent? 70 per cent?

    (b) Does this mean that businessmen prefer a higher tax rate so that they can minimize the net burden of their debt? Explain.

2 Wampeter, Inc., has earnings of $4 per share. The current market price of the stock is $80.

    (a) What is Wampeter, Inc.'s P/E multiple?

    (b) What is the firm's earnings yield?

    (c) What do you think would happen to the price of its common if Wampeter's management used the earnings yield as its cost of equity instead of its ROE of 20 per cent? (Hint: Be sure to include in your answer how the cost of equity—and capital—is used by management.) This question does not call for a precise answer.)

3 Duprass, Inc., has a capital structure like this:

Bonds (6 @ 6%)	$6,000
Preferred (5% coupon)	2,000
Shareholders' equity	2,000

Bonds, though originally issued at par, are now selling for $600 each and have ten years remaining to maturity. Preferred is quoted in the *Wall Street Journal* at $62.50 a share. Duprass last year earned 12 per cent on equity. Corporate tax rate is 40 per cent.

    (a) To maintain its present capital structure, how much of the increased capital must be generated from equity?

    (b) What is the market weighted average cost of capital for Duprass, Inc.?

    (c) If the capital structure grows 20 per cent, how much will be in each component at the end of the year?

    (d) Do you see an inconsistency in the fact that we use market values for debt and preferred, but a book value for cost of equity? Explain.

4 Beeper Amalgamated has total sales of $300 million. Management forecasts a sales increase to $420 million during 1974. (Assume all assets are fixed assets.) Its present capital structure, considered optimal, is:

Bonds (3% coupon)	$50 million
Preferred (7% coupon)	$25 million
Shareholders' equity	$25 million

New bonds will have a 10 per cent coupon rate of interest, twenty-year maturity, and will sell for $1,200 per bond. Preferred is selling at $50 per share. Management pays out 60 per cent of the firm's earnings in dividends. There are one million shares outstanding, and the *P/E* multiple is 8. Beeper has an after-tax profit margin of 2 per cent. The tax rate is 40 per cent.

(a) How much are earnings after taxes?
(b) By what percentage do sales, assets, and claims grow?
(c) For every $1 increase in sales, how much do assets and claims increase?
(d) To maintain its present capital structure, by what percentage and dollar amount must equity expand?
(e) What is the cost of equity?
(f) How much equity must be raised externally if management adheres to the same payout rate?
(g) How will the balance sheet look at the end of 1974?
(h) What is the market weighted average cost of capital?

5 One of your classmates in marketing comments on Figure 20–1, "Since management can maximize the firm's value by having a low k_a, it should seek a minimum ROE and use all equity. That would fill the bill."

(a) How do you respond to him?
(b) Do you agree that successful management puts pressure on itself to continue to be successful? Explain.

6 Financial analysts have noted that the premium of market price over book value of a common stock represents the market's recognition of superior management. How would you explain that assertion?

21

Short-Term Financing: Sources and Costs

Short-term finance is used by business for six months or less. The major sources of short-term business finance are trade credit, commercial banks, and commercial paper. Firms also can *raise cash* by reducing other assets. If a company holds marketable securities, they can be sold. Financial managers can usually obtain cash—for short intervals, at least—from accounts receivable and inventories. In unusual instances, fixed assets may be liquidated.

Sources: Increasing Liabilities

Businesses receive finance from an array of short-term creditors. The major sources are trade creditors, commercial banks, and commercial paper.

Trade Credit

Trade (or "book") credit arises when a business receives goods from a supplier without the requirement of immediate cash payment. A wholesaler may give his retailer-customer thirty days after receipt to pay for 100 dozen Titleist golf balls. Over the thirty days, the supplier is financing his customer; not, to be sure, lending him cash, but providing goods which the buyer can use for some time without paying for them.

For each party, the trade credit shows up differently on the books. For the grantor, the credit takes the form of an account receivable from his customer. The recipient's books will show the same amount as an account payable.

Trade credit is described by three elements: (1) the amount of a cash discount from the invoice price, (2) the time interval within which the discount applies (calculated from the day the invoice is received), and (3) the time when the gross amount of the invoice must be paid. For example, a company might receive an invoice for material of, for example, $10,000, with terms of 2/10, n30. That means the company receives a 2 per cent discount from the $10,000 gross amount if the invoice is paid within ten days, a $200 saving. However, should it not meet the ten-day deadline, it must pay the full $10,000 within another twenty days, or thirty days from receipt of the invoice.

Popularity

Trade credit is the most widely used source of short-term finance and the chief reliance of small- and medium-size firms. Three reasons explain this popularity.

1. Trade credit is automatic. A seller usually grants it because his competitors do.

2. Trade credit is convenient. To use trade credit, a firm need not go through the time-consuming, and perhaps embarrassing, procedure of applying for a loan. The firm can simply defer paying cash for its purchases.

3. Trade credit appears to be inexpensive. To many users, trade credit has no apparent cost; the only cost may seem to be the price of the goods purchased. However, the firm granting the credit incurs a cost by tying up its money in an account receivable, and it must cover this cost to stay in business. Since it is not charging interest on the trade credit, the firm granting it must recoup the cost by charging more for its products. Thus, a business that pays cash for its purchases without demanding a discount may be paying for something it is not receiving, never a happy circumstance.[1]

Cost

The cost of trade credit, as you can see, is usually concealed in the supplier's price. What if, in the $10,000 example above, the purchaser waits thirty days after the invoice and then pays the full $10,000? In so doing, he is paying 2 per cent ($200/$10,000) to use money an additional twenty days, the difference between the discount date and date of payment. Just how expensive this $10,000 is, can be disclosed by *annualizing* the interest rate involved. To annualize a rate

---

[1] In effect, the cash customer is subsidizing the credit customer. By paying cash, this customer induces the supplier to keep its prices lower than would otherwise be the case. The lower price is enjoyed not only by the cash customer, but also by the credit customer. Hence, the latter receives credit at a lower rate than he would otherwise have to pay, thanks to the cash customer. The same reasoning applies to the subsidy of credit card customers by those who prefer to pay cash.

is to state it on an annual basis rather than a portion of a year. This enables us to compare the cost of trade credit with other sources. To do so, we set up this proportion:

$$\frac{\% \text{ Discount}}{\text{Payment period} - \text{Discount period}} = \frac{\text{Annualized rate}}{360}. \qquad \text{(Eq. 21-1)}$$

Payment period minus discount period is the time interval for which the purchaser gets the use of the credit by foregoing the discount, and it is customary to use a 360 day year for ease of calculation. Substituting the figures above, we have

$$\frac{.02}{20} = \frac{x}{360}.$$

Solving for x, we find that the annual cost of failure to take the discount is 36 per cent. With trade credit so costly, a company should obviously make every effort to take the cash discounts offered. If necessary, it should borrow money from a bank to do this because the cost of bank credit is usually much less than 36 per cent.

If the buyer misses the discount date, should he pay as promptly as possible? Certainly not. He still owes $200 for the $10,000, no matter how soon he pays now. His effective rate of interest declines the longer he defers payment. Suppose, for example, that he pays forty days from invoice date—getting thirty days' use of the seller's funds. (Remember that the first ten days were free.) His cost, expressed as a rate on terms of 2/10, n30 becomes

$$\text{Cost} = \frac{.02}{30} = \frac{x}{360}$$
$$30x = 7.20$$
$$x = .24.$$

Thus, firms often try to avoid paying their accounts as long as possible, a practice known as "riding" credit. Of course, if they are habitually slow to pay their bills, they run the risk of impairing their credit rating. And, if the supplier becomes too impatient for his cash, a firm exceeding its credit period may be sued.

Table 21-1 shows the annualized cost of missing a cash discount. It assumes payments are made on the final due date.

Traditionally, trade credit has been used by large firms to finance inventories—and to some degree, receivables—for their smaller customers. Large firms have been able to borrow long-term funds and, in effect, lend them to their customers through liberal credit terms. Recently, however, the worm has turned. As you saw in chapter 7, small firms have been forced to finance big ones. In an economic power play, big companies have been riding their accounts payable to small suppliers. When the supplier remonstrates, the big reminds him, in effect, that "There are other suppliers of this product. If you don't appreciate our business, we can always buy from your competitors." Since a small firm may depend almost completely on sales to one source, it is. in no position to lose the large firm's business. The big firm, faced with terms of 2/10, n30, may pay its bill in seventy days and still take a 2 per cent discount!

Why would a big company resort to such tactics? Chiefly it does so because it is unable to procure finance as readily from other sources. It can exercise its economic power more readily in trade credit than in other financial markets. This is particularly true when the money and capital markets are squeezed by tight money. In 1969–70, the "payables slowdown" broke many small companies. Economic restraint fell, as usual, on those least able to bear it. This is the best reason why the government should avoid the monetary and fiscal excesses that inevitably make restraint necessary.

Table 21-1. Cost of Trade Credit

Terms	Credit Used	Cost
2/10, n30	20 days	36%
2/10, n20	10 days	72%
1/10, n20	10 days	36%
1/10, n30	20 days	18%

Determinants

The terms on which trade credit is granted are determined by the interplay of several forces. First, *competition* is a relevant factor. A new firm entering an industry will be forced to grant terms at least equal to those granted by its competitors. To do otherwise would limit the firm's sales. Second, the *nature of the product* affects trade credit. Products with very high turnover are sold on short credit terms. That is why, for example, the dairy industry has shorter credit terms than the steel industry. Third, *financial position* is important. A financially strong buyer will ordinarily receive liberal terms because the seller need not fear a default. If the buyer is financially weak, the seller runs a greater risk of default and will probably restrict both the amount and the terms of whatever credit he extends.

Widespread reliance on trade credit, despite its high cost, reflects the conflict between cost and availability of finance. Companies use trade credit because it is available, a factor often completely dominating cost. If businesses are unable to obtain finance elsewhere, they rely on suppliers to finance them. For many struggling firms, trade credit is the only source of external finance available and must be relied upon regardless of its cost.

Commercial Banks

Commerical banks stand second only to trade creditors in the volume of short-term funds supplied to business. To small- and medium-size firms, banks play a primary role in financing business growth because these firms do not have easy access to the capital markets. The following comment, made by an apparel manufacturing company president, is typical of the sentiments of many businessmen: "I believe in bank borrowing to the limit permitted," he states, "and in being constantly in a debt position with respect to banks."[2]

The bank loan market is a personal market in which borrower and lender meet face to face. Consequently, there is considerable room for attitudinal structuring on the borrower's part—he may be able to "brown-nose" the banker and so obtain funds on better terms. For this reason, a potential borrower is well advised to cultivate a strong relationship with his banker. As you saw in chapter 13, he can do so in several ways. He may refer other people to the bank, give it his personal and family accounts, use the services of its trust department, and so on. Most important of all, he can alert the bank to his firm's potential needs. Such anticipatory behavior increases the bank's confidence in the borrower's management capabilities. "We have tried," states a household appliance firm's financial executive, "to keep our banks fully informed well in advance of our need for working capital and intermediate financing, to assure ourselves of the availability of it when needed."[3]

In addition to being a source of finance, a commercial bank can give a businessman other valuable help. It may supply credit information on his customers. A knowledgeable banker will be familiar with developments in a particular industry or region and know much about business conditions in general. Often he is able to make a cool, rational assessment of profit potentials in a new undertaking—an ability often lacking in a businessman who may be too close to the trees to see the forest. Clear, objective advice from a good banker-advisor can be a major advantage to a businessman.[4]

Cost

Bank loans to businesses are made at quoted rates of interest consisting of a base rate, which only the biggest, most credit-worthy firms can qualify for, plus a percentage-point add-on based on the credit standing of the particular borrower. From the late 1930s until fall, 1971, the base rate was a *prime rate* set by a more or less informal agreement of the country's leading banks. The prime rate was not very mobile and followed market rates of interest up and down with a considerable lag. Late in 1971, some banks began substituting a "basic" or "floating prime" rate, typically one-half percentage point above the prevailing rate on four- to six-month commercial paper.[5]

The cost of a bank loan is computed using the relation between proceeds,

---

[2]Cited in Sorrell Mathes, *Growth Financing in the Smaller Firm,* Managing the Moderate-sized Company, Report No. 1, The Conference Board, 1967, p. 16.

[3]Cited in Patrick J. Davey and Francis J. Walsh, Jr., *High Interest Rates and Tight Money,* Managing the Financial Function, No. 6, The Conference Board, 1969, p. 16.

[4]You might keep this in mind, should you decide to become a banker. You can enhance your worth to both your bank and your clients by becoming as broadly informed as possible on both general business conditions and the economics of one or more particular industries. One of the authors had a friend who went from trainee to full vice president of one of the nation's largest banks in three years by so mastering the background of the motor freight industry that his advice to truckers became indispensable, and they flocked to do business with his bank.

[5]The banks' motive for this was the threat of interest-rate ceilings by the Nixon administration. Clearly, the bankers thought that government control of bank lending rates would be less likely if the prime rate were one linked to market rates rather than one arbitrarily set by the bankers themselves.

`dollar interest, and maturity. Proceeds are the funds that the borrower actually receives from the loan. The general formula is simply

$$C = \frac{D}{P},$$

(Eq. 21–2)

where

- D = dollar cost of interest,
- P = proceeds, and
- C = cost, or effective interest rate.

If a firm borrows $10,000 for twelve months and repays $10,600 at maturity, D is $600 and P is $10,000. This would be a loan at simple interest with a cost of 6 per cent. If the same loan had matured in eight months, it would be necessary to annualize the interest expense. Here the cost would be

$$C = \frac{6\%}{8 \text{ months}} = \frac{x\%}{12 \text{ months}} = 9\%.$$

Often the bank will choose to *discount* the loan. That is, the bank will deduct the interest in advance from the stated amount of the loan rather than letting the borrower wait until the end of the period to pay it. If the bank discounted the interest from the above $10,000 loan, then the proceeds would be $10,000 − $600 = $9,400. The *effective interest rate* would differ from the *nominal rate;* that is, the actual rate would differ from the quoted rate. The effective rate for the twelve-month loan is

$$C = \frac{D}{P} = \frac{\$600}{\$9,400} = 6.37\%.$$

The effective rate has moved up as a result of making the loan on a discount basis.

Bankers have other ways of increasing effective interest rates. One is through *compensating balances.* A compensating balance is an amount that must be left on deposit at the commercial bank at all times. It is supposed to compensate, or further reward, the banker for making a loan to a business firm. If a borrower is required to maintain a 20 per cent compensating balance, his cost of borrowing will be increased 25 per cent. In the 6 per cent simple-interest loan above, a 20 per cent compensating balance would mean that the bank would retain $2,000. Only $8,000 would be available to the borrower, and the effective cost of the loan would be

$$C = \frac{D}{P} = \frac{\$600}{\$8,000} = 7.5\%.$$

Had the loan been discounted, the proceeds would have been $10,000 − $600 − .20($10,000) = $7,400. The effective cost would have been

$$C = \frac{D}{P} = \frac{\$600}{\$7,400} = 8.1\%.$$

Finally, the banker may require his client to repay the loan in monthly installments rather than repaying in full at maturity. This arrangement almost doubles the quoted rate on the loan, since the borrower has, on average, the use of only about half the funds involved. On a $10,000 loan repayable in twelve monthly installments, the borrower would have the full $10,000 only for the first month; in the twelfth month, he would have the use of only $10,000/12, or $833.33. On average, he would have the use of ($10,000 + $833.33)/2 = $5,416.66. If his loan was neither discounted nor subject to a compensating balance, his effective rate of interest would be

$$C = \frac{D}{P} = \frac{\$600}{\$5,416.66} = 11.08\%.$$

Table 21–2 shows how the same nominal rate, 6 per cent, leads to widely different effective rates as bank loans are made on different terms.

Table 21–2. Nominal and Effective Rates of $10,000 Bank Loan

Type Interest	Nominal Rate	Proceeds	Effective Rate
Maturity	6%	$10,000	6.00%
Discounted	6%	$ 9,400	6.37%
Maturity with Compensating Balance	6%	$ 8,000	7.50%
Discounted with Compensating Balance	6%	$ 7,400	8.10%
Installment Repayment	6%	$ 5,417	11.08%

Line of Credit

In lieu of continuous borrowing, a financial manager may try to obtain a *line of credit.* In this case, the bank agrees to lend up to a certain amount of money any time the company requests it during some fixed future interval. The interest on the amount borrowed is usually stated as "prime plus," meaning that the borrower must pay the prime, or basic, lending rate, plus some extra percentage whenever he draws on his credit line. In addition, the borrower must pay the bank a small "standby fee," perhaps one-fourth or one-half of one per cent, on the unused amount of the line. For example, a firm may have a $200,000 line stated at prime plus 2 per cent, borrower to pay one-half of one per cent on the unused portion. If the firm borrows $100,000 when the prime rate is 6 per cent, it would pay 8 per cent on $100,000 and one-half of one per cent on $100,000.

Commercial Paper

Commercial paper is the unsecured promissory note of a large business of high credit standing, usually maturing in four to six months. Maturities longer than 270 days (nine months) do not exist because, beyond this time period, the issue must be registered with the Securities and Exchange Commission. Registration is an expensive and time-consuming process which would remove commercial paper's flexibility. The paper is issued in $5,000 multiples, although larger-denomination notes predominate.

There are two types of commercial paper. *Direct paper,* ordinarily accounting for about two-thirds of all issues, is sold by large sales-finance companies such as General Motors Acceptance Corporation and Aetna Finance. They sell their paper directly to buyers through a permanent sales force. *Dealer paper* is sold by borrowers through commercial paper dealers. Amounts of paper outstanding are usually much smaller for these borrowers. To move to direct placement, a company must ordinarily have at least $100 million of commercial paper outstanding. Until that level is reached, a direct sales force is uneconomical to support.

Use

Larger companies use commercial paper primarily as a substitute for bank borrowing. The interest rate on commercial paper is generally about one-half percentage point below the banks' prime rate. Since the effective rate on bank borrowings exceeds the nominal rate, owing to compensating balances, commercial paper stands as an attractively cheap source of finance.

Ordinarily, commercial paper is used to meet temporary needs: seasonal or cyclical bulges in asset requirements. But a company also uses it to meet unforeseen expenses and as temporary financing for long-term outlays. Later, when the company moves into the capital markets and sells stock or bonds to pay off the commercial paper, it is shifting from a short-term source of funds to a long-term source, a process known as *funding.*

Often, a company's use of commercial paper reflects the financial manager's ability to get the greatest mileage out of his firm's credit-worthiness. This is so because an issue of commercial paper must be backed by a line of credit with a commercial bank. The bank credit, however, need back only a part of the commercial paper issue, so the firm can obtain its maximum line of credit at the bank, then "multiply" this credit-worthiness in the commercial paper market. For example, if commercial paper must be backed 70 per cent by bank credit, then to borrow $100,000 in the commercial paper market the firm need have only a $70,000 line of credit at the commercial bank. Of course, the firm must pay a charge on the unused portion of its credit line, but the lower interest rate on commercial paper more than offsets this slight cost.

Who Buys

Commercial paper is bought by banks, other financial institutions, and non-financial corporations. They use it for liquid, interest-earning storage of short-term surplus funds. Since commercial paper *pays* no interest, it is bought at a discount from face (maturity) value. For example, the treasurer of Faithful Dobbin Dog Food may buy a $200,000, 90-day Household Finance Company note for $197,000. At maturity, the buyer will collect $200,000. His interest return is

$$\frac{\$3,000}{\$197,000} = 1.52\% \text{ for 90 days,}$$

or an annual rate of about 6.08 per cent.

The short maturity of commercial paper makes it impracticable for purchasers to make a prolonged analysis of the borrower's credit-worthiness, and its unsecured status involves obvious risk. Consequently, issuers are limited to companies whose soundness is accepted without question in the financial community.[6]

Sources: Decreasing Assets

Management can obtain cash to pay currently maturing debt by liquidating its current assets: inventory, accounts receivable, and securities. If it does so, both current assets and current liabilities decrease when it pays off the short-term debt. The result will be an increase in the firm's current ratio,[7] and no change in its working capital.

Accounts Receivable

A company which is against the wall money-wise can use its accounts receivable to generate cash immediately. Rather than waiting for the receivables to be paid off, management can either pledge or factor the accounts.

Pledging consists of borrowing money by putting up the accounts receivable as collateral. If a firm has $200,000 in accounts receivable, it may borrow perhaps $180,000 from a bank or finance company. The lender then has a *lien,* or legal claim, on the receivables and recourse against the borrower. *Recourse* means that if the receivables go bad, the borrower remains liable to the lender for any balance due on the loan. Risk of default on the receivables thus remains with the borrower.

Factoring involves the sale of accounts receivable without recourse. The purchaser of the accounts, called the factor, bears the risk of default; if customers do not pay, *he* absorbs the loss. To protect himself, a factor insists on giving prior approval to all credit sales made by a client-company. In other words, the factor assumes the credit function of its client. Thus, when the company receives an order, it must ask the factor for approval to make the sale on credit. If the factor says no, the company will refuse credit, making its customer pay cash. If the factor approves the credit of the purchaser, the firm will make the sale on credit, then discount that account with the factor. The factor will advance his client 85 or 90 cents on the dollar, enabling the businessman to recycle his funds back into inventory at once. The factor will collect the credit invoice at maturity, settling at that time any remaining amount due his client.

The cost of factoring receivables falls into two parts. First, the factor charges the customer from 1 to 2 per cent of the amount of each invoice as a basic factoring fee. Second, he charges his customer interest for the number of days in which the factor's own funds are tied up in the receivable. In addition, the factor deducts any amounts which the receivers of merchandise dispute as unsatis-

---

[6]The financial community's judgment is, of course, not infallible. The collapse of Penn Central and the resulting default on its commercial paper jolted the market in 1970. Such a mistake by the market, however, has been very much the exception and not the rule.

[7]Improvement of the current ratio depends on its being greater than 1:1 initially. If the ratio is exactly 1:1, then decreasing current assets and current liabilities by the same dollar amount will not change the ratio. And if the ratio is less than 1:1, then the current ratio will actually deteriorate. In each instance, working capital is constant.

factory, damaged, wrong items, and the like. After all charges are known, the factor will refund whatever is left owing his client.

Although factor-financing has the reputation of being high-cost financing, there is no overwhelming case that this is so. Interest charges made by factors are generally in line with those of other lenders. By factoring its receivables, a firm dispenses with both the worry and cost of a credit and collections department. Furthermore, factored accounts are much less likely to default on or delay payments, since factors work together and will blacklist a misbehaving company. However, factoring is the custom only in a limited list of industries: notably, textiles, leather goods, and food processing.

Inventory

Rather than waiting for inventory to flow through accounts receivable and into cash, management may be able—at a cost—to obtain cash immediately. It does this by pledging the inventory as collateral for a loan. One way is through *field warehousing,* where the inventory is kept on the borrowing firm's property, but in a walled or roped-off area. The lender will employ a third party to control the flow of goods into and out of inventory. Only the third party can permit the removal of any inventory. In *public warehousing,* the inventory is placed in a public warehouse as it is produced. There, it is controlled by an independent third party. Through warehousing, the lender has assurance that the collateral actually exists and is in the condition specified in the loan agreement. Costs of warehousing are charged against the borrower, making this sort of accommodation quite expensive unless very large amounts of inventory are involved.

Securities

Companies fortunate enough to hold marketable securities can, of course, raise cash by selling them. For government securities, the financial manager can find a ready market by calling his banker. For listed securities, i.e., those traded on a stock exchange, he will call his broker.

Debt securities involve a special consideration. If interest rates rise, their fall in price is directly proportional to their maturity. The wise financial manager will restrict his debt-security holdings to short maturities, thereby avoiding the capital losses that might result if long-dated debts had to be liquidated at a time of high interest rates.

To Remember

Annualized cost	Line of credit
Riding trade credit	Prime plus
Effective vs. nominal interest	Direct paper
Public and field warehousing	Dealer paper
Compensating balance	Recourse

Questions

1 Calculate the annualized cost of missing a discount whenever the paying firm receives terms of

   (a) 2/10, n30,
   (b) 1/20, n60,
   (c) 4/10, n20.

2 Bill McBain, the 73 year-old treasurer of Griffins Distributing Company, says to you, "We don't want to borrow from a bank to pay our bills within the cash discount period because a bank charges 8 per cent. Trade credit is free." How would you explain to him that it is *not* free, and that the firm might benefit from borrowing even though interest on the bank loan would show up on the income statement?

3 Calculate the effective rate of interest on a bank loan under the following conditions. The loan is for $1,000.

   (a) The loan is for six months, and the nominal rate is 6 per cent.
   (b) The loan is for six months, and the firm must repay $1,080.
   (c) The loan is for eighteen months, and the firm pays 6 per cent per annum discounted.
   (d) The loan is for twelve months at 6 per cent, and the firm must keep a $100 compensating balance.
   (e) The loan is for eighteen months, discounted at 6 per cent, and the firm must keep a $100 compensating balance.

4 Cacus Machinery Co. has an agreement with its bank allowing the company to borrow up to a total of $300,000 at any time. This line of credit costs Cacus Machinery 1½ per cent for the unused line, and prime plus 4 per cent for any used. The prime rate is 5%. Cacus is using $80,000 of the line. How much does it pay in interest?

5 Why is the cost of factoring accounts receivable usually overstated relative to pledging or bank borrowing?

22

Intermediate-Term
Financing and Leasing

Term Loans — *Development* — *Characteristics* — *Uses and Costs* — *Repayment* — Conditional Sales Contract — Leasing — *Types of Leases* — *Leasing vs. Buying*

This chapter is concerned with financing methods that are neither short- nor long-term, but either of intermediate duration (one to five years) or of the avoidance-financing sort. By avoidance financing, we mean some substitute for borrowing which still permits a businessman to obtain assets for his firm to use. One such device is leasing. A second is the conditional sales contract under which the seller finances and maintains ownership of the asset until the loan is paid. The chief form of intermediate-term financing is the term loan, a loan for more than one year which the borrower pays off in periodic installments, usually from the earnings of the asset(s) the loan financed.

Term Loans

The primary sources of term loans are commercial banks and insurance companies. Because loans from these two sources are similar in most respects, the following discussion will center on those from commercial banks.

Development

Term lending by commercial banks constitutes a break with both English and American banking tradition. Traditional doctrine, emphasizing banks' large *demand* liabilities, held that banks should make only short-term business loans to finance seasonal bulges in assets, usually inventories and receivables. To insure that loans were being used in this way, tradition decreed that banks enforce an annual clean-up of business loans. Once a year, then, each firm was supposed to pay its way completely out of debt to a bank.

Although that was long the nominal rule of the banker-business relation, actual practice was quite different. Businesses borrowed short-term funds to invest in long-term assets, fully expecting to renew the loan at maturity. And banks lent on a short-term basis with a full knowledge of what was happening: business A would extinguish its indebtedness to commercial bank B by borrowing on a short-term basis from commercial bank C, hence preserving the fiction of an annual clean-up. Such subterfuge had the redeeming value of showing that the borrower could get credit from other financial institutions. But it left both borrowers and banks dangerously vulnerable to unexpected money squeezes, and it intensified many of the financial panics of the nineteenth and early twentieth centuries.

Characteristics

Generally, the maturity of a term loan is three to five years, although New York banks occasionally have made them up to eight years. Term loans have three major characteristics. (1) The key to obtaining a term loan is *earning power*. The lender, in determining likelihood of repayment, looks to a firm's future earnings, rather than to pledged property or to its current financial strength. (2) A term loan involves a *direct relationship* between borrower and lender. There is a formal loan agreement stipulating terms of repayment to which both parties agree. Such face to face negotiation is in contrast to the stock and bond markets, where the borrowing firm rately contacts the supplier of funds personally. (3) A term loan involves *repayment in periodic installments* beginning no more than one year after the loan is made. This arrangement signifies the lender's insistence that the borrower make regular provision for repayment.

Uses and Costs

Firms use term loans to acquire permanent assets, as a form of interim financing, and to repay other borrowings. Often the permanently added assets take the form of increases in circulating (and working) capital. As interim financing, a term loan will be used to finance early stages of market development for a new product; then, when the market matures, the treasurer will *fund* the loan, shifting into a longer financial source. Proceeds from term loans are used to pay off short-term bank loans and, on occasion, to retire a bond issue. The latter occurs when the bond issue matures, or when it carries a high interest rate that the company wants to escape.

Term loans usually command higher interest rates than short-term loans. One reason is that they run longer, and bankers need to be compensated for their resulting loss of liquidity. Also, a term-lender incurs larger costs of credit investigation and loan supervision, and he adds these to the borrower's cost. Another possible cost, though not explicit, is that a borrower may be required to provide security for his loan. The pledging of security impairs a company's further borrowing ability. A majority of term loans, however, do not require security. The typical secured loan is smaller than the unsecured loan because it is made to a smaller firm and probably involves greater risk of non-repayment.

Repayment

More often than not, term loans are repaid in equal monthly or quarterly installments over the life of the loan. The loan is *amortized,* meaning that some of its principal is repaid in each period. The final installment of principal is repaid with the last payment. Relatively few term loans involve a "balloon"—a final payment much larger than the previous payments. By avoiding a balloon, the bank forces the borrower to provide for repayment of the loan at regular intervals instead of relaxing until a large lump of money is due at maturity.

Suppose that a firm borrows $5,000 for three years at 8 per cent interest, repayable in three annual installments. We can use present value calculations to determine how much each payment will be. If the firm were charged no interest, each payment would be $5,000 ÷ 3 = $1,666. But we know that each installment must be greater than $1,666, because the firm is paying 8 per cent interest. Since the payments will form an annuity, their amount can be calculated through the method suggested in chapter 5. Using Table A–4, annuity to present worth, we have

$$A = (CF_{pw\ to\ a})_{i\ =\ .08,\ n\ =\ 3,}$$
$$= \frac{PW}{(CF_{a\ to\ pw})_{i\ =\ .08,\ n\ =\ 3.}}$$
$$= \frac{\$5,000}{2.577},$$
$$= \$1,940.$$

The firm will make three equal payments of $1,940. Each payment will pay interest and principal as follows:

Year	Payment	Interest (.08)	Principal Amortized	Balance
1	$1,940	$400	$1,540	$3,460
2	1,940	277	1,663	1,797
3	1,940	143	1,797	–0–

In the first year, the firm pays $1,940; $400 is interest, and the rest ($1,540) amortizes principal. After reducing the principal, the balance remaining is $3,460, the amount which determines how much interest the firm will pay in the second year. Notice that the firm will repay a total of $5,820 for the $5,000 borrowed.

Because a term loan runs for an extended time, the bank protects itself by placing restrictions in the loan agreement. For example, the banker may stipulate that the borrower's current ratio must not fall below some specified level over the life of the loan. In addition, the bank may (1) restrict the borrowing firm's right to pay dividends, (2) make management changes within the firm contingent upon bank consent, and (3) subject future acquisition of fixed assets to prior bank approval (in order to keep funds from being sunk into fixed investments). These additional restrictions originate in bargaining between borrower and lender. As you might imagine, they are usually more pronounced in term loans to small firms than to large firms.

Conditional Sales Contract

A conditional sales contract is one in which the seller of an asset also finances it. The buyer does not receive title to the asset until the loan is completely paid off. The purchaser makes a down payment, then makes periodic payments of principal and interest to the seller. Contracts are of moderate duration, typically three years and rarely more than five. A substantial down payment, often one-third the contract price, gives the buyer a substantial stake and discourages him from defaulting. Both asset and obligation will show up on the purchaser's balance sheet, and if the purchaser defaults on a payment, the seller-lender can easily repossess the asset. Conditional sales contracts are widely used by manufacturers of machinery, dental and medical equipment, and certain kinds of vehicles. The seller has access to major sources of financing and so is able to finance his customers. This actually puts him in two businesses: manufacturing and equipment-financing.

Leasing

Leasing involves the use of an asset without assuming, or intending to assume, ownership. A firm acquiring the asset, called the *lessee,* obligates itself to pay the owner of the asset, called the *lessor,* a periodic money rental for its use.

Types of Leases

There are two major types of leases. A *financial lease* is one that does not provide for any maintenance services by the lessor and is not cancellable. *Sale and lease-back* is a special type of financial lease. Here, a firm sells an asset to a second company which, in turn, leases the asset back to the first firm. The lessee obtains cash from the sale of the asset and still maintains its use. Sale and lease-back is popular with companies wishing to raise cash on fully depreciated buildings which they still intend to occupy. Of course, the seller must then pay the lessor a rental, but rentals are tax-deductible expenses, and meanwhile the seller has greatly improved the cash position of his firm.

A *service lease* includes both financing and maintenance services by the lessor. Frequently, this type of lease is not fully amortized, meaning that the lessor will not fully recover the asset's cost through lessee payments. The lessor hopes to recover the remaining value by selling or re-leasing the asset after the present lease expires. In addition, a service lease often includes a cancellation clause permitting the lessee to cancel the contract and to return the asset. Cancellations before a certain specified date usually incur a cash penalty.

Leasing vs. Buying

Leasing as an alternative to owning an asset offers five advantages over buying. The first three advantages are real, the last two, we shall see, more apparent than real.

1. *Buying absorbs cash* when the assets are acquired, but leasing does not. This privilege of conserving cash by leasing is an unquestionable advantage of leasing over buying. Current ratio and working capital remain higher for the lessee, so that by leasing a firm may improve both profitability and liquidity. It is no wonder that so many firms during the 1960s began to turn toward leasing and away from buying.

2. Another advantage in leasing is that it is an *off-balance sheet transaction;* neither the assets nor the liabilities acquired show up on the firm's balance sheet. Reference to a lease is often relegated to an obscure footnote.[1] What difference does this make? A firm that leases will appear to have a greater return on assets and a lower debt-equity ratio than a firm that purchases the asset (assuming, of course, that the second firm borrows to finance the asset). For example, suppose that two firms have exactly the same balance sheets, as depicted below. Then, they both decide to use a $1,000 asset to take advantage of an opportunity yielding 10 per cent. Here are the two balance sheets before expansion:

Before Expansion

Trixie, Inc.			Rancor, Inc.		
Assets		*Claims*	*Assets*		*Claims*
	Debt	$5,000		Debt	$5,000
	Equity	5,000		Equity	5,000
$10,000		$10,000	$10,000		$10,000

Rancor, Inc., borrows $1,000 from a commercial .bank, and Trixie, Inc., leases the assets. After these transactions, their balance sheets look like this:

After Expansion

Trixie, Inc.			Rancor, Inc.		
Assets		*Claims*	*Assets*		*Claims*
	Debt	$5,000		Debt	$6,000
	Equity	5,000		Equity	5,000
$10,000		$10,000	$11,000		$11,000

Trixie's statement of financial condition is unchanged. Rancor's debt-equity ratio has increased, and its return on assets would now be lower than Trixie's. Trixie appears more profitable than Rancor and would probably possess greater financial maneuverability—it might be able to tap more debt financing in the future than could Rancor. Because most individuals prefer a secure stream of returns to a less secure one, Trixie's lower debt ratio may encourage investors to apply a higher price-earnings multiple to Trixie's shares than to Rancor's. For this reason, leasing has sometimes been used by managements as a subterfuge to push up the price of their common stock.

---

[1] Indeed, the effectiveness with which a CPA firm "rigs" a client's statement is in some degree measurable by how inconspicuous it can make this footnote.

3. Leasing *substitutes a variable cost for a fixed production cost,* depreciation. The lease contract can be written for a short period, or in the form of a
service lease permitting the lessee to cancel the contract at his option. In this
way, when business activity declines and sales fall, the lessee can turn the equipment back to the lessor and make no more payments. The lessee's operating
costs decline with the sales revenue. Leasing, then, reduces the degree of operating
leverage in a firm, and so reduces business risk.[2]

4. In an economy of rapid *technological change,* leasing seems to have
a further advantage over buying. A firm can lease an asset and, when it becomes
obsolete, terminate the lease and acquire a newer asset. The lessor then bears
the cost of technological obsolescence. For example, a firm may lease a computer
installation, then cancel the lease when a next-generation computer becomes
available, thus gaining at the lessor's expense. Of course, this advantage exists
only if the lessor underestimates the pace of technological change. If the lessor
anticipates the introduction of the next computer generation correctly, he will factor
this cost into his payment schedule.[3]

5. It is often said that leasing is advantageous because *lease payments* are
fully deductible for tax purposes. This is true since they are a cost of doing business.
However, tax-deductibility of payments does not settle the lease-versus-buy question in favor of leasing. Two annual charges associated with purchase of an asset
are also tax-deductible: depreciation, and interest on borrowed money.

Basically, there is a common sense answer to the lease-versus-buy question.
In essence, leasing is a *financial service* whose main benefit is to preserve a
firm's liquidity and lessen its business risk. Every benefit has a cost, and these
benefits cost the businessman. Increase in demand for leased assets has caused
the cost of leasing to increase—lessors build in a higher return to themselves
in the payment schedule of the leased asset. Thus leasing, in the long run, with
all charges considered, almost invariably costs more than buying. Current earnings
are invariably lower for a firm leasing than one buying. However, a cash-short
firm, or one already too deeply in debt, or one wanting to minimize the risks
of doing business, may find this added cost much more bearable than further
cash outflows, a further rise in debt, or increased business risk.

To Remember

Term loan	Service lease
Installments	Financial lease
Amortization	Off-balance sheet transaction
Conditional sales contract	

---

[2]The relation between fixed production costs and business risk is discussed in chapter 17.

[3]In all likelihood the lessor will not underestimate the pace of technological change. In the
computer industry itself, the market is dominated by one firm which not only does most of the leasing,
but also sets the pace for technological change. It is in a superb position to know when a major
change will occur and can thus write its lease agreements accordingly.

Questions

1. Incense International borrows $10,000 from the Hibernia State Bank. The loan is for three years at 10 per cent interest.
   (a) How much must each equal repayment be?
   (b) Complete a table showing the amount of principal amortized and interest with each payment.
   (c) What is the total amount paid to Hibernia State Bank?

2. "Leasing has disguised the fact that profitability in our economy is declining. If the truth were known, profitability is probably 20 per cent below what looking at financial statements indicates." Comment on this observation.

3. Two firms have a balance sheet like this:

Assets	Claims
	$200 Debt
	300 Equity
$500	$500

   Both firms had earnings before interest and taxes of $100 last year. Komus borrows $100 and acquires an asset; Atom-Tek leases a similar asset. The asset has earning power the same as the average for existing assets. The interest rate is 5 per cent and taxes are 40 per cent. Lease expenses are $5.
   (a) What are earnings after taxes for both companies *before* acquiring the new asset? What are ROA and ROE?
   (b) What are earnings after taxes, ROA, and ROE for each firm *after* acquiring the new asset? (Ignore depreciation.)
   (c) What has happened to maneuverability of each firm?
   (d) Now suppose Komus finances its acquisition by selling new common. What becomes of ROA and ROE?

4. Your classmate in accounting says, "I see no difference between leasing and a conditional sales contract." In what way are they similar? In what way do they differ?

5. Ecological Enterprises and Quester, Inc., both have a balance sheet like this:

Assets	Claims
	$200 Debt
	800 Equity
$1,000	$1,000

   Earning power (EBIT/TA) was 10 per cent last year. Quester borrows $500 and acquires an asset; Ecological Enterprises leases a similar one. The earning power remains 10 per cent, interest is 6 per cent, taxes are 40 per cent, lease payments are $40. (Ignore depreciation.)
   (a) What are the D/E ratios after acquiring use of the asset?
   (b) What are earnings after taxes, ROA, ROE for each after acquisition?
   (c) Explain the difference in profitability for Ecological Enterprises and Quester.

23

Long-Term Financing: Corporate Stock

Common Stock: Measures of Worth

In thinking of corporate stock, one generally has in mind common stock. Common shareholders are a corporation's real owners. They are the last to participate in the earnings stream—receiving their return after employees, creditors, and the government—and last to receive anything if the corporation is forced into liquidation. Because of this low priority, common shareholders bear the greatest risk in a corporation's financial structure.

Common stock has several measures of worth: par value, book value, market value, intrinsic value, and liquidation value.

Par Value

Par value is the most clear-cut of the measures of common stock worth, since it is fixed on the firm's books. It is an arbitrary dollar amount selected by management for showing common stock on the balance sheet.[1] Companies usually select as low a par value as possible, because some states tax corporations doing business within their boundaries according to par value of their stock.[2]

Par value has significance for the common shareholder. If stock is sold below par when it is issued, creditors in a bankruptcy proceeding can hold whoever *then* owns the stock liable for the difference between par and the lower original selling price (the discount).

Par value is one component of shareholders' equity. The number of shares issued and outstanding multiplied by par value per share governs the dollar amount entered on the balance sheet for common stock. In the balance sheet a few paragraphs below, for example, Perkison Enterprises has outstanding 100,000 shares at a par value of $5 per share, so the amount in common stock is $500,000.

Book Value

Book value of common stock is the accounting net worth, or shareholders' equity, of a corporation. Since net worth equals total assets less total liabilities, book value represents the shareholders' net claim on total assets. Recall that shareholders' equity itself is comprised of three components: common stock, paid-in capital in excess of par, and retained earnings. The first two components, sometimes called *external equity*, represent the amount a firm receives when it first issues its stock. Perkison sold its entire 100,000 shares for $7.50 per share, a total of $750,000. Consequently, it has entered 100,000 shares times $5 par value = $500,000 under common stock and the remainder ($750,000 – $500,000 = $250,000) under paid-in capital in excess of par.

Retained earnings, sometimes called *internal equity*, comprise that part of a company's past profits not paid out in dividends. It should be unnecessary to point out that retained earnings are not a cash fund but simply a *claim* that common shareholders have on a corporation's assets, a claim resulting from management's decision to plow earnings back rather than to pay them out in dividends.

Book value per share is total book value divided by number of shares outstanding. It can be figured either by subtracting total liabilities and preferred stock from total assets, and dividing this difference by the number of common shares, or by taking the sum of the common stock, paid-in capital in excess of par, and retained earnings, and then dividing this sum by the number of common shares. For Perkison Enterprises, book value per share is $50.

Perkison Enterprises

Total assets:	$10,000,000	Current liabilities	$ 3,000,000
		Long-term debt	1,000,000
		Preferred stock	1,000,000
		Common stock (100,000 shares at par value of $5)	500,000
		Capital in excess of par	250,000
		Retained earnings	4,250,000
	$10,000,000		$ 10,000,000

---

[1] See chapter 15 for a discussion of par value.

[2] Stock can be "no-par," meaning that management has assigned no par value to its common. If that is the case, many states levy the tax on an assumed $100 par value.

Market Value

Market value is the price at which the stock sells. It reflects the value a seller and buyer place on the stock. For a sale to occur, buyer and seller must ordinarily hold different expectations for future market value: the seller must expect the price to be lower in the future, the buyer, higher. (Of course, a seller might be forced to sell for other reasons: distress, more profitable use of funds, and so on.) If both parties held similar expectations, no exchange would occur because the owner would not release his shares. If a corporation's stock is listed on an exchange, then the most recent sale gives the approximate market value. Most daily newspapers list the market price of stocks traded on the New York and American exchanges.

What is the relation between book value and market value? Some stocks sell above book value, others, below. To a great extent, the difference between the two values is this: book value measures the accountant's estimate of the original contribution by shareholders in the past, including purchase of new issues and retention of earnings, whereas market value reflects investors' assessment of future earning power. When a firm's shares are priced in the market below book value per share, the firm is worth more dead than alive.

Intrinsic Value

Intrinsic value is an estimate of a stock's real worth, based on its apparent earning power, without regard to present market price. Theoretically, an investor guesses what earnings will be over a succession of future years and then *capitalizes* them, i.e., discounts them back to the present at a rate reflecting his desired rate of return plus some risk premium.[3]

Because it is subjective, the intrinsic value set by a particular person may have little relation to any of the other values. But it does affect market value. When one's estimate of intrinsic value exceeds market value, he will buy the share (if he has the money) because the present value of the expected stream of future earnings exceeds the present cost of obtaining that stream. If market value exceeds intrinsic value, he will not buy the stock; indeed, he will sell it if he already owns it. The net result is that market value will be driven toward people's marginal guess about intrinsic value.

Liquidation Value

Liquidation value is the estimated amount shareholders would receive if all assets were liquidated and all liabilities paid. This value reflects a stock's worth upon dissolution of the corporation. Since assets rarely sell for their full book value, liquidation value is usually below book value. In Perkison Enterprises, if assets in liquidation brought 50 cents on the dollar, claimants would receive $5,000,000. That would be enough to satisfy only the claims of the creditors, leaving nothing for common shareholders. In this instance, liquidation value is zero.

---

[3]We encountered this approach in discussing cost of equity, in chapter 20. Actually, investors short-circuit this academically popular valuation process by taking present earnings and applying to them a price-earnings multiple that incorporates their feelings about future growth, risk, and so forth.

Rights of a Common Shareholder

Corporations have legal obligations to their owners, the shareholders. Unlike proprietorships and partnerships, ownership and management in corporations are often separated. Large corporations employ professional managers who use the funds of thousands of stockholders. A system of checks and balances has developed over the years to prevent abuses. This system concerns the rights of common shareholders—the right to share in earnings, to vote for directors, to maintain their ownership position, and other rights discussed below.

Right to Participate

The most important right of shareholders is their right to participate in the stream of earnings which is left after all expenses. This participation comes in two ways: dividend payments and the reinvestment of earnings. While stockholders individually have little recourse to force directors to declare dividends out of earnings, once dividends are declared, they become a liability and must be paid.

Voting Right

Another important right of shareholders is the voting right. Each share a stockholder owns entitles him to one vote in corporate elections. Elections are held to elect directors and to vote on mergers, charter amendments, and other issues. However, voting control over management is often an empty formality. In large companies, the stock is spread among so many shareholders that individual shareholders—sometimes even a large number of shareholders—have virtually no voice in policy decisions. A large group of shareholders must unite in order to raise decisive voting powers.

Management or anyone else can solicit the right to vote in a shareholder's place in any corporate election. The document in which the shareholder delegates his voting right to another is called a *proxy*. A group wanting to force management or directors to change a policy may seek the proxies of shareholders. A proxy voter votes for the shareholder but votes his own desires unless the shareholder directs that he vote a particular way.

Traditionally, shareholders have given management their proxies when they are satisfied with company performance. If they have been dissatisfied, they have sold their stock. However, in recent years, a new militancy has arisen among stockholders seeking to change management through proxy fights. An independent group, discouraged by current management performance, might solicit proxies to replace the incumbents. Although a proxy fight may be unsuccessful in the sense that the dissidents cannot muster enough votes to win, the fight itself may prompt management to change its policy. Some recent proxy battles between corporation managements and social groups seeking greater ecological concern from firms are an example of the residual success of a proxy fight. Though the outsiders failed to achieve their direct objectives, they often succeeded in influencing management decisions.[1]

To maintain control, controlling stockholders have often established different *classes* of common stock with different voting rights. Often these classes are labeled

---

[1]Financial implications of pollution control are examined in some detail in chapter 30.

A and B, with one group entitled to vote and the other excluded from voting or restricted to voting on a minority of directors. Such devices are often employed when new capital is needed but current owners wish to preserve control.

Pre-emptive Right

Another means by which existing shareholders maintain control is through pre-emptive rights. The law has usually obliged corporations to offer existing shareholders the opportunity to preserve their pro rata, or percentage, ownership of the firm. They can do so by exercising their pre-emptive right, which allows them to buy new stock in proportion to their current holdings. This pre-emptive right also applies to securities convertible into common stock. Suppose that Global Corporation has one million shares of stock outstanding and Sidney Parsons owns 100,000 shares, 10 per cent of the total shares. If Global decides to sell an additional 10,000 shares, then Parson's pre-emptive right entitles him to buy 10 per cent (1,000 shares) of the new issue before it is offered publicly.

When pre-emptive rights exist, sale of a new stock issue is made through a special device called a _rights offering_. Each existing share of stock receives one right to maintain its pro rata share of ownership in the firm. These rights are options to buy the new stock at a specified price. A certain number of rights is needed to buy a new share and this number is determined by dividing the number of shares outstanding by the number of new shares to be issued.

Suppose the Falcon Company wishes to raise $10,000 by selling additional common stock through a rights offering. The company decides to offer this new stock for $100 per share, called the _subscription price._ One hundred new shares must be issued, determined in the following way:

$$\text{Total new shares} = \frac{\text{Capital required}}{\text{Price of stock}} = \frac{\$10,000}{\$100} = 100 \text{ shares.}$$

Falcon already has 1,000 shares outstanding at a market value of $150 per share. Consequently, the number of old shares, or rights, needed to buy one new share of stock is

$$\frac{\text{Old shares}}{\text{New shares}} = \frac{1,000}{100} = 10.$$

In other words, since there are 1,000 rights and 100 new shares to be issued, ten rights (old shares) are needed to buy one new share. Alternatively, since there are 1,000 old shares outstanding and 100 new ones to be issued, ten old shares will command one new share.

Valuing a Right

If a firm sells its stockholders new stock for less than the market value of the existing stock, then the privilege of buying this stock has a value. The market value of Falcon's existing stock is $150 times 1,000 shares, or $150,000 for all shares. The new subscription adds 100 shares at $100, bringing the average market value for Falcon stock to $160,000 for the 1,100 shares. Theoretically, the average market value of each share after the new issue will be $145.45.[5] With ten rights and $100, a share that is worth $145.45 may be purchased. The ten rights are worth this difference in value, $45.45; each right is worth $4.545. Here are the calculations:

Aggregate values:
Before offering	1,000 shares @ $150 =	$150,000	
New offering	100 shares @ $100 =	10,000	
After offering	1,100 shares	= $160,000	

To buy:

$$\$100 + 10R = \$145.45$$
$$10R = \$145.45 - \$100 = \$45.45$$
$$1R = \$\ 45.45/10 \quad = \$\ 4.545.$$

The formula below shortcuts the reasoning process and calculates, directly, the value of a right:[6]

$$R = \frac{M - S}{n + 1},$$

(Eq. 23–1)

where

R = value of one right,
M = market price of the stock selling with rights included,
S = subscription price, and
n = number of rights needed to buy 1 share of new stock.

For Falcon Company, the calculation for the value of a right is

$$R = \frac{\$150 - \$100}{10 + 1} = \frac{\$50}{11} = \$4.545.$$

If a shareholder does not wish to maintain his pro rata share in the firm, he can sell his rights. If he owns ten shares of stock, he has ten rights that he can sell for $45.45. The person buying the rights would put $100 in cash with the ten rights to buy one share of stock.

Did the holder of rights get something for nothing? At first blush, it might seem so, because he appears to have paid $145.45 for a $150 share. However, recall that *after* the flotation there are more shares outstanding than before, and theoretically, the resulting market price is $145.45 per share. In principle, an individual neither gains nor loses whether he exercises his rights or sells them. Only when he lets them expire does he lose. In our example, had our shareholder

---

[5]If the stockholders believed the proceeds from the flotation would be invested more profitably than other funds, then the price might reflect these feelings and remain at $150 per share or even increase.

[6]This formula gives the right's value when the old stock is selling "rights on." After the rights come out of it and the shares are issued, the market price will fall by the value of one right. The formula for the new market price after the flotation and without the right is $M_e = M_o - R$, where M_e is market price *ex rights,* or rights off, M_o is market price *cum rights,* or with rights, and R is the value of one right. The value of the right remains the same and is now equal to

$$R = \frac{M_e - S}{n} = \frac{\$145.55 - \$100}{10} = \$4.55.$$

with ten existing shares failed to exercise or to sell his rights, his wealth would have fallen as follows:

Before issue:	10 shares @ $150.00	= $1,500.00
After issue:	10 shares @ $145.45	= $1,454.50
	Loss	$45.50

Most states no longer require that shareholders be granted pre-emptive rights, so companies are removing this privilege from their charters through a ratifying vote of shareholders. Absence of this right gives management greater flexibility in marketing new issues and in negotiating acquisitions where payment in common stock is involved. You can imagine the problems involved if, every time a firm wanted to acquire another company by issuing new shares of common stock, it also had to make a rights offering.

Other Rights

Other rights granted stockholders include the right to be issued a certificate of ownership (stock certificate), to receive information on company operations through annual reports, to attend meetings of stockholders, and to transfer ownership. The right to transfer unwanted stock is especially important to the stockholder because transfer is an effective way to liquidate his investment.

New Flotations

As corporations expand, they need new equity. Creditors demand an equity base before they will lend money; the more ample the ownership stake in an enterprise is, the more readily creditors will furnish funds. Thus equity forms the foundation for all financial expansion.

Apportioning Funds

Suggested in Figure 20–1 (chapter 20) was the need for management to maintain an optimum debt-equity ratio. Maintaining such a ratio minimizes the firm's cost of capital. Thus, a financial manager must forecast his company's need for funds and determine how it should be apportioned between debt and equity. If a company is able to finance its equity needs entirely from retained earnings and still pay enough dividends to please its stockholders, then no external equity will be needed. However, if equity needs exceed projected retained earnings, the firm must sell additional stock.

Consider the example shown in Table 23-1. Superior Company anticipates an increase in its sales from $200,000 this year to $250,000 next year, a 25 per cent increase. Its assets now total $100,000. According to the per cent of sales forecasting method, if sales grow by 25 per cent, then assets must also grow by 25 per cent, to $125,000. Superior has found its optimal debt-equity ratio to be .50. Assets and financial needs will expand 25 per cent, or $25,000. To maintain the target debt-equity ratio, Superior Company's treasurer should finance $8,333 of the asset expansion from debt and $16,667 from equity. Table 23–1 shows the comparative balance sheets before and after expansion.

If Superior Company earns 3 per cent after taxes on sales, then profit after taxes will be .03 times $250,000 = $7,500. Paying no dividend, the treasurer must raise $16,667 – $7,500 = $9,167 from external equity. In other words, he must sell $9,167 in new common stock.[7]

Table 23–1. Superior Company Abbreviated Balance Sheet

Before Expansion			
Assets	$100,000	Debt	$ 33,333	33%
		Equity	66,667	67%
	$100,000		$100,000	100%
After Expansion			
Assets	$125,000	Debt	$ 41,666	33%
		Equity	83,334	67%
	$125,000		$125,000	100%

Timing

Once management decides to float a new issue of common, it must pick the best time to do so. Unfortunately, financial managers often follow the principle of least resistance in financing expansion and in timing the acquisition of external finance. Convenience dominates foresight. Treasurers raise funds, as long as possible, from commercial banks, because that is the easiest way; they ignore both the use to which funds will be put and the dangers of a loan renewal crisis; they fail to consider future conditions in the equity markets. As a result, they undertake sale of new equity only after they have been forced to because finance from other sources has become unavailable. With no concern for timing their firm's entry into the equity market, they are often obliged to obtain funds at the worst possible time, when the stock market is low or declining.

Falcon Company's management knows that it needs $10,000 in external equity in the coming year. Longer-range forecasts can help estimate equity needs for the next several years. Armed with this knowledge, Falcon Company's treasurer can plan to enter the equity market at a favorable time, selling new common stock when prices are high, expectations bouyant, and the market outlook generally favorable.

How significant is timing? It determines how much dilution of earnings and control will occur. In the rights problem discussed above, Falcon needed $10,000. At a market price of $100 per share, it needed to sell 100 new shares, but at a price of $125, it would need to sell only 80 new shares. Fewer shares can be absorbed more easily than can a large issue. Fewer shares also involve less dilution of earnings: future earnings will be spread over a smaller number of shares and future earnings per share will be greater. Less dilution may also keep the

---

[7]The amount of external equity needed is also affected by dividend policy, an influence discussed in chapter 24.

stock's price-earnings multiple higher. Finally, selling fewer shares means that present owners run less risk of losing voting control in the firm.

Preferred Stock

Preferred stock, like common stock, represents ownership in a corporation. The difference between these forms lies in the priority of their respective claims on the firm's earning stream and its assets. Preferred stock receives a stated dividend which must be paid ahead of any common dividends. In the event of liquidation, preferred shareholders recoup their investment at par before any funds can be allotted to common shareholders. Preferred owners usually have no voting rights unless the firm fails to pay them dividends for some interval. The preferred dividend is often *cumulative,* meaning that if it is missed for one or more periods, the arrearage must be paid, along with the current dividend, before any dividend can be declared on the common.

Debt or Equity?

Preferred has both debt and equity characteristics. Like interest on straight debt, the preferred dividend is a fixed charge. A firm obligates itself to pay *x* per cent annually on the par value of its preferred. However, missing a preferred dividend is not penalized to the extent that missing an interest payment is. Missed preferred dividends may accumulate, but they do not constitute default on a debt. By contrast, a missed interest payment may lead to bankruptcy.

Unlike straight debt, preferred has no maturity date. In this respect, preferred is a perpetuity, a security paying a fixed amount per year indefinitely. Unlike interest, preferred dividends are *not* tax deductible to the paying corporation. For this reason, use of preferred has declined relative to use of debt.

Like common stock, preferred receives a non-tax-deductible dividend. But because of its prior claim on both earnings and assets, preferred has less risk for investors. Consequently, an investor can expect a lower return on preferred than on common.

Should we treat preferred as debt or equity? Legally, and in an accounting sense, preferred is equity. Most managers, however, consider preferred as debt because of its fixed charge and leverage effect on common share earnings. Holders of common shares also think of preferred as debt, because of its superior claim, but bondholders consider it as equity because it supplies assets against their claims in case of liquidation. Generally, we believe it is more accurate to think of preferred as most corporation managers do, as debt.

Straight Debt vs. Preferred

We have seen, in Eq. 20–2, that deductibility of bond interest reduces the cost of debt to a corporation. Thus it can be argued that bonds are a cheaper source of capital than preferred stock, on which (with a 50 per cent tax rate) a company must earn $2 in taxable earnings for each $1 of dividend payments. This argument may be overturned, however, if the bond issue includes a sinking fund to retire the debt. For a twenty-year sinking fund debenture, 5 per cent of the issue would be retired annually, so that 95 per cent of the issue would be retired before maturity. Adding the sinking fund payment to the yearly interest payments of debt will sometimes result in a larger cash outflow than would preferred dividends, even when the tax implications are considered.

Less cash in the firm may impair future earnings. If the firm earns 10 per cent on assets, every $1 less in assets means 10 cents less in earnings. Thus, where bond investors would require sinking funds or other highly burdensome restrictions, management and shareholders alike may prefer to use preferred stock.[8]

To Remember

Par value	Subscription price
Book value	Timing
Intrinsic value	Apportioning funds
Market value	Preferred stock
Pre-emptive right	Straight debt vs. preferred

Questions

1. Sometimes, in referring to a stock that is selling below its book value per share, an analyst will say, "The firm is worth more dead than alive." Explain this statement.

2. Wadsworth Corporation has the following balance sheet:

Assets	Claims	
	Current liabilities	$ 2,000
	Bonds	4,000
	Preferred	1,000
	Shareholders' equity	
	Common stock (500	
	shares @ $2)	1,000
	Paid-in capital in	
	excess of par	500
	Retained earnings	1,500
$10,000		$10,000

(a) Calculate book value and par value per share.
(b) Wadsworth's common sells for four times book value. What is the market price? Explain the difference between market and book values.
(c) Calculate liquidation value if assets can be sold for (1) $8,000; (2) $7,000; (3) $3,000.
(d) How much external equity has Wadsworth raised? How much internal equity?
(e) An analyst's estimate of the intrinsic value of Wadsworth common is $140. Will he bid for any stock? What will subsequently happen to the relation between market and intrinsic values?

[8]For further discussion of the merits of preferred, see Gordon Donaldson, "In Defense of Preferred Stock," *Harvard Business Review* 40 (July–August 1962): 123–36.

3 The corporation itself bears the expense of proxy solicitation by management. Comment on the equity of this arrangement and its implications for success of those challenging management.

4 Economo, Inc., needs to raise $20,000 in external equity. Management decides on a subscription price of $8, and the market price of each of the 5,000 shares outstanding is $11.

(a) How many new shares will be issued?

(b) How many rights are required to buy one new share?

(c) What is the value of one right? Explain your answer verbally.

(d) What is the price of the stock *ex rights* (without rights) when the stock is finally issued? (Hint: Calculate the average price after the issue.)

(e) If no rights are exercised or sold and the issue is subsequently sold to the public at $10, what is the dollar decline of wealth suffered by existing shareholders?

5 Defend this statement: "Preferred stock is more like debt than like equity."

6 Mantissa Enterprises must decide between issuing preferred or bonds to raise $100,000. The final decision hinges on these facts: Debt will carry a 5 per cent coupon rate, have a ten-year maturity, and require a sinking fund of $10,000 per year. Preferred will carry a 7 per cent rate. The corporate tax rate is 40 per cent.

(a) Do you recommend that Mantissa sell bonds or preferred?

(b) If the tax rate were 60 per cent, which would you recommend?

24

Internal Financing and Dividend Policy

Internal Financing — Retained Earnings — Shareholders' Stake in Earnings — Dividend Determinants — *Risk Attitude* — *Personal Taxes* — *Reinvestment Opportunities* — *Liquidity* — **Dividend Policy** — *Cash Dividend* — *Stock Dividend* — *Stock Split* — *Other Dividends*

Internal Financing

By internal financing, we mean sources of funds available to the financial manager from year to year without raising them outside the company. For the short run, several internal sources of funds exist, as a review of the ''Sources and Uses of Funds'' statement in chapter 15 will show. These sources include depreciation (and other capital consumption allowances), funds from sale of fixed assets or investments,[1] and funds provided by retained earnings.

The first two of these sources represent funds only in a restricted sense. Consider depreciation flows first. Given a stable or rising sales level, depreciation recoveries cannot contribute in the long run to a firm's growth: they are destined eventually to replace the company's fixed assets.

---

[1] In the very short run, a firm can raise *cash* by running down its inventories and receivables, or by pledging or selling them, as we saw in chapter 21. We are using the word ''funds'' here in its accustomed sense of working (or net working) capital. For some applications, however, funds can be defined as cash with ''sources and uses'' tables drawn up on that basis.

This does not mean that depreciation dollars generated by a building, for example, cannot be used this year to buy a new machine—they can and will be. A look back at Table 20-1, in chapter 20, shows that in year-to-year financial planning, depreciation constitutes the largest single source of internal finance for business enterprise. In the short run, depreciation is the most flexible source of discretionary spending money at the financial manager's disposal. However, depreciation is an *encumbered source* of internal financing. Suppose that a series of new machine investments is financed by depreciation flows from a building. Eventually, the building itself will need replacement. Unless some provision has been made to generate the necessary funds, the company will encounter financial trouble.

Sales of investments or fixed assets—the second internal source of funds—are relatively infrequent and certainly not reliable as regular sources of funds, though a company with a large, liquid investment portfolio is in an enviably flexible position.

The remaining source of internal finance, retained earnings, is of major importance. From year to year, as Table 20-1 shows, it stands second only to depreciation in volume of funds provided. Furthermore, except in eras of rapid inflation (when earnings must be retained to supplement deficient depreciation allowances),[2] retained earnings usually represent an unencumbered source of funds, available to finance the firm's expansion or improvement.

The rest of this chapter will take a close look at retained earnings and—the other side of the coin—dividend policy. In the *retention versus dividends* decision, the pivotal principle is this: the ultimate goal is to maximize the long-run, sustainable price of a company's common stock. This is not only in the best interests of shareholders, it also keeps them happy with management: such shareholders rarely object to managerial discretion in bestowing large raises and bonuses.

Retained Earnings

The wide reliance of business managements on retained earnings for expansion is most plausibly explained by their ready availability. Retained earnings accumulate in the firm when earnings are not paid out in dividends. If earnings after taxes are not paid to shareholders, their retention is reflected in an increase in shareholders' equity on the *sources* side of the balance sheet, and in assets on the *uses* side.

Recall that retained earnings are not cash. They are simply a *claim* on a company's total assets, not matched by cash or any other particular asset. A firm can have large retained earnings (reflecting past profitability) but no cash (indicating present illiquidity).

Shareholders' Stake in Earnings

All earnings belong to a firm's common shareholders. Whether earnings should be paid out in dividends or retained to finance additional assets depends on which course will most benefit the majority of stockholders.

If earnings are paid out in cash dividends, shareholders can (after paying

---

[2]To review this point, see chapter 15.

income tax, each at his own rate) immediately enjoy them. They can spend the money to meet basic living costs (as retired people often must do), use it to buy luxuries they could not otherwise afford, or reinvest the dividend money in other ventures, thereby diversifying their money-making opportunities.

On the other hand, stockholders may benefit from having the company retain all, or a large part, of its earnings. This will be true if (1) the average stockholder does not need dividend income to live on, or (2) the company can earn a high return on reinvested earnings. If stockholders save their dividends, they will look for the most profitable way to reinvest them. But if their own company can outearn most alternative investments, they would do better to forego the dividends.

Stockholders' income tax considerations also frequently strengthen the case for a company's retaining its earnings. Dividends are subject to personal income tax at each stockholder's marginal rate. Out of each dollar of cash dividends one receives, only 50 to 70 cents may be available, after taxes, for reinvestment. By contrast, if the company does not distribute its earnings, but reinvests them directly in additional earning assets, the stockholder will have 100 cents out of each dollar working for him.

If a company that retains its earnings continues to earn a high return on equity, earnings per common share will rise rapidly without recourse to external equity sources. As earnings per share increase, so—across time—will the price per common share. Thus the income which stockholders forego in rejecting dividends will be more than compensated by growth in the market price of their shares. And, best of all, if they finally sell their shares, the increase in price will be subject only to the relatively low tax rate on capital gains, typically half the ordinary income tax rate that applies to dividends.[3]

For these reasons, retained earnings can be thought of as dividends waiting in the wings, to be paid in the future. However, stockholders live in the present, and not in the future. They may not be around long enough to receive earnings in the form of distant dividends. Most stock-value studies suggest that the average shareholder tends to have some preference for present dividends over future ones. Hence, most managements pay some dividends if they can. How much the dividend will be and how often it is increased depend, in final analysis, not only on the firm's earnings growth but also on management's "feel" for what the stockholders want. Dividend policy, like most other business decisions, is a compromise among contending influences. Management may prefer a high earnings-retention rate to accelerate the firm's growth, whereas stockholders may desire a year-to-year rise in their dividends. Actual policy must bring these conflicting wishes into amicable and stable balance.

Dividend Determinants

Whether shareholders prefer dividends or retained earnings heavily influences the firm's dividend decisions. In addition to "time" and taxes, mentioned in the preceding paragraphs, three other factors strongly affect dividend policy: the risk attitude of shareholders, reinvestment opportunities open to the firm, and the firm's liquidity.

---

[3]See the discussion of capital-gains taxes in chapter 14. Also, you may want to look again at Eq. 20–4 (chapter 20), where we first introduced dividend and capital gain returns.

Risk Attitude

A shareholder's attitude toward risk affects his preference either for taking his money now or at some future date. Future receipts are less certain than present ones because the likelihood of unforeseen misfortunes increases with time. If the shareholder is a risk averter, one who wishes to avoid risk, he will prefer to have his money now. A firm owned by shareholders who are avowed risk averters must emphasize dividends over earnings retention. Conversely, a firm whose shareholders consist principally of risk seekers, individuals who accept risk in the hope of larger pay-offs, would do well to emphasize retention. Its shareholders would receive net satisfaction from deferring dividend receipts if the chance was good that the dividends would be larger in the future.

Reinvestment Opportunities

The most important single influence on dividend policy is management's ability to use retained earnings profitably. So long as investments open to a company will yield a return greater than the investor could obtain by investing elsewhere, management ideally should retain the earnings.

For example, assume investments are available that yield the returns on equity depicted in Table 24–1. If shareholders can earn 14 per cent on some other investment, management should *not* accept the $25,000 project (E) because it yields only a 10 per cent return. If earnings after taxes are $200,000, the firm should—in the absence of other considerations—pay a $25,000 dividend and keep the other $175,000 to invest in the projects that yield shareholders a higher return than the 14 per cent they could obtain elsewhere.[4] Seen in this light, dividend payments would be a *residual* decision: management would first gauge the profitable internal uses of earnings, retain the necessary funds, and pay out the remainder to shareholders.

Table 24–1. Return from
Reinvested Earnings

Project	Investment	Return
A	$ 75,000	21%
B	80,000	20%
C	12,000	17%
D	8,000	15%
E	25,000	10%
	$200,000	

---

[4] If taxpayers are in the neighborhood of a 50 per cent ordinary income bracket, then even the 10 per cent project should be adopted. Why? The net amount they could invest would be reduced by one-half, making the after-tax return equal to .14(1 – .50) = .07. The 10 per cent they can get on reinvested earnings is obviously better.

To pay out too much to shareholders would not be in their best interest because it would call for selling additional stock to pay dividends. Suppose that the alternative return available to shareholders is 7 per cent; then all projects in Table 24–1 are acceptable. No dividend should be paid. But what if management pays a $25,000 dividend? Then it must turn around and sell $25,000 of common stock to exploit Project E.[5] In effect, the company has sold $25,000 worth of stock to pay shareholders a $25,000 dividend—and shareholders are worse off. Income taxes siphon off part of the $25,000 they receive. If their money had been left in the company, they would reap benefits from the full $25,000. By failing to observe the relation between the firm's internal return and the return available to shareholders from other investments, management has done its employers a disservice.

Liquidity

Paying a dividend depends not only on management and stockholder desires, but also on a firm's ability to pay. Although cash dividends are paid *out of* earnings, they are usually paid *with* cash. Thus only a firm with sufficient liquidity can pay a dividend.

In recent years the availability of cash for dividends has been curtailed by two influences. First, stop-and-go monetary policy has put firms through alternating spells of easy and tight money: money from financial markets has been readily available for a time and then has become almost impossible to acquire. Firms have had to store liquidity to be able to finance themselves during tight money interludes. Second, inflation has impaired companies' liquidity, restricting their dividend-paying ability. Price-level increases have made replacement of both fixed assets and circulating capital more costly. Firms planning to replace assets must make provision for doing so by retaining more earnings than previously. They must also accumulate enough *cash* to pay for the assets.

Dividend Policy

The usual notion of a dividend is that it is paid in cash, but dividends exist in other forms as well. The major ones are cash and stock, but these can be supplemented with stock splits and distributions of other assets. By expanding its dividend policy to include these other forms of dividends, management can more effectively achieve its objective of maximizing the sustainable market price of the firm's stock.

Cash Dividend

Part of the shareholders' claim consists of retained earnings, and these are legally available in their entirety for dividend payments. (Many state laws prohibit dividends that would reduce the common stock account, or paid-in capital in excess of par account.) However, as already noted, sufficient cash must also be available.

---

[5]This assumes that management insists on raising the amount from equity sources. It must do so, let us say, in order to maintain an optimum capital structure.

Suppose that management decides to pay a $100,000 dividend in cash. The effect on the company's balance sheet is illustrated below.

Before Dividend

Assets		Claims	
Cash	$500,000	Shareholders' equity:	
		Common stock (10,000 shares outstanding at $10 par)	$100,000
		Paid-in capital in excess of par	50,000
		Retained earnings	350,000
	$500,000		$500,000

After Cash Dividend

Assets		Claims	
Cash	$400,000	Shareholders' equity:	
		Common stock (10,000 shares outstanding at $10 par)	$100,000
		Paid-in capital in excess of par	50,000
		Retained earnings	250,000
	$400,000		$400,000

The payment reduces both cash and retained earnings by $100,000. If the company had distributed any other kind of asset as a dividend, then *that asset* and retained earnings would have shown similar declines.

Stock Dividend

A stock dividend is simply a means of redistributing the amounts in the shareholders' equity section of the balance sheet. For that reason, it is sometimes called a *recapitalization* (or permanent capitalization) *of earnings*. The asset side of the balance sheet is unaffected, retained earnings are reduced, and both common stock and paid-in capital in excess of par are increased.

Suppose the firm represented by the balance sheet above chose to pay a 10 per cent stock dividend rather than a cash dividend. Assume that its stock is selling on the market for $25 per share. The balance sheet after the transaction would appear as below. A 10 per cent stock dividend means that management will distribute .10 times 10,000, or 1,000 new shares: one additional share to each stockholder for every 10 formerly held.

Retained earnings will be lowered by 1,000 shares times the market price of $25, or $25,000. How much will be credited to common stock? Since par value is $10 per share, $10,000 will be allocated to the common stock component ($10 par times 1,000 shares). That leaves $15,000 ($25,000 dividend less $10,000 to common) that must be allocated to paid-in capital in excess of par.

Why declare a stock dividend? By so doing, management may have the best of all possible worlds: it can make the shareholders feel they are getting something of value, yet keeps funds in the firm which management can use as it sees fit. But notice that the shareholders actually receive nothing they did not have before. Book value per share (shareholders' equity divided by number of shares outstanding) is approximately 10 per cent less after the dividend than it was before ($45.45 versus $50), but each stockholder owns 10 per cent more shares. However, many people *believe* a stock dividend has value. Thus management can satisfy both those shareholders wanting dividends and those wanting the capital gains that come from plowing back earnings. Management keeps the funds in the company and invests them.

After Stock Dividend

Assets		Claims	
Cash	$500,000	Shareholders' equity:	
		Common stock (11,000 shares outstanding at $10 par)	$110,000
		Paid-in capital in excess of par	65,000
		Retained earnings	325,000
	$500,000		$500,000

Because there are more shares outstanding after the stock dividend, the market price per share declines.

The total market value of the firm's shares before the dividend was $25 per share times 10,000 shares = $250,000. Since shareholders were given nothing they did not have before, the total value of their claim theoretically does not increase. Hence, the new market price of their shares would be $250,000 divided by the 11,000 shares now outstanding, or $22.72.

Occasionally, a stock dividend may be declared in order to lower the stock price into a more active trading range. Since more people will buy a low-priced stock, the resulting increase in demand may make the stock sell higher in relation to book value. In this way, a stock dividend *may* increase the wealth of existing shareholders, even though the dividend simply means that the same pie is cut into a larger number of smaller pieces. In the example above, the price may decline only to $23.50, rather than to the theoretical figure of $22.72, as demand for the stock rises.

Stock Split

Another way management can lower the price of its stock, and hence increase trading activity, is to declare a stock split. In a stock split, no total dollar amount on either side of the balance sheet is affected. Only the two figures within the common stock entry are changed: number of shares and par value. Suppose our firm declares a two-for-one stock split. Here, management is in effect calling in all outstanding stock and reissuing twice as many shares.[6] The balance sheet would appear as below. After the split there are 20,000 shares outstanding.

Stock Split

Assets		Claims	
Cash	$500,000	Shareholders' equity	
		Common stock (20,000 shares outstanding at $5 par)	$100,000
		Paid-in capital in excess of par	50,000
		Retained earnings	350,000
	$500,000		$500,000

Since the total dollar amount in the common stock component is unchanged, par value must be halved (on a three-for one split, par would fall to one-third, on a four-for-one split, to one-fourth, and so on).

A stock split would probably increase trading activity in the stock. That could produce a windfall gain for existing shareholders, in the same way a stock dividend does. It could also help the firm sell new issues of its common stock more easily. A more active resale market enhances the appeal of new shares.

Other Dividends

In addition to cash and stock, management may declare other types of dividends. Any asset may be distributed so long as the distribution does not exceed the amount in retained earnings. The distribution of other assets can be in the form of stocks owned by the firm (called a "spin-off"), or products the firm produces. For example, liquor was a favorite dividend of liquor companies, and their shareholders, at the end of World War II. Such distributions are infrequent, however, compared with cash and stock dividends.

To Remember

Encumbered source	Stock split
Retained earnings and cash	Stock dividend
Risk attitude and dividends	Spin-off
Residual dividend policy	

Questions

1. You call your stockbroker about the possible dividend Exline Amalgamated will pay. He tells you, "Don't worry about their cash position, they have plenty of retained earnings available for dividends." What would you want to tell him?

---

[6]A two-for-one stock split is similar to a 100 per cent stock dividend in its impact on market price and book value per share.

2   Several investment advisory services calculate cash flow per share and emphasize the price-cash flow multiple rather than the *P/E* multiple.

(a) Why would an advisory service do that?

(b) Do you agree with the assertion that cash flow is a better measure than earnings of the return flowing to a shareholder? Why? What happens in the long run to the firm's earning power if it pays dividends equal to cash flow?

3   Libbey, Inc., has projects available yielding these returns on the firm's earnings after taxes:

Project	Amount	ROE
A	$10,000	25%
B	10,000	20%
C	10,000	15%
D	10,000	10%

(a) Shareholders can earn 18 per cent in investment elsewhere. What payout rate should Libbey, Inc., have?

(b) Now suppose the shareholders are in the 20 per cent tax bracket. What payout rate should Libbey have? (Assume capital gains are not taxed.)

(c) Finally, assume that shareholders are in the 50 per cent tax bracket. Again omitting taxes on capital gains, what payout rate should Libbey have?

(d) What is the implication of questions (b) and (c) for the payout rate and the tax bracket of shareholders? Is it consistent with the chapter discussion?

4   Most firms pay a cash dividend and sell common stock at the same time.

(a) In what way does such a policy diminish shareholders' wealth?

(b) Defend this policy.

5   Curran, Inc., has an abbreviated balance sheet like this:

Assets		Claims	
Cash	$ 200	Shareholders' equity:	
Other	1,800	Common stock (100 shares	
		outstanding, $5 par)	$ 500
		Paid-in capital in	
		excess of par	1,000
		Retained earnings	500
	$2,000		$2,000

Curran's stock sells for $40 per share on the Exchange. Show the balance sheet after:

(a) A $1 per share cash dividend is declared and paid.

(b) A 10 per cent stock dividend is declared and paid.

(c) A four-for-one stock split occurs.

(d) A one-for-four reverse stock split occurs.

6   If the objective of financial management is to maximize the sustainable market price of the firm's common stock, how can you defend a stock split as sound financial policy?

25

Long-Term Financing: Bonds and Notes

Bond Usage — *Reasons for Use — Limitations on Use — Role of Trustees* — Bond Types — *Mortgage Bonds — Collateral Trust Bonds — Equipment Trust Certificates — Other Types — Debentures — Subordinated Debentures — Capital Notes* — Computing Interest Coverage — Bond Ratings — Bond Sweeteners — *Convertible Bonds — Market Price of Convertible Bonds — Bonds With Warrants — Convertibles vs. Bonds With Warrants — Convertible Preferred: A Note*

Bond Usage

A glance back at the sources of funds in Table 20–1 shows that bonds are an important source of long-term funds for business. Why? We have touched on some of the reasons while describing other sources of funds; now it is time to examine systematically the role of bonds in business finance.

Reasons for Use

There are five main reasons why companies use bonds in their financial structures.

1. The growth rate of a company's sales and assets may be so rapid that it cannot be supported entirely from retained earnings. To acquire additional assets, management must go outside the firm for finance, and bond financing is often prefera-

ble to short-term debt, common or preferred stock, or other modes of financing.[1]

2. An increase in financial leverage may lead to a desirable increase in ROE.[2] So long as leverage is favorable, management can use debt financing to increase the return accruing to the shareholders of the firm. Of course, greater financial leverage means greater risk, but so long as the expected return increases proportionately more than the risk premium shareholders apply, the share's value should increase. For example, expected earnings may now be $1 per share for infinity. Discounted at 10 per cent, the intrinsic value is $1/.10 = $10. If financial leverage raises the average return to shareholders 20 per cent to $1.20 and the discount rate 10 per cent to 11 per cent, the intrinsic value rises to $10.90.

3. Reduced fears of depression and long intervals of easy money have made businessmen less fearful of downturns in economic activity. Monetary and fiscal policies are biased in an expansionary direction. This expansionary bias is interpreted by businessmen to ensure that sales revenues will be high enough to meet interest expense and that leverage will be favorable. Hence, businessmen have turned increasingly to the use of debt, including bonds, rather than equity financing.

4. Interest expense on bonds is tax-deductible. Only one dollar before interest is needed to meet a dollar's worth of bond interest expense, versus two dollars to pay one dollar in preferred dividends or to provide one dollar of earnings on common. Recall Eq. 20–2, which suggests that the cost of debt (interest) is reduced by the firm's tax bracket. That means that if everything else is equal, the financial manager chooses to use bond financing rather than preferred or new common stock.

5. Finally, inflation has encouraged businessmen to use more long-term debt, since repayment is likely to be made in cheaper dollars. So long as lenders do not tack on a large price level premium to protect themselves from loss through inflation, borrowers gain at their expense.

The last two points, inflation and the tax-deductibility of interest, may reduce the burden of interest payments appreciably. A general formula for calculating the *real burden* of interest from its *nominal cost* is

$$i_R = i_N(1-t) - p, \qquad\qquad\qquad \text{(Eq. 25–1)}$$

where

      i_R = real interest rate,
      i_N = nominal (quoted) annual interest rate,
      t = corporation's tax bracket, and
      p = annual percentage increase in the price level.

For example, if the nominal rate on a firm's debt is 8 per cent, it is in the 50 per cent tax bracket, and inflation is 3 per cent per year, the real burden of interest is .08 (1 – .50) – .03 = 1 per cent.

---

[1]How rapid growth forces firms to rely on external financing is covered in chapter 30.

[2]Recall that changes in sales are multiplied into larger changes in earnings before interest and taxes through use of fixed costs in production. In turn, changes in earnings before interest and taxes are multiplied into larger changes in earnings before taxes through the use of interest bearing funds. See discussions of these relations in chapters 17 and 19.

Limitations on Use

There are four major limitations on the use of bonds for long-term financing. First, conservatism in management can restrict the desire for long-term debt. Some managers are inclined to follow religiously the maxim, "Neither a borrower nor a lender be." In principle, they prefer to owe no one, and in practice, as risk averters, they avoid any significant degree of debt. Second, inflation cuts two ways: it may encourage management to make long-term debt commitments, but it can also curtail the use of debt. If lenders are sufficiently farsighted, they will tack on a percentage adjustment equal to the rate of price level increase. If they overestimate the rate of inflation, they may add an exorbitant premium to the real rate. In such circumstances, management would shun debt. Third, creditors may make various non-interest demands to compensate for being repaid in cheaper, inflated dollars. One such demand creditors may make is for an equity kicker, or privilege, in the debt instrument—for example, a provision permitting the creditor to acquire some of a company's common stock at some future date. (Equity kickers are discussed later in this chapter when we turn our attention to convertibles and warrants.) Management may be unwilling to accept such a provision, and so avoid the use of debt by limiting the firm's growth to what can be financed out of internally generated funds, new common stock, and short-term borrowing.

Lastly, credit stringencies resulting from a tight monetary policy may force companies to restrict long-term debt. At times, debt capital is simply not available to weaker borrowers. At other times, funds are so scarce that lenders can insist on crippling restrictions: eliminating dividends over the life of the loan, approving changes in executive management, putting a bondholder's representative on the board of directors, and so on. For example, the following is appended in an obscure footnote to the Kearney-National, Inc., *Annual Report* for 1970:

> The loan agreement provides, among other things, for limitation on additional funded debt, requirements for the maintenance of working capital at the greater of $9,000,000 or 100% of consolidated senior funded debt, and certain restrictions with respect to the payment of dividends and the purchase or redemption of capital stock. Under the most restrictive of these agreements $337,170 of retained earnings was free of such restrictions at December 31, 1970.

Such demands by lenders raise the effective cost of borrowing, and so discourage the resort to debt.

Role of Trustees

The bond market, unlike the bank loan market, is impersonal, in the sense that lenders and borrowers rarely meet in person. Individuals in St. Paul, Spokane, Miami, and New Dime Box, Texas, may buy the bonds of a corporation in Philadelphia without ever contacting that firm's management or stockholders. To protect the widely dispersed creditors, a *trustee* is appointed. He must act at all times to protect the interest of bondholders.[3] The trustee, usually a bank officer, has three primary responsibilities. (1) He certifies the bond issue by making sure that it conforms with legal requirements. (2) He makes sure that the corporation fulfills all responsibilities set forth in the *indenture,* the legal document specifying all phases of the agreement between lender and borrower (property pledged, form

---

[3]This is his legal obligation under the Trust Indenture Act passed by Congress in 1939.

of bond, restrictions, and so on). (3) He takes suitable action in the bondholders' behalf if the corporation defaults on principal or interest, or violates any of the loan restrictions.

Bond Types

Several bond types exist, reflecting a variety of creditor and borrower positions and desires. The different types have evolved through bargaining and maneuvering in the new issues market, as businessmen and investment bankers have innovated in order to reconcile companies' needs with those of bond investors.

The most important classes of bonds are mortgage bonds, debentures, and collateral trust bonds. Of closely related character are equipment trust certificates and corporate notes.

Mortgage Bonds

A mortgage bond is backed by a pledge of fixed assets. Such a pledge is called a mortgage. If the borrower defaults on repayment of principal and/or payment of interest, the lender can claim the pledged property. To restrict a borrower from pledging the same asset for another loan, the lender may require that the issue be a *closed-end issue*. This means that no new claims can be issued against the pledged assets. The lender may also insist that any fixed assets acquired in the future be pledged as collateral for the loan. Such a requirement is called an *after-acquired property clause*.

To reassure lenders that the firm will be able to repay the debt, the borrower may be required to provide a sinking fund, a periodic payment of money into a fund for retirement of the bonds. Bonds are retired in three ways. First, sufficient funds may be accumulated by the trustee to cover retirement of the bonds when they mature. Second, the trustee-manager of the sinking fund may buy back bonds in the open market and then retire them. Or, if the bonds are redeemable (callable), particular bonds may be periodically selected by lot for call-in and retirement.

Where a sinking fund is provided, management can estimate through present value calculations how much must be invested each year to ensure the issue's retirement at maturity. Suppose, for example, that a firm will retire a $10,000 issue in ten years. Management wants to know what amount must be set aside each year in order to have $10,000 on hand at the end of ten years. The amount depends on the rate at which annual deposits in the sinking fund are expected to earn interest. Let us assume 5 per cent. Using the method suggested in chapter 5, to accumulate a future value of $10,000 in ten years, the required annual deposit is

$$A = FW \, (CF_{fw \; to \; a}) \; i = .05, n = 10,$$

$$= \frac{FW}{(CF_{a \; to \; fw}) \; i = .05, n = 10,} \quad 1$$

$$\doteq \frac{\$10,000}{12.578},$$

$$= \$795.$$

The firm can deposit $795 per year and, earning 5 per cent on each deposit, accumulate $10,000 in ten years.

As an alternative to contributing to a sinking fund, a corporation may issue *serial bonds.* Under this arrangement, bonds are redeemed in order of their serial numbers. A certain portion of the issue matures each year and is paid off. The chief example of serial bonds is the equipment trust certificate, described a few paragraphs below. Finally, it should be noted that bond issuers are often free to use retained earnings (if there is cash to match) to buy back their bonds in the open market.

Sinking funds and serial bonds reduce lenders' worry. When such features are incorporated in loan agreements, lenders know that the borrowing corporation will be repaying the loan periodically or accumulating the wherewithal to repay it when due. Reduced uncertainties concerning repayment typically result in a lower interest rate.

Collateral Trust Bonds

Collateral trust bonds are similar to mortgage bonds, but are secured by a list of securities (either stocks or bonds) deposited with a trustee, rather than by fixed assets. They are used primarily when a company wishes to borrow on the pledge of securities it would find inconvenient or impossible to sell, for example, the common stock of its subsidiaries.

Equipment Trust Certificates

In contrast to mortgage bonds, which are secured by fixed assets, equipment trust certificates are secured by mobile equipment. They are issued chiefly by railroads and airlines to finance purchase of locomotives, cars, and aircraft. As with other bonds, equipment trust certificates have a trustee to represent the holders. These certificates differ, however, in that they are issued with serial maturities. For example, in a $15,000,000 railroad issue, $1,000,000 worth of certificates may be dated to mature each year for fifteen years.

The purchaser of equipment must make a substantial down payment, typically 20 to 25 per cent, and the serial certificates are paid off at a faster rate than the equipment depreciates. This substantial equity in the equipment gives borrowers a strong financial incentive not to default, and they rarely do. If they should default, the equipment is highly mobile and easily resold to satisfy the debt.

Certificate holders (lenders) enjoy prompt recourse to the equipment in case of default. The railroad or airline holds the equipment only under a lease contract until the last certificate is paid off. Since the lessee does not have legal title, the property is easily reclaimed by its legal owner, the trustee of the issue. Certificates thus enjoy a very high investment standing.

Today, probably more aircraft are owned by equipment trusts than by airlines. For example, TWA has outstanding $70 million, 10 per cent issue to mature in 1985.[4] It is secured by eight Boeing 727s and two Boeing 747s.

Other Types

There are many other bond types, and we shall mention only a few more. First, *income bonds* are promises to pay only if interest is earned. If the firm

---

[4]See the *Wall Street Journal* for the current price of these certificates. They are listed under *New York Stock Exchange Bonds* this way: TWA 10s85. If the current price is 101%, it means that the price is $1,016.25. For practice, using Eq. 20-2, calculate the *yield to maturity* if its market price is 101% and it has ten years until maturity.

does not earn enough revenue to cover all expenses, then no interest is legally due.[5] *Revenue bonds* are issued by municipalities or government divisions and pay interest out of the revenue generated from the specific project financed by the bond. Turnpikes and municipal sports arenas are examples of assets financed with revenue bonds. *General obligation bonds* are backed by the general taxing power of a municipality, and usually enjoy a higher rating than revenue bonds. Interest received on revenue and general obligation bonds is exempt from federal taxation.

The interest yield on a tax-exempt bond is often computed as a taxable yield equivalent, which means the yield necessary for a taxable bond to provide the same after-tax yield as the municipal, or tax-exempt, bond. Taxable yield equivalent is computed as $Y_m/(1 - t)$, where Y_m is the yield on the municipal and t is the investor's tax bracket expressed as a decimal fraction. A 60 per cent tax-bracket investor would need a 10 per cent taxable bond to get as high a yield as a 4 per cent tax-exempt bond would give him.

Debentures

A debenture bond is a promise to pay backed only by the general credit of the issuer. Not backed by the pledge of any specific asset, it is simply an IOU of the issuing corporation. Usually, the credit of a firm selling debentures is so strong that investors are willing to forego a pledge of assets.

Subordinated Debentures

A subordinated debenture has a claim to interest and principal after that of any claim to which it is specifically subordinated. In bankruptcy, claims of a senior and its subordinated issue are lumped together. In this way, the subordinated creditors receive nothing until the senior claim is completely satisfied, and they usually come out worse than general creditors. All debt claims, including accounts payable, are classed as general creditors unless the indenture specifies a lien on property or subordination. Without subordination, each creditor class would receive cash equal to its percentage composition of the firm's liabilities. Of course, any mortgage bondholders (mortgagees) receive the liquidated value of the mortgaged asset, and any of their remaining claim is placed in the pool with general creditors.

How subordination works can be illustrated this way. Assume that a firm has debentures specifically subordinated to a note and has a balance sheet like this:

Claims	Amount	% of Total	Unsubordinated Allocation	Subordinated Allocation	% Claim Satisfied
Note	$ 400	40%	$200	$300	75%
Subordinated debentures	$ 200	20%	$100	–0–	–0–
Trade creditors	$ 400	40%	$200	$200	50%
	$1,000	100%	$500	$500	50%

---

[5] Whether interest accumulates depends on the particular indenture.

Note and subordinated debenture holders comprise 60 per cent, and trade creditors 40 per cent of the claims. Where $500 is available for distribution, $300 and $200 are the two units' claims. Noteholders receive $300, subordinated debenture holders zero, and trade creditors $200. If $800 were available, noteholders would receive $400, subordinated debenture holders $80, trade creditors $320.

Because subordinated debentures increase assets, but have an inferior claim, senior creditors like to see a firm issue them. However, since interest on a subordinated debenture must be met just like that on any other debt, senior debt holders become concerned if too many debentures are issued, subordinated or not.

By issuing debentures rather than mortgage bonds, a firm strengthens its ability to obtain future trade and bank credit in larger amounts. That is, it will still have assets available to pledge, should this become necessary. Interest cost of a debenture is higher than for a mortgage bond, however. To reduce their interest rates, debentures are often made convertible or warrant-bearing, two equity kickers which we shall examine shortly.

Capital Notes

Rather than consume time and expense in registering its bonds with the Securities and Exchange Commission, an issuer may choose to sell its bonds privately.[6] Five or six large life insurance companies (or bank trust departments) may buy an entire $50 million issue of these non-marketable bonds, called capital notes. On such issues, the purchasers negotiate terms (payment of principal, maturity, and so on) to meet their preferences. The issuer can obtain its money quickly. Since the issue is not registered, it can not be sold in the open market, so purchasers are buying an illiquid asset. To compensate them for this illiquidity, the issuer pays a higher interest rate than on comparable marketable bonds. Issues of privately placed notes have, and need, no trustee since purchasers are few and knowledgeable.

Computing Interest Coverage

In chapter 17, we examined the ratio of earnings before interest and taxes (EBIT) to interest expense. This ratio measures the margin by which interest is covered and indicates a firm's risk of default. Where more than one debt issue is outstanding, the ratio must be adjusted to measure the coverage of the different issues. A junior issue is not as secure as a senior one, and to reflect this an analyst must use the cumulative method of computing interest coverage.

Assume that Kyklos Corporation has three bond issues outstanding, presented here:

First mortgage 7%, due 1984	$2,000,000
General mortgage[7] 8%, due 1977	1,000,000
Debentures 10%, due 1990	500,000
	$3,500,000

---

[6]Private placement is discussed in detail in chapter 29.

[7]A fancy name for a second (or third) mortgage.

The analyst would expect the first mortgage bond to be covered more times than the general mortgage or debentures, because the first mortgage holder has a superior claim. The cumulative (or overall) method of computing coverage of interest expense takes the interest requirement on a particular issue *plus the requirements on all issues senior to the one in question,* and divides this sum into earnings before interest and taxes.

Suppose Kyklos Corporation had earnings before interest and taxes of $600,000. Then interest coverage on the three above issues would be as follows:

1. First mortgage bonds: $\dfrac{\$600,000}{\$140,000} = 4.29$ times.

2. General mortgage bonds: $\dfrac{\$600,000}{\$\,80,000 \,+\, \$140,000} = 2.73$ times.

3. Debentures: $\dfrac{\$600,000}{\$50,000 \,+\, \$\,80,000 \,+\, \$140,000} = 2.22$ times.

The cumulative method of calculating times interest earned yields what one intuitively expects: each issue shows better coverage and a stronger position than those inferior to it.

Bond Ratings

How do creditors judge the investment merit of a bond? The easiest way is to rely on the bond ratings provided by Standard & Poor's Corporation and Moody's Investor's Service, Inc., the two major rating services. These agencies examine an issuer's profitability, total size of his debt, cyclical and other risks of his business, "average year" and "worst year" interest coverage on the bonds in question, strength of the bondholder's indenture protection, and so forth, and then assign letter ratings to indicate the bond's probable quality.

Moody's uses these symbols: Aaa, Aa, A, Baa, Ba, B, Caa, Ca, C.[s] The first three classes designate the least investment risk, the last three, the greatest. These two agencies do not rate all bonds, only those they are specifically requested to examine (sometimes the issuer will ask them to do so), or those they believe will receive widespread attention. Moody's covers over 15,000 issues. For example, the TWA issue mentioned above was rated Baa.

Moody's and Standard & Poor's sometimes rate the same firm differently. This happens—even though both undertake much the same analysis that we covered in chapters 16 and 17, carry out on-site inspections, and hold interviews with management—because subjectivity and intuition inevitably creep into the evaluation.

Receiving a high bond rating is important to a company for two reasons.

---

[s]Standard & Poor's uses AAA, AA, A, BBB, BB, and so on. The first five ratings translate roughly as follows: Aaa or AAA: unusually thick protective margins, no possibility of impairment foreseen. Aa or AA: good margins, though not so thick as above; no likelihood of impairment foreseen. A: protective margins all right for now; future impairment possible, though unlikely. Baa or BBB: definitely in trouble in a major depression or industry setback, Ba or BB: definitely speculative and future interest highly uncertain.

First, the higher the rating is, the lower the interest the issuer will pay.[9] Second, many institutional buyers are restricted to securities of investment grade only, which usually means the top three ratings. If an issue falls below these three, it loses a large potential demand and its bonds will sell at a lower price (and have a higher yield).

Bond Sweeteners

During intervals of credit stringency, corporations try to encourage purchase of their bonds by adding "sweeteners" to their straight debt issue. A sweetener is a financial benefit provided the creditor in addition to interest. Two frequent sweeteners are conversion privileges and warrants.

Convertible Bonds

Convertible bonds are exchangeable, at the bondholder's option, for the common stock of the issuing corporation. The conversion feature is usually expressed as a *conversion ratio,* which states the number of common shares into which each bond can be converted. For example, a $1,000 par bond may have a conversion ratio of 20:1. One bond can be presented to the corporate treasurer, who must give twenty shares of common stock in exchange. The *conversion price* is the price at which the common stock is received in conversion. Since a $1,000 bond is the equivalent of twenty shares of common stock, the conversion price is $1,000/20 = $50 per share. Given the conversion price, one can find the conversion ratio and vice versa. A constant conversion price may prevail over the life of the bond, or the price may increase (and ratio decrease) at intervals. *Straight-debt value* is the value of the bond without its conversion privilege. This value can be approximated by examining the price of straight bonds of comparable issuers. Finally, *conversion value* is the value of the bond in terms of its stock equivalent. If the market price of the stock is $60, then the bond's conversion value is 20 times $60 = $1,200.

How is the conversion price of a new bond decided? A financial manager will consider the following factors:

1. Current price of the firm's common stock.
2. The expected rise of the firm's earnings and, hence, of the common stock price.
3. How popular the conversion feature currently is with investors.
4. Desired duration of the conversion privilege.

The greater each of these is, the higher the conversion price will be.

The firm will want to place conversion price *above* current market price, but not so far above it as to be unattainable. If conversion price exceeds current market price by too wide a margin, investors will not buy the sweetener since it will have no apparent value. If the sweetener is substantially worthless, then the firm might as well sell straight debt. Conversely, management must not place the conversion price so close to the current price of the common as to provide

---

[9]Recall from Eq. 20-1 that any return is equal to a pure return plus a risk premium. The higher the rating is, the lower the risk premium, and vice versa.

for almost immediate conversion. In that case, management would do as well to sell common stock.

The point to note is this: a convertible bond has both common stock and straight-debt features, and the issuer should set the conversion price at a level that takes advantage of both features. Doing so ensures that investors will buy the convertibles on a lower yield basis than straight debt would sell for, thus reducing the firm's cost of debt.

Besides serving as a sweetener, convertibility is an indirect way for management to sell common stock. If the market price of the common is below what management considers its fair value, the firm can issue convertible bonds and await a stock-price recovery to produce conversion into common. The company's debt-equity ratio will increase at first, then diminish as conversion occurs. To force conversion, the issuer can make the bonds *callable.* That means the issuer can buy back the bond at a predetermined price. Suppose, for example, that a $1,000 par convertible bond is callable with a 10 per cent premium, meaning at $1,100. Suppose also that the bond now has a conversion value of twenty shares times $60, or $1,200. If the treasurer calls the bond, he can be sure the holder will not present the bond for cash, but will take twenty shares of stock instead.[10] Conversion will in effect be forced on the creditor.

Not only convertibles, but all other kinds of bonds can be made callable. Making an issue callable enables the issuer to *refund* it if interest rates decline. For example, if his firm has a 10 per cent issue outstanding and interest rates fall to 6 per cent, he can call the issue, pay the call premium, and replace it at 6 per cent, saving a 4 per cent interest expense.

Market Price of Convertible Bonds

As we saw above, a convertible bond has two theoretical values. It will sell in the market at a price at least equal to the higher one. Its floor is set by the price at which it will sell solely on its merit as a fixed-income investment, its *straight-debt value.* Thus, a twenty-year, 5 per cent convertible bond would not sell below $703.10 if straight bonds of equal quality were selling to yield 8 per cent to maturity. But if the bond were convertible at $50, i.e., into twenty common shares, and the common was selling at $40, the bond could not sell for less than its *conversion value* of $800 (20 times $40). If it sold below $800, market participants would immediately buy the bond, present it for its 20 shares of common, and make a profit. This type of transaction, in which opposite positions are taken in separate markets—here, buying and selling the stock, is called arbitrage. For example, if the bond were selling for $750, arbitragers would make a gross profit of $50. By taking advantage of the situation, they drive the market price toward its conversion value. Actually, if the common price were $40, the bond would probably sell for somewhat more than $800, the gap between the market price and conversion value of $800 representing a *conversion premium.* In soaring stock markets, convertible bonds may rise far above the theoretical conversion values because speculators can buy convertible bonds with a smaller brokerage fee than on the equivalent common stock.

---

[10]The calling of a convertible bond issue is subject to advance notice, so the bondholder would ordinarily have thirty days in which to convert.

Bonds with Warrants

A *warrant* is the privilege of purchasing a firm's common stock at some specified price, called option price. A newly-issued bond may have a warrant attached entitling the holder to buy one share of common stock at, for example, $50. When the bond is issued, the option price stipulated on the warrant is *always* above the current price of the common. In our example, the option price of $50 might reflect a market price of $30.

Like the conversion privilege, warrants (1) enable an issuer to float his bonds at lower interest, and (2) add a speculative flavor to bond ownership. If the common rises well above the option price before warrants expire, warrant holders may make large profits.

Warrants may be detachable or non-detachable. The first sort can be detached from the bond and sold separately in the market. Non-detachable warrants can be sold only with the bond.

Convertibles vs. Bonds With Warrants

When a conversion privilege is exercised, the debt-equity ratio falls, and there is no change in a firm's total assets. When warrants are exercised, the firm's debt-equity ratio likewise falls, but its *total assets increase.* To exercise the privilege of obtaining common from a warrant, the investor must pay in cash. In our example, $50 must be paid to obtain a share of common.

Converting a bond issue may increase a firm's earnings by eliminating interest expense, though the resulting increase in number of common shares also tends to dilute earnings on a per-common-share basis. On the other hand, the exercise of stock-purchase warrants brings new cash into the company, at least partly offsetting the "dilution effect" of additional shares. In general, bonds with warrants attached appear more beneficial to shareholders, present and future, than convertible bonds.

Convertible Preferred: A Note

Like bonds, preferred stock may be convertible into common. The logic of conversion ratios, prices, and values for preferreds precisely parallels that of bonds and does not require further explanation here. Preferred stocks may also be subject to call prices and sinking funds. Again, these features closely resemble such features in bonds.

To Remember

Reasons for bond usage	Cumulative method of interest coverage
Trustee	Conversion ratio and price
Mortgage bonds	Callable
Debenture	Convertible floor
Warrant	

Questions

1 The formula for calculating the real burden of interest from the nominal rate implies that corporation managers would favor an increased tax rate.

    (a) Show this formula and demonstrate the impact of an increased tax rate.

    (b) Assume a firm has $100 EBIT. Interest expense is $60.

        (1) Calculate the cash outlay associated with interest and taxes at a 60 per cent tax rate.

        (2) Calculate the cash outlay associated with interest and taxes at a 40 per cent tax rate. (Hint: Do not use the formula. Construct a brief income statement.)

    (c) Do you believe corporate managers favor a higher tax rate? Explain.

2 Precision Machinery is in the 48 per cent marginal tax bracket. The nominal cost of interest is 9 per cent. Phase II controls on the economy have slowed the pace of inflation to 3.5 per cent per annum.

    (a) What is the real burden of interest?

    (b) At whose expense do debtors gain from inflation?

3 Bildo, Inc., issues $100,000 in closed-end mortgage bonds with an after-acquired property clause. The bonds have a twenty-year life. Management must, according to the indenture, contribute annually equal sums to a sinking fund.

    (a) If the sinking fund is held in idle cash, earning no interest, how much must each deposit be?

    (b) If the fund earns 4 per cent, how much must each deposit be?

    (c) If the fund earns 8 per cent, how much must each deposit be?

4 Tackacs, Inc., has the following financial structure:

Bank loan	$ 3,000
Debenture	5,000
Subordinated debenture	4,000
Shareholders' equity	8,000
	$20,000

The subordinated debenture is inferior to all debts of the firm.

    (a) Assets are liquidated for $10,000. How much does each claimant receive?

    (b) Assets are liquidated for $8,000. How much does each claimant receive?

5 Ricardo Chavez, treasurer of Rebus Amalgamated, asks you to calculate coverage of interest expense on the firm's bonds. Here are the issues:

First mortgage, 5% due 1987	$10,000
Debenture, 6% due 1981	4,000
Subordinated debenture, 8% due 1980	6,000
	$20,000

The subordinated debenture is subordinated to the other two issues. Rebus Amalgamated's earnings after taxes are $2,040. The firm's tax rate is 40 per cent. Using the cumulative method, calculate the coverage of each issue.

6 Rolo and Nelso, a conglomerate firm, has outstanding a subordinated convertible debenture. The conversion ratio is 40, par value, $1,000.

(a) What is the conversion price?

(b) If the stock is selling for $40, what is the bond's conversion value?

(c) Suppose that in question (b), the bond is selling for $1,700. What is the conversion premium? Why does a convertible have a conversion premium?

(d) Now assume the bond is selling for its straight-debt value, $1,500. What would arbitragers do?

7 Defend this statement: "Use of bonds with warrants is more beneficial to existing shareholders than convertible bonds."

26

Capital Allocation and Budgeting

We move now to a firm's *use* of its financial resources. Having raised funds, how should it employ them? This chapter examines two parts of the answer: (1) the *theory* of capital allocation, and (2) the *administrative* procedures for handling long-term outlays. (Chapter 27 describes specific methods of *selecting* long-term investments, and chapter 28 considers circulating capital and its effective employment.)

Capital Allocation

Capital allocation means the way management arranges assets and claims against assets. The purpose is to achieve maximum present value for the firm's ownership interest, which is generally taken to mean maximum sustainable price for its common stock. In theory, common stock price is determined by the *amount* of future earnings and dividends investors expect and by the *discount rate* investors apply to these expected flows. In this chapter, some systematic relations between costs and returns are analyzed to show how earnings are theoretically maximized.

Costs and Revenues

Maximizing net return is based on a fundamental principle: marginal costs must equal marginal revenues. You will remember that marginal cost is simply the change in total cost that results from producing one additional unit, while marginal revenue is the additional revenue obtained by selling one more unit. The cost curves you studied in economics looked like those in Figure 26-1. Average cost is total cost divided by the number of units produced.

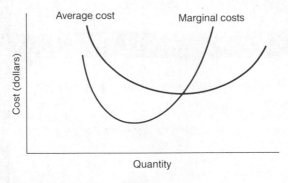

Figure 26-1. Cost Relations

Average cost at first falls, reaches a minimum, then rises, because marginal cost first falls, then rises. So long as marginal cost is below average cost, each new unit produced will pull average cost down; once marginal cost exceeds average cost, each additional unit will force average costs up.

Why does average cost first fall, then rise? It falls because as output increases, fixed costs are being spread over more units. Once buildings and machines are in place, each unit produced incurs only the variable cost of labor, materials, supplies, and the like. As fixed costs are prorated over more units, the fixed cost chargeable to each unit falls, rapidly at first, then more slowly. You can see through a simple example how this happens. If fixed costs are $100, and I produce one unit, the fixed (overhead) cost per unit is $100. With ten units of output, the overhead per unit drops by $90, to $10 per unit. But going from ten units to 100 units, the overhead per unit drops only $9 more, to $1 per unit. But so long as variable cost per unit holds steady, average cost per unit continues to decline. However, with the effort to produce more and more units from a given setup of buildings and machines, a point of congestion is finally reached where the plant gets crowded and efficiency declines: people get in each other's way, overtime must be paid and less productive grades of labor hired, materials waste increases, percentage of defective items rises, and so on. Diseconomies of scale occur. At this point, variable cost per additional unit rises, more than offsetting the slow decline in fixed cost per unit. Marginal cost therefore rises, often steeply, pulling up average cost behind it.

The revenue curves associated with output (under conditions of imperfect competition) have the shapes depicted in Figure 26-2.[1] Average revenue is total revenue divided by total output. Since total revenue is equal to price times quantity, average revenue must be equal to price. Marginal revenue is the change in total revenue.

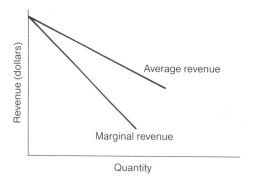

Figure 26-2. Revenue Relations

Combining all of the curves, we get Figure 26-3, in which several points are evident. First, by carrying production forward to the point where a rising marginal cost meets a falling marginal revenue, the firm maximizes its total profit. Graphically, the rectangle *KRPT* represents the maximum profit area attainable within the system of curves depicted. Second, to implement this decision the firm produces *OQ* units of output. Third, both average and marginal revenues fall continuously over the whole range of sales. Fourth, average and marginal costs both fall at first, then rise, with the marginal cost curve rising much more steeply. Finally, of course, the marginal cost curve cuts the average cost curve at its lowest point.

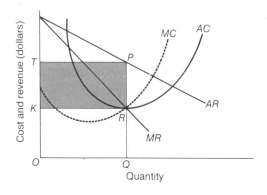

Figure 26-3. Cost and Revenue Relations

---

[1]Under imperfect competition, revenue curves decline because it is possible to increase sales revenue by cutting price to attract competitors' customers. Under perfect competition, average revenue, marginal revenue, and price would be equal and represented by a straight, horizontal line.

Marginal Cost and Return: Invested Capital

The cost and return (revenue) curves you studied in economics dealt with a company's *output* decisions. Now we shall see how analogous curves—and logic—describe its capital investment decisions.

Marginal Return

A firm will discover, through proper analysis of its product market and its production costs, that certain money-making opportunities (which we shall call projects) are open to it. The investments required for these projects, and the returns expected from them, can be "guesstimated," and these guesstimates incorporated in figures.[2] The projects can then be ranked in order of expected profitability. This has been done in Table 26–1 for five hypothetical projects, each involving a $10,000 outlay. Included in each project are (1) outlay required, (2) marginal return, i.e., the *added* profit the company would make by adopting *that* project, (3) the company's total return from that project plus all projects above it, (4) the average return on all projects down through the one in question, and (5) the marginal and average returns at that point, expressed in percentages.

Table 26–1. Return on Investment as a Function of Amount of Investment

Investment Project	Outlay	Dollars Marginal Return	Total Return	Average Return	Per Cent Marginal Return	Average Return
A	$10,000	$2,500	$2,500	$2,500	25%	25.0%
B	10,000	2,000	4,500	2,250	20%	22.5%
C	10,000	1,500	6,000	2,200	15%	20.0%
D	10,000	1,000	7,000	1,750	10%	17.5%
E	10,000	500	7,500	1,500	5%	15.0%

In Table 26–1, return means the difference between total revenues (TR) and total costs (TC), which do not here include the cost of capital.[3] Notice that the relation between marginal and average return is such that if marginal return is above average return, the average will be increasing; if the marginal return is below the average, the latter will be declining, as Figure 26–2 indicates it should. In Table 26–1, however, marginal return is always below average return.

"Laddering" prospective investment projects in their order of profitability,

---

[2]The detailed process by which these guesstimates are assembled and evaluated will be described more fully later in this chapter and in the next. Suffice it to note here that a project, such as a new product or expanded output of a present product, will oblige the company to acquire various additional assets: land, buildings, plant, equipment, and additional circulating capital. The cost of these plus wages, materials and other "current" outlays must be weighed against expected sales revenue to estimate expected profits. Prospective sales revenues will depend on forecasts of unit sales volume and selling prices.

[3]The returns shown here are all received in the year in which the outlay is made. We thus avoid the problem of discounting receipts from future years, a problem taken up in chapter 27.

as we have done, enables management to proceed logically with its decision how much to invest. It is in position to take advantage of projects yielding higher returns before moving on to those with lower yields. If the company's supply of investible funds is limited, it can skim the cream off the investment opportunities open to it. (Investible funds are restricted by capital rationing, a phenomenon discussed later in this chapter.) Otherwise, it will continue to accept and undertake projects until doing so is no longer profitable.

When will further projects become unprofitable? To decide this question, a firm must examine the behavior of its cost of capital—specifically how its cost of capital behaves as more and more capital is raised for investment.

Marginal Cost

We have already noted, in Figure 20–1, that a firm's cost of capital is probably stable over some fairly wide range of financial leverage. However, the problem we are considering here is different: How does cost of capital behave as a firm endeavors to raise more and more capital within a relatively short time?

The cost rises because capital markets are imperfect. That means a single firm is faced with a cost of capital function that is upward sloping the more finance it seeks. An extreme case is capital rationing, in which the loanable funds are limited by the unwillingness of the lender to supply more than a certain amount no matter what yield is offered. A firm can borrow only so much unless it expands its equity. Equity can expand only so fast by means of retained earnings. Of course, a company can sell new shares to enlarge its equity base to support more borrowing. But here again, the stock market will absorb additional shares only at a higher rate. If a company tries to evade these limitations, its cost of capital is bound to rise. If it cuts dividends to retain more earnings, the stock price may fall and new stock may become more expensive to sell. If it tries to sell too many new shares, the market price will also fall as investors shout "dilution." And if, without duly expanding the equity base, the company tries to sell more bonds, the quality rating of its bonds tumbles, interest cost goes up, and shareholders add a higher risk premium to the rate of return they require from the firm.

Table 26–2 gives an exaggerated impression of how a firm's cost of capital rises as additional chunks of investment are undertaken and have to be financed

Table 26–2. Cost of Capital as a Function of Amount of Investment

Capital Unit	Capital Raised	Dollars Annual Cost	Total Cost	Average Cost	Per Cent Marginal Cost	Average Cost
1	$10,000	$1,000	$1,000	$1,000	10%	10.0%
2	10,000	1,000	2,000	1,000	10%	10.0%
3	10,000	1,400	3,400	1,133	14%	11.3%
4	10,000	2,100	5,500	1,375	21%	13.7%
5	10,000	3,000	8,500	1,700	30%	17.0%

within a relatively short interval. The amounts reflect the relations depicted in Figure 26-1.

Table 26-2 underscores the point that diminishing returns from a schedule of investment possibilities are not the only concern a management confronts in making its investment selections. It must also consider the possibility that trying to expand too rapidly, attempting to crowd too much new investment into a particular time interval, may increase its cost of funds from investors.

Capital Cut-Off

The cost of capital is the cut-off point in project selection. Management will accept all projects with returns exceeding the cost of capital, but cut-off, or reject, all those with returns below this cost.

What list of investment projects should our sample company's management accept? Clearly, it will want to accept project A, for this project will return 25 per cent on the $10,000 which capital unit 1 will provide at only a 10 per cent cost. Similarly, it should accept B, with a 20 per cent return, financed by unit 2 at a 10 per cent cost; and C, with a 15 per cent return and a 14 per cent cost through financing via unit 3. What about D? No. D returns only 10 per cent on an investment that would have to be financed through unit 4 at a 21 per cent cost. Still less will management want E's 5 per cent return at the 30 per cent cost required by capital unit 5.

What is the principle involved in this decision? It is the same one you probably learned in economics: equalizing (as nearly as possible) marginal cost (MC) with marginal return (MR). The principle works whether you are dealing with output decisions (marginal cost of product versus marginal revenue from product) or investment decisions (marginal cost of capital versus marginal return from investment).

Maximizing Total Return

By following the *MC = MR* rule, a company will maximize the total profit open to it. The following schedule demonstrates this for our sample firm:

Investment Project	Capital Unit	Marginal Return	Total Return	Marginal Cost	Total Cost	Total Profit = Total Return minus Total Cost	Marginal Profit
A	1	$2,500	$2,500	$1,000	$1,000	$1,500	$1,500
B	2	2,000	4,500	1,000	2,000	2,500	1,000
C	3	1,500	6,000	1,400	3,400	2,600	100
D	4	1,000	7,000	2,100	5,500	1,500	-1,100
E	5	500	7,500	3,000	8,500	-1,000	-2,500

Maximum profit is achieved when project C, whose marginal return is $1,500, is financed with capital unit 3 at a cost of $1,400. Here the equalization of marginal cost and return cannot be brought into closer balance because both capital and projects occur in relatively large chunks. This is usually true in the real world.

The Real World: Uncertainty and Imprecision

Theoretical principles often cannot be applied precisely to the real world or to actual decisions, and so it is with setting $MC = MR$ in capital investment.

The example above appears precise because we assume that the cost of capital is definitely known and the investment returns are sure to occur. We are working under comfortable conditions of hypothetical certainty.

Let us turn to real life and real business. You are a flesh-and-blood businessman. What will your new product sell for three years hence? What will unit sales be four years from now? What will manufacturing costs be in five years? You throw up your hands. No businessman can do more than guess at these answers.[4] Yet your forecasts of what your projects will return depend on just such precarious guesses: guesses based on all sorts of implicit (and usually unconscious) assumptions about customer preferences, the state of business, competition, labor costs, fashions, technological changes, and so on. Rarely are all, or even a majority, of such assumptions borne out by events.

Nor will calculating the marginal cost of capital for your firm as a whole tell you what return a particular project should aim at. Theoretically, the uncertainties surrounding every project call for some "allowance for risk." This means that to realize, on average, a 14 per cent return on *this kind of project,* management should not accept it unless it promises to yield about 20 per cent.[5] The six extra percentage points are like "Kentucky windage" in rifle shooting: aiming upwind to hit the target. But how fast the wind is really blowing, the businessman never knows. So the "Kentucky windage" he adds to his project-return requirement is, like the return itself, guesswork.

Thus despite the fine guiding logic of the marginal principle, the real businessman decides his investments in a changing, unpredictable world of inaccurate data, large uncertainties, and incalculable odds. In this environment, intuition and experience are often more reliable guides to an effective allocation of capital than the precise-appearing textbook rules which we review in chapter 27.

Administering Outlays for Long-Lived Assets

A firm's outlays on fixed assets demand closest attention because they are virtually irrevocable. Once they are made, a company must live with its decisions or accept—usually—large losses, if it chooses to liquidate its committments. To

---

[4]John Maynard Keynes, greatest of twentieth century economists, wrote, "Most, probably, of our decisions to do something positive, the full consequences of which will be drawn out over many days to come, can only be taken as a result of animal spirits—of a spontaneous urge to action rather than inaction, and not as the outcome of a weighted average of quantitative benefits multiplied by quantitative probabilities. Enterprise only pretends to itself to be mainly actuated by the statements in its own prospectus, however candid and sincere. Only a little more than an expedition to the South Pole, is it based on an exact calculation of benefits to come." *The General Theory of Employment Interest and Money* (New York: Harcourt, Brace & Co., 1936), pp. 161–62. The quotation is from chapter 12—in the authors' opinion the greatest and truest analytical account of business and the investment markets ever written by man. Other excellent work on uncertainty in business decisions has been done during the past thirty years by G. L. S. Shackle. See, for example, his *Uncertainty in Economics* (Cambridge: Cambridge University Press, 1968).

[5]We present two methods of dealing with uncertainty at the end of chapter 27.

insure due care, procedures used in planning long-lived investments often are formal and quite complex.

The following discussion describes typical procedures in a large firm. In smaller companies, capital allocation decisions are much simpler. In tiny firms, these decisions may be made informally by one man, the president. And, since he bears many other simultaneous responsibilities, his decisions may be hasty and illogical. The following discussion describes ideal procedures.

Allocation of a company's capital is formally controlled through a capital budget, formal authorization of expenditures, reviews of projects in progress, and, finally, post-completion audits. Each component will be discussed in turn.[6]

Capital Budget

The capital budget lies primarily within the controller's province of financial management. It is prepared annually and indicates the dollar amount of funds the company will devote to capital outlays for the coming year. It details the projects, assets, and activities in which the company will invest these outlays. Approval of the budget does not authorize the actual expenditure of funds.

The capital budget answers four questions for management:

1. *What* are the long-lived *asset needs* of the firm?
2. *What* capital *funds* will the firm *need* during the coming year?
3. *When* will these funds be *spent?*
4. *Who* will be *responsible* for the expenditures?

Although primary responsibility for drawing up the budget rests with the controller, he gets his information by requesting plant and division managers and others to submit lists of the proposals they consider necessary. Individuals supporting a project are called *sponsors.* In turn, the controller will screen the proposals, consolidate them into a companywide proposed capital budget, and submit it to top management for final approval. This procedure will be completed during the closing weeks of the firm's fiscal (business) year.

Step One

The first step is for department heads to submit their requests on a standard form like that in Figure 26–4. The controller reviews these requests in a meeting with each department head to make sure he has classified each proposal correctly and understands its nature. Usually, department heads can sense, through past experience with the budgeting process, how much money they will be allowed to spend—the principle that when you've played the game before, you have an idea of what it takes to win. Department heads have a feel of what to ask for and what not to ask for.

Some companies provide for a blanket inclusion of smaller items. These need not be justified separately, but may be included in a cluster, either because (1) individually they cost less than a certain amount, or (2) collectively they comprise less than a certain percentage of the division's proposed budget. This arrangement relieves management of having to examine a multitude of small expenditures and

---

[6]The rest of this chapter relies heavily on Norman C. Pflomm, *Managing Capital Expenditures,* Studies in Business Policy, No. 107, The Conference Board, New York, 1963.

Figure 26–4.

Dept.	Check One		General description of item or project	Estimate of total cost	Completion date	How many years will it take net savings to pay for the item or project?	Justification and remarks
	Addi- tion	Replace- ment					

CAPITAL EXPENDITURES BUDGET PROPOSAL FOR THE FISCAL YEAR ENDING DECEMBER 31, 19____

Reprinted from Norman Pflomm, *Managing Capital Expenditures,* Studies in Business Policy, No. 107, 1963. By permission of The Conference Board, New York.

gives division heads a welcome freedom of action in deciding smaller outlays.[7]

Divisions are usually required to assign priority ratings to their projects. Projects will be listed on proposed division budgets in descending order of need. For example, in Figure 26–4, priorities would be explained in the column headed "Justification and Remarks."

Priorities might be classified as:

A. Absolutely essential. Legally required, replaces facilities physically exhausted, necessary for health or safety.
B. Necessary. Expenditure that may be delayed temporarily, but cannot long be avoided.
C. Economically desirable. Results in cost savings, needed for new products, or expands capacity.
D. General improvement. Needed for morale, prestige, etc.

Step Two

After the controller has evaluated each division's needs, he submits the budget to top management for final review and approval. Although the board of directors usually gives final approval, the real work is typically done by a capital expenditures committee consisting of the president of the firm and other senior officers.

Authorizing Capital Expenditures

Before funds are actually spent on a project, management gives a second look to see that the situation has not changed since the original budget was approved. The division manager will submit a form like the one in Figure 26–5. On it he must show exactly how much of the total expenditures approved in the already approved capital budget his project will require. In preparing the appropriation request form, he will consult with engineers, sales managers, accountants, and other staff specialists. Questions and suggestions from the staff experts can refine the proposal and stimulate project sponsors to think of profitable alternatives.

The division head will usually have to submit an economic analysis of the project if it is intended to increase the firm's profitability.[8] In addition, he often must list alternative methods of reaching the objective, stating why such methods

[7]A blanket inclusion is the application of the exception principle discussed in chapter 19.

[8]Economic analysis, or ranking and selecting projects, is the subject of the next chapter.

Figure 26–5.

AUTHORIZATION FOR CAPITAL EXPENDITURE
(SEE REVERSE SIDE FOR INSTRUCTIONS)

ORIGINATOR	DATE	AUTHORIZATION NUMBER

1. DESCRIPTION OF PROPOSAL:

CAPITAL EXPENDITURE BUDGET DATA	DIVISION	DEPARTMENT OR ASSET CLASS	ASSET SUBCLASS
2. TOTAL APPROVED CAPITAL EXPENDITURE BUDGET	$	$	$
3. TOTAL AUTHORIZATIONS APPROVED - YEAR TO DATE			
4. AMOUNT THIS AUTHORIZATION			
5. UNAUTHORIZED CAPITAL BUDGET BALANCE			ITEM NO.

6. THIS EXPENDITURE ☐ IS ☐ IS NOT INCLUDED IN CAPITAL BUDGET FOR YEAR

7. REASON(S) FOR REQUEST:

☐ REPLACEMENT   ☐ NEW OR CHANGED PRODUCT   ☐ HAZARD ELIMINATION
☐ REDUCTION IN COST   ☐ INCREASED FACILITIES   ☐ OTHER (EXPLAIN BELOW)

8. EXPLAIN NECESSITY OF PROPOSED EXPENDITURE:

FOR COST ACCOUNTING DEPARTMENT USE ONLY	REQUESTED BY:	DATE
	RECOMMENDED:	DATE
	RECOMMENDED:	DATE
	RECOMMENDED:	DATE
	APPROVED:	DATE

Reprinted from Norman Pflomm, *Managing Capital Expenditures,* Studies in Business Policy, No. 107, 1963. By permission of The Conference Board, New York.

QUANTITY	DETAILS OF ITEMS and ESTIMATED COSTS	AMOUNT

INSTRUCTIONS

Prepare Authorization for Capital Expenditure in quadruplicate as follows:

ITEM

1. Supply concise summary of capital asset(s) to be secured.

2. Insert total amount of Capital Expenditure Budget approved for your department for the calendar year in column headed "Department or Asset Class". Manufacturing Division will use columns headed "Division", "Department or Asset Class" and "Asset Subclass". Research and Engineering Division originators will complete information required in column headed "Department or Asset Class" and will forward all copies of Authorization to Research and Engineering Accounting Manager who will insert information required in the Division column.

3. Total all previous Authorizations approved during calendar year.

4. Insert total amount of expenditure being requested for approval.

5. Deduct total of Item 3 and 4 from Item 1.

6. Place an "X" in appropriate box and insert calendar year.

7. Check one or more reason(s) for the request.

8. Explain necessity and benefits of proposed expenditure in detail.

Originator will secure approval in accordance with Item D of S.P.I. 95.

FOR COST ACCOUNTING DEPARTMENT USE ONLY	DATE DISTRIBUTED
COPY NO. 1 COST ACCOUNTING DEPARTMENT	COPY NO. 3
COPY NO. 2	COPY NO. 4 ACCOUNTS PAYABLE AND PAYROLL SECTION

are less desirable than the project he proposes. Frequently, this is the single most difficult step in justifying an appropriation request.

When a proposal reaches this stage, it is usually well supported and its justification appears persuasive.

Who gives final approval? Figure 26–6 shows how one company operates under a system of dollar limits which permits each manager to approve projects up to a stated dollar amount. This is typical practice.

What do firms do when an emergency arises—a plant explosion or major machine breakdown occurs—and quick expenditures are required? The division head usually proceeds to spend the money, then submits an appropriation request, *ex post facto.* If the expenditure is extremely large, he will naturally obtain verbal approval for his proposal first.

Figure 26–6. Dollar Limits on Capital Expenditure Approval

| | Limits of Final Approval* | | | | |
	Office Furniture & Equip.	Machinery and Equipment	Land	Building	Investment
Plant Manager	$ 500	$ 1,000	NA	$ 1,000	NA
Division Vice President	1,000	5,000	NA	5,000	NA
Division Controller	1,000	NA	NA	NA	NA
Division President or Senior Vice President	5,000	15,000	NA	15,000	NA
Parent Company Controller	5,000	NA	NA	NA	NA
Executive Vice President	25,000	25,000	NA	25,000	NA
Chairman Exec. Committee	50,000	50,000	NA	50,000	NA
Executive Committee or Board of Directors	No Limit	No Limit	No Limit	No Limit	No Limit

*Except for sale of converting equipment which requires Executive Vice President approval for all amounts up to $25,000 and regular approvals for amounts over $25,000.

NA No authority to give final approval.

Source: Reprinted from Norman Pflomm, *Managing Capital Expenditures,* Studies in Business Policy, No. 107, 1963. By permission of The Conference Board, New York.

Controlling Projects in Process

Even though funds have been committed, management is far from finished with its control of an investment. The financial manager is responsible for seeing that projects are carried out as proposed with respect to cost, purpose, and timing of expenditures.

Controlling projects in process is usually the direct responsibility of a company accountant. He will assign an authority number to each appropriation request, and all documents reflecting charges against this project will bear the same number. All documents pertaining to the project will be kept together and all expenditures posted as they come in. In addition, the accountant will advise the division manager and the controller whenever expenditures total, for example, 75 per cent of appropriations.

Higher management also will want to know the exact status of all major projects, especially if they are directed toward cost-saving or profit-improvement.

Delays in beginning or completing such projects will result in permanent loss of profits.

The common weakness of status reports is that they fail to give senior management meaningful information. Often, the division manager will calculate how much of the project is completed by determining how much of the appropriation has been expended. If 50 per cent of the funds have been spent, he will be tempted to say the project is 50 per cent completed, but that may not be so. The progress should also be reported in physical terms with an engineer's estimate of per cent physical completion.

Supplemental Appropriations

In an inflationary economy, actual expenditures often exceed budgeted amounts. Not only will capitalized outlays increase, i.e., fixed assets, but also expense items, outlays that are *not capitalized*. Both kinds of overruns must be dealt with. Sometimes, if the overrun does not exceed perhaps 10 per cent of the original appropriation, the division manager need not make a supplementary expenditure request. This practice allows for unforeseen outlays and for errors in forecasting costs. But it may also encourage loose handling of estimates, budgets, and outlays.

Completion Report

Whoever originally submits the appropriation request (the sponsor) is responsible for submitting a completion report. This report notifies all parties concerned that work has been completed. It often consists of an original and five copies, one each for sponsor, controller, works manager, production, purchasing, and chief engineer.

Besides notifying interested parties, the completion report accomplishes three other objectives. (1) It compares actual with estimated costs, forcing the sponsor and division manager to explain any discrepancy. (2) It obliges senior management to approve any cost overrun and thus scrutinize it closely. (3) It forms the basis for proper accounting entries on the company's books. Some expenditures will be recorded as expenses, reducing income in the current period, while others are entered as capital outlays, reducing profit in subsequent periods through depreciation.

Post-Completion Audit

The post-completion audit is sometimes called a performance report. Its importance is reflected in its purposes:

1. To verify resulting savings or profit.
2. To reveal reasons for project failure.
3. To check on the soundness of managers' proposals.
4. To aid in assessing the effectiveness of future capital acquisitions.

The audit should take place after enough time has elapsed for the project to "iron out all the bugs." Usually, if the project is below a certain size, for example, $10,000, it can be audited locally, that is, by the division manager's own staff. If it exceeds that amount, it should be carefully audited by headquarters.

Senior management should make a continuous use of audits to evaluate the effectiveness of its capital allocation program. Audits should also be reviewed when promotions are on the line. The lower manager who has been effective in selecting his projects and controlling their completion should be rewarded.

Asset Disposal

Technology in our economy changes rapidly. Often, one device for accomplishing a task is no sooner introduced than a better one is announced. Companies are forced to dispose of obsolete assets and invest in new ones able to perform the same task more efficiently. Controlling asset disposal thus becomes an integral part of the capital management program.

For orderly operation, formal requests to dispose of assets should be used. Figure 26–7 illustrates a suitable form. The division manager submits it. The form notifies all concerned parties of the impending action, provides a basis for proper entries in accounting and inventory records, and minimizes interoffice correspondence. The procedure thus becomes routinized.

Figure 26–7.

REQUEST FOR APPROVAL TO DISPOSE OF FIXED ASSETS

Date _____

Originating Plant or Office, etc.   Request No. _____

Disposition Requested

Department   Building Number and Designation

| Description and Asset Number | Estimated Salvage Value | Book Value |

Requested by   Approved—Engineering Division   Department Approval

Executive Approval   Noted—Comptroller's Department   Recorded

Reprinted from Norman Pflomm, *Managing Capital Expenditures,* Studies in Business Policy, No. 107, 1963. By permission of The Conference Board, New York.

To Remember

Marginal cost and return	Sponsor
Laddering projects	Authorization
Diminishing returns	Completion report
Capital budget	Post-completion audit

Questions

1 Magic Vacuum, Inc., can invest in various $1,000 projects that yield the following returns including costs of capital:

A $300
B $200
C $200
D $100
E $ 50

Magic Vacuum has a cost of capital on each $1,000 lump that goes like this:

1 $ 50
2 $100
3 $200
4 $300
5 $400

(a) Why should the marginal cost of capital increase and the marginal return on investment fall?
(b) What is the last project the firm will accept? Calculate the average return and average cost of capital at that point.
(c) Sketch a chart depicting total, average, and marginal returns and costs for Magic Vacuum. Shade in the profit area.

2 Spiro Markowicz, treasurer for Whiz Chewing Gum, wants his firm to diversify by entering a new industry. He points out that returns on every $1,000 should be 20 per cent, and Whiz can raise finance at 18 per cent. Why might the presence of uncertainty cause Whiz management to refuse the suggestion?

3 What might be some reasons for firms to submit an appropriations request in addition to an expenditures budget?

4 G. W. Pollack is the sponsor of a $50,000 investment proposal. The project has been under construction eighty days, and $30,000 has been expended. He files a status report indicating the program is 60 per cent completed based on the percentage of appropriated funds expended.

(a) If Pollack is correct, in how many more days will the program be complete?
(b) How should Pollack determine the status of the project?

5 To check on the soundness of managers' proposals is one of the aims of the post-completion audit. Do you agree with this aim? Why?

6 Which do you consider to be more important, the ability to forecast demand and costs accurately, or precision in calculating marginal cost and return? Why?

27

Ranking and Selecting Investment Proposals

Profit — Requisites — Methods — *Payback — Average Rate of Return — Internal Rate of Return — Profitability Index* — Adjusting for Uncertainty — *Risk Adjusted Discount — Certainty Equivalent* — A Misplaced Emphasis — Summary — Appendix

---

Fixed asset selection is one of the financial manager's most crucial decisions. Fixed assets require large outlays of money and last many years. These decisions, as we have noted, are largely irrevocable.

This chapter discusses the most publicized phase of fixed-asset investment: the ranking and selection of investment proposals. It concentrates successively on three topics: (1) ambiguity of the profit concept as a ranking and selection criterion, (2) the various ranking and selection methods business firms use, and (3) the problem of adjusting the ranking-selection process for what is loosely called risk, but is actually uncertainty.

Profit

In the capitalist system, a company's objective is usually stated as "maximizing profit." A firm maximizes profit by responding to market demand, to spreads between prices and costs, and by producing what the market says is most urgently wanted. In this way, productive resources are put to their best uses and society reaps the benefit.

If profit maximization is so widely accepted as the firm's objective, what difficulties can it present as a criterion for ranking and selecting investment projects? There are, in fact, three difficulties to note: its ambiguity, its abstraction from uncertainty, and its neglect of time. Let us examine each in turn.

1. There is no consistent or universally useful measure of profit. Chapter 16 examined several measures, each useful in a specific context. Which is most useful in judging returns from fixed assets? Not the *total* earnings resulting from an investment, because this figure pays no attention to (a) how big an investment it took to produce the earnings, or (b) how the investment was financed. What about *some rate of return* on investment? What rate should be used? The rate before taxes or after taxes? Does depreciation affect the rate of return? Does the time-pattern of earnings affect the measure of profit? Clearly, the profit-measure question is a knotty one.

2. Profit maximization abstracts from uncertainty. All of the above mentioned measures of profit fail to recognize the uncertainty present in the investment. Although two assets may offer the same return by the above measures, the *quality* of return will vary according to the uncertainty involved in owning each asset. For example, the return on a government bond is more certain than that on a share of common stock. Even though both may be yielding at present $20 per year, they cannot be considered equally desirable.[1]

A recognition that uncertainty is present in any project evaluation method shows how fallible any attempt to maximize earnings can be. Suppose that a firm is earning $2 per share and has an opportunity to invest in a project that might increase earnings per share to $3, but might also reduce them to zero. Should management accept the project? The theoretical answer depends on the relative probabilities of different earnings results, the likelihood of a loss large enough to be catastrophic, and management's risk attitude.[2] There is a chance that despite a substantial rise in earnings per share the share price itself will decline. Shareholders may consider the enlarged returns so shaky and so uncertain of continuing that they will capitalize, i.e., discount, these returns at a sufficiently higher rate to drop the stock price.

Thus, in assessing the prospective earnings of investment projects, businessmen must recognize the presence and likely impact of uncertainty.

3. Profit *per se* neglects time. The financial manager must never forget that money has time value. To say that two projects yielding $15,000 and costing $10,000 are equal would obviously not be correct if one yielded its $15,000 this year, and the other two years hence.

---

[1] Recall that when genuine risk is present (rather than uncertainty), it can be measured by the standard deviation of expected returns. The larger the standard deviation is, the larger the risk will be.

[2] Given the probability of an occurrence, we can tell whether someone is a risk seeker or averter by comparing the odds at which he can bet (objective odds) with those he believes are correct (subjective odds). For example, assume there is 1 chance in 10 of a successful outcome. Here, the objective odds are 9:1. Out of 10 tries, you will lose $1 on 9 bets and win $9 on one, leaving a zero net gain. The expected value recognizes that, if you win, you will have $10, if you lose, zero. It is calculated: $.10(\$10) + .90(0) = \$1$. A risk seeker will accept the wager even though the subjective odds exceed the objective ones. A risk averter will accept only if the odds seem "too high," that is, the objective odds exceed the subjective odds. See the discussion in Kenneth Boulding, *A Reconstruction of Economics* (New York: Science Editions, Inc., 1962), pp. 118–20.

Requisites

If profit (or its synonyms, earnings and return) is unsuitable for ranking and selecting fixed assets, what principle should be used? Before answering this question, let us ask another: What properties should a ranking and selection criterion ideally possess? There are four. The criterion should:

1. Recognize the time value of money by preferring an early receipt of money to a later one.
2. Consider the cash flows over a project's entire life.
3. Incorporate the firm's cost of capital.
4. Weigh the uncertainty involved in the project.

Financial managers have developed several methods of evaluating investment proposals, each having both advantages and disadvantages. Keeping our four requisites in mind, let us examine four major approaches and compare their merits.

Methods

Table 27-1 calculates the expected cash flows from a $2,000 investment outlay with five-year life and straight-line depreciation. Cash flow consists of earnings on capital, minus taxes and plus depreciation.[3] To calculate it, you must first subtract depreciation (and interest on bonds, if it is paid) from operating income to get income subject to tax. After subtracting taxes to obtain profit after taxes, you must add back depreciation and interest payments to get cash flow. Seen in this light, cash flow is simply the sum total of cash which an investment returns for two purposes: (1) to replace the cash put into the investment, and (2) to pay the providers of equity and debt capital a reward for use of their money. Table 27-1 shows cash flows on this basis.

With the information in this table, we can illustrate the four main ways of ranking and selecting investment proposals.[4]

Payback

The payback method calculates the length of time required to recapture through cash flows the firm's outlays on a project. In our example, the payback period is approximately three years and three months. You calculate it this way. You need to recover $2,000. The first three years' cash flows make $1,850. You need only $150 of the third year's flow of $650—about one-fourth of another year. Thus the period is three years and three months.

How is payback used to rank and select projects? The ranking step occurs when investment proposals are lined up according to payback periods, beginning with the shortest. Then projects are selected on the basis of an acceptable maximum time period. Suppose with the Table 27-1 project, the maximum acceptable period is three years. Then this project will be rejected. If its period had been three years, it would have been accepted.

---

[3]The earnings portion of cash flow, as the term applies to *an investment proposal,* must include all recompense to suppliers of capital. For this reason, as the next sentence points out, it is necessary to include *interest* in cash flow. Interest is the recompense to suppliers of debt capital.

[4]The $2,000 is a net figure. If the asset were replacing another, the $2,000 would be net of liquidation, an adjustment examined in this chapter's appendix.

Table 27–1. Net Benefits From a $2,000 Outlay

Year	1	2	3	4	5
Earnings Before Interest, Depreciation and Taxes	$700	$700	$800	$600	$400
Less: Interest	100	100	100	100	100
Less: Depreciation	400	400	400	400	400
Earnings Before Taxes	$200	$200	$300	$100	($100)
Less: Taxes (50%)	100	100	150	50	–0–
Earnings After Taxes	$100	$100	$150	$ 50	($100)
Add: Depreciation and Interest	500	500	500	500	500
Cash Flow	$600	$600	$650	$550	$450[5]

How does payback stand as a ranking-selection criterion? Theoretically, it is not good because it possesses none of the four ideal properties:

1. It does not consider the time value of money. It treats all cash flows as equivalents.
2. It does not consider flows over the project's entire life. Once payback has occurred, further flows are ignored.
3. It ignores the cost of capital.
4. It does not *explicitly* recognize uncertainty.

The point, of course, is that payback is not a measure of profitability at all; it measures *speed of capital recovery,* which an accountant would call return *of* capital, as opposed to return *on* capital.

Yet in practice, payback is a popular method. It appeals especially to cash-short companies and to firms operating in the face of large uncertainties. If a management must recover its cash quickly to avoid going broke or suffering great financial strain, a short payback standard is not only sensible but mandatory. Firms confronted with large, sudden, unpredictable changes in demand, technology, or price—for example, makers of fashion-goods, users of machinery subject to sudden obsolescence, innovators in products capable of rapid imitation—also find payback a reasonable and fruitful standard. Since only near-term cash flows can be forecast with any accuracy, it makes little sense for these companies to rely on flows projected for distant years.[6] Thus, a short payback period is a buffer against uncertainty.[7]

---

[5] The fifth year cash flow is $450 rather than $400 because of the company's loss on this project in its fifth year. This will either (a) reduce income taxes by $50 on earnings from other company projects, or (b) entitle the company to a $50 tax refund of past taxes.

[6] "It would be foolish, in forming our expectations, to attach great weight to matters which are very uncertain. . . . Our knowledge of the factors which will govern the yield of an investment some years hence is usually very slight and often negligible. If we speak frankly, we have to admit that our basis of knowledge for estimating the yield ten years hence . . . amounts to little and sometimes to nothing; or even five years hence. In fact, those who seriously attempt to make any such estimate are often so much in the minority that their behavior does not govern the market." John Maynard Keynes, *The General Theory of Employment Interest and Money* (New York: Harcourt, Brace & Co., 1936), pp. 148–50. He makes a similar observation in "The General Theory of Employment," *Quarterly Journal of Economics* 51 (February 1937): 213–14.

[7] A point persuasively argued by G. L. S. Shackle in a landmark article, "Interest Rates and the Pace of Investment," *Economic Journal* 56 (March 1946): 1–17.

Average Rate of Return

The widely used average rate of return (ARR) method estimates profitability of an investment through a ratio between average return after taxes and average outlay. The computation runs

$$ARR = \frac{\text{Average income after taxes}}{\text{Original outlay}/2} \qquad \text{(Eq. 27–1)}$$

In our example, average income after taxes amounts to $300 divided by five years, or $60 per year. Average investment in the project, which begins life at $2,000 and ends at zero, is $2,000/2, or $1,000. Thus we have

$$ARR = \frac{\$60}{\$1,000} = 6\%.$$

Variations of the same method are average return before taxes on average investment ($140/$1,000 = 14 per cent); average return after taxes on total investment ($60/$2,000 = 3 per cent); and average return before taxes on total investment ($140/$2,000 = 7 per cent).

Sometimes the ARR method is called the accounting rate of return because it emphasizes the accounting notion of return (earnings).

Although the ARR method considers returns over the whole project life, it ignores time value of money, cost of capital, and uncertainty. Just the same, it continues to be widely used by businessmen in an unpredictable world where a man is usually content simply to be generally right or wrong about a project's outcome, rather than arithmetically precise about its returns.

Internal Rate of Return

A project's internal rate of return (sometimes called marginal efficiency of capital) is the discount rate that equates the present value of its cash inflows (returns) with its cash outflows (outlay).[8] It is an iterative, or trial-and-error, method in which the project sponsor tries several discount rates until he hits on one that brings the two streams into equality. Mathematically, this process solves the following equation for k:

$$PW = \sum_{i=1}^{n} \frac{CF_t}{(1 + k)_i} \qquad \text{(Eq. 27–2)}$$

where

$$PW = \text{present worth of project outlays,}$$
$$CF = \text{each cash flow,}$$
$$k = \text{internal rate of return,}$$
$$i = \text{year in which each flow occurs,}$$
$$n = \text{project life in years, and}$$
$$t = \text{each year.}$$

---

[8]Although in our illustrations all outlays are made at the beginning of the project's life (time period zero), real-life projects sometimes call for outlays at later points in time. These cash outflows must be discounted for futurity in the same way a distant cash inflow is discounted. Assume that the time value of money is 10 per cent. Then, just as a return of $1,000 in five years has a present value of $621, so an outlay of $1,000 that must be made in five years has a *present cost* of $621.

In our example, the sponsor might begin by trying a discount rate of 20 per cent. He would then "solve" the equation below by substituting for *k*:

$$\$2,000 = \frac{\$600}{(1 + k)^1} + \frac{\$600}{(1 + k)^2} + \frac{\$650}{(1 + k)^3} + \frac{\$550}{(1 + k)^4} + \frac{\$450}{(1 + k)^5}$$

Of course, rather than using the mathematical equation, he would use a solution table like Table 27–2. Here, *k* represents his guess what the internal rate of return will be. A starting point can be estimated by finding the ratio of cash outlay to the undiscounted present value of the cash flows. By looking in the future worth to present worth table along the row where *n* = the *middle year* of the life of the project, find the ratio you calculated. Then, read up the column and you have an approximate *k*. In our example $2,000/$2,850 = 0.70. Looking across the table where *n* = 3 (the middle year), we find 0.70 is close to *k* = 14 per cent.

Table 27–2. Solution Table, *k* = 20%

Year (*n*)	Cash Flow	CF (*k* = 20%)	PW
1	$600	.833	$ 499.80
2	600	.694	416.40
3	650	.578	375.70
4	550	.482	265.10
5	450	.401	180.45
			= $1,737.45

Since, as Table 27–2 demonstrates, the present value of the future cash flows is not equal to the cash outlay, the sponsor knows that the internal rate of return is not 20 per cent. He must try another rate. Should it be higher or lower than 20 per cent? Since at 20 per cent the present worth of cash flows was too low, he should decrease *k*. He tries 14 per cent, as in Table 27–3. Now PW is still below the outlay. His next move is perhaps to try 12 per cent, to

Table 27–3. Solution Table, *k* = 14%

Year (*n*)	Cash Flow	CF (*k* = 14%)	PW
1	$600	.877	$ 526.20
2	600	.769	461.40
3	650	.675	438.75
4	550	.592	325.60
5	450	.519	233.55
			= $1,985.50

sandwich the IRR between two specific discount rates. At 12 per cent, the PW is $2,081.75. The sponsor now knows that the internal rate of return lies between 12 and 14 per cent. Linear interpolation would give about 13.68 per cent.[9]

The capital budgeting committee can rank proposals according to IRRs, and deem acceptable all those which *exceed* the firm's cost of capital. If capital is rationed so that not all projects can be accepted, then management will accept those with the greater IRR until all funds have been used up.

IRR is widely used by firms that operate in stable business environments or pride themselves on great precision in evaluating capital spending proposals. The IRR method satisfies most theoretical criteria. Clearly, it recognizes money's time value and all cash flows from a project. It can adjust for uncertainty either by arbitrarily reducing the flows estimated for distant years or by demanding that speculative projects yield extraordinarily high IRRs. (Methods of adjusting cash flows for uncertainty are discussed a few paragraphs below.)

The chief fault of the IRR method is in failing to discount all flows at the company's cost of capital. The point is somewhat technical and requires a slightly sophisticated understanding of compound interest theory, but it amounts to this: whatever IRR is computed is the assumed rate at which all cash flows will be *reinvested* over the project's life. This may not bias the valuation of a project when the IRR differs little from the firm's cost of capital. But what of exceptionally high-yielding projects? Suppose an IRR calculation comes to 40 per cent when the company's cost of capital is considered 12 per cent? A 40 per cent IRR means that as money is recovered from this project, it can be reinvested in others to yield 40 per cent. This assumption seems very doubtful for a company that appears happy to make 12 per cent. So the implicit assumption about what reinvested flows will earn makes IRR theoretically less perfect than the profitability index, our fourth method. In practice, however, the two methods usually rank projects in exactly the same order.

Profitability Index

The profitability index (PI) is the ratio of the present worth (PW) of cash flows to original outlay (I). Cash flows are discounted at the firm's *cost of capital.*

Assuming a 10 per cent cost of capital for the firm, the project sponsor would use a solution table like Table 27–4. The present value of cash flows discounted at a 10 per cent cost of capital is $2,184.25.[10] Now, we can use the PI formula:

$$PI = \frac{PW}{I} = \frac{\$2,184.25}{\$2,000.00} = 1.09.$$

---

[9]Some writers (including the authors) argue that such interpolation is unnecessary, even unwise, because it suggests accuracy in a process that at many points is based on sheer guesswork. Even though we think an approximate solution suffices, here is how we got 13.68 per cent. With 14 per cent, you have present worth of $1985, at 12 per cent, $2,081. The difference is $96. From either present worth figure you need to get $2,000. To get there from $2,081 (12 per cent), you must move the IRR up by 81/96 of two percentage points, or by about 1.68. From $1,985 (14 per cent IRR), you must move the IRR down by 15/96 of two percentage points, or by about .32. Either calculation brings you to 13.68 per cent.

[10]If cash flows were all equal, they would constitute an annuity and our solution would have been simpler.

Table 27-4. Solution Table, $k = 10\%$

Year (n)	Cash Flow	CF (k = 10%)	PW
1	$600	.909	$ 545.40
2	600	.826	495.60
3	650	.751	488.15
4	550	.683	375.65
5	450	.621	279.45
			= $2,184.25

Given alternative investments, management may accept all projects with a PI greater than 1. Or, if investment funds are limited, it accepts first the project with the largest PI and moves down the rankings until funds are exhausted. The profitability index satisfies all theoretical criteria for a project ranking device because it accepts the time value of money, considers cash flows throughout the project's life, incorporates the cost of capital, and can be easily modified to include an explicit adjustment for uncertainty. Also, since the PI is a ratio, the ranking it gives is not affected by the sizes of the different projects.

Adjusting for Uncertainty

Let us now consider how the businessman, ranking and selecting investment proposals, may adjust for the uncertainties that beset a project's future.

Risk Adjusted Discount

One approach, called *risk adjusted discount,*[11] adjusts denominators in Eq. 27-2. Management adds a premium to the firm's cost of capital, extra percentage points assigned according to type of project being assessed and based on management's intuition and judgment.[12] For example, for replacement of existing assets, where management knows from experience what losses to expect, a sponsor may use zero risk premium; for new projects in a similar line of business, a sponsor may assign a 5 per cent premium; and for projects in a completely different line of business, he may assign a 10 per cent premium.

By adding this premium to the cost of capital, management is using Eq. 16-1, adjusting the pure rate of return (here, the market weighted average cost of capital we calculated in chapter 20) by a risk premium. Management in effect is saying, "The greater the uncertainties of a project, the greater the prospective return must be to persuade us to accept it." Thus, the hurdle rate which each project must clear varies directly with its uncertainty. If a firm's cost of capital

---

[11]Correctly, it should be called *"uncertainty* adjusted discount."

[12]Actually, there are precise ways to adjust cash flows for risk. Most begin with the standard deviation and make probabilistic adjustments, as implied in footnotes 1 and 2 above. We choose to deal here only with uncertainty, leaving statistically sophisticated adjustments to advanced finance courses.

is 10 per cent and it is faced with projects having the premiums mentioned, then each project's future cash flows would be discounted as follows: replacement, 10 per cent; new project in a similar line of business, 15 per cent; new projects in a different line of business, 20 per cent.

Certainty Equivalent

Alternatively, the businessman might adjust *numerators* in the present worth equation. That is referred to as the *certainty-equivalent* approach.[13] Management will assign a certainty-equivalent factor, which is a subjectively determined probability, to each cash flow. This certainty equivalent will range between 1, indicating certain occurrence, and 0, indicating no possibility. In calculating, management will add to the solution table two new columns, titled "certainty-equivalent factor" and "certainty equivalent." Treating the $2,000 project in Table 27–4 as a new project in a similar line of business, this kind of adjustment for uncertainty might produce Table 27–5.

Table 27–5. Solution Table, k = 10%

Year (n)	Cash Flow	Certainty-Equivalent Factor	Certainty Equivalent	CF (k = 10%)	PW
1	$600	.9	$540	.909	$ 490.86
2	600	.8	480	.826	396.48
3	650	.5	325	.751	244.08
4	550	.3	165	.683	112.70
5	450	.1	45	.621	27.95
				=	$1,272.07

Each cash flow is multiplied by its certainty-equivalent factor to yield its certainty equivalent. Then, each certainty equivalent is discounted at the firm's weighted average cost of capital. Notice that the certainty-equivalent factors decline year by year: this is what you would expect, because less certainty attaches to an expected occurrence as its remoteness in time increases. The profitability index is 0.64 ($1,272.07/$2,000); clearly an unacceptable project.

Where do the certainty-equivalent factors come from? The financial manager must estimate them, drawing on his experience and intuition. How accurate will they be? Time alone can tell.

Like the risk adjusted discount approach, the certainty-equivalent method compels the manager to include uncertainty explicitly in his estimate. In coming up with a specific factor, he must at least consider all of the elements which make a given cash flow uncertain: competition, technological change, altered consumer preferences, inflation, government restrictions, cost changes, ecological problems, and so on. In the end, however, even though he comes up with a seemingly precise figure, everyone should recognize that it is only quantified guesswork.

---

[13]G. L. S. Shackle first used this term in *Expectations, Investment, and Income* (Oxford: Oxford University Press, 1938).

A Misplaced Emphasis

Authors of finance texts, who want their books to appear precise and authoritative, usually devote too much space to the ranking and selection step in capital budgeting. Actually, estimating the cash flows, which is the task of the engineering, production, and marketing people, is far more important than ranking and selection, which the finance man handles. Given reasonably correct cash flow estimates, very rough methods of ranking and selection guided by common sense will get the job done quite adequately. But applying the most sophisticated methods to inaccurate or utterly uncertain cash flow estimates carries the great danger that businessmen may take precise-looking results seriously and so be trapped into relying on them blindly.

To Remember

Payback	Profitability index
Average rate of return	Role of the cost of capital
Internal rate of return	Risk adjusted discount
Reinvestment rate	Certainty equivalent

Questions

1 "Good grief," says Bud Minard, President of Minard Food Stores, "we cannot afford any new taxes or competition. We have a profit margin of only 1 per cent already." How would you counter this comment to indicate that profit is really better than 1 per cent?

2 Gehrsbach, Inc., is evaluating a project which will reduce labor costs in its production process. Earnings before interest, depreciation, and taxes on the $4,000 project will be $2,000 in each of the first two years of its life, $3,000 in each of its last two. Interest expense is $300 per year and the tax rate is 40 per cent. Gehrsbach, Inc., uses straight-line depreciation and its cost of capital is 12 per cent.

   Evaluate the project using
   (a) payback,
   (b) average rate of return,
   (c) profitability index,
   (d) internal rate of return.

3 "To evaluate a project, you should use net cash flow (profit after taxes plus depreciation), not·cash flow plus interest." Do you agree? Why or why not?

4 "This method," says the instructor's manual to the textbook," is really a return of capital, not a return on capital."
   (a) Which method is being discussed?
   (b) How would you distinguish between the two returns?

5 A project has a 30 per cent IRR. The firm's cost of capital is 10 per cent.
   (a) Should the project be accepted?
   (b) What will probably happen to the firm's stock price when it is accepted?
   (c) If management cannot select future projects which yield so high a return, might the stock price drop after this highly profitable project expires?

6 A project we are considering has a PI of .70. The present worth is $4,700. What is the outlay?

7 Bill Temple, treasurer of Eolian Amfonics, is evaluating a $1000 project with expected cash flows of $500, $700, and $300, in years 1–3, respectively. Eolian Amfonics' cost of capital is 6 per cent. Projects of this risk nature carry a 4 per cent premium. Temple assigns a certainty-equivalent factor of .9, .7, and .4 to each of the years, respectively. Calculate the profitability index (PI) using

(a) risk adjusted discount approach,
(b) certainty equivalent approach.

Summary: Solving Capital Budgeting Problems

I.   Cash Flow
A. *Determine net cash outflow* for the project by adding all outlays, including working capital.
B. *Determine net cash inflow* for each year of the project:
  1. If the net cash inflow after taxes is given, this is the desired figure, so use it.
  2. If net income after taxes and depreciation is given, add depreciation and allocable bond interest to net income to get net cash inflow.
  3. If earnings before depreciation, interest, and taxes is given, subtract depreciation, interest and taxes to obtain net income, then add back depreciation and interest to get net cash inflow.
II. Methods
A. To calculate *payback period:*
  1. Simply figure the number of full years and fraction it will take to recover the net cash outflow out of net cash inflows. (A listing by years of *cumulative* net cash inflows will make this calculation easy.)
  2. If payback period is quicker than cut-off, the project is acceptable.
B. To calculate *average rate of return:*
  1. Average the annual *net income after taxes* (do not use cash flows or present value) over the project's life.
  2. Figure the average investment in the project over its life. If there is no salvage value and no additional investment in later years, this can be found by taking half the original cost since the project begins at original cost and ends, fully depreciated, at zero.
  3. Divide average net income by average investment to get the average rate of return after tax on average investment.
C. To calculate *internal rate of return:*
  1. Divide the net cash outflow for the project by total undiscounted net cash inflow for the project. Look in the future worth to present worth table for the row where n = middle year of this project. Find the figure nearest the ratio. Look up the column. This is your best starting estimate of the project's internal rate of return.
  2. Starting at this estimated return, sandwich the outlay between two discounted amounts.
  3. If the internal rate of return > cost of capital, the project is acceptable.

D. To calculate *profitability index:*
1. Discount all outlays for the project at the firm's cost of capital. (The factor will be 1.0 if all outlays occur at the beginning of the project.)
2. Discount the net cash inflows at the cost of capital.
3. Divide the present worth of the inflows by the present worth of the outlays to get the profitability index. If the profitability index exceeds 1.0, the rate of return on the proposal exceeds the cost of capital, and it is an acceptable project.

Appendix: The Replacement Decision

To decide whether or not to replace an existing asset or project, a businessman considers marginal costs and benefits. The four elements of the decision are 1) comparison of cash flows from operation of present vs. replacement machine, 2) cash retrieved from disposal of the present machine, 3) tax effects of disposal, and 4) salvage values.

Here is an example. Downman Enterprise has been using a machine tool for two years originally acquired for $20,500. The machine was expected to have a useful life of five years and a $500 salvage value. The machine generates $8,000 a year before interest, depreciation, and taxes. The firm uses straight-line depreciation.

Now management has an opportunity to buy a new machine tool for $16,000 with a three-year life and $1,000 salvage value. It will replace the present one and permit one worker to spend part of his time on another project, reducing labor expense $2,000. The machine tool distributor offers a $9,500 trade-in on the present machine.

Comparing Cash Flows

Look at the cash flows with and without replacement. (The normal tax rate is 50 per cent.)

	With Replacement	Without Replacement
Earnings Before Depreciation and Taxes	$10,000	$8,000
Less: Depreciation (straight-line)	5,000	4,000
Earnings Before Taxes	$ 5,000	$4,000
Less: Taxes (50%)	2,500	2,000
Earnings After Taxes	$ 2,500	$2,000
Add: Depreciation	5,000	4,000
Cash Flow	$ 7,500	$6,000

The *marginal* cash flow from operations is $1,500.

Cash From Disposal

Now consider the cash from liquidating the existing machine. The original $20,500 asset has a $12,500 book value. Selling the asset (or trading it in) for $9,500 permits Downman to retrieve all but $3,000 of the original outlay. This $3,000 is a sunk cost.

Tax Implications

Although $3,000 cannot be retrieved, Downman shareholders receive a benefit from it. The loss offsets a gain elsewhere in the firm and reduces tax outlays, or generates a tax refund through the carry-back provision. Still assuming a 50 per cent tax rate, the marginal tax benefit is $1,500.

Salvage Values

Disposing of the present machine, Downman Enterprise foregoes its future $500 salvage. But with the new machine, the firm will receive an estimated $1,000 from salvage. The net change is $1,000 − $500 = $500.

Tabular Presentation

Here are all the cash flows associated with the decision, along with the periods in which flows occur:

	With Replacement	Without Replacement	Period
1. Purchase New	− $16,000		0
2. Disposal Present	9,500		0
3. Tax Reduction or Rebate	1,500		0
4. Cash Flow New	7,500		1–3
5. Cash Flow Present		$6,000	1–3
6. Salvage New	1,000		3
7. Salvage Present		500	3

Now the task is to allocate the marginal flows with replacement. Here is how the businessman does that:

Marginal Outlay[1]		Period
1. Purchase New	$16,000	0
2. Sell Existing	(9,500)	0
3. Tax Reduction	(1,500)	0
Net	$ 5,000	

Marginal Inflows		
4. Cash Flow	$ 1,500	1–3
5. Salvage	500	3

For capital budgeting purposes, the marginal outlay is $5,000, marginal cash flows from operations are $1,500, and marginal salvage flow is $500.[2]

The businessman evaluates these marginal flows. The payback period is three years. The IRR is the rate of discount that equates the $5,000 outlay with the future cash inflows of $1,500 in each of the next three years (an annuity) and

---

[1]This will help you to remember the flows under outlay: purchase is *always* an *outflow;* selling the old is *always* an *inflow.* Taxes are an *outflow* when the old is sold for a *gain,* an *inflow* (or a reduction in an outflow) when sold for a *loss.*

[2]What if Downman Enterprise could sell the old asset for $15,500? Then, the adjustments to the $16,000 outlay would be (1) a cash inflow of $15,500, (2) a tax outlay of $1,500 (on the $3,000 gain). The net cash outlay would be $16,000 − $15,500 + $1,500 = $2,000. The gain is taxed at the normal rate because the gain does not exceed accumulated depreciation.

$500 at the end of three years. Since $5,000 = $4,500 + $500, the IRR of this project is zero, so only in the unlikely case where capital is free (cost of zero), or the firm is paid to borrow money (cost less than zero), should replacement be made.

Question

Houyhnhnm International has a production system that is now generating earnings before interest and taxes (gross benefits) of $40,000 per year. This project has a remaining estimated life of six years. Straight-line depreciation and zero salvage are used, and the tax rate is 40 per cent. (Use 20 per cent for capital gains). Two years ago, when the system was new, Houyhnhnm's management paid $280,000 for it.

Now, management has the opportunity to acquire a new production system for $280,000 that will permit the firm to use two fewer employees. This improved system will lower annual operating expenses $22,000. The new system has an estimated salvage value of $40,000 at the end of its six-year life.

(a) Decide whether or not Houyhnhnm should replace the existing system under each of the following conditions (its cost of capital is 8 per cent):
   (1) It sells the old system for $180,000.
   (2) It sells the old system for $240,000.
   (3) It sells the old system for $310,000.

(b) Now suppose that the new system *increases* labor costs $40,000 per year. What is your decision if management can sell the old machine for $365,000?

28

Administering Circulating Capital

Cash — *Transactions Balance* — *Precautionary Balance* — *Speculative Balance* — *Investment Balance* — *The Cash Budget* — *A Cash Budget Illustration* — *Excess Cash* — Accounts Receivable — *An Illustration* — *Collection Practices* — Inventory — *Inventory Control Illustrated* — *Economic Order Quantity* — *Safety Stock* — *Total Cost of Maintaining Inventory* — *Order Point*

Managing circulating capital, or current assets, is the financial manager's most time consuming job. It requires time because, with its short turnover, circulating capital is continually absorbing and releasing cash.

To minimize his company's investment, the financial manager should keep circulating capital at the lowest level consistent with profitability and safety. In so doing, he will enable the firm to increase its asset turnover and produce a higher rate of return on assets.

Circulating capital consists of cash, accounts receivable and inventory. Each of these assets presents unique managerial problems, and for each, accepted methods of management have been developed.

Cash

Holding cash is a necessary evil. Cash earns no return, so having it on hand lowers the average return the firm earns on total assets. Why, then, hold cash? We examined the primary reasons in chapter 3, but they merit reiterating.

Transactions Balance

A firm needs a pool of cash because its receipts and expenditures are not perfectly synchronized: a company usually pays its bills before it receives cash from its own sales. This pool of cash is known as a transactions balance. The most advantageous size of this balance is calculated by using a cash budget, a managerial tool we shall look at shortly.

Precautionary Balance

Management cannot forecast the future infallibly. Unexpected losses or emergencies may occur. To guard against these, a company needs a rainy day fund of cash, a precautionary balance. Through this reserve, it can prevent a *linkage of disasters* wherein failure to meet one cash obligation, however small, can bring other debts due and so lead to collapse of the firm. For example, failure to pay a $3,000 advertising bill could arouse the fears of other creditors, causing them to press for payment.

Speculative Balance

A business must also keep cash on hand to take advantage of unexpected opportunities. Cash cannot always be borrowed when needed, and exceptional opportunities are most likely to arise when almost no one has, or can procure, cash. How large this speculative cash balance need be depends on a company's holdings of liquid, marketable securities, its lines of credit at commercial banks, and its ability to squeeze cash out of its operations by delaying payables, running down inventories, and so on. But some reserve of money itself is always advisable.[1]

Investment Balance

The final reason for holding idle cash is for future investments. Financial managers must marshal large-scale finance in advance of paying for a large investment, for example, a $300,000 building. Here, management would build up a pool of $300,000 in cash, however temporary, to pay for the building.[2]

The Cash Budget

The prudent financial manager forecasts his cash on a monthly, weekly, sometimes even daily basis. His tool is the cash budget.

The cash budget is a detailed forecast of expected cash flows stretching

---

[1] It is said that in 1932 Gulf Oil Company missed the chance to buy much of the great East Texas oil field at a bargain price for lack of ready cash. Management never forgot the lesson. As depression gave way to recovery and, later, to war boom, the company piled up cash and marketable securities awaiting another opportunity. It came in 1946. Gulf was able to buy a half interest in the fabulous Kuwait oil concession at a "distress" price from the nearly bankrupt Anglo-Iranian Oil Company.

[2] Both the amount and duration of cash holding would be relatively low in view of the availability of very short-term, interest-earning investments.

Table 28–1. Gladstone Company, Cash Flow Worksheet for 1974

	Jan.	Feb.	Mar.	Apr.	May	June	July	Aug.	Sep.	Oct.	Nov.	Dec.
Sales (Net)	$10,000	8,000	22,000	24,000	9,000	5,000	5,000	10,000	12,000	12,000	30,000	33,000
Receipts												
1st mo., 30%	3,000	2,400	6,600	7,200	2,700	1,500	1,500	3,000	3,600	3,600	9,000	9,900
2nd mo., 70%		7,000	5,600	15,400	16,800	6,300	3,500	3,500	7,000	8,400	8,400	21,000
Total	3,000	9,400	12,200	22,600	19,500	7,800	5,000	6,500	10,600	12,000	17,400	30,900
Purchases (80% of Next Month's Sales)	6,400	17,600	19,200	7,200	4,000	4,000	8,000	9,600	9,600	24,000	26,400	6,400
Payments (Total from Preceding Month)		6,400	17,600	19,200	7,200	4,000	4,000	8,000	9,600	9,600	24,000	26,400

several periods ahead. It summarizes in a single view the factors expected to affect cash inflows and outflows. It serves not only to forecast expected levels of cash, but also to indicate when management should take steps to deal with an impending shortage or excess.

A Cash Budget Illustration

Gladstone Company has already forecast next year's total sales. But to set up a cash budget, it must forecast sales on a monthly basis. Suppose that the bulk of sales comes in early spring and, because of an elaborate sales campaign, in late winter. Gladstone extends trade credit to its customers. A 1 per cent discount can be taken if the customer pays within thirty days. Historically, 30 per cent of sales are paid for during the month the goods are sold, and the remaining 70 per cent within the second month.

Purchased materials and parts amount to 80 per cent of sales. Materials and parts are purchased during the month preceding the sales, to provide for assembling, and paid for in the month in which sales are made. Wages, rent, and taxes are the other variable outlays—variable in the sense that they are geared to sales. However, another outlay looms on the horizon: Gladstone must repay $15,000 in bonds during June. Finally, the financial manager has decided that, to ensure minimum liquidity, Gladstone's cash level should not fall below $3,000.

Table 28–1 presents a worksheet of expected cash flows for Gladstone Company over the coming year. It shows clearly when anticipated sales will be collected and when contemplated purchases will be paid for. Since cash receipts flow into the firm during the month sales are made and the following month, the worksheet has two entries for receipts. For example, March sales of $22,000 generate receipts in March of $6,600 (30 per cent of sales) and in April of $15,400 (70 per cent of sales). Gladstone must pay for its purchases during the month following purchase, and this timing accounts for bottom-line entries. March purchases of $19,200 (80 per cent of anticipated April sales) are paid for in April.

Combining the purchases-payments and sales-receipts data with other cash outlays and receipts, and entering the desired cash level, completes the budget. Table 28–2 shows Gladstone's cash budget in final form. The receipts and payments rows of figures have been transferred directly from the worksheet (Table 28–1). Wages and salaries, taxes, and the bond retirement of $15,000 have next been entered. Payments for these outlays have then been deducted from receipts to give the cash gain or loss from the month's transactions. Adding a net cash gain to, or subtracting a net cash loss from, the beginning cash balance gives the ending cash balance for each month. To complete the budget, each month's anticipated ending cash balance is compared with the desired balance to see how available cash compares with requirements.

The bottom line in Table 28–2 highlights the relation between actual and desired cash. Each month's entry is a cumulative total measuring cash shortages (and so borrowings) or excesses (and so near-cash investments). Each month's dollar amount is the total borrowings (if shortage) or investments (if excess) outstanding at that time. You will notice that the *changes* in the final line of Table 28–2 equal the cash gain (loss) during a month. The rationale is that any cash excess is used to discharge debt, any shortage is covered by borrowing.

Gladstone can expect a $6,200 excess of cash during February which it can temporarily invest, but in March, outlays will exceed receipts by $8,900. This

Table 28–2. Gladstone Company, Cash Budget for 1974

	Jan.	Feb.	Mar.	Apr.	May	June	July	Aug.	Sep.	Oct.	Nov.	Dec.
Receipts*	$ 3,000	9,400	12,200	22,600	19,500	7,800	5,000	6,500	10,600	12,000	17,400	30,900
Outlays												
Payments*		6,400	17,600	19,200	7,200	4,000	4,000	8,000	9,600	9,600	24,000	26,400
Wages & Salaries		800	1,500	1,500	850	800	800	900	1,000	1,000	2,000	2,500
Other Payments												
Taxes			2,000			2,200			2,000			3,000
Bond Repayment						15,000						
Total Payments		7,200	21,100	20,700	8,050	22,000	4,800	8,900	12,600	10,600	26,000	31,900
Cash Gain (Loss)		2,200	(8,900)	1,900	11,450	(14,200)	200	(2,400)	(2,000)	1,400	(8,600)	(1,000)
Beginning Cash		7,000	9,200	300	2,200	13,650	(550)	(350)	(2,750)	(4,750)	(3,350)	(11,950)
Ending Cash (Assuming No Adjusting)		$9,200	300	2,200	13,650	(550)	(350)	(2,750)	(4,750)	(3,350)	(11,950)	(12,950)
Cash Level Desired		3,000	3,000	3,000	3,000	3,000	3,000	3,000	3,000	3,000	3,000	3,000
Cumulative Cash Excess (or Shortage)		6,200	(2,700)	(800)	10,650	(3,550)	(3,350)	(5,750)	(7,750)	(6,350)	(14,950)	(15,950)

*From Table 28–1.

net outlay would pull the cash balance down to $9,200 less $8,900, or $300—$2,700 below the desired level. Gladstone's treasurer will borrow $2,700 to meet his firm's target cash level. In April cash receipts exceed outlays by $1,900. Adding this amount to March's $300 ending balance (assuming no adjusting), the treasurer sees that his firm will end April with an unadjusted balance of $2,200. Comparing this amount with the desired, he sees that he must have borrowings of $800 in April. Since he needs a loan of $800, he can pay down the $2,700 loan he had in March. How much will he reduce the loan and where do the funds come from? He will reduce it by $1,900 with funds from operations: the excess of receipts over expenditures.

Relations among the rows and figures are easily traced, and you should pause now to work through some of them to make sure you understand their sequence and meaning. For example, the $11,450 cash gain in May will be used to pay off the $800 loan outstanding, leaving a net excess of $11,450 – $800 = $10,650. The $14,200 cash deficit in June less the $10,650 cumulative excess means that $3,550 must be borrowed to bring July's beginning cash balance to the $3,000 desired level.

Here is another perspective on Table 28–2. The cash gain or loss in any month can be found by looking at the changes in the Cumulative Cash Excess or Shortage row. Take, for example, May:

May cumulative cash excess	$10,650
Add: April cumulative shortage	800
May cash gain	$11,450

Since Gladstone begins May with $800 in borrowings outstanding (to have its desired $3,000 opening balance), and ends May with a $10,650 excess, it obviously gains $11,450 cash from operating receipts and outlays in May.

A cash budget forces management to be explicit in its cash planning. Management must forecast all factors that influence cash flows in the planning period. Then, the treasurer plans his action to cope with a cash gain or loss, investing or repaying a loan with a gain and borrowing or liquidating investments to cover a shortage. Aware that such forecasts cannot be accurate, the treasurer must build flexibility into both worksheet and cash budget. This can be done through use of variable budgets, which recognize that some expenditures will vary at different levels of sales—for example, wages and taxes.

Excess Cash

What should a firm do with its excess cash? The answer depends on the economic outlook in general and on management's particular degree of conservatism. The safest short-term investments for cash are Treasury bills, short-term obligations of federal agencies, commercial paper, short-term tax-exempt obligations of state and local governments, and certificates of deposit. If the cash is permanently in excess, i.e., will not be needed in the predictable future, management probably should use it to acquire fixed assets, retire debt, or enlarge dividends.

Accounts Receivable

The administration of accounts receivable reflects a firm's credit policy. Trade credit is justified only to the extent that a firm's profits are improved by selling on terms rather than for cash only.[3] This means that the marginal return from granting trade credit must exceed its marginal cost.

The marginal return from trade credit is simply the gross profit (before credit costs) that a company makes on the additional sales. Trade credit involves three marginal costs: (1) cost of money tied up in trade receivables, (2) credit losses, and (3) handling expense. Bearing these costs in mind, a credit manager will classify his firm's customers according to (1) interval of payment (which shows the cost of money for each class), (2) probability of non-payment (which measures expected loss on each class), and (3) allocable processing and collection cost.

An Illustration

Suppose a company's marginal return from credit sales·is 10 per cent of invoiced amount. Its weighted average cost of capital is 10 per cent per year. It can sell $10,000 worth of merchandise to each of the five classes of customers shown in Table 28–3.

Table 28–3. Customer Classes and Expenses

Customer Class	Expected Payment Period (in days)	Expected Per Cent Uncollectable	Allocable Collection Expense (% of invoiced revenue)
A	10	0	0
B	30	1	¼
C	60	2	1
D	90	5	3
E	120	10	4

To which classes of customers can the firm profitably make credit sales? For Class A, the only expense is the cost of financing the increase in accounts receivable for ten days,[4] $(10/360) \times .10 \times \$10,000 = \$28$.[5] The marginal return is $\$10,000 \times .10 = \$1,000$; and the marginal profit from credit sales to this class of customers is $\$1,000 - \$28 = \$972$. For Class B, cost of money for thirty days is $(30/360) \times .10 \times \$10,000 = \$83$. To this must be added the cost of uncollectibles, $.01 \times \$10,000 = \$100$, and allocable collection costs of $.0025 \times \$10,000 = \$25$, for a total marginal cost of $208. Against marginal return of $1,000, Class B customers produce a marginal profit of $792. Making similar calculations for other classes, the credit department will complete a table similar to Table 28–4.

Using Table 28–4, the credit manager could see that expansion of sales to Classes A, B, and C would be profitable, to D and E, unprofitable. For these last two classes, the credit manager might insist on full payment in advance for

---

[3]We are here discussing trade credit as a *use* of funds. In chapter 23, it was discussed as a *source* of funds.

[4]Since the rise in receivables is expected to be permanent, it should be financed from a permanent source.

[5]The annual cost of capital is calculated for only the days it is used. For Class A, the cost is $(10/360) \times .10 = .0028$; for Class B, $(30/360) \times .10 = .0083$.

Class E, and specific approval from his office before any orders are shipped to Class D. Before giving his approval, he would make the credit terms more stringent (for example, net 10 days) and demand partial payment in advance.

Table 28–4. Customer Classes and Marginal Profit or Loss

Customer Class	Cost of Money	Loss on Uncollectibles	Collection Expense	Total Marginal Cost	Marginal Return	Marginal Profit or Loss
A	$ 28	0	0	$ 28	$1,000	$972
B	83	$ 100	$ 25	208	1,000	792
C	166	200	100	466	1,000	534
D	249	500	300	1,049	1,000	−49
E	332	1,000	400	1,732	1,000	−732

Collection Practices

Sound customer classification must be accompanied by effective collection practices. Credit sales must be collected approximately within the allowed payment period. Effective collections treatment of overdue accounts is always an exercise in diplomacy as well as firmness. Many accounts with "slow pay" reputations are nonetheless sound, and their business much too valuable to lose by abrupt or insulting efforts to collect money a few days sooner than they genuinely intend to pay.

Most collection procedures are based on a series of perodic and gradually stronger reminders to customers that payment is due. Notices, letters, and telephone calls from management officials are the usual sequence. Collection treatment begins sooner and quickly becomes more insistent, of course, for customers in lower credit classes than those in higher ones. In our example, class D customers approved for credit might receive a reminder notice even before bills are past due, a phone call from the credit manager the day payment is due, and a letter threatening suit five days later.

Inventory

The objective of inventory management, like accounts receivable management, is to minimize the firm's investment while at the same time maximizing the firm's return from holding the asset.

Companies hold inventories to give flexibility between production and sales. A firm may experience a strike by production employees, shortages of raw material, or delays in delivery of equipment, all of which will delay production. Thus precautionary stocks of raw materials and goods in process, as well as finished goods, are advisable. On the other hand, unforeseen surges of demand for the firm's product must be satisfied or sales may be lost permanently. By holding inventory, then, management reduces uncertainties surrounding both production and sales.

Inventory Control Illustrated

Figure 28–1 illustrates ideal inventory behavior. At the beginning of each time period, inventory has just been delivered. Maximum inventory is on hand, 230 units. Now, as time passes, goods will be sold from inventory. This is reflected in the down-sloping line from *A* to *B*. At *B*, only 30 units are left in inventory. At that point, a new delivery of merchandise arrives (either from a supplier or from the firm's own assembly line)—vertical line *BC*—and boosts inventory back to 230 units. Then the process begins again.

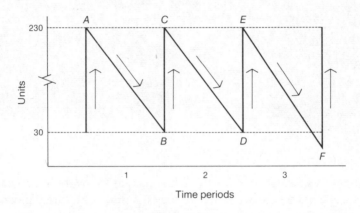

Figure 28–1. Inventory Model

Here, the merchandise delivered at the beginning of each inventory period is 200 units. Why? This question leads to two others. First, how did management set its order size at 200 units? Second, how did it decide on an ending inventory of 30 units? Let us examine both questions.

Economic Order Quantity

The number of units a firm ideally orders in each ordering interval is called the *economic order quantity* (EOQ). This is the number management must order each time if it is to minimize its total inventory cost: storage costs plus ordering costs.

Storage costs arise from holding inventory; for example, insurance, warehouse space, interest on funds tied up in the inventory, and spoilage, obsolescence, or pilfering losses. *Ordering costs* are those of order preparation and checking, and the inspection and shelving of the goods when delivered.

The simplest formula for figuring EOQ runs

$$EOQ = \sqrt{\frac{2TO}{PS}},$$

(Eq. 28–1)

where

    T = total sales for the year in units,
    O = order costs (per order),
    P = price (per unit), and
    S = storage costs as a per cent of price.

Notice that if ordering costs (which affect the numerator) rise relative to storage costs (which are in the denominator), a company should increase its order size and pay to store more units. In so doing, it saves more through less frequent ordering than it loses through additional storage costs. Conversely, as storage costs increase relative to ordering costs, management will reduce EOQ and place orders more frequently. Reducing EOQ lowers the average inventory size (lowering storage costs), and increases the number of orders. Average inventory (A) is found by dividing EOQ by 2, or

$$A = EOQ/2. \qquad \text{(Eq. 28–2)}$$

The relation between EOQ and annual number of orders (N) is inverse. The larger the EOQ, the fewer will be the number of orders placed, and vice versa.[6] Specifically, the annual number of orders is found by dividing total sales in a year (T) by EOQ, or

$$N = T/EOQ. \qquad \text{(Eq. 28–3)}$$

Now, let us supply some numbers to see how levels used in Figure 28–1 were calculated. Big Endian, Inc., sells 2,000 units per year to its single customer, the federal government. Ordering costs are $4. Big Endian must pay $2 per unit for goods, and storage costs are 20 per cent of this price. Substituting in the formula, we see that

$$EOQ = \sqrt{\frac{\text{Ordering costs}}{\text{Holding costs}}}$$

$$= \sqrt{\frac{2 \times 2,000 \times \$4}{\$2 \times .20}}$$

$$= 200.$$

Since 200 units are ordered each time, the annual number of orders is 2,000/200 = 10.

Safety Stock

Figure 28–1 shows that each period except E ends with 30 units in inventory. Thirty units represents the level of safety stock. That is the number of units management has decided to maintain as a cushion against unforeseen surges in demand or delays in delivery. A safety stock boosts the average size of inventory and so increases storage costs. For Big Endian, storage costs without safety stock are holding cost times average inventory, or $.40 × 100 units = $40. But with a safety stock of 30 units, Eq. 28–2 is modified like this: (200/2) + 30 = 130. Storage costs become $.40 × 130 = $52. The increase is 30 per cent. Management should weigh the marginal benefit of not missing sales against this $12 marginal cost to assure itself that keeping safety stock is actually profitable.

---

[6]If you have mathematical intuition, the EOQ formula will tell you an important principle about the behavior of inventories. Note that all variables determining EOQ are under the square root radical. This means that inventory needs increase not in direct proportion to sales, but in proportion to the *square root* of annual sales. The EOQ formula is derived by an elementary application of calculus to an expression for total inventory cost.

Total Cost of Maintaining Inventory

Since the cost of *maintaining* inventory is the sum of ordering and storage costs, we can see how much it is costing Big Endian to maintain its inventory. With the thirty-unit safety stock, here are the calculations.

1. Order costs per year:
   Number of orders × Cost per order
   10 × $4 = $40.
2. Storage costs per year:
   ~~Number of inventories × Cost per inventory~~
   ~~10 × $52 =~~   ~~$520.~~

$$S(P)\left(\frac{EOQ}{2} + SS\right)$$

$SS = Safety\ Stock$

Total annual cost of inventory maintenance is ~~$560.~~ *92* This is the optimum, or least-cost, combination of ordering and storage costs. Notice that it is not the cost of inventory, but only the cost of maintaining inventory.

Order Point

As you can perceive, there is a calculation to tell you at what level to order new inventory so as to receive it just as the safety stock is reached. The formula is

$$OP = (\text{Delivery period} \times \text{Use rate}) + \text{Safety stock}. \qquad \text{(Eq. 28–4)}$$

OP is the order point expressed in inventory level. Delivery period is measured in weeks. Use rate is the number of units the firm sells per week. Assume, in our example, that delivery time takes two weeks. Big Endian will sell 2,000/50, or 40 units per week.[7] This amounts to 80 units during the delivery period. Hence, it will place an order for 200 units whenever its inventory reaches 80 + 30, or 110 units, expecting delivery when inventory reaches 30 units, bringing the beginning inventory once again to 230 units.

To Remember

Cash budget	EOQ
Cash balances	Safety stock
Marginal costs of trade credit	Order point

Questions

1 Ebenezer, Inc., has the following situation. Sales will be $10,000 in January, $15,000 in February, $30,000 in each of March and April, and $10,000 in May. The treasurer insists on a $4,000 minimum cash balance. On January 1, Ebenezer, Inc., has a $6,000 loan from the bank. The firm has $6,000 beginning cash. All sales revenue is collected in the month after sales are made. Wages and

---

[7]Fifty weeks are used for a year rather than fifty-two, for ease of calculation. The obsessive compulsive is welcome to use fifty-two, if he so desires.

purchases of merchandise are paid for in the month preceding a given month's sales. Merchandise purchases and wages are 90 per cent of the subsequent month's sales. Prepare a cash budget covering the four months beginning in January. Assume that collections in January are $16,000. What is the largest loan Ebenezer, Inc., makes to cover cash shortages?

2 The Suno Corporation's cash budget shows the following entries for cumulative cash excess or shortage: September $6,000; October $2,000; November ($2,000); December ($6,000). What cash gain or loss from its operations did Suno have in October, November, and December?

3 Foma, Inc., has a 20 per cent cost of capital. It has four classes of customers with the following payments pattern. It receives a 15 per cent return on the $10,000 sales it makes to each class.

Class	Period (days)	% Uncollectible	% Collection Expense
1	20	1	2
2	60	4	3
3	90	6	5
4	150	10	15

(a) How do you explain "per cent collection expense"?
(b) To which customer classes should Foma's credit manager continue to sell on existing terms?
(c) What policy do you suggest the credit manager follow with respect to the currently unprofitable classes?

4 Aphrodite, a company that traps and sells tiggers to a fanatical clientele, has determined that the cost to keep a tigger is 20 per cent of its $20 selling price. It costs Aphrodite $2 to order a tigger and the company sells 3600 tiggers a year.
(a) Calculate the EOQ.
(b) How many orders does Aphrodite place per year?
(c) What is the total annual cost of inventory control?
(d) It takes Aphrodite three weeks to receive delivery of tiggers. At what inventory level should Aphrodite order its tiggers?

5 List and discuss the three dimensions of trade credit cost. How would you explain "allocable collection expense?"

29

Marketing New Security Issues

A firm trying to raise money by floating stock or bonds faces both marketing and legal problems. It wants to get the best price for its issue, and it must conform to the laws and regulations that govern new issues.

Legal Restrictions

Restrictions placed on new issues, debt or equity, stem largely from the 1929 stock market crash. The preceding bull market years (1927–29) had brought massive corporate security flotations. Congressional investigations after the crash revealed that many abuses and no few frauds had occurred in the new-issues market. To prevent such abuses in the future, Congress enacted regulatory legislation. Every financial manager must be familiar with the resulting federal rules and requirements before his firm markets a new security issue.

338

Securities Act of 1933

The Securities Act of 1933, which applies to the primary, or new issues, market, is a full disclosure act. It requires issuers of all securities, except those specifically exempted, (1) to file a registration statement (called an S-1) with the Securities and Exchange Commission (SEC),[1] and (2) to deliver a prospectus (actually, a condensed S-1) to any prospective security buyer before he purchases the security. Exempt securities include intra-state issues (new issues sold in one state only); governmental securities; securities of companies regulated by some federal commissions (such as railroad securities, which are regulated by the Interstate Commerce Commission); issues of non-profit organizations; and issues below $500,000 or those sold to twenty buyers or less.

An S-1 is a detailed statement of information about a firm—its management, directors, divisions, finances, accounting, history, operations, earnings, and so on—which might have a bearing on the value of the security being offered. The SEC is not concerned with profit potential of the firm, price at which its security is being offered, or even the legality of its operations. It *is* concerned that such information be made available to prospective purchasers. However, although the SEC can order the seller to send buyers prospectuses, no way has been found to make buyers read them. Quite possibly, 90 per cent do not.

Securities Exchange Act of 1934

The Securities Exchange Act of 1934 applies to the *secondary*, or existing issues market. It regulates the securities exchanges, provides for control over corporate insiders (by requiring them to file reports of their stock transactions), and empowers the Federal Reserve to set margin requirements on stocks listed on exchanges. Margin is the amount of cash a buyer must put up to purchase stock on credit. The stock itself is collateral.

Blue Sky Laws

In addition to Federal regulation of new securities issues, all fifty states have regulations restricting new securities issues within their borders. The state regulations are called *blue sky laws*. Kansas passed the first such act in 1911. A state congressman at the time commented that the laws should prevent unscrupulous stock salesmen from promising the blue sky to unsuspecting citizens. Issues must comply with these regulations before securities can be offered in particular states.

Marketing a New Issue

Once management has decided to raise money in the capital, or long-term financial market, it faces the task of marketing its security. Though it is possible for firms to sell new securities directly to investors, the usual route is through investment bankers.

---

[1] Before passage of the Securities Exchange Act of 1934, which established the SEC, the Federal Trade Commission was responsible for registering new issues.

Investment Banking Functions

An investment bank is a financial intermediary that links suppliers of long-term funds with firms needing them. Investment banking may be a misleading term, for an investment banking firm typically invests its own funds in a new issue only while distributing it. It does not make loans or permit checks to be written on its liabilities, as a commercial bank does.

How do companies select their investment bankers? The law requires railroad companies and utilities doing interstate business to select investment bankers on the basis of competitive bidding: the banker who bids the highest price (or lowest yield) wins the issue. Industrial firms typically select their investment bankers through private negotiation with one or more candidates. Table 29–1 shows the division of recent-year new issues between competitive and negotiated underwritings.

Table 29–1. Corporate Negotiated and Competitive Bid Security Offerings (in millions of dollars)

	Negotiated		Competitive	
	Volume	*Number*	*Volume*	*Number*
1964				
Bonds	$2,444	140	$1,736	104
Preferred	117	16	44	6
Common	1,374	314	59	4
1966				
Bonds	$4,316	174	$3,898	136
Preferred	416	18	41	5
Common	3,101	311	105	6
1969				
Bonds	$8,568	314	$4,706	193
Preferred	405	22	150	11
Common	8,486	1,786	231	6
1970				
Bonds	$18,463	389	$5,486	160
Preferred	1,083	37	232	19
Common	4,931	766	533	12
1971				
Bonds	$17,683	409	$7,953	189
Preferred	1,371	37	797	40
Common	10,715	1,113	630	15

Source: *Investment Dealers' Digest.* Derived from various tables.

An investment banker has four main functions: (1) originating the issue, (2) underwriting, (3) syndicating, and (4) distributing. (A fifth function, not uncommon, is to make an "after market" in underwritten securities by acting as a dealer. The securities dealer's role is outlined in chapter 32.)

Originating

Originating an issue means planning for it through negotiations between investment banker and issuing firm. Originating occurs only on negotiated issues. For those, the investment banker is present in the planning stage to advise on questions such as debt versus equity, premium versus discount pricing, what indenture provisions, timing, and so on. On competitively bid issues, a company must usually decide what features its security will have, then put its "design" out for bids.

In a negotiated issue, the investment banker helps the issuer get his financial position in order before the securities are offered by arranging for an audit and legal services. An accounting firm audits the corporate records and prepares financial reports. Attorneys prepare registration papers for the SEC. The investment banker obtains a printer familiar with the exacting forms in which the prospectus and other documents must be set.

In originating issues, an investment banker protects his reputation carefully. He makes certain that all required information is included in the registration data, and assures himself that the offering is sound. If buyers trust his financial judgment, they will be inclined to view favorably any issue he offers.

To price an issue, the investment banker considers how the market is performing and the prices similar issues are commanding. He brings his expertise to bear in a disagreement with management over pricing an issue. Managers sometimes have inflated ideas of the worth of their firm's shares or bonds, and want a higher price than the investment banker deems advisable. The banker must reconcile the issuers' demands with those of his other clients, the security buyers. Buyers are happiest if the price of a new issue increases after they buy it. Thus, the banker tries to price an issue somewhat below the absolute maximum the issue could command so that its price will move up in subsequent trading.

Timing an issue depends on the length of time needed to prepare the issue and conform with registration requirements, and on conditions in the capital markets. The average time lapse after first contact between originator and issuer is six months. But new issues are often delayed due to market conditions: a jammed new-issues calendar,[2] badly declining market, or investment banker's advice to wait for a better opportunity can effectively stall an issue. Contrariwise, issues can be accelerated if conditions seem unusually favorable.

Underwriting

Underwriting means the outright purchase of an entire new issue of securities, by an investment banker or group of investment bankers, for resale to clients. Through this device, an issuer frees himself of the risks and uncertainties ordinarily present while an issue is being sold to investors. The instant an underwriting agreement is signed, whether the transaction was negotiated or bid competitively, the issuer is "home free." It has obtained a firm price for its securities, and risks of future market fluctuations—or a completely unsaleable issue—now fall on the underwriter.

---

[2] A new-issues calendar gives a three-month preview of announced flotations. As a matter of practice, an issuer selects a date in advance, lists its name there, and claims the date as its own.

Naturally, the underwriter bids a lower price for the securities than the price at which he expects to resell them. But competition among underwriters has usually kept this gross spread, or total compensation, relatively small. Thus, underwriting is at best a hazardous business, calling for supremely accurate judgment. In the early 1970s, gross spreads were ranging from 1 per cent on negotiated bond offerings to 6 per cent on industrial equity offerings.[3] In the volatile stock and bond markets since 1965, investment banking firms have often run large and prolonged losses on both competitively bid and negotiated underwritings.

Underwriting hazards are magnified by the fact that underwriters operate largely on *borrowed* capital. This heavy use of financial leverage multiplies the chance of loss when an issue fails. If an investment banker borrows $9 for every $1 of his own capital going into a new issue, then a 1 per cent loss on the gross price of the issue will cost him 10 per cent of his own capital.

This excessive amount of leverage serves to induce investment bankers to restrict the volume of new issues during periods of monetary restraint, thereby restricting the supply of loanable funds. An investment banking firm is loathe to buy a $200 million, 30-year debt issue if he believes interest rates will increase during the flotation. The capital losses on such an issue might jeopardize its solvency. If the issue is a competitively bid one, the investment banker may choose not to bid. If it is a negotiated issue, he will probably advise his client to wait until the market "cools off."

How narrow spreads may become in competitive bidding is illustrated by one large issue in 1962. On a $300 million debenture flotation by AT&T, Halsey, Stuart & Company won the bid over Morgan Stanley & Company, 101.07 to 100.66. That is, Halsey, Stuart offered AT&T $1,010.70 per bond, and Morgan Stanley offered only $1,006.60 per bond. Halsey, Stuart reoffered the bonds at 101.767, or a spread of $6.97 per $1,000 par bond. On 30,000 bonds, the total spread was $209,100.

Syndication

Several investment banking firms usually band together on a given issue to spread the risks and pool their capital. Such a temporary combination is called a *syndicate*. It exists only for a single issue, though on Wall Street the same firms are found together in syndicates time after time. The firm that organizes the syndicate—the one that has gotten the business on a negotiated underwriting—is the manager. The manager assigns syndicate shares, usually on a reciprocity basis, i.e., you included me in your last syndicate so here's a piece of mine.

Syndication enables an investment banker to spread his capital among several underwritings instead of gambling all his capital on the outcome of a single flotation.

Syndication also increases the equity investment in an issue, and so reduces the degree of financial leverage and risk associated with the flotation. For example, if Halsey, Stuart handled the entire distribution of the above $300 million issue without benefit of a syndicate, it would give AT&T 300,000 bonds times $1,006.60, or $301,980,000. Where would Halsey, Stuart get the money? Some would come

---

[3]These estimates are from Samuel L. Hayes III, "Investment Banking: Power Structure in Flux," *Harvard Business Review* 49 (March–April 1971): 137.

from its own funds, but most would be borrowed on a call loan basis from a New York bank. Perhaps $280 million would be borrowed in this flotation. By forming a syndicate, other investment bankers can put up some of the cash for the issue and borrow only what they need or desire. In this way, the total borrowing necessary is reduced. For example, it may fall to $75 million in the AT&T issue.

A syndicate continues until the issue is either sold out at its offering price, or until it becomes evident that sale at this price is impossible. In the latter case, the syndicate breaks up, each member taking his share of the unsold securities[4] and selling this residue at the best obtainable price. Each then licks his own financial wounds.[5]

In addition to regular underwriting, there are agency marketings (sometimes called "best-efforts" deals) and stand-by underwritings. In *agency marketings*, the investment banker does not take title to the new issue, but acts simply as the issuer's agent and tries to sell all he can. Beyond an outlay of time and sales personnel, he makes no investment and assumes no risk in the flotation. A *stand-by underwriting* is one in which a syndicate agrees to buy a forthcoming issue at a predetermined price (usually considerably below the expected one) if the issuer himself is unsuccessful in selling his new securities. This arrangement is typically used to guarantee an issuer of rights that all rights will be exercised: the underwriters agree, for a stated fee, to take up all unexercised rights, exercise them, and resell the new securities at whatever price they can get.

Distribution

Distribution means selling a new issue to investors, be they individuals or financial institutions. Syndicate members enlist other firms to help distribute, or sell, the issue. These distributors (called the selling group) are merely agents, or functional middlemen, who do not take title to the securities they sell. Underwriters, in contrast, are merchant middlemen who actually take title.

Payment

No fixed formula exists for apportioning the spread (between resale price and price paid for a new issue) among manager, underwriters, and selling group members. Generally, 20 per cent of the spread goes to the manager, 30 per cent to the underwriters, and 50 per cent to the distributors.[6] Why do selling group members get so large a share when they assume no risk? They do because the manager and underwriters know that the best way to get inventory off their hands quickly is to have salesmen out beating the bushes. The bigger the commission is, the harder salesmen will beat the bushes. Of course, the manager also serves as an underwriter and distributor, so if he can sell some of the securities, he stands to make the entire spread on the securities he sells.

In the AT&T $300 million issue won by the syndicate managed by Halsey,

---

[4]How unsold securities are allocated among syndicate members is spelled out in advance by the syndicate agreement.

[5]From March through May 1966, when bond yields were sky-rocketing, thirteen competitively bid utility issues in a row failed to sell out at syndicate prices.

[6]Hayes, "Investment Banking," p. 137.

Stuart, the $6.97 spread per bond might have been distributed as in Table 29–2. On each bond Halsey, Stuart sold, it would have made $6.97; on each bond it underwrote, but sold through a selling group member, $3.48; on each bond underwritten and sold by other firms, $1.39 as manager. In 1971, Merrill, Lynch managed or co-managed $9.91 billion in new security flotations, making it the number one firm, dollar-wise, in the industry. First Boston Corporation was second, with $9.42 billion.

Table 29–2. Hypothetical Distribution of Gross Spread on $300 Million AT&T Debenture Issue

	Amount	Per Cent
Manager (Halsey, Stuart)	$1.39	20
Underwriters	2.09	30
Distributors	3.49	50
	$6.97	100

Flotation Costs

The cost of floating a new issue varies with its size and type. Cost falls as a per cent of issue price as issues become larger. There are two reasons for this. First, fixed expenses—underwriting investigation, registration, legal fees, and so on—are spread over more units. Second, smaller underwritings involve less well-known companies and so require greater sales effort. By type of issue, cost is highest for common stock, next for preferred, and lowest for bonds. Common stock is most expensive because price and market risks are larger, and because stock issues are typically smaller than bond issues and so must bear a larger share of fixed cost per unit. Equity offering costs, as a per cent of gross market value, are shown in Table 29–3. For large issues, they average around 5 per cent. By contrast, large bond issues are often floated for less than 1 per cent of market price.

Table 29–3. Equity Flotation Costs as a Per Cent of Issue

Size	Cost
Less than $500,000	27%
$500,000—less than $ 1,000,000	22%
$1,000,000—less than $ 2,000,000	14%
$2,000,000—less than $ 5,000,000	10%
$5,000,000—less than $10,000,000	6%
$10,000,000—less than $20,000,000	6%
$20,000,000—less than $50,000,000	5%

Source: Securities and Exchange Commission.

Placement

If a firm chooses to sell new securities itself, by *direct placement,* it uses no investment banker. Direct placement of *public offerings* seldom occurs. Only AT&T has had a large enough demand from investors to use direct placement frequently in public offerings. Ordinarily, a firm uses direct placement in a *private offering* in which securities are sold to one or more financial institutions (fewer than twenty to avoid registration). The issuer does not offer the securities to the public. A private offering is exempt from registration under the Security Act of 1933, since purchasers are few and presumably sophisticated enough to protect their own interest.

What determines the choice of placement? There are several considerations. Since a private placement, under most circumstances, is not subject to the legal requirements of a public placement, a firm can place securities privately more quickly and with less bother. For purchasers, however, a privately placed issue is less liquid than a publicly placed one for two reasons. First, the issue is not widely distributed: it lacks the public market that might readily absorb the issue if the institutional buyer wanted to sell its holdings. Second, before the institution can sell the issue to the public, the issue must be registered with the SEC, a time-consuming process. Because of lower liquidity, a privately placed issue must yield more than one sold publicly—a factor that partly offsets the absence of underwriting and registration costs. An issuer, then, must weigh the benefits of private placement against a higher yield requirement. He also must recognize that in foregoing a public market for his securities, he forfeits the public relations advantage that arises from a wide list of security-holders.

The extent to which private placements outyield public bond issues depends on whether insurance companies, pension funds, and other institutional buyers have substantial excess funds. When they have, they bid aggressively for private placements, and the spread narrows. When institutions are short of funds (as they were in 1966), the spread widens; institutions then get their fill of bonds in the public market. At that point, they ordinarily prefer marketable issues to private placements, and thus drop out of the private placement market.

Listing Securities

Marketing stocks (and sometimes bonds) is easier if they are listed on a national securities exchange and therefore widely known to investors. Listing, however, involves certain costs and risks. Thus, a company contemplating repeated trips to the capital market faces the question: to list or not to list. In deciding, it must weigh the potential advantages and disadvantages. If a firm decides to trade on an organized exchange,[7] it must then take steps to comply with that exchange's particular listing requirements.

Advantages and Disadvantages

Listing is generally considered to have the following advantages:

1. A wider market for the firm's stock through wider ownership.

---

[7]The alternative of having a good public market "over-the-counter" is discussed in chapter 32.

2. Enhancement of the firm's reputation through wider publicity.
3. A higher stock price through the increased liquidity, more frequent quotations, and greater notice among brokers that exchange-trading brings.

The disadvantages of listing are:

1. Loss of old-owner control by spreading a company's ownership among a larger group.
2. Additional expense and disclosure. The company must pay initial and annual fees to the exchange, and must reveal more of its affairs, in financial and proxy statements, than it has in the past.
3. Unnecessary and unjustified price changes in the stock. These may result from speculative activity on the exchange, or from ill-founded buy and sell recommendations by brokerage houses.

Listing Requirements

Each organized exchange has unique requirements for listing. However, all listing requirements provide for:

1. Full public disclosure of information that might affect value of the firm's shares, including events as they occur and periodic (usually quarterly) financial reports.
2. Maintenance of transfer facilities, so that when a security is sold, the ownership title can be switched promptly. The *registrar,* which maintains a list of shareholders entitled to dividends, and the *transfer agent,* which destroys the old stock certificates and issues new ones, must be separate firms.
3. Some stipulated level of profit over a number of years and a minimum number of shareholders. For example, for original listing, the New York Stock Exchange requires a firm to have a pre-tax profit of at least $2.5 million in its latest fiscal year and a minimum 2,000 holders of 100 shares or more.

Whenever any of these requirements is violated, shares may be deleted from trading on the exchange.

To Remember

Securities Act of 1933	Distributing
Securities Exchange Act of 1934	Stand-by underwriting
Originating	Agency marketing
Underwriting	Direct placement
Syndicating	Private offering

Questions

1 Is the New York Stock Exchange (NYSE) a *primary* market? Explain. Must stocks sold on the NYSE conform to the Securities Act of 1933? Why or why not?

2 List and briefly describe the four functions of an investment banker. Why are stocks sold mainly through negotiated agreements?

3 Can an investment banker make any money buying a bond from an issuer to yield .0735 and selling it at 0731. Will he lose .004, or not? Explain.

4 A new $10 million issue is acquired by a syndicate at a 7 per cent current yield. It is sold to yield 6.8 per cent, its coupon rate.

   (a) Explain why the company did not sell the bond directly to the public and save 11 per cent ($28.57) on each bond.

   (b) Show a hypothetical breakdown of the dollar spread among the manager, underwriters, and distributors.

   (c) Should the issuer privately place the issue and so save the spread? Why or why not?

   (d) What offsets the saving that the firm might reap through a private placement?

5 All firms are not listed on one of the organized exchanges. Why is this so?

6 What is meant by the illiquidity of a private placement?

30

Financial Difficulties and Financing Growth

Life Cycle of a Firm — Types of Growth — Difficulties Stemming From Internal Growth — *Anticipating Financial Needs — Cash Level* — External Growth — *Financing a Combination —A Purchase* — *Pooling* — Financial Difficulties — *Inflation — Inflation and the Short-fall of Depreciation — Inflation and Inventories — The Environmental Problem: Financial Implications*

This chapter focuses on the special financial problems produced by corporate growth, inflation, and growing public demand for environmental control. Such problems are particularly subtle and likely to escape timely notice in the flurry of day-to-day decisions geared to immediate operating exigencies. Yet their long-run consequences may prove crippling, even fatal, for managements unaware of the lurking dangers.

Life Cycle of a Firm

In theory, a business firm, like a person, has a life cycle comprising birth, youthful exuberance, middle-aged maturity, and finally, senility and death. Figure 30–1 shows the hypothetical life cycle of a firm across time.

In the early stages, as a firm begins to penetrate its market, growth is usually quite rapid. When maturity sets in, market saturation and competition reduce the growth rate. Although sales still increase, they increase at a diminishing rate.

Finally, in senility, sales turn down. With the downturn, the firm no longer needs its former volume of assets, since asset needs change as sales change; it can thus begin paying back its capital.

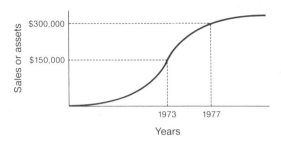

Figure 30-1. The Life Cycle of a Firm

Types of Growth

Two kinds of corporate growth are possible. With *internal growth,* an increase in sales results from expansion of a company's own assets. *External growth,* on the other hand, results from acquiring the assets, customers, and products of other firms.

Internal growth reflects an increase in the economy's net investment, as firms increase their assets. External expansion does not expand a society's total business assets; it simply shifts them from one firm to another. Only claims against existing assets are altered.

Difficulties Stemming from Internal Growth·

There is a saying in finance that "a firm can grow itself into bankruptcy." So it can, if the demands of growth are permitted to ride roughshod over considerations of liquidity and financial balance. Thus growth, for all its opportunities, also entails major hazards.

The two major financial difficulties associated with internal growth are (1) failure to anticipate the need for external finance, and (2) failure to provide for an adequate level of cash.

Anticipating Financial Needs

So long as a company is not growing (unit sales are constant), and inflation is not serious, internally generated funds usually suffice to finance asset needs. Depreciation reserves will cover fixed-asset replacements. If assets are growing slowly, automatic sources of finance (accounts payable and accruals), together with retained earnings, often meet a firm's financing needs. But when growth accelerates, the increase in asset requirements will outstrip the finance available from these sources, forcing the company to go outside to raise new money. Here is how a financial executive of a metals wholesaler states the problem:

> Very few companies realize how much additional capital is required to support even a modest growth. In addition to the capital requirements for sales growth, we have found it necessary and desirable to invest in additional machinery and

equipment, for such things as greater automation in our materials handling and installation of computers and related machines for accounting, statistics, and invoicing.[1]

The more rapid a company's growth is, the more finance it will need to acquire—and must *plan* to acquire—from external sources.

For example, consider the two firms, Amalgamated Enterprise and Barthe Battery, whose balance sheets as of January 1, 1973 are shown in Table 30–1. For 1972, both firms had the same sales and same profit margin. Days sales invested in each kind of asset are simply the dollar amount of that asset divided by average daily sales.

If Amalgamated's sales in 1973 expand by 20 per cent, the new level of sales will be 1.20 × $720,000 = $864,000, as Table 30–2 shows. The rise in sales is $144,000. Since every dollar of sales requires 80 cents in assets, and hence financing, the company will need .80 × $144,000 in new finance, or $115,200. Where will it come from? Part will come from automatic sources, accounts payable and taxes payable. They will supply .15 × $144,000 = $21,600. This means that $93,600 is needed from other sources. Of this amount, $34,560 will come from retained earnings, 4 per cent of *total* sales. Amalgamated still needs $59,040.

Now consider Barthe. If its sales in 1973 expand by 5 per cent, sales volume will be 1.05 × $720,000 = $756,000. Again, each additional dollar in sales requires 80 cents in assets and financing. Barthe needs .80 × $36,000 in new financing, or $28,800. For Barthe, 15 per cent of $36,000 will come from automatic sources, a total of $5,400. Of the remaining $23,400 needed, Barthe will have $30,240 in retained earnings. It can use the excess of $6,840 ($30,240 − $23,400) to pay a dividend, to repay some of its debt, or to build up assets, perhaps by buying securities.

The balance sheets in Table 30–2 show both firms at the end of the year. Through major rises in loan and bond financing, Amalgamated has increased its reliance on external funds from $108,000 to $167,040. (Of course, the actual division between loans and bonds would depend on such considerations as suitability, availability, and costs.) Barthe reduced these accounts from $108,000 to $101,160, but Barthe might have used the funds to pay a dividend. If Amalgamated had grown more slowly, it would have required less financing from external sources. Had Barthe grown more rapidly, it would have had less funds available for discretionary purposes.

Cash Level

Rapid growth has an irresistible tendency to swallow cash. Many profitable opportunities cry out to be satisfied. If, for example, sales at a 20 to 40 per cent profit margin are to be realized, plant and equipment must be expanded, inventory increased, and labor force and raw materials enlarged. But all such outlays absorb cash. Because they do, management must give primary attention to its cash budget and cash position. The company that chases the pretty baubles of rapid growth and profit, without regard to liquidity, may find itself unable to pay its bills and wind up with neither.

---

[1]Cited in Sorrell Mathes, *Handling Company Growth,* Managing the Moderate-Sized Company, Report No. 5. The Conference Board, 1967, p. 16.

Table 30-1.

Amalgamated Enterprise, January 1, 1973: Total Sales = $720,000; Daily Sales = $720,000/360 = $2,000; Profit after taxes = .04.

Assets	Amount	% of Sales	Days Sales	Claims	Amount	% of Sales	Days Sales
Cash	$ 36,000	5	18.0	Accounts Payable	$ 72,000	10	36
Securities	14,400	2	7.2	Taxes Payable	36,000	5	18
Accounts Receivable	216,000	30	108.0	Loans	72,000	10	36
Inventory	165,600	23	82.8	Bonds	36,000	5	18
Plant and Equipment	144,000	20	72.0	Stockholders' Equity	360,000	50	180
				1. Paid in Capital in Excess of Par			
				2. Common (at Par)			
				3. Retained Earnings			
	$576,000	80%	288		$576,000	80%	288

Barthe Battery, January 1, 1973: Total Sales = $720,000; Daily Sales = $720,000/360 = $2,000; Profit after taxes to sales = .04.

Assets	Amount	% of Sales	Days Sales	Claims	Amount	% of Sales	Days Sales
Cash	$ 36,000	5	18.0	Accounts Payable	$ 72,000	10	36
Securities	14,400	2	7.2	Taxes Payable	36,000	5	18
Accounts Receivable	216,000	30	108.0	Loans	72,000	10	36
Inventory	165,600	23	82.8	Bonds	36,000	5	18
Plant and Equipment	144,000	20	72.0	Shareholders' Equity	360,000	50	180
				1. Paid in Capital in Excess of Par			
				2. Common (at Par)			
				3. Retained Earnings			
	$576,000	80%	288		$576,000	80%	288

Table 30-2.

Amalgamated Enterprise, December 31, 1973: Total Sales = $864,000; Daily Sales = $864,000/360 = $2,400; Profit after taxes = .04.

Growth = 20%

Assets	Amount	% of Sales	Days Sales	Claims	Amount	% of Sales	Days Sales
Cash	$ 43,200	5	18.0	Accounts Payable	$ 86,400	10.0	36.0
Securities	17,280	2	7.2	Taxes Payable	43,200	5.0	18.0
Accounts Receivable	259,200	30	108.0	Loans	101,520	11.7	42.3
Inventory	198,720	23	82.8	Bonds	65,520	7.6	27.3
Plant and Equipment	172,800	20	72.0	Shareholders' Equity	394,560	45.7	164.4
				1. Paid in Capital in Excess of Par			
				2. Common (at Par)			
				3. Retained Earnings			
	$691,200	80%	288		$691,200	80%	288

Barthe Battery, December 31, 1973: Total Sales = $756,000; Daily Sales = $756,000/360 = $2,100; Profit after taxes to sales = .04.

Growth = 5%

Assets	Amount	% of Sales	Days Sales	Claims	Amount	% of Sales	Days Sales
Cash	$ 37,800	5	18.0	Accounts Payable	$ 75,600	10.0	36.0
Securities	15,120	2	7.2	Taxes Payable	37,800	5.0	18.0
Accounts Receivable	226,800	30	108.0	Loans	65,160	8.6	31.0
Inventory	173,800	23	82.8	Bonds	36,000	4.8	17.1
Plant and Equipment	151,200	20	72.0	Shareholders' Equity	390,240	51.6	185.9
				1. Paid in Capital in Excess of Par			
				2. Common (at Par)			
				3. Retained Earnings			
	$604,800	80%	288		$604,800	80%	288

External Growth

External growth was a common phenomenon in the late 1960s. In fact, the period was dominated by merger mania. In increasing numbers, firms acquired assets, personnel, and products by combining with other firms through merger or consolidation. A *consolidation* is an agreement by which two or more companies agree to unite and become a new corporation, combining the assets and claims of the predecessor firms into one balance sheet. A *merger* is the absorption of one or more corporations by another, with the acquiring firm maintaining its corporate identity.

Why do companies merge or consolidate? Some reasons are:

1. To eliminate a competitor.
2. To ensure a stable source of supply.
3. To diversify a product line, either to reduce sales variability (for example, an air conditioner manufacturer merging with a heating manufacturer), or to offset a declining growth rate and delay senility.
4. To acquire key personnel or assets. Since it cannot buy them separately, the corporation may "buy the cow to get the calf," through acquisition or merger.
5. To procure finance, either cash or the improved access to capital markets that a larger firm has.[2]

Financing a Combination

One company can acquire another in several ways, but the most widely used involve either purchase or pooling. To see how these work, consider the balance sheets of the two companies below. Note that Acquired has assets of $500, liabilities of $300, and shareholders' equity of $200.

	Acquirer				Acquired		
Assets		*Claims*			*Assets*	*Claims*	
Cash $	500	$10,000	Equity	Cash	$500	$300	Debt
Other	9,500					200	Equity
	$10,000	$10,000			$500	$500	

Let us examine a purchase first.

A Purchase

Suppose Acquirer buys Acquired for $200 in cash. (Purchase can also be made with stocks, bonds, and other forms of payment.) The cash price equals Acquired's equity, and changes in Acquirer's balance sheet would be:

Acquirer	
Assets	*Claims*
Cash −$200	
Subsidiary	Subsidiary
assets + 500	liabilities + $300
Change $300	Change $300

---

[2]For a readable and informative analysis of the benefits involved in mergers, see Frank M. Butrick, "Is That Firm for Sale?" *Conference Board Record* (June 1971): 30–32.

What if Acquirer had paid more than book value for Acquired? Suppose Acquirer paid $300 for the $200 shareholders' equity. Changes would read:

Acquirer

Assets		Claims	
Cash	−$300		
Subsidiary assets	+ 500	Subsidiary liabilities	+ $300
Goodwill	+ 100		
Change	$300		$300

Goodwill is simply a balancing item and represents the excess or premium over book value paid by Acquirer. It would be amortized, or written off, over a number of years, thus reducing future profit. In this respect, it is handled like the depreciation of an asset. But unlike depreciation, amortized goodwill is *not* a tax-deductible expense. The full amount of the expense is a reduction in earnings after taxes.

Acquirer also can make its purchase with common stock or debt, thus conserving cash. However, if the acquisition is a purchase at more than book value, it still reduces future earnings as noted above.

Pooling

To avoid adverse earnings effects from goodwill, firms may choose to pool their interests. *Pooling* may occur whenever the companies meet certain SEC requirements, for example, roughly equal shareholders' equity and assets, and continuation of both managements. Stock or debt of Acquirer is issued for the equity of Acquired, as in a purchase, but an important difference is this: goodwill does not arise. The only adjustment is in the shareholders' equity account of Acquirer. Other assets and liabilities are simply pooled. After a pooling of interests by the above firms, the new balance sheet would read:

Acquirer

Assets		Claims	
Cash	$ 500	Liabilities	$ 300
Other	9,500	Equity	10,200
Acquired assets	500		
	$10,500		$10,500

In market value of its stock, Acquirer may pay a very large premium over shareholders' equity. Nevertheless, after the combination, assets and claims are no more than the sum of the individual assets and claims. No goodwill arises, and future earnings are not diminished by amortized goodwill.[3]

Financial Difficulties

Two major challenges facing business in the early 1970s were inflation and public demand for environmental control. Each posed major financial problems

---

[3]For a further discussion, the interested student is directed to Myron Gordon and Gordon Shillinglaw, *Accounting: A Management Approach,* 4th ed. (Homewood, Ill.: Richard D. Irwin, Inc., 1969), pp. 468–78.

for managements and appeared to call for determined programs of financial stewardship.

Inflation

Inflation has four main adverse effects on a business firm: (1) increased operating costs, (2) increased borrowing costs, (3) unstable financial markets, and (4) a "mining" of the company's real assets. The first three we deal with briefly; the fourth, at length.

Inflation increases a company's current operating costs. Outlays for labor, material, supplies, and services rise. The financial manager must recognize early in the inflationary cycle that the firm's circulating capital needs are increasing—and that the increase is almost certainly permanent. He will be wise, therefore, to raise the needed funds from long-term sources.

Inflation pushes up interest rates, thus increasing a company's borrowing costs. Here again, a financial manager must anticipate events to stay ahead of the game. If he foresees an inflationary cycle of appreciable duration, he is wise to do his *permanent* borrowing (and nail down firm lines of credit) while interest rates are still low and borrowers are not queued up in the long-term debt markets.

The financial manager must also recognize that as inflation forces interest rates higher, his company's debt coverage ratios may fall, lowering the quality rating of its bonds and forcing it to pay still higher yields for debt money.

Debt coverage ratios fall because interest charges rise and a given volume of earnings before interest taxes covers the charges fewer times. Suppose that a company has $100,000 in fixed debt and EBIT of $20,000. If interest on the debt averages 5 per cent, interest charges are covered four times and bonds are high-grade. If interest averages 8 per cent, coverage is only two and one-half times and bonds are medium- or low-grade.[4]

There also is much to be said for selling common stock before inflation explodes. People formerly thought that inflation was good for the stock market, but it is quite obvious that the Johnson and Nixon inflations both knocked it for a loop.

Inflation also results in unstable financial markets. Because the Treasury continues to run deficits even during inflationary booms, the burden of stopping price rises increasingly falls on the Federal Reserve and tight money. But the Federal Reserve has acted erratically, first stamping on the monetary brake, bringing on a credit crunch and collapsing stock market, then panicking and pushing the money-supply accelerator harder than ever, so all financial markets go up and down like roller coasters. Thus the financial manager must cleverly manage his timing, knowing when to borrow money most cheaply, whether to borrow for long- or short-term, when to sell new stock, and so on. He must ignore what presidents, cabinet officers, Federal Reserve spokesmen, and other public-relations experts are saying, examine the cold facts with an independent mind, and decide realistically what financial moves he must take to keep his firm liquid and in the black.

Inflation and the Short-fall of Depreciation

The most serious (because most stealthy) injury that inflation can inflict on a business firm is to weaken ability to replace its real capital, particularly its fixed

---

[4]The sharp rise in interest rates during the late 1960s resulted in widespread reductions of quality ratings on public utility bonds in the early 1970s.

assets.[5] There is a *short-fall of depreciation:* funds provided by depreciation are not sufficient to finance the asset's replacement. Depreciation is calculated on the *historical* cost of assets, and, therefore, makes no allowance for the effect of inflation on future replacement costs. If the replacement in kind for any asset costs more than the original, funds provided through depreciation will prove insufficient.

Consider, for example, the asset described in Table 30–3, which has a five-year life. At the end of five years, the firm will have received total depreciation accruals of $5,000. But if the price level has increased 5 per cent annually, replacement cost for the asset will have risen to $6,380, or 27 per cent more than the amount supplied by depreciation.

Table 30–3. Original Outlay and Depreciation

Investment	Year	Depreciation
$5,000	1	$1,000
	2	1,000
	3	1,000
	4	1,000
	5	1,000
	Accumulated	$5,000

How, then, can replacement be handled? The firm must finance the short-fall from other sources: retained earnings, or new flotations of stock or bonds. It should *not* use a short-term source, such as bank loans, for that would violate the principle of suitability. But what about the availability of retained earnings, that other component of funds generated from operations? Inflation and the understatement of depreciation have an impact here, too. Since depreciation is understated, it follows that earnings are *overstated.* That part of reported earnings equal to the short-fall in depreciation is not earnings at all, but merely the *uncovered cost* of correcting depreciation. Since profit is overstated, taxes are excessive.[6] Also, if the illusory nature of reported earnings is not recognized, the company may pay larger dividends than could be justified in constant dollars. The result is that fewer dollars will be available for reinvestment.

How can a financial manager cope with this problem? One step, as you saw in chapter 18, is to keep (for management use only) a second set of books in constant dollars, and base financing and dividend decisions on what they show. On these books, the financial manager can revalue each asset each year and increase its depreciation allowance.

---

[5]Two outstanding discussions of this problem are Harold Bierman, Jr., *Financial Accounting Theory* (New York: The Macmillan Company, 1965), pp. 271–80, and George Terborgh, "Inflation and Corporate Profits," Essay 4, in *Essays on Inflation* (Washington, D. C.: Machine and Allied Products Institute, 1971), pp. 48–56.

[6]This argument is often summarized by this statement: "The government is taxing away the capital base of the economy."

In our example above, let us assume that the financial manager foresees 5 per cent inflation annually over the asset's entire life. Depreciation charged in each year should be increased 27 per cent, because with a five-year asset life and 5 per cent inflation, ultimate replacement cost will rise 27 per cent. The asset itself should be marked up $250 in year 1, to reflect the 5 per cent increase in replacement cost, to $5,250. To keep both sides of the balance sheet equal, the increased valuation of the fixed asset is reflected in shareholders' equity as a $250 "capital increment."[7] Net assets will then be $5,250 – $1,270 = $3,980. The net impact on shareholders' equity will be $250 (increment) – $1270 (depreciation) = – $1,020, the same as the *net* change in assets. Here are these changes:

	Assets			*Shareholders' Equity*
	$5,000	Beginning of year		$ 250	Capital increment
Less	3,980	End of year	Less	1,270	Depreciation
	$1,020	Reduction		$1,020	Reduction

On the income statement, the company shows $270 in additional depreciation expense. Earnings before taxes are shown as $270 less.

Accelerating depreciation and shortening asset lives are of little benefit in coping with the problem. Both permit *faster recoveries* of funds invested in fixed assets. Total recovery is still limited to the historical cost. The only advantage of accelerated depreciation is that a company recovers its outlays through cash flows sooner. Once recovery is complete, however, the firm's income taxes on returns generated by the asset rise because the depreciation shield has expired.

In an effort to spur capital spending, Congress has occasionally permitted businessmen to deduct from their tax liability a percentage of their current capital outlays. If this *investment tax credit* is, for example, 7 per cent, then a $10,000 capital outlay permits a firm to reduce its tax payment by $700.[8] Funds so provided ease the cash drain that inflation causes. The asset-replacement problem still remains, however.

Despite all palliatives, the financial manager faced with inflation has only one course of action. That is to appropriate retained earnings for fixed-asset replacement. Doing so will not keep inflation from draining the firm's real capital, for the company must still overstate its earnings and pay excessive taxes. But appropriation will inform stockholders that part of the reported profits are not real—that is, not available for dividend payments—but must be retained to supplement insufficient depreciation allowances. Bookkeeping entries for a $50,000 appropriation would be as follows (all within the shareholders' equity section):

Before appropriation

Common stock (10,000 shares	
at $10 par value)	$100,000
Paid-in capital in excess	
of par	50,000
Retained earnings	70,000
	$220,000

---

[7] Robert K. Jaedicke and Robert T. Sprouse, *Accounting Flows: Income, Funds, and Cash* (Englewood Cliffs, N.J.: Prentice-Hall, 1965), p. 70

[8] Of course, the firm would have to owe at least $700 in taxes to receive this much credit.

After appropriation

Common stock (10,000 shares at $10 par value)	$100,000
Paid-in capital in excess of par	50,000
Retained earnings	20,000
Appropriation: for replacement of capital assets	50,000
	$220,000

The appropriation does not mean that an amount of cash corresponding to the amount of retained earnings has been set aside for asset replacement. Remember that retained earnings are merely a balance sheet claim, not a fund of money. Hence, the financial manager also has the task of watching his cash, not frittering it away, and making sure that when the time comes to replace the assets cash for that purpose is available.

Inflation and Inventories

Inflation can influence stated business profit through inventory valuation and cause businesses to lose funds in higher tax payments. As a point in evidence, one study has indicated that taxable corporate profit would have been $48.4 billion less between 1945 and 1970 if the effects of inflation on inventory values were removed.[9] At a 50 per cent tax rate, corporate tax payments would have been reduced $24.2 billion.

There are two principal ways inventory may be valued. The FIFO method (first in, first out) says that the first units acquired are the first ones sold; units used in calculating cost of goods sold are the "oldest" units, and those remaining in inventory are the "newest" ones. The LIFO method (last in, first out) says that the last units acquired are the first ones sold; units used in calculating cost of goods sold are the "newest" units, those remaining, the "oldest." If LIFO is used for tax reporting, the IRS requires its use in financial reporting.

An example will show the difference between the two methods of accounting for inventory. A firm has 500 units in inventory on January 1, the beginning of its selling period, each valued at $6. Purchases are as follows:

February	3	500 units @ $6.00 =	$ 3,000
May	4	1,000 units @ $6.50 =	$ 6,500
July	1	3,000 units @ $7.00 =	$21,000
December	5	1,000 units @ $8.00 =	$ 8,000

At the end of the year, December 31, the firm has 1,000 units on hand. Since the firm had 500 units on hand at the beginning, bought 5,500 units during the year, and had 1,000 units at the end of the period, it sold (beginning + purchases) – ending = 5,000 units.

Using FIFO, the following goods would be treated as sold:

Beginning inventory	500 @ $6.00 =	$ 3,000
Purchases	500 @ $6.00 =	3,000
	1,000 @ $6.50 =	6,500
	3,000 @ $7.00 =	21,000
Cost of goods sold	5,000	$33,500

⁹Cited in Ronald M. Copeland, Joseph F. Wojdak, and John K. Shank, "Use LIFO to Offset Inflation," *Harvard Business Review* 49 (May–June 1971); 93.

By contrast, use of LIFO would give a substantially higher value:

Most recent purchases	1,000 @ $8.00 =	$ 8,000
	3,000 @ $7.00 =	21,000
	1,000 @ $6.50 =	6,500
	5,000	$35,500

If the firm's sales had been $40,000, and cost of goods sold the only cost, the two methods of accounting for inventory would have resulted in the following reported earnings and tax liabilities.

FIFO	Sales	$40,000
	Cost of goods sold	33,500
	Net profit before tax	6,500
	Federal income tax (50%)	3,250
	Net after tax	$ 3,250

LIFO	Sales	$40,000
	Cost of goods sold	35,500
	Net profit before tax	4,500
	Federal income tax (50%)	2,250
	Net after tax	$ 2,250

The FIFO firm reported $2,000 more in earnings before taxes, so it must pay a $1,000 larger tax payment. Conversely, the LIFO firm stated $2,000 less in net profit before tax, but its net after tax is only $1,000 less because its tax outlay was smaller.

A firm using FIFO under the inflationary conditions implied above will pay higher taxes because its earnings will be overstated. The income-producing ability of the FIFO firm will deteriorate because its circulating capital is being taxed away.

How would inventory be valued on the balance sheet? Using FIFO, the firm would have 1,000 units at $8 each, or $8,000; using LIFO, 1,000 units at $6 each, or $6,000. Thus, in periods of rising prices, LIFO understates inventory value on the balance sheet, while FIFO records it more accurately. However, deficient inventory values on the balance sheet do not penalize a firm on tax payments, while deficient estimates of cost of goods sold do. Therefore, in choosing to undervalue balance-sheet inventory rather than cost of goods sold, a company is choosing the lesser of two evils.

Since there seem to be such obvious advantages to using LIFO rather than FIFO, you probably believe that surely all businesses must use LIFO. That is not the case. As of 1968 only about 17 per cent of the value of manufacturing inventory was being stated at LIFO costs.[10] Evidently management is more concerned with stated earnings—which are lower with LIFO—and their direct impact on share prices than with conserving cash in the firm.

The Environmental Problem: Financial Implications

Economics teaches that for every benefit there is a cost. The benefits of high-level consumption, a comfortable environment, and leisure living have been bought, at least in part, by contaminating and bespoiling the environment. The public has become increasingly aware of these costs. Through its elected representatives, it is initiating a get-tough policy toward businesses that contaminate

[10]*Ibid.*, p. 92.

their surroundings. A strong move in this area was passage of the Clean Air Act of 1970. This act gave greater scope and powers to the Federal Environmental Protection Agency, made state government involvement in pollution matters mandatory, and initiated stricter air pollutant emission standards.

The magnitude of pollution control costs is evident in the following figures. Over the years 1966–71, Standard Oil of New Jersey spent on pollution control $1.5 billion; the electrical utility industry expects to spend $2 billion during 1972–76; Dow Chemical has spent almost $1 million for control of effluents at one plant and expects company-wide expenditures to total $25 million over a three-year interval. At the macroeconomic level, the Environmental Quality Council estimates that cumulative costs of fighting pollution in the years 1970–75 will exceed $105 billion. Of this, $23.7 billion will be allocated to reduce air pollution. Water pollution control will cost about $38 billion, solid waste, about $43.5 billion.

What are the financial implications? If firms are obliged to invest in costly pollution-control systems and devices, their assets will increase, and, assuming the same dollar earnings, return on assets will be diminished. But the same dollar earnings will *not* occur, because pollution-control devices will be depreciated, thereby reducing earnings. This additional depreciation will be the *explicit cost* of controlling pollution.

We say explicit cost because an implicit, unspecified cost of pollution has been and continues to be borne by those on whom pollution damage falls. Society is moving to have pollution costs reflected on the income statements of industrial polluters. The costs will then be incurred by those receiving the benefits of the production: the customers (through higher prices), and the shareholders (through lower returns).

To the extent companies can pass their added costs along to customers through higher product prices, the war on pollution need not hurt their earnings, nor jeopardize their finances. But not all companies will be so fortunate. Some, facing elastic customer demands or cut-throat competition, will have to absorb cost increases through reduced earnings. How will such companies be affected? Finance will become harder to obtain. A drop in earnings per share will disenchant investors. Larger fixed costs (depreciation charges) will raise operating leverage and increase risk. Where companies finance pollution-control outlays with debt, their financial leverage also will increase. These three elements will interact to raise costs of capital and make the financial manager's job more difficult. Ultimately, lower earnings will reduce the flow of capital into the industry, and the industry will shrink.[11]

To Remember

Internal growth	Purchase vs. pooling
External growth	Inflation and replacement
Impact of rapid growth	Inflation and inventory

---

[11]Of course, the picture is not bleak for everyone: producers of pollution-control equipment will enjoy a new and growing market. The saying, "It's an ill wind that blows no good," applies as well to economic trends as it does to other aspects of life.

Questions

1 What are the primary sources of finance during each stage in the life cycle of a firm? Why might a dynamic firm in the exuberance of youth want to merge with a ''dying'' firm?

2 Here are abbreviated balance sheets of two firms (SHE is shareholders' equity):

Gordus				Memnon			
Assets			Claims	Assets			Claims
Cash	$ 800	SHE	$1,000	Cash	$500	Debt	$600
Other	200			Other	200	SHE	100
	$1,000		$1,000		$700		$700

Gordus *purchases* Memnon with cash, paying $300 for Memnon's equity. Last year, Gordus had earnings before taxes of $200, Memnon, $100. The tax rate is 40 per cent.

(a) Show Gordus' balance sheet after merger.

(b) Assume goodwill is amortized (written down) over a two-year period. If earnings of each division remain the same, what will earnings be after the purchase?

3 If a merger is made to diversify a firm's operations, and so reduce risk, why might the *P/E* multiple applied to the post-merger firm increase?

4 Bogus Distributors buys a building for $200,000 in 1968. It depreciated the building on a twenty-year basis toward a zero salvage value. The price level increases 3 per cent per year over the twenty-year period.

(a) What is the replacement price of the building at the end of its life?

(b) How much should depreciation expense be each year to prevent the short-fall of depreciation?

(c) What do you suggest Bogus Distributors do to avoid dissipating its earning power?

5 Explain how LIFO can protect a firm's earning power during inflation.

6 The Mitchell Company begins the year with 500 air conditioners in inventory, valued at $50 each. It makes these purchases:

March	200 units @ $60
June	100 units @ $66
November	200 units @ $70

The year ends with 200 units on hand. Total sales in the year are $58,000. The tax rate is 40 per cent.

(a) Show comparative closing balance sheets and costs of goods sold using LIFO and FIFO.

(b) How much will the difference be in taxes paid under each method?

(c) Which method will yield a greater return on assets?

7 What is meant by a firm's circulating capital being taxed away?

8 How might the installation of pollution-control equipment increase both the operating and financial leverage in a firm? Do you believe this will cause an increase in firms' cost of capital? Why?

31

The Money, Bond, and Mortgage Markets

The Money Market — *Liquid Storage of Funds* — *The Treasurer's Problem* — *Choice of Instruments* — *Issuing Commercial Paper* — The Bond Market — *Bond Yield Fluctuations* — *Bond Market Strategy: An Illustration* — *Secular Yield Trends* — *Bond Market Technicalities* — The Mortgage Market

---

Chapter 7 dealt with the money and capital markets as part of the monetary mechanism. This chapter views them from the standpoint of the corporate financial manager. It emphasizes the money market as his main reliance for the interest-bearing investment of short-term surplus funds; though it points out that he may also *raise* short-term funds there by floating commercial paper. His main activity with respect to bonds is floating them to finance long-term capital requirements. Mortgages are ordinarily of greater interest to home buyers than to corporate treasurers, but this book would not be complete without some further brief account of them.

The Money Market

This short addendum on the money market is intended to answer four questions. (1) How does the corporate treasurer use the money market? (2) What is his chief problem in dealing with it? (3) What outstanding properties of money market instruments fit them for particular uses? (4) How should money market investments be decided?

Liquid Storage of Funds

Corporations accumulate temporary funds for dividend payments, tax installments, and other purposes. Reduced circulating capital requirements pile up idle cash in slack periods. Such sums today are capable of earning substantial interest returns over short intervals, provided they can be invested with safety and liquidity. These properties are provided in varying degrees by money market instruments.[1] While the money market is not the only place a corporate treasurer can turn for short-term investments, it is ordinarily his safest and most familiar recourse.[2]

Selection rather than timing is the treasurer's main problem in making money market investments. We have seen that short-dated, high-grade debt securities typically provide high yields in boom periods, low yields in recessions: rising yields when business is expanding, falling yields as the economy contracts. But the availability of corporate funds for short-term investment typically moves counter to the "juiciness" of yields. Business firms have the most surplus money to lend at interest during times of slack business—at recession bottoms when yields are low. When yields are invitingly high, as they are during booms, corporate needs to finance peak levels of inventories and receivables are typically large: firms are much more likely to be borrowers in the money market—sellers of commercial paper—than lenders to it.

The Treasurer's Problem

Since the timing of money market investment is decided almost automatically by the timing of corporate cash flows, the main problem facing the treasurer is not when to invest but *what to invest in?* In large degree, the decision comes down to the classic financial dilemma illustrated in Figure 17–3: yield versus liquidity.

Money market instruments differ with respect to (1) ease of resale, (2) how closely maturities can be tailored, or at least selected, to meet an investor's need, (3) yield, and (4) to some degree, safety. The extent to which a trade-off between yield and liquidity is necessary depends on predictability of the lender's need for cash.

If a treasurer needs his cash back to meet a dividend date or tax payment, and is sure no intervening need will arise, then he is free to pick the highest-yielding instrument among those of the right maturity. If, however, he is merely "storing money at interest" against *unpredictable* needs, then questions of marketability and liquidity arise. The investor can get a better yield by buying a longer-dated instrument. This may cause him no embarrassment or loss if the instrument is highly marketable, as U.S. Treasury bills typically are. He might get a better yield on bills maturing five or six months hence than on one- or two-month bills; and if he had to sell them after a month or so, he might come out no worse on his interest return for the period. But if he bought five- or six-month commercial paper (which ordinarily has no resale market), he might suffer an actual loss getting someone to take it off his hands a month or two later.

---

[1] Introduced by name and generally described in chapter 7.

[2] Small corporations may invest in small denomination CDs at commercial banks (under $100,000 and non-negotiable), in savings and loan shares, or small-loan company certificates.

Table 31–1. Money Market Instruments

		Obligation	Denominations
United States Treasury Bills		U.S. Government obligation. U.S. Treasury auctions 3- and 6-month bills weekly. Also offers, through special auctions, one-year maturities and tax anticipation bills.	10M to 1MM
Commercial Paper 1. Prime Sales Finance Paper		Promissory notes of finance companies placed directly with the investor.	5M to 5MM
2. Dealer Paper	I. Finance	Promissory notes of finance companies sold through commercial paper dealers.	5M to 5MM
3. Dealer Paper	II. Industrial	Promissory notes of leading industrial firms sold through commercial paper dealers.	5M to 5MM
Prime Bankers Acceptances		Time drafts drawn on and accepted by a banking institution, which in effect substitutes its credit for that of the importer or holder of merchandise.	25M to 1MM
Negotiable Time Certificates of Deposit		Certificates of time deposit at a commercial bank.	500M to 1MM
Short-term Tax-Exempts	I. Temporary & preliminary notes of local public housing agencies.	Notes of local agencies secured by a contract with federal agencies and by pledge of "full faith and credit" of U.S.	1M to 1MM
Short-term Tax-Exempts	II. Tax & bond anticipation notes.	Notes of states, municipalities, or political subdivisions.	1M to 1MM

Source: Reproduced with permission from *Money-Market Investments: The Risk and the Return,* copyright 1970 by Morgan Guaranty Trust Company of New York.

Choice of Instruments

Table 31–1 displays the significant characteristics of leading money market instruments. It deserves your careful study, and there is little we need add to its catalogue of facts.

Issuing Commercial Paper

For the medium- or large-size company, commercial paper is a possible source of short-term funds. Assuming the company's credit standing is high enough (and the Penn-Central experience suggests that this really is mostly a matter of

Table 31–1. Money Market Instruments, Cont'd.

Maturities	Marketability	Basis
Up to 1 year.	Excellent secondary market.	Discounted. Actual days on a 360-day year.
Issued to mature on any day from 3 to 270 days.	No secondary market. Under certain conditions companies usually will buy back paper prior to maturity. Most companies will adjust rate.	Discounted or interest-bearing. Actual days on a 360-day year.
Issued to mature on any day from 30 to 270 days.	No secondary market. Buyback arrangement usually can be negotiated through the dealer.	Discounted or interest-bearing. Actual days on a 360-day year.
Usually available on certain dates between 60 and 180 days.	No secondary market.	Discounted. Actual days on a 360-day year.
Up to 6 months.	Good secondary market. Bid usually ⅛ of 1% higher than offered side of market.	Discounted. Actual days on a 360-day year.
Unlimited.	Good secondary market.	Yield basis. Actual days on a 360-day year. Interest at maturity.
Up to 1 year.	Good secondary market.	Yield basis. 30-day month on a 360-day year. Interest at maturity.
Various, usually 3 months to 1 year from issue.	Good secondary market.	Yield basis. Usually 30 days on a 360-day year. Interest at maturity.

size), it can sell commercial paper. The yield on commercial paper is typically less than the prime loan rate at the banks, and the sale of paper involves no compensating balance requirement, so the borrower enjoys the use of all the funds he pays for. The main disadvantages of commercial paper are (1) that it includes none of the advisory services a good bank can provide, and (2) that lender-borrower relations are impersonal, i.e., there is no "loyalty" required or expected on the part of lenders. Lenders can be expected not to renew their loans when the paper matures if better lending opportunities occur elsewhere. As we noted in chapter 21, commercial paper is usually backed with standby credit lines at commercial banks, so that if the paper cannot be renewed, funds to pay it off are assured.

The Bond Market

Whereas business firms use the money market both for storage and borrowing of funds, most of them use the bond market only to borrow. Since bond sales always involve intermediate- or long-term borrowings, timing is a crucial factor in a decision to sell bonds.[3] Thus an understanding of price trends and yield movements is of key importance to the businessman involved in bond issues or refundings.

Bond Yield Fluctuations

Chapter 6 dealt with interest-rate fluctuations in general. Like other interest rates, bond yields rise in booms, fall in recessions: a *cyclical* pattern of movement. This means that firms can sell bonds at a smaller interest burden in times of recession, while bonds floated during booms typically carry much higher interest burdens. This behavior of bond-interest costs injects a basic difficulty into the timing of bond financing. Firms are most likely to need long-term debt (and other financing) during booms and least likely to need it in recessions. Thus the basic movement of bond yields makes "bond money" most expensive when it is needed and least expensive when it is unneeded.

Availability, as well as cost, of bond money moves contrary to needs. In a deep recession, few bond issues are coming to market and the calendar of offerings is clear and uncluttered. But at the peak of a boom, as in August–October 1966, or in November 1969, it may be "standing room only" in the new issues market. In fact, so many firms may be lining up to sell debt issues that there isn't room for all of them. In this case, only companies with the biggest names and best credit ratings are able to sell bonds—there aren't enough bond buyers to take care of the rest. Companies may come to their investment bankers with proposals to market $15–$20 million worth of new bonds only to be told that "There isn't room on the calendar because a $250 million Telephone issue, several large power companies, and a couple of mammoth industrial concerns (like GE and Texaco) have preempted all the debt funds in sight for the next two months." In such case, smaller, less well-known issuers must usually postpone their bond sales, and either seek temporary, substitute financing (bank loans or possible commercial-paper sales), cancel their projects for lack of finance, or seek a merger partner.

Not only cost and availability, but *terms of indentures* also are geared to the business cycle. In recessions, money is cheap, abundant, and looking for bonds to be invested in. Savers and investors are glad to find bonds that will pay them a half-way decent interest rate, and they are not inclined to debate an issuer's reasonable requirements regarding call period, call premiums, sinking funds, and other provisions of the indenture. By contrast, in boom times, a "buyer's market" for bonds exists. More issues are looking for buyers than the market

---

[3]Some people would say the crucial question is whether to sell stock (common or preferred) or bonds in the first place, and this is undeniably important. But given the decision to finance with debt, the problem then becomes one of timing. If it is not a good time to sell bonds—too many issuers, or much lower rates expected soon—a strong company can always substitute short-term borrowings temporarily while awaiting a better opportunity in the bond market. (Of course, the judgment that waiting will pay off must be right.)

can accommodate. Buyers can pick and choose and bargain with issuers for the most advantageous terms. Since yields are temporarily much above the average expected over the next few years, bond buyers almost invariably demand "call protection": an indenture provision prohibiting the company from redeeming the bonds for five to ten years. This, of course, insures that the buyer will continue to collect his contracted high rate of interest for this interval, even though "market" bond yields fall drastically. If a company refuses to make its issue "noncallable," then it may have to pay an extra one-half or three-quarters percentage point of coupon interest. And in tight bond markets, other indenture provisions—working capital requirements, dividend restrictions, limitations on other debt financing, and so on—are likely to be tighter simply because investors are in the driver's seat.

Bond Market Strategy: An Illustration

These considerations suggest that one key to effective bond financing by the corporation is proper foresight: a willingness and ability to look far enough ahead to foresee a need for debt capital and avoid both high yields and traffic jams in the bond market. An noteworthy instance of such foresight was turned by Texas Instruments, Inc., in October 1965, as the big updraft in bond yields was just beginning. This professionally managed company sold $50 million in new debentures on a 4.80 per cent interest basis, and the day the treasurer, George Livings, went to New York to pick up the check from the underwriters, he "stored" the money in New York bank CDs at 5.00 per cent. Through the next six years of soaring yields and recurring credit crunches, TI rode comfortably liquid at painlessly low cost.

Indeed, through much of the time from November 1965 through mid-1971, the *Treasury bill rate* was substantially above TI's cost of long-term debt money. The company could enjoy the rare luxury of borrowing long and lending short, the safest of all financial practices—in contrast to the oft-fatal mistake of borrowing short and lending long, i.e., making long-term loans with money borrowed at short-term with continual risk of non-renewal. It is very much to this company's credit that liquid as it was through the 1966–69 era, it did not squander its money on acquisitions that later had to be "eaten" or sold at very large losses.

Foresight to time bond-market forays advantageously comes primarily from a sound understanding of interest-rate history, recurring business-cycle patterns, and conditions in one's own industry. It also calls for correctly forecasting both when a company will need debt capital and what the future movement of interest rates will be. A careful study by one of the authors suggests that in 1966 a majority of companies had not even attempted to make these forecasts, but had permitted themselves to be propelled into the market at the worst possible time when their need for borrowings became desperate.[4] Since 1966, companies have shown more desire to forecast both future bond market conditions and their own needs. This was a major factor preventing the prolonged or deep decline of bond yields during the 1970–71 recession. The Federal Reserve was pumping up the money supply at a frightful rate and firms could see faster inflation and much higher interest

---

[4]See Peyton Foster Roden, "Financial Management and the 1966 Credit Crunch: A Study of Financial Myopia" (Ph.D. dissertation, North Texas State University, 1970); also "A Misplaced Emphasis in Financial Management," *North Texas Business Studies* (Fall 1971): 30–44.

rates not far ahead. So even though business was not improving dramatically, major companies continued to sell new bonds in record amounts.

Secular Yield Trends

Chapter 6 discussed the secular (or super-cyclical) trend in interest rates: persistent moves upward or downward lasting through several business cycles and carrying yields far above or below their starting level. Such trends, of course, affect suppliers and users of long-term funds more drastically than they do money market participants. Bonds are issued and held for longer intervals; decisions to issue or purchase them must be lived with for decades rather than months or years. Subsequent changes in yields may produce immense fluctuations in bond prices; subsequent changes in the buying power of money may also vastly alter both the real burden to bond-issuers and the real return to bond-holders.

Only the main implications of secular swings in bond yields can be mentioned here, but you should see at once the advantage of being on the right side of these prolonged moves: issuing bonds early when yields are trending up (and money is falling in value) and buying bonds early (as an investor) when a fall in yields (and rise in money's value) is under way. For example, corporations that sold large volumes of long-dated bonds in 1946–47 at yields of 2½ to 2¾ per cent have been riding a whole generation practically free. The average inflation rate of slightly more than 3 per cent per year has actually exceeded the interest rate on these borrowings, effectively reducing the real rate of interest to less than zero. Additionally, as Eq. 25–1 shows, income taxes cut the nominal interest rate almost in half, measured in after-tax dollars. By contrast, companies that failed to anticipate the secular movement of yields, and postponed their heavy bond borrowing until 1969–70, had to float bonds at 8 to 10 per cent near what may turn out to be the top of a long cycle of rising bond yields. If it is, and if bond yields fall and inflation changes into deflation, then the real burden of bonded debt contracted (1) at high interest rates, and (2) in cheap money, will rise painfully, since it will have to be paid back in an era of low interest rates in "dear" money. Many a company might not survive the experience.

The Federal Reserve Bank of St. Louis cites evidence indicating that since 1952 inflation has exerted a strong and prompt influence on interest rates.[5] Since 1961, the influence has become prompter and more pronounced. Why the two years, 1952 and 1961? The former is important because it was the first full year in a decade that the Federal Reserve was able to use open market operations to absorb bank reserves. In 1951 the Treasury and the Federal Reserve reached an accord, relieving the Federal Reserve of the responsibility it had assumed in 1942 of supporting the price of federal securities near par. With the accord, monetary policy began to exert an independent influence on the economy, and open market operations became a full-fledged tool of monetary policy. In 1961 began the great wave of inflation that characterized our economy throughout the 1960s and early 1970s. Rather than shifts in underlying saving and investment, inflation has accounted for nearly all the increase in interest rates since 1961.

Why has the price level effect become more pronounced? Probably for two

---

[5]William P. Yohe and Denis Karnosky, "Interest Rates and Price Level Changes, 1952–1969," Federal Reserve Bank of St. Louis *Review* (December 1969): 18–38.

reasons. First, awareness of price level movements is more widespread. The news media publicize price level indices, and this knowledge can be more rapidly incorporated by creditors into their required rate of return calculated along the lines of Eq. 16–1. Second, the frame of reference that participants use to structure price level expectations is dominated by inflation. Since 1961, there has been an absence of price level cycles—inflation, deflation, inflation—so that debtors and creditors focus on inflation. Since that year, there has been no deflation to dampen the expected movement of interest rates.

What will happen if bond yields keep going up from their level in 1969–70? The answer is that the bond market would probably cease to exist, with long-term debt capital becoming unobtainable. If it becomes evident to long-term creditors that they are continually underestimating the price level premium, savers may refuse to make long-term loans at any rate of interest. Then, as in many European countries today, businessmen will be able to obtain only short-term loans, which lenders can refuse to renew—or up the interest rate on—if they find inflation accelerating. Since this would cluster all of a firm's debt maturities within the few months or years immediately ahead, the business picture would become increasingly unstable, and susceptible to panic and collapse. However, the politicians and central bankers who have master-minded our economy have failed to recognize this simple fact of history, and for all their fine words and empty rhetoric, they do not really seem in the least anxious to curtail inflation. So, there is a valid question to raise here: Will there always be a bond market?[6]

Bond Market Technicalities

The foregoing account of how a businessman should look at the bond market gives only a simplified, high-spot impression. If you were contemplating an issue of bonds, many problems not yet mentioned would confront you. Not only would you have to decide your timing, but a host of other questions as well. Should you put a low coupon on your bond and sell it at a discount, a high coupon and sell it at a premium, or a "current" coupon and sell it at par? Sometimes the market favors one, sometimes another. To what extent should you trade a longer non-callable period for a lower interest coupon? Should your bonds have a sinking fund, be convertible into common stock, have an indenture permitting management greater freedom at the cost of a higher yield? There is also registration with the SEC to consider. As you can see, the actual design and selling of a bond issue is a complicated proceeding. If the issue is a negotiated underwriting, your investment banker can offer much worthwhile advice.

The Mortgage Market

The chief fact of life surrounding the mortgage market is its residual, contra-cyclical position. It is residual because long-term loan money flows strongly into mortgages only after the demands of stronger bidders—corporations, the Treasury, and federal agencies (through which the government does its "back door" financ-

---

[6]This was the actual title of a discerning article written by Fegus McDiarmid in *Public Utilities Fortnightly*, September 29, 1966, pp. 40–48. See also, George A. Christy, "Doom over the Bond Market," *Business Perspectives* (Fall 1970): 4–10.

ing)—are satisfied. These strong bidders are not handicapped by artificial ceilings on the interest rates they can pay; hence in times of tight money, they pay what the market requires to get funds and so "suck" money away from mortgages. Then, when recession comes and corporations, particularly, are no longer selling bonds aggressively, more money becomes available for mortgages. This gives rise to the contra-cyclical pattern of money availability: plentiful money for mortgage financing in recessions, less in booms.[7]

Like bond yields, mortgage interest rates rise and fall with the business cycle and with interest rates generally, but their moves tend to be "stickier" and more restrained. Mortgage rates are administered rates, set by lending institutions and changed rather infrequently, in contrast to bond yields, which reflect daily bond trades in the open market. Mortgages compete with corporate bonds for investment by several kinds of financial institutions, notably life insurors. The spread between mortgage and bond yields largely regulates the flow of life insurance money between the two investments. When bond yields skyrocket, as they have in recent booms, life insurance companies desert the residential mortgage market to invest in higher-yielding bonds.[8] Commercial and industrial mortgages fare less poorly because here the lender may demand "a piece of the action," in the form of some sweetener or automatic inflation hedge. Thus an apartment-builder may obtain a mortgage loan at, for example, 9 per cent interest plus 1 per cent of gross receipts. If inflation continues and rentals rise, the lender will automatically share in the apartment's increased income.

Since individual home ownership has long been a goal of government policy, Washington has tried in various ways to support and fortify the residential mortgage market. The Federal National Mortgage Association (formerly a quasi-government institution, but now largely privately controlled, known as Fannie Mae) has functioned as a kind of central bank for government-backed FHA and GI mortgages. Using its strong borrowing power as a government agency, it has raised large sums in the bond and money markets when housing loans were tight and used the funds to buy mortgages from insurance companies, savings and loan associations, and other lenders; these lenders then recycled the cash into new mortgages. As noted in chapter 12, this operation has been very profitable, since Fannie Mae bought mortgages when yields were high and prices were cheap and later resold many of them when yields were low and prices high again. A new federally-owned institution to share this task with Fannie Mae, the Government National Mortgage Association (Ginnie Mae) commenced operations in 1970.

Because the government's deficits and bloated money supplies have sent interest rates skyward and demoralized the residential mortgage market, proposals were heard during 1970 to force institutional lenders—life insurance firms, pension funds, and the like—to lend a certain portion of their assets on mortgages as the price of continued tax exemption or favored tax treatment. The advisability

---

[7]This fact has tended to make the housing industry a so-called automatic stabilizer of business since World War II. Automatic stabilizers are discussed in chapter 33.

[8]A rule of thumb is that to compensate the mortgage lender for the added bother of servicing the mortgage—monthly collections and accounting for the loan—he needs about 150 "basis points" (equal to 1½ percentage points) more on a mortgage than he can get on a high-grade corporate bond.

of so straight-jacketing the lending rights of these institutions was promptly questioned by those who saw in it a first step toward a regimented capital market and socialized economy. The proposal has been shelved.

Another problem for mortgage financing arises from the vulnerability of savings and loan associations to major rises in interest rates. The associations trade on the difference between the rates at which they borrow money from "depositors" and the rates at which they lend on mortgages. However, mortgages are very long-term loans and are repaid only slowly. Consequently, the *average rate* at which a savings and loan association has its money out on loan will change very slowly and may be very different from the rate being charged on new mortgage loans. This means that the rate which associations can afford to pay their "depositors" cannot exceed their average rate over the past eight or ten years, minus perhaps two percentage points to reflect operating costs. But if all interest rates are going up, and the associations fail to pay more for share accounts, then savers will both boycott the associations and pull money out of them to buy Treasury bills, bank CDs, and even small batches of high-yielding corporate bonds: a process identified in chapter 10 as *disintermediation.* Thus the sharp rise in interest rates during 1969 sharply reduced the flow of funds to savings and loan associations and, consequently, the availability of new money for residential mortgages.

To Remember

Liquid funds storage	Secular yield trend
Bond market timing	Residual position of mortgage market

Questions

1. Why is selection, rather than timing, the corporate treasurer's chief problem in making money market investments? How does this involve the classic financial dilemma, yield versus liquidity?

2. Discuss the merits and shortcomings of commercial paper as a *source* of short-term funds.

3. Distinguish between cyclical and secular fluctuations in bond yields and describe the characteristic pattern of both fluctuations.

4. How do cost, availability, and indenture provisions of bond flotations typically change over the business cycle?

5. Does inflation make bond financing cheaper and easier for corporations? Discuss.

6. What features of a bond issue must the issuer design to fit the market? Where can he get advice on best design?

7. Why does the availability of funds for residential mortgages appear to move contra-cyclically?

8. Why do commercial and industrial mortgages fare better in times of tight money than residential mortgages?

32

The Stock Market

By the *stock market* we mean the market for common and preferred stocks, which are equity interests (ownership rights) in incorporated companies. This market comprises the whole apparatus dedicated to helping people buy, sell, price, select, and finance the securities in which they invest or trade. This apparatus embodies brokers, dealers, investment bankers, security analysts, portfolio managers, professional investment advisors, banks and other financial institutions, the organized stock exchanges, the over-the-counter securities market, state securities commissions, and the Securities and Exchange Commission in Washington, D. C.

Customers of the Stock Market

Customers of the stock market include both individuals and institutions. Individuals hold an estimated three-fourths of the total dollar volume of stocks, and institutions hold the other one-fourth. However, the proportion of stocks held by institutions has risen year by year, and the proportion held by individuals is slowly falling, as pension funds, investment companies and other institutional investors have progressively bid a rather static supply of shares away from individual holders.[1]

Institutions trade in the stock market at a faster pace than individuals; on the New York Stock Exchange, institutional buying and selling has recently accounted for about half the total share turnover. These trends in institutional ownership and activity are largely accounted for by two facts: (1) the rapid growth of pension funds and mutual funds, which invest most of their money in common stocks, and (2) the rising vogue of performance in the stock market, which encourages institutions to "trade the market" for quick profits instead of holding stocks passively for long-pull investment gains.

Major institutions active in the stock market include the following:

1. Investment companies, notably the mutual funds. These organizations are actually intermediaries for individual investment, with the company providing professional portfolio management, stock selection, and market timing. Since these companies pool the funds of thousands of individual investors, they can also diversify their investments far more widely than individuals are able to.
2. Bank-administered trust funds.
3. Pension, profit-sharing, religious, charitable, and college and university endowment funds.
4. Fire and casualty—and to an increasing extent, life—insurance companies.

Over-the-Counter and Listed Markets

Stock trading facilities are furnished both by the organized stock exchanges —the New York, American, Midwest, Pacific Coast, and others—and by the over-the-counter markets. The latter are a loosely organized, nation-wide network of many thousands of security dealers and dealer houses which make markets (by quoting bids and offers) on perhaps 50,000 different stocks. In general, the stocks of large, well-known manufacturing, mining, merchandising, railroad, airline, and utility companies are listed (admitted to trading) on the nation's major stock exchanges. Stocks of secondary companies, including many bright and rising younger firms, are typically traded over-the-counter. However, a majority of the nation's bigger bank and insurance company stocks are also traded over-the-counter. (Actually, "over-the-counter" is a misnomer; most trading in such issues is over-the-telephone.) Let us look more closely at trading processes in the two markets.

---

[1]The rather static supply of shares since World War II has reflected corporations' preference for bond financing. During the later 1960s, however, many companies took on more debt than they could comfortably service during the 1970–71 slump. As a result, beginning in early 1971, offerings of new common stock by corporations increased sharply. With debt still comprising much more than its historic average share of corporate capital, prospects for a rapid enlargement of common stock available to investors seem likely during the 1970s.

The Over-the-Counter Market

The key man in the over-the-counter market is the middleman called a *dealer*. A dealer is one who makes a market in something by buying and selling it for his own account and risk. A securities dealer makes a market in one or more stocks by standing ready to buy at one price (called the bid) and to sell at another—and slightly higher—price (called the offer). The difference between bid and offer is termed the spread. This comprises the dealer's expected gross profit on any transaction. Customers use the over-the-counter market by buying stock from a dealer, who maintains an inventory of shares for sale, or by selling their stock to a dealer when they want to dispose of it. The dealer makes his market by trying to keep his bid and offer, and the spread between them, at prices where the amounts of stock he buys and sells are roughly equal through time. If he starts buying more stock than he sells, he responds by dropping both his bid and offer. This discourages customers from selling him so much stock and encourages them to buy more stock from him. If he finds he is selling out his inventory, then he raises his bid and offer prices to restore balance.

Dealers' bids and offers are published in newspapers, stock quotation sheets, and elsewhere, but published spreads must be interpreted merely as general indications of prices at which business can be done. The published figures may not be current or accurate, due to (1) delays in printing, and (2) the fact that *very large* bids or offers will almost invariably oblige dealers to change their quotations.[2] The prices quoted by different dealers are kept in rough alignment by forces of competition. Trading is by a process of private negotiation: usually one party is a private investor and the other a dealer, although dealer can—and often does—trade with dealer. Dealers may charge their customers a commission, adding it to the offer price or subtracting it from the bid, or they may quote a net price which includes the equivalent (or more) of a commission.

The Listed Market

Almost any stock can trade over the counter, but, as chapter 30 noted, to be eligible for trading on an organized exchange a stock must first be listed. This means that the company whose stock is involved must apply for trading privileges and meet certain requirements set by the exchange. Companies list their stocks to obtain more active markets for them and to enhance their prestige.

The listed market relies on a process known as "auction" trading. The key man here is the broker, who serves merely as his customer's agent to buy and sell stock. Unlike a dealer, a broker does not take title to the stock he handles. The firms that brokers work for are members of one or more stock exchanges.

When you give your broker an order to buy or sell stock, he sends the order to the trading floor of the exchange. There, an exchange member representing your broker's firm takes the order to the particular station, or post, where your stock is traded. Trading in this stock is conducted by another exchange member called a "specialist." A specialist's function is to make a market in one or more

---

[2]Technically, most over-the-counter quotations are bids to buy, and offers to sell, 100 shares at the stated prices. Larger or smaller transactions are subject to further negotiation.

stocks. He does this mainly by acting as a broker for people who want to do business at prices above or below the present market. Suppose Dr. Pepper Company is trading around $50 a share. People who want to buy at prices under 50 leave their buy orders (bids) with the specialist; people who want to sell at prices above 50 leave their sell orders (offers) with him; the specialist's "book" thus reflects the structure of bids and offers around the market. A specialist may also buy and sell for his own account, subject to rules that prohibit him from competing unfairly with orders left by customers.

The "Auction" Process

We can illustrate the "auction" process with the following example. Suppose you give an order to buy 100 shares (a round lot) of Dr. Pepper "at the market." This means at the best price immediately available. A stock exchange member representing your firm walks to the post where Dr. Pepper is traded and, in a voice audible to all around the post, asks, "How's Dr. Pepper?" The specialist responds by quoting the highest bid and lowest offer on his book, perhaps 49½ and 50¼. Your floor broker now knows that he cannot buy Dr. Pepper "off the specialist's books" for less that 50¼. He also knows he must bid more than 49½, because another customer has made a prior bid at this price. So your broker tries to work between bid and offer by shouting, "Bid 50 for 100." He hopes some other broker in the crowd around the post will sing out "Sold!" or that the specialist himself will sell stock (short or from his inventory) at a price below the lowest customer offer on his books. If no one else offers stock at 50 or 50⅛, your broker will simply say "Take it at a quarter," and buy the lowest-offered stock on the specialist's books, 50¼.

Odd-lots of stock, less than 100 share amounts, trade at a price based on the next round-lot transaction to occur after the odd-lot order is received on the trading floor. On substantial amounts of stock, New York and American Stock Exchange commissions run around one per cent of the value of stock bought or sold. (Both buyer and seller pay a commission.)[3]

Regulation of Stock Trading

Several agencies, governmental and otherwise, supervise and regulate the stock markets, largely in hope of preventing—or at least punishing—fraud and manipulation. Each organized exchange has its own machinery, including a board of governors and various committees, to police the business ethics of its members. These officials try to make sure that trading is fair and that customers are dealt with honestly. The National Association of Security Dealers (NASD), organized under a federal law, aims at similar surveillance of the over-the-counter market.[4]

---

[3]On $200 worth of stock the NYSE commission is $7.50. On $1,000 worth it is $22.50. Both figures apply to odd-lot trades and include the 50 per cent surcharge imposed in 1970 to keep member firms from going broke.

[4]The 1938 Amendment to the Securities Exchange Act of 1934, generally referred to as the Maloney Act of 1938, provided for the NASD.

In addition, there are federal and state laws regulating securities transactions. Both of these sets of laws were discussed in chapter 29.

Stock Market Behavior

How you describe the movement of the stock market depends on the time interval you have in mind. Four general kinds of movements in stock prices have long been noted: (1) secular, (2) primary, or cyclical, (3) secondary, or technical, and (4) day-to-day.

Secular Movement

Secular, or very long-term, movement appears to have been raising stock prices an average of about 2½ per cent per year since 1871. This average rise, however, applies only to broad, representative groups of stocks, not to individual issues. It is also dependable only over very long intervals of time—spans of three to four decades, equal roughly to the working lifetime of a college graduate. Stocks have risen historically at this rate because the earnings and dividends of the nation's major stockholder-owned companies have also trended upward through time at about 2½ per cent. In addition to the 2½ per cent growth, stocks over most of the past century have paid dividends averaging about 5 per cent on current price. This has given long-term stockholders a total return over the years of around 7½ per cent. In recent years, inflation seems to have speeded up the growth rate of earnings to around 4 per cent yearly; but the big rise in stock prices since 1949–50 has reduced dividend yields to an average of about 3½ per cent on current price.[5] This is still an overall return (dividend yield plus earnings growth) of about 7½ per cent.

Primary Movement

Primary, or cyclical, movement of stock prices reflects investors' expectations for business conditions six months or so ahead. Typically, this trend is geared to anticipated swings of the business cycle and accompanying changes in corporate profits and dividend payments. Usually the stock market moves in advance of, or leads, the business cycle, but not always. Market breaks in 1946, 1962 and 1966, for example, were false alarms: they were not followed by the expected recessions. The lead of stock prices over changes in business also varies widely from one market cycle to the next.

Since World War II, *bull markets*—cyclical rises in stock market averages—typically have lasted two to three years. *Bear markets*—cyclical declines in the prices of most stocks—have lasted something less than a year. Thus the stock market spends the majority of its time rising; however, when it falls, it falls much faster than it rises. It should be emphasized that these statements about bull and bear markets apply only to broad averages of stock prices, which reflect, of course, the behavior of a majority of stocks. But always some individual issues are able to buck the trend: to rise when the general market is falling, and fall when it rises.

---

[5]Yields have fallen even though dividends have risen because prices rose much faster than did dividends during the 1950s.

Secondary Movement

Secondary, or technical, movement consists of irregular rises and declines extending over several weeks' time. If we visualize the primary trend up or down as a straight line, then the secondary movement appears as a wavy line (sine wave, to those who know trigonometry), swinging first above and then below the main trend line. This secondary movement seems largely based on trader and investor emotion, on people's tendency to "overbuy" or "oversell" stocks: a prolonged move by stocks makes their prices overly responsive to unexpected news and vulnerable to profit-taking by traders who have had the market move their way. So-called weak buyers or sellers tend to come into the market only after a rise or fall has lasted some time. These people are the market's chronic money-losers, lacking the judgment to trade profitably. When the market becomes cluttered with these unfortunate amateurs, it is said to be "technically weak." A market is technically strong after most such traders have been washed out by a "healthy reaction," or downturn, in prices.

Day-to-Day Movement

Day-to-day movement in stock prices depends on small, random changes in the daily pressures of supply and demand. It is relatively unimportant and is best ignored by all but the most trigger-happy short-term traders. Often, of course, the daily papers account for a few points rise or fall in the market averages by citing attention-getting events in the day's news: earnings reports by major companies, promises or threats of legislation by Congressmen, pronouncements by the Federal Reserve or industry spokesmen, release of business statistics by government bureaus, and the like.

Examples of these four kinds of market movements are illustrated in Figure 32–1.

"Discounting" the News

The reason why a single day's news seldom has an enduring effect on the market is that most so-called news has been discounted in advance by the stock prices already prevailing. It comes about in this way.

The future is not altogether a closed book. Some traders in the market often have advance knowledge of coming events or make accurate assessments of their probability. To the extent that future developments can be foreseen, they are always acted upon *immediately* by alert traders, who alter their bids or offers accordingly. In addition, "insiders" in the companies or government bureaus where news first breaks can often profit illegally by buying or selling before the news is made public. The result is that prices have often changed in anticipation of news before the news itself is widely known.

Market-wise, therefore, there are two kinds of news: discountable and non-discountable. *Discountable news* may affect the market weeks or months in advance of its public announcement. By contrast, *non-discountable news* takes the market by surprise. This distinction provides an important yardstick for assessing the market's reaction to news announcements. Discountable news, when finally made public, is (in traditional market metaphor) water over the dam—knowledgeable traders have long since acted on it. Thus its influence is pretty certain to be

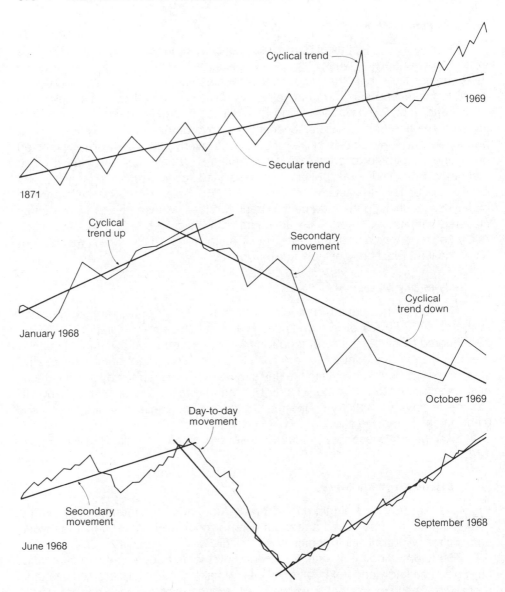

Figure 32–1. The Four Kinds of Market Movement: Secular, Cyclical, Secondary, and Day-to-Day

temporary. On the other hand, if announced news is of a kind that no one could have known about in advance or predicted, then its effect may be more lasting. For this reason, the most important question for a trader or market analyst to ask when news breaks is: Could this news already have been discounted?

Two Principles of Market Pricing

Stock exchanges merely provide a marketplace where anyone, acting through a qualified broker, can offer money for stocks or stocks for money. Nor does the exchange set stock prices or control them in any way. Stock prices, like most other prices in an enterprise economy, are set by the forces of *supply and demand*. They are also an instance of what economists term *marginal pricing*. A correct understanding of these principles is so important that we now discuss them at some length.

Supply and Demand

Whatever the background forces at work (boom, bust, Federal Reserve, taxes, profits, mergers, foreign buying, war scare, whatnot), the immediate determinants of stock prices are always supply and demand. Only through stocks bid for or offered at definite prices in the market can so-called ultimate factors affect the pricing process. Thus if some new influence in the market is noted, your first question should always be: How will this affect supply and demand? Will it cause buyers to offer, or sellers to accept, lower prices? If so, the market will move down. Or is it likely to persuade sellers to demand, and buyers to pay, higher prices? In this event, the market can be expected to move up.

Marginal Pricing

Securities markets differ from commodity (goods and services) markets in that *total supply* is relatively fixed. Companies issue new stock only at infrequent intervals. Meanwhile, of course, somebody has to hold all the shares currently outstanding. This means that one way to look at the present price of any stock is to recognize that this is the price to which the stock must fall to get someone to hold that last share in existence. This holder of the final share is called the marginal holder, and the principle involved is termed marginal pricing.

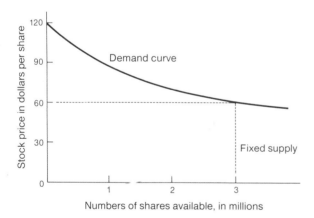

Figure 32–2. Supply-Demand Pricing of Common Stock, General Gismo Corporation

Figure 32–2 illustrates the marginal pricing principle. The rather horizontal curve is really a demand curve laid on its side, but a special kind of demand curve. It is based on the supposition that successive shares of the stock could be auctioned off according to how much buyers would pay for them if the buyers thought each share was the last share available. The curve shows that while someone would pay as much as $120 per share for the first share of General Gismo Corporation, the price per share would fall as more shares became available. Since 3,000,000 shares are on the market, and it takes a price of $60 to get the three-millionth share held, General Gismo now trades at exactly $60 a share.

Usually, most shares of stock issued by a company are simply held by investors and do not trade at all. But to the extent that any part of the total supply is offered for sale, the price must fall until a buyer is found. Similarly, if anyone wants to buy the stock, he must continue raising his bid until a price is reached which will pry stock loose from some present holder.

This means two things. First, stock prices are set by the small or marginal portion of the issue that actively trades. Second, if markets are "thin" (buyers and sellers few and far between), wide swings in prices may take place. If, for example, few buyers are bidding for a stock and a substantial amount of it is offered for sale, the price is likely to fall a long way before enough buyers can be found to absorb the dumped supply. Such stocks and their markets are called "volatile." In contrast, broad, active markets are manned by numerous buyers and sellers. Here price changes usually occur in small fractions and large bids or offers may be absorbed by the market without noticeable price variations.

Margin Trading and Short Selling

Two other factors which affect the demand for listed stocks are margin trading and short selling. These two facilities are not usually available to traders in over-the-counter stocks.

Margin trading is simply the privilege of borrowing a certain percentage of the purchase price when you buy stock. Literally, *margin* refers to the money you must put up out of your own pocket: what you borrow is termed your debit balance or broker's loan. Margin requirements on original purchases of stock are regulated by the Federal Reserve Board. If the margin requirement is 70 per cent, then you would have to put up $7,000 in cash to buy $10,000 worth of stock.

By controlling margin requirements, the Federal Reserve regulates the flow of credit into the stock market and thus helps prevent speculative excesses from developing. If you borrow money from a broker to buy stock, you must pay interest on the loan. Sometimes interest charges on margin accounts rise very high, and this has a tendency to cool off speculation in the market.

Besides the initial margin requirement imposed by Federal Reserve regulations, your broker also requires you to preserve a certain maintenance margin in your account. This is the *difference* between the value of the stock in your account and the amount of your broker's loan. Typically, maintenance margin requirements run at least 25 per cent. Suppose, for example, you had borrowed $3,000 to buy $10,000 worth of stock. The maintenance margin requirement is 25 per cent. How low could your stock fall before your broker sent you a "house call"—a demand for more maintenance margin to protect his loan? The answer is $4,000. At $4,000, you would owe your broker $3,000, and your remaining equity in the stock would be only $1,000—exactly 25 per cent of the market value of your stock. If the stock dropped to $3,900, you'd get a house call for $100 more in maintenance margin. There is an old stock market saying that "The only sure tip from a broker is a margin call."

Technically, *short selling* is defined as any sale of a security which is consummated with the delivery of a borrowed certificate. Seculative short selling involves selling securities one does not own, in the hope of profiting on a future fall in price. Actually, the procedure simply reverses the usual one of buying low and selling high by selling high first and then buying back low. Since the original sale is completed with a borrowed certificate, the short seller owes dividends on the borrowed stock as they come due. There is no time limit on how long a seller can remain short. Sometimes so much stock in a particular issue is sold short that the stock can no longer be borrowed. Then, if the lenders demand their stock back, the short sellers have to "buy in" the short shares at whatever prices holders of the stock demand. This predicament is called a "squeeze." It is a main reason why stocks of smaller companies with only a few hundred thousand shares outstanding should not be shorted; squeezes are too easy to engineer in such stocks.

Do margin trading and short selling benefit the market? There is much argument on this issue. Some people say these practices contribute to a more liquid market by enlarging the volume of trading. Short selling is defended on the ground that it helps keep prices from rising too high in bull markets. On the other hand, critics complain that these tactics aid speculators rather than investors and thus contribute to instability and wider price swings in the market. The overall issue is still unresolved.

Patterns of Stock Prices Through Time

Historically, the stock market's course has been marked by wide swings in prices, earnings and dividends per average share, and in the multiples of earnings and dividends investors have been willing to pay. Examples of this volatile behavior appear in Table 32–1.

Table 32–1. Standard & Poor's 425 Industrial Common Stocks, Selected Statistics, 1928-69

Year	Price Dec. 31	Earnings Per Share	Dividends Per Share	Price-Earnings Ratio	Yield	Market Peak (P) or Bottom (B)
1928	20.85	1.20	.73	17.37	3.48	P
1932	5.18	.31	.39	16.97	7.55	B
1936	16.50	.92	.67	17.93	4.09	P
1941	8.75	1.10	.68	7.92	7.76	B
1945	16.72	.65	.61	19.74	3.66	P
1948	15.06	2.34	.91	6.45	6.02	B
1961	75.72	3.57	2.08	21.21	2.75	P
1962	66.00	4.07	2.20	16.22	4.07	B
1965	98.47	5.58	2.85	17.65	2.89	P
1966	85.24	5.77	2.98	14.77	3.50	B
1968	113.02	6.35	3.18	17.80	2.81	P
1970*	79.89	5.83	3.29	13.70	4.12	B

*End of second quarter.
Source: Standard & Poor's Corporation.

Notice the general pattern of variation between market peaks and bottoms over the years. The largest source of variation seems to be the change in price-earnings ratios—the multiples of earnings investors are willing to pay, given their expectations for business profits in the next year or so. Because price-earnings ratios shrink with pessimism, stock prices can fall—as they did in 1966—even when earnings and dividends are rising. In most bear markets, dividend yields also rise because prices fall faster than dividends, which most companies try to maintain. Conversely, in bull markets the price rise outstrips the gain in either earnings or dividends, so that price-earnings ratios increase and yields fall.[6]

The supply of stock consists both of issues already outstanding and the annual volume of new issues. In some years during the 1960s, corporations retired (through repurchase) more stock than they issued. This produced a relative scarcity of stock available to buyers, which helped account for the relatively high level of stock prices prevailing through the 1960s. To redress badly balanced capital structures and weakened working capital positions, corporations have begun selling larger quantities of stock in the new-issues market.

The willingness of existing holders to sell their stock also affects the supply available to purchasers. An important question at any time is: What kind of stock-holders predominate? Are they mainly investors, who hold their shares firmly? If so, traders will have to bid aggressively higher prices to dislodge the supply of stock. Or are stocks widely held by such unstable holders as perform-ance-minded mutual funds and unseasoned speculators ("spring lambs ready for the shearing") waiting to sell on the next rise? If so, the first bad news may jar loose a huge supply of stock in a cascade of selling. Another factor affecting willingness to sell is the expectation of present stockholders for economic stability and/or earnings growth. If investors are confident that good business will continue, stocks will be hard to buy and their prices will rise strongly on any aggressive buying. On the other hand, expectations of coming recession, falling corporate earnings, or profit-shrinking wage-push inflation will make investors more willing to sell, and stock prices will have less upthrust behind them. Finally, of course, the present tax structure reduces investors' willingness to sell. Taxation of long-term capital gains often freezes investors into stocks which have already achieved large increases, a phenomenon known in the brokerage trade as "tax rigor mortis."

Demand for Stocks

The demand for stocks can be analyzed from two standpoints. First, as already noted, total demand can be divided into _individual_ and _institutional_ components. Since 1950, the percentage of common stocks owned by institutions has risen steadily, and the percentage owned by individuals has declined. Institutional de-mand was long considered more consistent and more conservative than individual demand; flows of investible funds to such institutions as pension funds and fire and casualty companies were almost automatic; and these institutions dealt in the market as long-term investors in high-grade stocks. In recent years, however, institutions have become more performance-minded, often playing the market's

---

[6]You may be curious about the high P/E ratio (16.97) prevailing at the end of 1932. This was due almost entirely to the fact that earnings had all but vanished, so that very low stock prices still resulted in a substantial price-earnings multiple. Yield is dividend ÷ price.

shorter swings in "go-go" (highly speculative) or other second-quality stocks. Mutual funds typically try to get out of stocks when they see bear markets coming and load into them again when a new bull market starts.

A second way to look at stock market demand is to consider the variables that influence *all* demands, whether individual or institutional. One such factor is the size and rate of financial saving in the economy, since this furnishes the pool of funds with which stocks are bought. A second factor is the amount of credit available to individuals and partnerships who buy on margin, and to dealers and investment bankers to finance their inventories of unsold securities. A third influence is people's relative desire for holding equities versus holding debt obligations. This in turn reflects their expectations with respect to (1) prosperity or recession, (2) the trend of corporate earnings, and (3) inflation or deflation in the price level.

Short-Period Price Changes in Stocks

Predicting short-term price movements is very difficult. If it were easy, few people would need to work for a living, least of all stockbrokers. The market's shorter swings depend heavily on the kinds of participants who dominate the trading, for different sorts of operators have very different goals, strategies, and methods.

In general, those who buy and sell stocks can be classified either as investors or traders. Investors are people who buy stocks to hold a long time and who aim at gradual capital growth with dividends while they wait. Traders, on the other hand, aim to buy low and sell high over relatively short periods of time (or sell high and buy back low, if they operate as short sellers). As a class, traders include the following:

1. Major-swing traders, who try to buy in recessions (when stocks are cheap) and sell in booms (when their prices are high).
2. Short-term traders, whose holding periods may run anywhere from a day to more than six months (the dividing line for long-term capital gains). This category contains the "performance" and "hedge" funds.
3. Dealers and stock exchange specialists.
4. Special situation traders, who trade in "turn-around" companies (an earnings reversal is expected), acquisition candidates, companies about to announce new inventions. stock splits, and other bullish news.

Stock Selection and Timing

Both traders and investors in the stock market face two main problems: what to buy, and when to buy it; problems, respectively, of selection and timing. Of the two, timing seems clearly the more crucial and difficult. Correct timing is closely associated with two factors: (1) price level, and (2) group action. At or below some bargain price, the stock of any solvent company becomes a worthwhile purchase. On the other hand, even a stock like IBM or Xerox selling at 100 times earnings can be dangerously overpriced.[7] Investors must always bear in mind

---

[7]RCA sold at 100 times earnings in 1929. People who bought this fine "growth" company at this inflated level waited nearly 35 years to break even on price alone.

that the strongest-looking companies can suffer misfortunes that reduce their earnings and take the "bloom" (meaning high price-earnings ratio) off their stock.[8] However, the fact that a stock is selling at a bargain price does not mean people will immediately recognize its true worth and drive the price back up to where it belongs. "Undervalued" stocks often "lie on the bottom" a long time before the market awakens to their merit. A trader, interested in a quick move, must satisfy himself not only that a stock is soundly priced but also that the market is becoming conscious of its attractiveness so that it will move upward fairly soon. One evidence of a coming move in a stock is increasing interest by traders and/or investors in the group (that is, industry or type—such as conglomerates) to which the stock belongs.

Selecting stocks and timing their acquisition fall into two broad categories: fundamental and technical methods. Each method offers answers to the central problems of selection and timing, but the data used are very different.

Fundamental Analysis

Fundamental analysis relies on economic data. Essentially it asks: What are stocks worth in view of the economy's expected behavior and the earnings outlook for particular companies?

Fundamental analysis relies on quantitative standards of value derived from historical experience. One looks back on a stock's previous record to see what average yield and P/E ratio it has sold at, what its earning power has been in good and bad years, and what growth its earnings and dividends have had in the past decade or so. From these data an *intrinsic value* is computed: typically, its normal, or average-year, earnings at the present time times its average price-earnings ratio of the past five or ten years. If the stock is selling below this appraised value (say as much as 20 per cent), it should be bought. If it is selling above its intrinsic value, it should be sold and the funds switched to an undervalued issue.

Consider, for example, Babcock and Wilcox Company near the end of 1969.

Year	Average Price	Earnings	Average Price-Earnings Ratio	Dividend	Average Yield
1964	32	$2.04	16	.96	3.0
1965	39	2.38	16	1.07	2.7
1966	36	2.67	13	1.21	3.4
1967	46	2.69	17	1.33	2.9
1968	41	2.04	20	1.36	3.3
1969	30	.80	38	1.36	4.5

At a price of 23 in 1970 the stock was far cheaper statistically than at any time in the preceding six years. Of course, it was selling 29 times the current year's estimated earnings (23/.80 cents) and the company was running delays

---

[8]For example, consider the case of Litton Industries. For years, this company's earnings rose like stairsteps. Then from 1967 to 1968, earnings per share tumbled from $2.66 to $1.79. The stock's price fell from 120 down to 37. Earnings fell 33 per cent. Price fell 69 per cent.

and large losses on its deliveries of nuclear generating equipment. But these difficulties seemed temporary. Meanwhile the company appeared to have normal earning power well above $2.00 per share and a well-established tendency to sell 16 or more times earnings. An investor might well have bought BAW at 23 in confidence that its normal value was at least 16 times $2, or $32 per share. In mid-1971, it sold at 42.

Technical Analysis

Advocates of technical analysis reject the notion that economic data have power to predict stock prices. They contend that such "fundamental" developments as sales, earnings, and dividends are typically discounted in price changes well before they are published by the financial press or reporting services. And since, as statisticians have long noted, no other statistical series runs dependably ahead of the stock market, technicians argue that only the market itself is able to predict the market. Technical approaches therefore rely on data generated by the market's own behavior. They include a number of charting methods and doctrines which may be applied either to the overall market or to the behavior patterns and statistics of particular stocks. Since the technical market doctrines are part of the Wall Street tradition, it seems fitting to close this discussion by briefly reviewing the more prominent ones.

1. *Support and resistance points.* Stocks show strength by overcoming resistance (prices that have stopped previous rises) or by holding support (prices which have arrested earlier declines). Symptoms of weakness are opposite, i.e., failure to overcome resistance or a penetration of support levels.

2. *Price-volume relation.* "Trend goes with the volume," is a market adage. If volume of trading rises (in the market or in a particular stock) as the price rises, strength is indicated and an upward trend will follow; a rise accompanied by dwindling volume will not hold.

3. *Advance-decline ratio.* A dominant proportion of stocks advancing signals a continuing rise for the overall market. A preponderance of declines suggests a market downtrend.

4. *New highs and lows.* A large proportion of new highs for the year to new lows for the year suggests a strong market. A majority of new lows has opposite implications.

5. *Breadth of market.* This is the number of different stocks trading on a particular day. The broader the market, the more significant the direction in which the market moves that day.

6. *Reaction to news.* A strong stock (or market) holds its ground on receipt of bad news and rises on good news; a weak one falls on bad news, refuses to rise on good news.

7. *Leadership.* The most active (heavily traded) stocks are called the market leaders. If stocks of high quality and price are leading the market upward, it is a sign of strength. Poor leadership (cheap or speculative stocks) on a rise suggests coming weakness.

8. *Short interest.* A large short interest (stock sold short and not yet bought back, or "covered") is considered bullish. If prices fall, the shorts must buy back their borrowed stock in order to take profits, and this will cushion the decline.

If prices rise, the shorts will be panicked into covering, which will force prices still higher.

9. *Contrary opinion.* A near-unanimous opinion about the market is usually wrong. Do the opposite of what "everybody" recommends. This is Bernard Baruch's celebrated principle.

10. *Odd-lot theory.* Odd-lot (less than 100 shares) traders have the reputation of typically doing the wrong thing at major turns in the market, e.g., selling heavily as a bear market changes to bull, or buying heavily in a bull market's last stages.

11. *Cash reserves of mutual funds.* When these are high (say 10 per cent of total fund assets), the market is due to rise because the funds cannot long afford to hold so much idle cash and must soon reinvest. When funds' cash reserves are low, the market is vulnerable to profit-taking by the funds as they try to rebuild their depleted cash positions.

12. *Ratio of New York Stock Excahange to American Stock Exchange volume.* When volume in the more speculative ASE stocks rises to 50 per cent or more of NYSE volume, the market structure is shaky.

The Market's Role in the Economy

Whole volumes have been written on the stock market without beginning to exhaust the subject, so we can only scratch the surface in these few pages. But in closing we should say something about the market's broad usefulness and potential hazards in the economy as a whole.

There seems little question but that over the decades the stock market performs two great services. It is (1) a barometer of economic conditions, and (2) a guide for allocating economic resources among different industries and companies. The gradual rise of major market averages mirrors the country's economic progress. The market's ups and down give convenient warnings of coming recessions and recoveries; and sometimes—as when speculation becomes excessive—stock prices serve as a thermometer of fever in the economic body. The greater profitability and growth over time of certain industries is advertised by the superior performance of their stocks, and this makes it easier for companies in sectors of rising demand to obtain resources for expansion. It is easier for a "growth" company, or a consistently profitable one, to raise money by selling new stocks or bonds than for a company with only a drab record to show.

On the other hand, the stock market's structure and machinery undoubtedly lend themselves to gambling and even to occasional speculative excess. Keynes wrote:

> Speculators may do no harm as bubbles on a steady stream of enterprise. But the position is serious when enterprise becomes the bubble on a whirlpool of speculation. When the capital development of a country becomes a by-product of the activities of a casino, the job is likely to be ill-done.[9]

---

[9]John Maynard Keynes, *The General Theory of Employment Interest and Money* (New York: Harcourt, Brace & World, Inc., 1936), p. 151. Anyone wishing to understand the role and occasional dominance of speculation in the stock market should read the whole of chapter 12, from which this quotation is taken.

The greatest fear, of course, is that someday the market will blow up into another balloon of speculation like 1929 and then collapse, ruining hundreds of thousands of people, destroying billions of dollars worth of collateral values, wiping out the financial institutions that have lent to speculators, and plunging the country into deep depression. Some people say this could not happen again because there are laws on the books to prevent it, but one should also remember that unpopular laws can be ignored or repealed, and that this would probably happen if the nation ever got well launched on another speculative joyride.

All in all, the stock market is like other human institutions. The mechanical system it represents is morally neutral; whether the institution works for good or evil depends, in the final analysis, on the morality and good sense of the people operating it. A right-thinking, right-doing citizenry needs few laws to keep its lives straight, while all the laws in history cannot keep a shortsighted or cynical people from destroying itself.

To Remember

Listed market

Over-the-counter market

Auction market

Negotiated market

Odd-lot

Discountable news

Margin

Short sale

Selection and timing

Fundamental analysis

Technical analysis

Questions

1 What kinds of institutions are active in the stock markets?

2 Distinguish between "auction" and "negotiated" markets. Does this parallel the difference between the stock exchanges and the over-the-counter markets? Explain.

3 Discuss briefly the regulatory philosophy of the SEC.

4 Name and describe the four main kinds of common-stock movements.

5 Why is it said that the market usually "discounts news?" Why do "discountable" and "non-discountable" news have different effects?

6 Name and describe the two main principles of stock-market pricing.

7 What is margin? In what ways is margin trading regulated?

8 What is a short sale? How does a short seller obtain stock to deliver to the buyer?

9 Distinguish between fundamental and technical analysis of the stock market.

10 List six principles for judging the market's technical position.

33

The Business Cycle

The Business Cycle

For at least two centuries, alternate expansions and contractions have marked the course of the business system. We call this phenomenon the business cycle, even though the term *cycle* implies a regularity of timing and amplitude seldom present in business fluctuations.

The business cycle typically consists of an interlude of prosperity rising into boom, peaking out, sliding into recession, recovering, and launching into a new phase of prosperity. Although the length and breadth of its phases have differed widely from one cycle to another, this general pattern has repeated itself with little variation. The business cycle is accompanied by wide swings in the main economic and financial variables—incomes, output, employment, business profits, interest rates, and stock prices.

The cycle is a major factor in business and financial decisions. Its massive changes lie far beyond control of the individual business manager, indeed largely beyond the control of government. Since he is powerless to alter these fluctuations,

388

the manager must accommodate himself and his enterprise to their swings. A good motto to remember in thinking about the business cycle would run: "Swing with business cycles, not against them."

The Financial Manager and the Cycle

Although lines of business differ in their sensitivity to the cycle, all industries are in some degree affected. Sales volume, operating costs, and the cost of money all change over the cycle with noticeable impact on a firm's profit and outlook. Unlike internal conditions, which are susceptible to a firm's control, the business cycle is an intractable external influence to which, in large measure, a business can only adjust.

The financial manager must know how the business cycle affects both business in general and his own industry and firm. He must pay particular attention to the cycle's impact on money supply, interest rates, and stock prices. He must be aware of how drastically the cycle's successive phases may change the cost and availability of borrowed funds and the firm's cost of equity capital. He must also recognize and be able to forecast how his own firm's need for funds will change over the cycle. Finally, he must develop his timing skill so that the firm's additions and retirements of fixed and circulating capital can be timed advantageously in relation to cyclical change.

Some people, of course, say that application of modern theory has tamed the business cycle. They point out that since World War II, U.S. recessions have been less serious than earlier. Nevertheless, significant slowdowns in economic expansion took place in 1962, 1966, and 1970, with sharp impact on business profits and stock prices. In both 1962 and 1966, the Dow Jones Industrial average of stock prices fell some 25 per cent within a few months; in 1970, the decline was 38 per cent. The 1966 and 1970 slowdowns were preceded by credit crunches in which short term interest rates rose by as much as 50 per cent in a year's time. Managers who were able to forecast these changes and anticipate their consequences brought large savings and other advantages to their firms and prevented costly mistakes that hurt less vigilant competitors.

Business Cycle Theories

Many theories have sought to explain business cycles by means of a single dominating cause. Business cycle theories fall in two broad classes: *exogenous theories,* in which the cause lies in a factor outside the economy itself; and *endogenous theories,* in which destabilizing forces within the economy generate the cycle.

Most exogenous theories have as central to their thesis foreign trade and exchange. Usually some foreign shock occurs, such as imposition of trade barriers by a foreign country or a business collapse abroad, and a domestic collapse or recovery is set in motion.

An example of another type of exogenous theory is the "Sun Spot" theory propounded a century ago by the British economist-astronomer, W. S. Jevons.[1]

---

[1]William Stanley Jevons, *Investigations in Currency and Finance* (New York: A.M. Kelley, 1964), a reprint of the original 1884 edition.

Jevons found significant correlations between the number and size of sun spots, weather conditions on the earth, demand for British exports of farm implements, and the long historical series of booms and depressions in England.

Endogenous theories of the business cycle are popular now. Let us briefly review six of the many types advanced in the twentieth century.

1. *Over-investment theories.* These theories stress the fact that factory owners, home builders, automobile buyers, and other creators and purchasers of durable goods do not invest at a uniform rate. Instead, capital formation comes in waves—"bucket-fulls," as a German economist once said—leading to alternating surpluses and shortages of durable items. The surpluses generate recessions and the shortages generate booms. A depression begins when capital formation is overdone and ends when large numbers of durable assets have worn out and must be replaced.

2. *Under-consumption (over-saving) theories.* These theories stress the inability of consumption at the peak of a boom to keep pace with all the goods which newly expanded production facilities are putting on the market.

The propensity, or inclination, to consume falls as income rises. The economy drowns itself in cream as a wealthier people become satisfied with the level of consumption they have reached. They begin to save an increasing share of their current income. Higher saving means lower spending. Lower spending in turn means that businesses make fewer sales. Faced with sagging sales, businessmen cut back on production and try to eliminate excess inventory. To cut back on production, they lay off workers. As employment falls, income and consumption fall, plunging the economy into a depression.

3. *Psychological theories.* These theories stress the instability of businessmen's emotions and expectations. Central to these theories is the self-fulfilling prophecy: anticipation of an event makes it happen, because when a person anticipates an event, he acts in such a way as to bring that event about. For example, businessmen may lose confidence and anticipate a recession. They try to insulate themselves against a recession's consequences by building up liquidity now. Increasing liquidity and curtailing current investment plunge the economy into recession.

4. *Credit theories.* Credit theories emphasize the flow of money and credit in:

(a) permitting a boom to get underway,
(b) throttling a boom at its peak, and
(c) enforcing liquidation during the recession.

The changing role of money supply and interest rates over the business cycle is strongly emphasized. What businessmen can do depends heavily on the availability of credit, and the degree of ease or tightness in the banking system becomes the barometer of the cycle's next stage. Low interest rates and easy money help the boom to start and feed it on its way. Tight money and high interest rates choke off boom and inflation at their peaks.

5. *Innovations theories.* These theories stress the role of new inventions, products, production processes, machines, markets, and so forth, in creating the business opportunities on which booms are often based. These new business innovations or opportunities come in clusters, introducing a process of creative destruction: a new production process makes old methods obsolete, so business-

men get rid of the obsolete assets and compete to acquire the new. When markets are finally saturated, the boom fades. Innovations theories of the business cycle are invariably associated with Josef Schumpeter, an Austrian economist who taught at Harvard University.[2]

Unquestionably, innovations do help to explain the strength both of particular business cycles and of the forces of business expansion over prolonged periods. Much of the vigor of business growth in the United States from 1830 to 1880 was based on the building of railroads. From 1900 to 1930 the American economy was powerfully propelled by the development of electric power and the automobile. Since World War II, major innovations have included television, the computer, aero-space technology, and even the cold war.

6. *Price-cost relations and profit margin theories.* These theories stress the favorable relation between prices and production costs at the start of an expansion, the early tendency for profits to rise faster than wages and other costs, and the role of expanding profits in generating a boom. The boom continues until, amid labor shortage and increasing capacity, wages and other costs begin to overtake price increases. Margins and profits then fall, collapsing the boom. Similarly, during recessions the cost-price relation gradually grows more favorable and the decline ends with profit margins largely restored.

This explanation of the business cycle was strongly emphasized by Keynes in *A Treatise on Money,* published in 1930.[3] Keynes pointed out that booms begin as profit inflations and end as wage inflations. When rising wages overtake fading profits, the boom ends. The great American business cycle theorist, Wesley C. Mitchell, also developed this basic explanation.

Modern business cycle theories are usually eclectic—that is, a blend of two or more theories. All observers see the same things happen in a business cycle, and the main difference is in what each chooses to emphasize. It is probably fair to say that all of the above theories are helpful in understanding the cycle, yet it is certainly true that none explains it single-handedly.

What brings a boom to an end makes a big difference. If it is choked off by tight money, the economic outlook in years immediately ahead is favorable. The boom was choked off before it ate too deeply into future opportunities for capital formation, i.e., for business and consumer investment. There is a backlog of demand for houses, factories, buildings, machines, automobiles, and appliances. But if a boom "dies a natural death," the outlook is black indeed. Such a boom has already borrowed too many investment opportunities from the years ahead. Capital formation has been overdone and the economy must now pass through a period of subnormal investment. This principle almost certainly explains the severity of the 1929-33 depression, and the economy's general sluggishness from 1958 through 1964.

Cycle Phases

Now let us apply some of the preceding theory to an examination of a representative business cycle. Although each business cycle is unique, all contain

---

[2]Joseph Schumpeter, *The Theory of Economic Development* (Cambridge, Massachusetts: Harvard University Press, 1955).

[3]John Maynard Keynes, *A Treatise On Money,* (London: Macmillan & Company, Ltd., 1930).

sufficiently similar characteristics to permit us to generalize about them. In the following model, the cycle has four phases: (1) upswing, (2) upper turning point, (3) downswing, and (4) lower turning point.

The Upswing

We begin with the economy emerging from recession. Conditions for business expansion are highly favorable. A prolonged spell of subnormal business has depleted inventories for both merchants and manufacturers. Shelves and warehouses must finally be restocked. Factories also need repairs, and in many instances replacement, of buildings and machinery. Interest rates are low. The demand for money has been light and money is readily available for borrowing. Consumers, long fearful of losing jobs or suffering reduced incomes, must finally replace worn-out goods: the old shoes, bed sheets, car, and so forth, bought before the recession have now reached their limit of usefulness.

Business revival begins slowly at first, then gains momentum. Merchants order to restock their shelves; this stimulates manufacturers' activity. The recalling of laid-off workers to their jobs adds to payrolls, wages, and spending power. New incomes, flowing into the hands of consumers, bring a rise in retail sales, increasing merchants' orders for still more inventory. Business activity rises in a kind of push-pull interplay between consumer demand, manufacturing activity, and increasing incomes. As idle capacity comes into use, fixed costs per unit of output tumble, and profit margins and profits soar. Early in recovery, profits outstrip all other economic series in percentage rate of climb.

Gradually, as business returns to normal and then becomes extremely good, demand begins to press on existing manufacturing capacity. Businessmen foresee a need for more plant and equipment to handle the rising tide of orders, and soon capital investment committees are busy placing orders for new buildings and new machines. In spite of a continual increase in manufacturing output, consumer buying absorbs inventory as fast as merchants can stock it.

Other evidences of prosperity become noticeable. The cost of money begins to rise. Merchants commence to borrow heavily at banks to finance larger inventories and receivables, and consumers enlarge their borrowings to acquire more houses, automobiles, and appliances. The upsurge in plant and equipment expenditures by business firms brings a flood of new bonds to market, and bond yields begin to rise.

A spirit of optimism takes over as incomes increase faster than the supply of goods and services. Prices begin to rise. Wages also rise, and the government begins to show concern over symptoms of inflation.

At this point the rise in business becomes self-reinforcing. To the extent that economic resources are employed to create new plant and equipment, they are not available to enlarge the supply of consumer goods. However, the investment in new plant and equipment generates large additions to people's incomes. Since their resulting expenditures meet a limited supply of goods, this pushes prices up at an accelerating rate. Much of the accelerated price rise is due to the speculative buying of goods: merchants order inventory in excess of needs because they expect to make a speculative profit on the continuing rise in prices. The ready availability of credit strengthens this speculative buying, and merchants and manufacturers gladly pay the rising interest rates charged on loans.

Speculation now flows over into the securities and commodities markets. The stock market, which typically rises ahead of business anyway, leaps into a real boom. Speculators buy stocks not only in anticipation of better business earnings, which will lead to higher dividends, but also in the hope of selling to other speculators at inflated prices. Similar speculative price rises grip the commodity and real estate markets.

The general rise in prices strengthens the collateral value of all sorts of pledgible items, reinforces the confidence of both lenders and borrowers, and increases the availability of credit while lowering credit standards.

The Upper Turning Point

What forces end the upswing? Basically, the fact that a business boom cannot sustain itself indefinitely. The boom develops because businessmen are adding to their productive capacity and building inventory at an abnormally rapid rate. But at some point, all the capacity that can profitably be used will have been created, and inventories will have become large enough to meet all forseeable needs. Indeed, much new plant and equipment creation and inventory enlargement will have been prompted by speculation rather than by the economy's real needs; thus, it is quite probable that the expansion of both new capacity and inventories will have been badly overdone. When this discovery is made, a rush may develop to cancel projects and orders already under way. This rush will not only precipitate a downturn in business, but also give the downturn much momentum.

Price-level and monetary factors also play large parts in reversing a business boom. The central bank reacts to inflation by slowing down the growth of money supply. Money begins to get tight, and interest rates rise. As money becomes expensive and hard to borrow, many people—merchants, manufacturers, home builders, and home buyers—begin to think twice about borrowing. As interest rates soar to ration an inadequate supply of funds, mortgage borrowers begin to be priced out of the market.[1] With markets for corporate bonds congested, many companies heed the advice of their investment bankers and postpone their issues.

Meanwhile, the Treasury and federal government may also restrain the boom by increasing income taxes (personal and business) and by cutting expenditures. Since a Treasury surplus withdraws funds from the economy, it can aid powerfully in putting brakes on the boom.

Presently, the stock market and business profits begin to suffer. Stocks have already climbed a long way before the business boom begins. For a while during the boom they move higher. But rising interest rates and tight money make margin accounts more difficult to finance, and falling bond prices and rising bond yields make bonds an increasingly attractive alternative to stock investment. Finally, far-sighted investors and speculators perceive that the rate of gain in profits for many companies is slowing down and preparing to reverse itself. They begin to sell their stocks, and soon stock prices are falling. Falling stock prices discourage speculators who hold stocks on margin, and their selling soon becomes contagious, leading to a real break in the stock market.

---

[1]This happens because, as noted in chapter 31, residential mortgage yields do not rise sufficiently to meet the competition of yields on either corporate bonds or commercial and industrial mortgages.

At the same time, the rate of gain in business profits starts to slow down. The capital goods ordered at the start of the boom become available. The economy's ability to produce consumer goods now expands. Supply begins to overtake demand, and manufacturers, goaded by unused capacity, compete vigorously against each other for consumer markets. Price rises become harder and harder to achieve in the face of intensifying competition and tightening money. Meanwhile, the economy has reached the limit of its labor supply. Workers are difficult to hire. Labor discipline becomes difficult; if workers are fired for loafing on one job, another is easy to find. Employers compete vigorously against each other for a limited labor supply, driving wages up sharply at a time when price increases are difficult to come by. This puts profit margins under great pressure, and profits generally begin to fall. The boom ends in a great flurry of "profitless prosperity," with rising labor costs devouring the gains businessmen had hoped to make.

The boom has now reached its peak and begins to fade rapidly. Businessmen cancel their orders for plant expansion and for new inventory. Some companies, hit with declining profits, and even losses, cut their dividends. Reports of reduced earnings, falling dividends, some business failures, and the still-prevailing reign of tight money all drive the stock market down at an accelerated rate. Confidence escapes businessmen, speculators, and consumers alike. Everyone now expects the worst to happen,[5] and the swing of expectations from over-optimism to pessimism now drives business into a rapid decline. Sales fall, workers are laid off, and many people reduce their spending to conserve cash for a "rainy day."

The Downswing

Once the downswing in business is under way, reinforcing influences accelerate its decline. Businessmen liquidate inventories and do not replace them. Some inventory may have to be sold to pay pressing debts; dumping it on the market depresses prices. Having liquidated inventory, and fearing further declines in both prices and sales, merchants buy only on a "hand to mouth," as-needed basis. Weak inventory ordering backs up on the factories. Manufacturers cut production runs. Employees lose overtime, get short-timed, or laid off. As people lose jobs and go on unemployment compensation, their incomes and buying power fall, further reducing economic demand and business activity.

Business profits fall along with sales. Since most firms are affected by both operating and financial leverage, the percentage decline in profits is typically a

---

[5]The contagiousness of pessimistic expectations was rife and recognized even in Shakespeare's time. Consider, for example, the following dialogue from *King Richard the Third,* act 2, scene 3:

> *First Citizen:* Come, come, we fear the worst; all will be well.
> *Third Citizen:* When clouds are seen, wise men put on their cloaks;
> When great leaves fall, then winter is at hand;
> When the sun sets, who doth not look for night?
> Untimely storms make men expect a dearth.
> All may be well; but, if God sort it so,
> 'Tis more than we deserve, or I expect.
> *Second Citizen:* Truly, the hearts of men are full of fear:
> You cannot reason almost with a man
> That looks not heavily and full of dread.

multiple of the percentage decline in sales. Some firms meet the fall in profits by reducing their dividends. Some firms may experience such large losses that they are unable to meet bond or bank interest or to pay other fixed charges. They go into receivership or bankruptcy.

Pessimistic expectations darken the future outlook of both businessmen and consumers. Demand for borrowed funds dries up. Speculation in the stock market comes to an end and the volume of stocks bought and sold falls to a trickle. Liquidity preference is high; everyone would rather own cash than stocks or inventories. Real estate and commodity prices fall along with stock prices, and the lower level of collateral values makes borrowers less credit-worthy. Lenders become highly selective and only "preferred risks" can borrow money.

One bright spot shows up even as the downturn is under way. Interest rates begin to ease. Alarmed by signs of recession, the central bank reverses its tight-money policy and begins an aggressive program to lower interest rates and increase the availability of loanable funds. Meanwhile, borrowers at banks and other financial institutions hasten to pay off their loans and get out of debt. As spending by businessmen and consumers slows down, money begins to pile up in the banks in idle pools. Conditions gradually become super-liquid and interest rates fall to low levels.

Meanwhile, of course, the government also uses fiscal policy to fight the recession. Taxes for individuals and corporations are cut, government spending for unemployment relief and public works is increased, and a large government deficit is fueled by massive Treasury borrowings at the banks. The proceeds of the deficit are promptly spent by the government in an effort to provide jobs and to prevent an excessive slowdown in the economy.

The Lower Turning Point

Even without intervention by the central bank and government, the downswing must eventually end. There are three primary self-limiting factors, and several lesser ones come into play.

1. The end of inventory liquidation and the fall of inventories to an irreducible minimum oblige merchants to place new orders for goods. Even though ordering begins on a "hand to mouth" basis, this replenishment in inventories brings a step-up in factory activity.

2. Time, wear, and obsolescence oblige manufacturers to begin replacing plant and equipment. The resulting orders for new capital goods are a powerful spontaneous force in bringing about revival.

3. People's consumption does not fall as much as their income. As incomes decline, families cut back on their savings and spend a higher fraction of their income to maintain accustomed living standards. Thus, the fall in wages, salaries, dividends, and profits is matched by a less than proportionate fall in demand. This helps keep the economy going even in the darkest days.

In addition, a kaleidoscope of recovery begins. The liquidity of the system improves and the stream of business failures gradually subsides. With increased output, labor productivity increases. Businesses increase output without resorting to hiring, so capacity utilization rates rise. And even during recession, the stock market begins to rise as market participants begin to "look over the valley" at impending prosperity.

All of these factors work together to end the decline and produce a gradual upturn. Invisible at first and recognized by only a few, this upturn gradually gathers strength as new orders, new hirings, new incomes and new sales begin to spread in ever-widening circles.

Are There "Super Cycles"?

In the past, once in each lifetime, the U.S. economy has undergone a depression of exceptional severity. This generation-long business cycle is often called the super cycle. The troughs, or depressions, of these super cycles fall precisely thirty-six years apart: 1857, 1893, and 1929. Although no such major adjustment has followed World War II, no one can be absolutely certain that modern techniques of economic control have forever banished the possibility.

The theory of why these "gully washers" have come is simple and plausible. The economy, like any other machine, accumulates maladjustments as it goes along. If people were entirely far-sighted and provident, these maladjustments would be corrected as soon as they appeared. However, the correction of such evils as inflation, badly planned investment, excessive speculation, too much debt, out-of-line wages and salaries, and so on, is always painful. People wish to postpone the readjustment as long as possible, and they typically elect to office politicians who use palliatives and stop-gaps to put off the evil day. Thus sand and grit are not removed from the economic gears. Gradually, the nation's economic machinery becomes so overloaded with maladjustments that something gives way. A collapse of speculation, for example, may undermine business and consumer positions already weak from too much debt, and a string of bankruptcies will follow. This in turn collapses consumer demand, sales fall, unemployment rises, incomes plummet. A contraction of business brings on more bankruptcies. A "once in a generation" downswing starts and does not stop short, as ordinary business recessions do, but continues downward until all weak or overextended positions are wiped out: unsound debt is cleared away, poorly planned investment written off, and excessive wages, inefficient management, and prices out of line with costs are wrung out of the economic structure. Then, with the economy once more on a sound foundation, another generation of growth can take place, broken only by recessions of no more than moderate severity.

Financing Tactics Over the Cycle

To the financial manager, the business cycle is a fact of life. He must accept it because he cannot change it. Since he cannot control its action, he must therefore adjust his own actions to it. How does he do this?

The financial manager's main strategy is simply to move with the cycle, taking advantage of his knowledge of what the next stage will be. Clearly, he does not want his company to complete an expensive new plant or saddle itself with a huge inventory just as a recession is beginning. On the other hand, he does not want his company to enter a period of good business without ample manufacturing capacity, or without the ability to finance an increasing volume of inventory and receivables. Decisions to expand the company's scale of operations are not made by the financial manager alone, but his voice can powerfully influence the votes and decisons of the firm's other officers.

What is good financial strategy over the typical business cycle? As the downturn ends and the company is very liquid, it is a good time to begin thinking about lines of banking credit and possible future bond issues. The company does not need to add to its idle funds right now. But better business lies ahead and should be planned for.

As business revival begins, inventories and receivables start to increase. This brings a rise in the company's need for circulating capital. Before long, too, demand may be pressing on factory capacity. Operating executives may be thinking about adding to plant and equipment. Each of these projects is likely to call for outside financing. Where should this financing come from? Most of the new financing need is likely to be permanent. Plant and equipment, being long-lived assets, must be financed from permanent sources. Most of the increased need for circulating capital is likely to prove permanent, for the firm will grow over the next few years and it is doubtful whether the next recession will carry circulating capital needs back down to their present level. Thus, the bulk of the new financing will be permanent. At this stage of the cycle it should be done through a bond issue. Bond yields are still low and rising only slowly. The bond market is broad and uncongested. Investment bankers are eager for business and will give an issue better attention. It is a good time to sell bonds.

As the stream of recovery widens into prosperity, it may be well to market one or more additional issues of bonds before bond yields go out of sight (as they typically do at the peak of a boom). By now the need to finance rising levels of inventory and receivables has grown to large dimensions. The economy—and likely your business—have begun to operate above balanced levels. Now if a drop were to come, your inventories and receivables would face a sharp contraction. It makes no sense to use permanent financing for needs that may evaporate with a change in the cycle. From this point on, circulating capital needs should be met from temporary sources, preferably bank loans or factoring agreements.

Now prosperity climbs into boom. The stock market approaches a peak. This is the time for the astute financial manager to sell new common shares for two or three times the price he could have gotten during the recession, using some of the proceeds to retire debt. Bond financing has become very costly with tight money, high interest rates, long intervals of non-refundability, and stringent indenture restrictions on borrowers. It is a good time to stay out of the bond market, and the astute financial manager will have timed his financing at this point to consist of common stocks.

Common stock financing at the peak of a boom is not only cheap, it also provides an equity base for debt financing during the next recovery. By entering the recession period with a comfortable equity-to-debt ratio, the company not only minimizes its financial risk, but also impresses future lenders with a large "cushion" of equity to protect their loans.

Now the boom peaks out and recession is underway. The stock issues sold at the boom's peak, plus ample lines of bank credit, make the company comfortably liquid despite the downturn. As the recession gathers headway and sales begin to drop, the company's need to finance inventories and receivables declines. This decline is met by retiring bank loans—the temporary source of circulating capital. Liquidity is maintained but excess liquidity is avoided as the company slips down into the nadir of recession.

From here the financing cycle will begin again.

To Remember

Speculative buying

Exogenous theories

Endogenous theories

Over-investment theories

Under-consumption theories

Psychological theories

Credit theories

Innovations theories

Profit margin theories

Eclectic theories

Super cycles

Questions

1. Is it correct to call recurring business fluctuations "cycles"? Explain.

2. What relations typically exist between the business cycle and a firm's financial position?

3. Describe a typical business upswing. Why doesn't it continue indefinitely?

4. What particular parts do financial factors play in limiting a business expansion?

5. Describe the downswing of the cycle. Why doesn't it continue indefinitely?

6. Would a downswing in business go on forever even if the Federal Reserve and Treasury failed to act? Why or why not?

7. Why is it better for a boom to be killed with tight money than to "die a natural death"?

8. Describe in detail the proper general tactics for the financial manager to pursue over the business cycle.

9. Have "super cycles" existed in the past? Why? What purpose have they served?

34

Financing International Business Transactions

Foreign Exchange Markets — *Structure of Exchange Markets — Cross Rates and Arbitrage Among Currencies — Exchange Rate Fluctuations and Their Consequences — Exchange Rate Hazards in Lending and Investing* — Spot and Forward Exchange Markets — *Movements of Spot and Forward Rates — Hedging Exchange Risk — Hedging on the Forward Market* — International Investment and Interest Arbitrage — *Covered Interest Arbitrage — Interrelation of Exchange and Interest Rates — Interest Rate Parity — Factors Assisting and Obstructing Interest Parity*

So long as business transactions keep within the boundaries of one country, a single, predictable system of laws and money values applies. But when sales or purchases, loans or investments, cross national frontiers, additional and sometimes unforeseeable hazards arise. They arise from three sources. First, laws and business customs (including the ethics of dealing with foreigners) differ widely from one country to another. Second, each nation is a sovereign power with the right under international law to repudiate contracts with citizens of other countries, confiscate their property, or subject them to punitive or discriminatory regulations. Third, each country has its own currency, the value of which may change suddenly or unpredictably in relation to the world's other currencies. The possibility of such changes introduces into international business transactions the element of currency, or exchange, risk. For example, if I agree to sell gismos to Pierre at five francs a piece when five francs exchange for one dollar, I wind up losing money if, by the time I collect, five francs exchange for only 80 cents.[1]

Foreign Exchange Markets

The discussion of the international monetary system and the U.S. balance of payments in chapter 11 pointed out that most countries set and ordinarily maintain par, or declared, values for their currencies. We have seen that each country keeps the value of its currency within the IMF "bands" by buying and selling it and foreign currencies in the world's currency markets. If, for example, Ruritanians spend, lend, invest, or give away too many florins (their currency unit) abroad, foreigners will get rid of their excess florins by selling them for some more desirable currency, perhaps dollars or Graustarkian guilders. That is the reason why countries maintain international currency reserves. When foreigners dump florins on the world's foreign exchange markets, the Ruritanian central bank (or "exchange equalization authority") must have a supply of guilders or dollars with which to buy up unwanted florins. Conversely, if foreigners desire to accumulate more florins than Ruritanians are making available through regular business and government transactions, the florin is strong. Then the Bank of Ruritania will pay out florins in exchange for the guilders and dollars being offered by foreigners, and Ruritania's international reserves will go up instead of down.

Foreign exchange markets are thus the foci of all influences acting to strengthen or weaken the position and price of the world's currencies in relation to each other. Since all currencies are free to fluctuate in limited degree, and since any currency can be drastically devalued or revalued if it becomes very weak or very strong, the foreign exchange markets and their fluctuations are of great interest and importance to international businessmen. Profit or loss on international transactions often depends more on one's astuteness in forecasting the future movement of foreign exchange rates—or in hedging against their unfavorable moves—than on the quality of one's goods, effective salesmanship, or astute pricing.

Foreign exchange rates can be quite sensitive and may change rapidly when people are busy getting out of one currency and into another. The foreign exchange markets are very "broad" markets because in ordinary circumstances they can absorb large volumes of buying and selling with minimal price changes. To understand why, let us look briefly at the structure of these markets.

Structure of Exchange Markets

Foreign exchange markets are centered in the great commercial banks of cities like New York, London, and Tokyo. These banks act as dealers in the world's currencies. They buy and sell currencies on bid and offer prices which are typically only a few hundredths of a per cent apart. Banks make "retail" markets with individual businessmen or tourists, and "wholesale" markets with other banks and with central banks.

---

[1]This example illustrates a 20 per cent devaluation of the franc between the time a contract is written for international exchange of goods and the time of delivery and payment. A quick calculation will show that the exchange value of the franc has been cut from 20 U.S. cents to 16 cents.

As dealers, banks ordinarily try to maintain a balanced position in the foreign currency markets, i.e., to keep their foreign currency assets and liabilities roughly in balance on a day-by-day or week-by-week basis.[2] A bank does this by netting out its foreign exchange position. First, it tries to balance foreign exchange purchases and sales among its own customers. If it has an excess of sales or purchases, it may next look for banks in its own city or country with an offsetting excess of purchases or sales; the two banks may "swap" excess positions. Finally, if a majority of banks in the home country have an imbalance of purchases or sales, they will look to banks abroad in order to net out their foreign exchange positions.

In striving for balance, a bank may vary its bid and offer prices for foreign currencies slightly—either to its own customers or to other banks—in order to encourage or discourage purchases from it or sales to it. These small variations in foreign exchange quotations create minute but profitable opportunities for foreign exchange traders in the different banks to buy from one bank while simultaneously selling the same currency to another—a process called arbitrage.

Arbitrage is defined as the act of buying and selling an asset simultaneously in different markets at different prices with the effect of assuring a guaranteed, or "locked in," profit when deliveries are completed and payment is received. Let us examine exchange arbitrage.

Cross Rates and Arbitrage Among Currencies

In the world's foreign exchange markets, practically every rate in the world is quoted against every other rate. Since there are more than 100 different currencies, this leads to some very complicated patterns of cross rates. How, for example, does the Swedish krona stay in balance simultaneously with the U.S. dollar, Dutch guilder, Mexican peso, and Japanese yen? The answer is arbitrage. Foreign exchange traders are ever-alert to money-making opportunities momentarily present through divergencies in exchange values.

Suppose, for example, a trader at First National City Bank of New York notices the following quotations:

Franc costs in dollars	.2000,
Peso costs in dollars	.1010,
Peso costs in francs	.4995.

He instantly recognizes that the peso has higher value in terms of dollars than of francs. Thus he can make a profit by swapping dollars for francs, using francs to buy pesos and converting the pesos back into dollars. Specifically, he might, if quick enough, make the following transactions:

Sell $1,000,000 for 5,000,000 francs.
Sell 5,000,000 francs for 10,010,010 pesos.
Sell 10,010,010 pesos for $1,011,011.

Our alert trader has thus picked up $11,011 for his bank in a quick stroke of

---

[2]Exceptions to this rule of balanced positions arise when banks have strong reason to believe that a currency will move persistently in one direction for a prolonged time, or that it may even be devalued or revalued. Then the traders in a bank may seek to accumulate or short the currency in question through an excess of purchases or sales. However, these objectives are satisfied mainly through contracts to buy or sell forward exchange as explained a few pages hence.

exchange rate arbitrage. We must note, of course, the price effects of these transactions. By selling francs to buy pesos, he acts to raise the peso's value against the franc. By selling pesos to buy dollars, he acts to lower the peso's value against the dollar. Since the peso is a relatively small currency, a few more transactions of this size would almost certainly raise the peso against the franc and diminish it against the dollar to the point where arbitrage would no longer be profitable. If, at the same time, the supply of francs available for dollars at exactly 20 cents was highly elastic, rates would soon settle at the following three-way balance:

Franc versus dollar	.2000.
Peso versus dollar	.1000.
Peso versus franc	.5000.

What are called broken cross rates (divergences in exchange values) would no longer exist.

Exchange Rate Fluctuations and Their Consequences

Although foreign exchange trading, including arbitrage, is ordinarily a stabilizer of exchange rates, it cannot (and will not) long maintain a rate where economic forces say it should not be. Although the present international monetary system is based on fixed exchange rates, economic laws often decree that rates have to be lowered or raised in order to prevent hopeless long-term imbalances between the supply of a nation's currency and the demand for it. Nations may differ greatly from their neighbors in the policies they pursue with respect to money supplies, price levels, international lending or investing, interest rates, and overseas giveaways or military spending.

The variety of economic policies adds to the uncertainties faced by the international businessman. Consider what can happen on different transactions. An American exporter may agree to deliver a certain machine in three months to a buyer in Liverpool, England, at a price of £100,000, thinking he will get $280,000 in U.S. money, since the pound is quoted at 2.80 on the dollar. But it is fall, 1967, and right after Thanksgiving the pound is devalued to $2.40. So the £100,000 received on December 15 converts into only $240,000, and our U.S. businessman has lost his shirt on the deal.

Consider also what can happen on an import transaction. It is mid-summer, 1969, and you contract to buy a shipment of West German glassware for 100,000 marks. In September, however, the Germans cut the mark away from the old par of about 25 cents on the dollar and let it float, i.e., let its price be decided solely by the market forces of supply and demand. So on October 1, when you have to pay for your purchase, marks are selling for almost 27 cents. Your merchandise winds up costing you about 7 per cent more than you had planned —enough to erase most of your expected profit.

Exchange Rate Hazards in Lending and Investing

Exchange rate fluctuations need not amount to major devaluations to produce losses on many kinds of international financial transactions. Even moves by exchange rates between the upper and lower parity limits can prove costly to short-term investors abroad.

Suppose, for example, an American investor sees U.S. three-month Treasury bills yielding 5¾ per cent versus 6 per cent for three-month British bills on the London market. At the same time the pound is quoted at $2.40. So, hoping to pick up the extra one-fourth percentage point of yield, the investor sells his U.S. bills and buys British ones: he sells $240,000 worth of U.S. bills and buys £100,000 of British bills. Now, suppose that at the end of three months, the pound has depreciated against the dollar to a price of $2.39.[3] At 6 per cent interest, the British T-bills mature to yield £101,500. But since a pound will now buy only 2.39 dollars, the investor winds up with only $242,585, as your multiplication will show. This is nearly $1,000 less than the $243,450 he could have realized by staying in U.S. T-bills at 5¾ per cent over the three months. This last example illustrates the hazards in what we shall soon identify as uncovered interest arbitrage.

Spot and Forward Exchange Markets

Before we discuss the ways of hedging against foreign exchange risk, we must acquaint ourselves with the division of foreign exchange transactions into *spot* and *forward* markets. This division is almost precisely analogous to the separation of domestic commodity-trading facilities into actuals and futures markets. The spot foreign exchange market deals in foreign exchange available for immediate or almost immediate delivery. (Foreign exchange bought and sold can take many forms: currency, checks, bills of exchange, cable transfers of funds, and the like.) The forward market deals only in *contracts* to buy and sell: binding contracts by which one party agrees to deliver, and the other to accept, foreign currency at a specified price on a stated future date.

Forward contracts are typically entered into for periods of up to one year, although thirty-, sixty-, and ninety-day contracts are most common. Typically, one party to a forward contract is a businessman or investor, and the other is a major bank (which is also, of course, a dealer in the spot market and may use its forward contracts as offsets or hedges against subsequent spot transactions). For example, I buy £100,000 thirty days forward at 2.5513 from the Chase Manhattan Bank of New York. This means that thirty days hence they will pay me £100,000 for which I must pay them $255,130. This agreement will be honored regardless of what happens to the dollar-pound exchange rate in the meantime. The risks inherent in such transactions will be discussed shortly.

Movements of Spot and Forward Rates

Ordinarily, spot and forward rates on a currency move in the same direction, depending on whether the currency is strong or weak in the exchange markets. However, spot rates can move only within their IMF bands; when a spot rate reaches its floor, the central bank or exchange stabilization authority must support it; at the ceiling, it must be halted by unlimited purchases of foreign currencies. No such limits restrain the movement of the forward rate; it is free to fall as far below, or rise as far above, the parity limits as traders are willing to buy and sell it.

[3]Recall that a currency *depreciates* when its price falls as a result of market action. This term should be carefully distinguished from *devaluation*, which is the formal act of a government in reducing the stated or par value at which it agrees to "defend" its currency.

Where the forward rate stands in relation to the spot rate has forecasting significance. A forward rate below the spot rate suggests expectations of future weakness in the spot rate; the greater the "forward discount" (amount by which the forward rate is below spot), the more ominous the outlook for the spot rate. Where traders greatly fear that a currency will soon be devalued, the thirty-day forward rate may be 5 or 10 per cent below the spot rate. This is mainly because (1) merchants who are due to receive the weak currency in the next few weeks are selling it forward in order to avoid still larger losses if devaluation occurs, and (2) speculators are selling the weak currency forward hoping that it will be devalued before their contracts come due (in which case they can buy the currency at a *new* spot price below the delivery price on the forward contract, and so profit from the difference). Analogously, a currency is considered strong if the forward rates are above spot.

Hedging Exchange Risk

Now we are ready to consider the hedging of exchange risk, a tactic the international businessman or investor often uses to shrink the uncertainties of his transactions to acceptable size. What is the basic principle of hedging? It is to protect a liability by creating an offsetting asset of corresponding size—or to protect an asset by creating an offsetting liability. Before turning to hedges in the forward market, let us look at a hedge in the spot market.

Here, for example, is the Paris office of U.S. Gismo and Widget Corporation. It holds 5,000,000 francs in accounts receivable. If the franc stays at 20 cents, the receivables are worth $1 million; but if the franc (as some observers fear) is devalued 20 per cent, these receivables will be worth only $800,000, and swoosh!—down the drain go the last two years' profits of the French Division. How can the division controller hedge his receivables—an asset expressed in francs? He can do so simply by creating an offsetting liability, also expressed in francs. One way is to go to The Last National Bank of Paris and borrow 5,000,000 francs for sixty or ninety days, or whatever the crisis period is expected to be. He then uses the 5,000,000 francs to buy $1,000,000 in U.S. Treasury bills (whose interest payments will roughly offset the interest charge on the French bank loan). Now he is hedged. If the franc is devalued 20 per cent, U.S. G & W loses $200,000 on its receivables, which fall in value from $1 million to $800,000. But an offsetting profit is made on the bank loan; the Treasury bill is still worth $1 million (neglecting interest), and it now costs only $800,000 to repay the 5,000,000 franc bank loan. So $200,000 lost on receivables is offset by $200,000 made on the proceeds of the borrowed francs.

Hedging on the Forward Market

Another tactic the U.S. G & W controller might have used to hedge would have been to sell approximately 5,000,000 francs ninety days forward. (Let's say, to make our example easy, that he sells them forward at par, 20 cents). This obligates the company to deliver 5,000,000 francs ninety days from now in exchange for $1,000,000. If the franc is not devalued, then ninety days hence it will cost the firm $1,000,000 to buy the spot 5,000,000 francs; it will then deliver the francs and get $1,000,000—the forward contract price—in return. Nothing gained, nothing lost. But nothing gained or lost either on the 5,000,000 francs in receivables which—since there has been no devaluation—are still worth $1 million. Suppose the franc had been devalued 20 per cent. The receivables would shrink to $800,000 in U.S. money. But an offsetting gain would be made on the forward hedge. The controller at the end of ninety days could in effect buy up the 5,000,000 francs he owed for $800,000. The forward buyer of the francs (who is, by virtue of this fact, a forward seller of dollars) has agreed to pay $1,000,000 for these francs. So the forward hedge yields a $200,000 profit, precisely equal to the loss sustained on the receivables.

In one respect, this example is oversimplified. In an actual case of devaluation jitters, the forward franc-dollar rate would be far below the spot rate. The spot rate would not hold at par but would almost certainly be jammed against the floor by flight from the weak currency. If devaluation did not occur, then the spot price would rally strongly—possibly approaching the upper limit of its parity band—as people who had sold the franc forward subsequently flocked into the spot market to buy francs to deliver against their forward contracts.

Indeed, selling a doubtful currency forward can involve substantial loss if devaluation does not occur. Suppose, for instance, we sell francs ninety days forward at 19 cents, expecting a devaluation from 20 cents to 16 cents. (Remember that the spot price could not fall below 19.55 cents—2¼ per cent below par—but the forward rate is usually sagging badly by the time devaluation fears are widespread.) But after ninety days the franc has not only escaped devaluation but, owing to energetic balance of payment correctives applied by the French government, it has become very strong. The spot franc, formerly at its floor of 19.55 cents, has begun to rally. Now speculators and others who sold forward at 19¼ cents, 19 cents, or 18½ cents are going to have to deliver spot francs to satisfy their contracts. They can only buy them in the spot market. Their concentrated buying lifts the spot franc rapidly—19.7 cents, 20.0 cents, 20.3 cents—all the way to its ceiling at 20.455 cents. We (the unlucky forward seller) must now pay 20.455 cents for francs that will yield us only 19 cents on delivery.

The point to emphasize is this. If you hedge or speculate in the spot market, your potential loss is limited to swings within the parity bands of the foreign currency. If you use the forward market, your risks are much larger because there are no fixed limits to fluctuations in the forward price. It may be far below the floor of the spot market. If you buy or sell forward at a price outside the bands, and a change of par in the doubtful currency does not take place, you may suffer a large loss from having to buy or sell this currency in the spot market to make delivery against your forward contract.

You should also visualize other hedging transactions in which the forward market is useful. Suppose that the franc is shaky. A U.S. merchant due to be paid francs two months from now guarantees himself a fixed dollar price by selling his franc proceeds forward. A U.S. exporter making a contract to be paid in francs ninety days from now checks the forward market, calculates the cost to sell francs forward, and adds this cost to the price he quotes in francs.[4] Or suppose, on

---

[4] For example, I want $30,000 for my merchandise. The spot franc is 20.0 cents; ninety-day forward is 19.50 cents. To gross $30,000 at par my price would be 150,000 francs. To "lock in" proceeds of $30,000 by selling enough francs forward today to guarantee this number of dollars, I would need 30,000/.195, or 153,846 francs. The 3,846 franc difference between $30,000 converted into francs at spot and $30,000 converted at the ninety-day forward price comprises my cost of cover on the transaction.

the other hand, that the German mark seems headed for revaluation. An American importer, who is committed to pay in marks when he receives German goods forty-five days hence, can protect himself through a forward purchase of marks at today's dollar price. Typically, a U.S. merchant who commits himself either to pay or receive an unstable foreign currency at a distant date will not only protect himself with an appropriate hedge in the forward market; he will plan his hedge at the same time he prices his transactions, and will allow for the cost of forward cover in the price he quotes or agrees to pay

International Investment and Interest Arbitrage

In addition to transactions in goods and services, international business includes a myriad of investment transactions across national boundaries. American companies buy British subsidiaries, U.S. and German companies participate in joint manufacturing ventures, French and Swiss citizens buy common stocks in U.S. companies, American investors buy the bonds and bills of the British Treasury. International investment is too varied and too complex to discuss in its entirety here, but one phase does deserve special notice because of its world-wide influence on money markets and interest rates. This is the matter of interest arbitrage.

Opportunities for gainful lending do not stop at the water's edge. Today, a person, company, or financial institution with short-term funds to invest at interest has money markets throughout the world bidding aggressively for his funds. If treasury bills or commercial paper in London yield more than equivalent short-term investments in New York, the exchange markets offer a quick, reliable vehicle for moving funds to London where the better bargain exists. However, we have already seen that ordinary or "uncovered" interest arbitrage is beset by risks of exchange rate fluctuation. Experienced investors rarely if ever engage in international short-term lending transactions without taking effective steps to eradicate these risks. The method employed is known as *covered interest arbitrage.*

Covered Interest Arbitrage

Covered interest arbitrage is the process of hedging in the forward market interest returns in a foreign currency. Let us again raise the situation described earlier, in which our investor lost money buying British three-month Treasury bills at a 6 per cent yield (against a 5¾ yield on U.S. bills) because during the three months the pound fell vis-à-vis the dollar. Could the U.S. investor have done anything to hedge his risk and "lock in" an improved yield at the very instant he completed his transaction? The answer depends not only on how interest rates in the two money centers compare, but also on how the spot and forward rates of foreign exchange stand in relation to each other.

Suppose, for example, that at present *both* the spot and three-month forward pound are selling at $2.40. It is then possible for the interest arbitrager to guarantee himself a profit on the switch from U.S. to British Treasury bills by the following steps:

1. Sell his 5¾ per cent U.S. Treasury bills for $240,000 cash.
2. Buy £100,000 spot at $2.40.
3. Invest the £100,000 in British Treasury bills at 6 per cent.
4. Sell £101,500 forward at $2.40.

His forward sale of £101,500 (proceeds of £100,000 invested at 6 per cent for three months) will bring him $243,600. This is $150 more than the $243,450 he would have obtained at maturity from $240,000 left in 5¾ per cent U.S. three-month Treasury bills. And—this is the point—the profit is assured from the instant the proceeds of the foreign investment are *sold forward* at a sufficient price.

Of course, a check of the forward exchange market might quickly have shown that forward cover was lacking and that there was no opportunity for safe arbitraging operations despite the yield advantage of London over New York. Suppose, for example, the forward pound had sold at $2.39. A forward sale of the £101,500 proceeds of the British bill investment would have brought only $242,585 when converted back to dollars, much less than the gross from the U.S. bills.

Interrelation of Exchange and Interest Rates

The foregoing examples of interest arbitrage suggest that exchange rates and interest rates in different countries are related in a systematic way. Such intuitions are correct. The forces of covered interest arbitrage, always present among foreign exchange dealers and knowledgeable traders, are a powerful influence affecting both interest and exchange rates and the alignment that exists between the two. To see why, let us look at a somewhat novel situation in which an international investor can make money by moving his funds from a country where interest rates are higher to one where they are lower. Does this seem nonsensical? It is only when we fail to consider the way in which interest rate and exchange rate comparisons are systematically linked through the forces of covered interest arbitrage.

Suppose, for example, that an American businessman has $100,000 excess cash that he does not need for six months. Currently, six-month U.S. Treasury bills are yielding 6 per cent, while six-month West German bills are yielding 4 per cent. However, the spot mark is selling at 25 cents, while the six-month forward mark is quoted at 25.5 cents. Then covered interest arbitrage from New York to Bonn will be profitable even though interest rates in Bonn are lower. Let us trace the transaction:

1. With the $100,000 he buys 400,000 spot marks and invests them in 4 per cent, six-month Germany treasury bills.
2. Simultaneously, he sells forward the guaranteed proceeds of his German bills, 408,000 marks, for $104,040. This is $1,040 more than the $103,000 he would have had sitting six months in 6 per cent U.S. bills.

The point, of course, is that while the businessman loses money on the interest side of his transaction he more than makes it up on the exchange portion. Experienced traders are understandably indifferent to which part of the transaction actually gives them their profit so long as the overall arbitrage arrangement is profitable.

Interest Rate Parity

The preceding discussion suggests there is an equilibrium relation between interest and exchange rates in two countries—a relation in which the gain from shifting funds for interest advantage would be exactly offset by a loss on the sale of proceeds on the forward exchange market. Such an equilibrium relation does indeed exist. It is called *interest rate parity.* In fact, the relation of interest and exchange rates between two international money centers always tends to move toward interest rate parity. The incentive is provided by covered interest arbitrage.

To portray systematically the role of interest rate parity, the circumstances under which covered interest arbitrage will flow, and the direction in which it will flow, let us make two simple assumptions. We shall assume (1) that all interest rates are expressed in terms of annual yields, and (2) that the premium or discount at which forward exchange is selling in relation to spot exchange also is expressed as an annual percentage figure.[5] We can then say that the interest rate differential in favor of the foreign country is so many percentage points per year, while the premium or discount on forward foreign exchange is some other number of per- centage points per year. In this way we are able to make a direct comparison between interest rate differentials and rates of premium or discount on forward exchange.

The results of such a comparison are systematically presented in Figure 34–1. The chart shows interest parity as a line along which the interest rate gain is always exactly offset by forward exchange loss, and vice versa. If, for example, the interest differential favors the foreign country by 2 per cent, interest parity calls for the forward rate on the foreign currency to be at a 2 per cent discount. The chart also illustrates the various combinations of interest rates and forward premiums or discounts at which covered arbitrage will flow in or out of a country. For example, even though the interest rate differential favors the foreign country by 1 per cent, arbitrage will flow into the home country if the forward discount on the foreign currency is more than 1 per cent. On the other hand, even if the interest differential favors your country by 2 per cent, arbitrage will flow out if the forward premium on the foreign currency exceeds 2 per cent.

Factors Assisting and Obstructing Interest Parity

Movements of funds under covered interest arbitrage tend to restore interest parity. We can see this by considering what happens at point A on Figure 34–1. Interest rates in the foreign country are 1½ per cent higher than those in the home country, while the forward discount on the foreign currency is only one-half of 1 per cent. Consequently, a transfer of funds abroad with exchange risk covered would net an additional 1 per cent per year return. But the actual movement of funds abroad forces both interest and exchange rates back toward interest parity. Interest rates rise in the home country as people sell bills here; they fall in the foreign country as people buy bills there. The forward discount on the foreign currency widens as interest arbitragers buy the foreign currency spot to make their investments and sell it forward to bring the proceeds home.

One might think that opportunities for covered interest arbitrage would disap-

---

[5]Assume, for example, that the spot mark is 25 cents and the six-month forward mark is 25½ cents. Then six-month forward marks are $(.255/.25) - 1 = 2$ per cent higher than spot, which would equate to a twelve-month premium of 4 per cent.

pear quickly as vigilant traders took advantage of them. But they are often quite persistent because their presence reflects other influences besides investment incentives. International interest rate comparisons also are affected by what governments and central banks wish to accomplish for their domestic economies, with inflows and outflows of international capital a secondary consideration. The relation between a country's spot and forward rate is affected by numerous factors besides covered interest arbitrage: by the balance of payments, by merchants hedging commercial transactions, by international businessmen and long-term investors investing and disinvesting in foreign countries, by currency speculators speculating on the rise or fall of exchange rates. Each of these influences contributes its own supply and demand pressures to the spot and forward rates for every currency, with the result that arbitragers are not always able to close even highly profitable departures from interest rate parity.

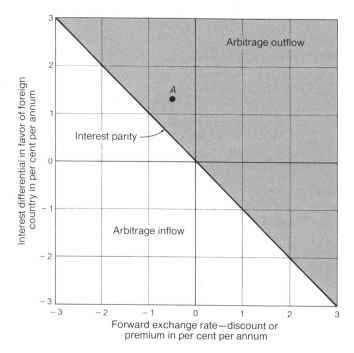

Figure 34–1. Interest Rate Differentials, Forward Exchange Rates, and Covered Interest Arbitrage

Central banks may also manipulate arbitrage opportunities as a means of monetary control over their domestic economies. By intervening massively in either the spot or forward market, a central bank can often provide or deny forward cover for interest arbitrage operations inward or outward. Thus central banks can stimulate inflows or outflows of short-term funds and so influence liquidity conditions and interest rates in their home money markets.

To Remember

Exchange risk
Retail and wholesale markets
Cross rates
Arbitrage
Spot rate

Forward rate
Hedging
Interest arbitrage
Covered interest arbitrage
Interest rate parity

Questions

1 Describe the source and nature of exchange risk.

2 Describe how the exchange trader in a major bank tries to "net out" his position. Does he ever deliberately seek an unbalanced position? When? Why?

3 Illustrate how broken cross rates give rise to opportunities for exchange arbitrage.

4 Briefly explain the nature of a forward exchange contract.

5 What is the basic principle of hedging? Illustrate two ways in which a merchant owning or due to receive a weak foreign currency could hedge his exchange risk.

6 Explain this: "Traders always try to contract debts in overvalued currencies and credits in undervalued currencies." What effect do these efforts exert on the structure of exchange rates?

7 What is interest rate parity? Give an illustration of it.

8 What is arbitrage? Covered interest arbitrage?

9 Illustrate a situation in which it is advantageous for an investor to move funds from a high-interest money center to a low-interest center.

Appendixes

Glossary

Definitions of terms not included in the glossary may be
found by consulting the index for text references.

Amortize	To pay off a debt by installments. An amortized loan is repaid in regular installments, each payment consisting of some principal and some interest.
Arbitrage	Simultaneously buying and selling the same or equivalent securities in different markets to profit from a divergence in their prices.
Bankers acceptance	Businessman's short-term promise to pay which has been guaranteed for payment (accepted) by his bank. Used largely in foreign trade to substitute a bank's known credit for the unknown credit of an individual or firm.

413

Bill	Short-term, non-interest-bearing promise to pay, issued by a business or government to borrow money. If sold on the open market, it is bought at a discount, the holder obtaining his "interest" when it matures at face value.
Bond	A promise to pay issued by a corporation or government body to borrow money for five years or longer. It pays a stated rate of interest at regular intervals, usually six months, and repays its face amount (ordinarily $1,000) at maturity.
Budget	Plan or schedule that adjusts spending over a coming period to expected income or available funds.
CD (Certificate of deposit)	Interest-bearing time deposit in a commercial bank, usually maturing in one to six months, and typically negotiable when made in large amounts. Often used by businesses for temporary investment of surplus funds.
Capital budget	Company plan of expenditures on assets whose returns are expected to extend beyond one year.
Capital note	Interest-bearing, long-term promise to pay issued by a corporation to borrow money, but differing from a bond in that it has no trustee to represent the creditor.
Capitalize	To calculate the present value of expected future income.
Central bank	A government-owned or government-controlled bank that holds the reserves of commercial banks, issues currency, and regulates a country's supply of money and credit. The Federal Reserve System is the U.S. central bank.
Commercial finance company	A non-bank lender to business firms. Chiefly, it makes short-term loans secured by inventory or receivables and raises funds by selling its own securities in the open market.

Commercial paper	Promissory notes, usually maturing within six months, used by major corporations to raise short-term funds. Non-interest-bearing, they are sold at a discount to investors as liquid investments for temporary funds.
Dividend	A distribution to stockholders of part of their claim to a corporation's net worth, usually from profits and typically in cash.
Equity	Ownership interest in a business. In a corporation, equity consists of the sum of stockholders' claims.
Eurodollars	Dollars deposited in a bank abroad.
Factor	Quasi-lender to business firms that supplies short-term funds by buying their accounts receivable.
Fiscal policy	Government's effort to regulate the economy through federal spending, taxation, and public debt management.
Funding	Converting short-term debt to long-term, usually by selling new long-term securities to replace maturing short-term ones.
Investment banker	Financial intermediary that helps corporations sell new securities.
Liquidity	Ease of conversion into cash with little chance of loss.
Marginal	Economist's term meaning "one more." Marginal cost is the cost of producing one more unit; marginal revenue, the income derived by selling one more unit.
Monetary policy	Central bank's effort to regulate the economy by varying the cost and availability of money and credit.
Note	IOU used to evidence a loan. May be long- or short-term.
Private placement	Selling new securities to a few large buyers rather than to the general public.

Prospectus	Briefed-down summary of a firm's registration statement, which is sent to prospective buyers of new securities.
Proxy	Document in which a stockholder yields his voting power to someone else.
Short sale	Any sale of a security which is consummated by delivering to the buyer a borrowed certificate. Usually made in hope of profiting from expected decline in a security's price, which will enable the seller to replace the borrowed security at a lower price.
Registration	Process by which issuer of new securities is required to file descriptive information with some government authority and obtain its approval before securities can be publicly offered.
Risk	Calculable chance of loss. Usually used incorrectly by writers on finance to mean "uncertainty," which is ignorance of the expected outcome.
Short-term	Maturing in less than one year.
Sinking fund	Periodic payment by a debtor corporation to a bond-issue trustee, usually used to buy in bonds or call them by lot for retirement. A means of retiring the bulk of a bond issue before maturity, and so strengthening the bonds that remain outstanding.
Stock	The equity or ownership interest in a corporation, represented by certificates for transferable shares. Divided into preferred stock, which has limited rights to earnings and assets ahead of common stock, and common stock, which represents the residual interest in earnings and assets after all other claimants have been allowed for.
Term loan	Bank or insurance company loan to a business firm for several years, which is repaid in periodic installments.

Trade discount	A reduction, ordinarily of one or two per cent, in the billed price of goods, which a supplier offers his business customer in return for prompt payment.
Treasury bill	A short-term, non-interest-bearing promissory note sold to investors at a discount by the U.S. government to finance its debt.
Underwriting	Purchase of an entire issue of new securities by investment bankers for reoffer to investors at a mark-up in price.

Tables

Table A-1. PRESENT WORTH TO FUTURE WORTH,
Compound Sum of $1

Year n	1%	2%	3%	4%	5%	6%	7%
1	1.010	1.020	1.030	1.040	1.050	1.060	1.070
2	1.020	1.040	1.061	1.082	1.102	1.124	1.145
3	1.030	1.061	1.093	1.125	1.158	1.191	1.225
4	1.041	1.082	1.126	1.170	1.216	1.262	1.311
5	1.051	1.104	1.159	1.217	1.276	1.338	1.403
6	1.062	1.126	1.194	1.265	1.340	1.419	1.501
7	1.072	1.149	1.230	1.316	1.407	1.504	1.606
8	1.083	1.172	1.267	1.369	1.477	1.594	1.718
9	1.094	1.195	1.305	1.423	1.551	1.689	1.838
10	1.105	1.219	1.344	1.480	1.629	1.791	1.967
11	1.116	1.243	1.384	1.539	1.710	1.898	2.105
12	1.127	1.268	1.426	1.601	1.796	2.012	2.252
13	1.138	1.294	1.469	1.665	1.886	2.133	2.410
14	1.149	1.319	1.513	1.732	1.980	2.261	2.579
15	1.161	1.346	1.558	1.801	2.079	2.397	2.759
16	1.173	1.373	1.605	1.873	2.183	2.540	2.952
17	1.184	1.400	1.653	1.948	2.292	2.693	3.159
18	1.196	1.428	1.702	2.026	2.407	2.854	3.380
19	1.208	1.457	1.754	2.107	2.527	3.026	3.617
20	1.220	1.486	1.806	2.191	2.653	3.207	3.870
25	1.282	1.641	2.094	2.666	3.386	4.292	5.427

Table A–1. PRESENT WORTH TO FUTURE WORTH,
Compound Sum of $1, Cont'd.

Year n	8%	9%	10%	12%	14%	15%	16%
1	1.080	1.090	1.100	1.120	1.140	1.150	1.160
2	1.166	1.188	1.210	1.254	1.300	1.322	1.346
3	1.260	1.295	1.331	1.405	1.482	1.521	1.561
4	1.360	1.412	1.464	1.574	1.689	1.749	1.811
5	1.469	1.539	1.611	1.762	1.925	2.011	2.100
6	1.587	1.677	1.772	1.974	2.195	2.313	2.436
7	1.714	1.828	1.949	2.211	2.502	2.660	2.826
8	1.851	1.993	2.144	2.476	2.853	3.059	3.278
9	1.999	2.172	2.358	2.773	3.252	3.518	3.803
10	2.159	2.367	2.594	3.106	3.707	4.046	4.411
11	2.332	2.580	2.853	3.479	4.226	4.652	5.117
12	2.518	2.813	3.138	3.896	4.818	5.350	5.936
13	2.720	3.066	3.452	4.363	5.492	6.153	6.886
14	2.937	3.342	3.797	4.887	6.261	7.076	7.988
15	3.172	3.642	4.177	5.474	7.138	8.137	9.266
16	3.426	3.970	4.595	6.130	8.137	9.358	10.748
17	3.700	4.328	5.054	6.866	9.276	10.761	12.468
18	3.996	4.717	5.560	7.690	10.575	12.375	14.463
19	4.316	5.142	6.116	8.613	12.056	14.232	16.777
20	4.661	5.604	6.728	9.646	13.743	16.367	19.461
25	6.848	8.623	10.835	17.000	26.462	32.919	40.874

Table A-1. PRESENT WORTH TO FUTURE WORTH,
Compound Sum of $1, Cont'd.

Year n	18%	20%	24%	28%	32%	36%	40%
1	1.180	1.200	1.240	1.280	1.320	1.360	1.400
2	1.392	1.440	1.538	1.638	1.742	1.850	1.960
3	1.643	1.728	1.907	2.067	2.300	2.515	2.744
4	1.939	2.074	2.364	2.684	3.036	3.421	3.842
5	2.288	2.488	2.932	3.436	4.007	4.653	5.378
6	2.700	2.986	3.635	4.398	5.290	6.328	7.530
7	3.185	3.583	4.508	5.629	6.983	8.605	10.541
8	3.759	4.300	5.590	7.206	9.217	11.703	14.758
9	4.435	5.160	6.931	9.223	12.166	15.917	20.661
10	5.234	6.192	8.594	11.806	16.060	21.647	28.925
11	6.176	7.430	10.657	15.112	21.199	29.439	40.496
12	7.288	8.916	13.215	19.343	27.983	40.037	56.694
13	8.599	10.699	16.386	24.759	36.937	54.451	79.372
14	10.147	12.839	20.319	31.691	48.757	74.053	111.120
15	11.974	15.407	25.196	40.565	64.359	100.712	155.568
16	14.129	18.488	31.243	51.923	84.954	136.97	217.795
17	16.672	22.186	38.741	66.461	112.14	186.28	304.914
18	19.673	26.623	48.039	85.071	148.02	253.34	426.879
19	23.214	31.948	59.568	108.89	195.39	344.54	597.630
20	27.393	38.338	73.864	139.38	257.92	468.57	836.683
25	62.669	95.396	216.542	478.90	1033.6	2180.1	4499.880

Table A–2. FUTURE WORTH TO PRESENT WORTH,
Present Worth of $1

Year n	1%	2%	3%	4%	5%	6%	7%	8%	9%	10%	12%
1	.990	.980	.971	.962	.952	.943	.935	.926	.917	.909	.893
2	.980	.961	.943	.925	.907	.890	.873	.857	.842	.826	.797
3	.971	.942	.915	.889	.864	.840	.816	.794	.772	.751	.712
4	.961	.924	.889	.855	.823	.792	.763	.735	.708	.683	.636
5	.951	.906	.863	.822	.784	.747	.713	.681	.650	.621	.567
6	.942	.888	.838	.790	.746	.705	.666	.630	.596	.564	.507
7	.933	.871	.813	.760	.711	.665	.623	.583	.547	.513	.452
8	.923	.853	.789	.731	.677	.627	.582	.540	.502	.467	.404
9	.914	.837	.766	.703	.645	.592	.544	.500	.460	.424	.361
10	.905	.820	.744	.676	.614	.558	.508	.463	.422	.386	.322
11	.896	.804	.722	.650	.585	.527	.475	.429	.388	.350	.287
12	.887	.788	.701	.625	.557	.497	.444	.397	.356	.319	.257
13	.879	.773	.681	.601	.530	.469	.415	.368	.326	.290	.229
14	.870	.758	.661	.577	.505	.442	.388	.340	.299	.263	.205
15	.861	.743	.642	.555	.481	.417	.362	.315	.275	.239	.183
16	.853	.728	.623	.534	.458	.394	.339	.292	.252	.218	.163
17	.844	.714	.605	.513	.436	.371	.317	.270	.231	.198	.146
18	.836	.700	.587	.494	.416	.350	.296	.250	.212	.180	.130
19	.828	.686	.570	.475	.396	.331	.276	.232	.194	.164	.116
20	.820	.673	.554	.456	.377	.312	.258	.215	.178	.149	.104
25	.780	.610	.478	.375	.295	.233	.184	.146	.116	.092	.059

Table A-2. FUTURE WORTH TO PRESENT WORTH,
Present Worth of $1, Cont'd.

Year n	14%	15%	16%	18%	20%	24%	28%	32%	36%	40%
1	.877	.870	.862	.847	.833	.806	.781	.758	.735	.714
2	.769	.756	.743	.718	.694	.650	.610	.574	.541	.510
3	.675	.658	.641	.609	.579	.524	.477	.435	.398	.364
4	.592	.572	.552	.516	.482	.423	.373	.329	.292	.260
5	.519	.497	.476	.437	.402	.341	.291	.250	.215	.186
6	.456	.432	.410	.370	.335	.275	.227	.189	.158	.133
7	.400	.376	.354	.314	.279	.222	.178	.143	.116	.095
8	.351	.327	.305	.266	.233	.179	.139	.108	.085	.068
9	.308	.284	.263	.226	.194	.144	.108	.082	.063	.048
10	.270	.247	.227	.191	.162	.116	.085	.062	.046	.035
11	.237	.215	.195	.162	.135	.094	.066	.047	.034	.025
12	.208	.187	.168	.137	.112	.076	.052	.036	.025	.018
13	.182	.163	.145	.116	.093	.061	.040	.027	.018	.013
14	.160	.141	.125	.099	.078	.049	.032	.021	.014	.009
15	.140	.123	.108	.084	.065	.040	.025	.016	.010	.006
16	.123	.107	.093	.071	.054	.032	.019	.012	.007	.005
17	.108	.093	.080	.060	.045	.026	.015	.009	.005	.003
18	.095	.081	.069	.051	.038	.021	.012	.007	.004	.002
19	.083	.070	.060	.043	.031	.017	.009	.005	.003	.002
20	.073	.061	.051	.037	.026	.014	.007	.004	.002	.001
25	.038	.030	.024	.016	.010	.005	.002	.001	.000	.000

E / 5,000

Table A-3. ANNUITY TO FUTURE WORTH,
Compound Sum of a $1 Annuity

Year n	1%	2%	3%	4%	5%	6%	7%
1	1.000	1.000	1.000	1.000	1.000	1.000	1.000
2	2.010	2.020	2.030	2.040	2.050	2.060	2.070
3	3.030	3.060	3.091	3.122	3.152	3.184	3.215
4	4.060	4.122	4.184	4.246	4.310	4.375	4.440
5	5.101	5.204	5.309	5.416	5.526	5.637	5.751
6	6.152	6.308	6.468	6.633	6.802	6.975	7.153
7	7.214	7.434	7.662	7.898	8.142	8.394	8.654
8	8.286	8.583	8.892	9.214	9.549	9.897	10.260
9	9.369	9.755	10.159	10.583	11.027	11.491	11.978
10	10.462	10.950	11.464	12.006	12.578	13.181	13.816
11	11.567	12.169	12.808	13.486	14.207	14.972	15.784
12	12.683	13.412	14.192	15.026	15.917	16.870	17.888
13	13.809	14.680	15.618	16.627	17.713	18.882	20.141
14	14.947	15.974	17.086	18.292	19.599	21.051	22.550
15	16.097	17.293	18.599	20.024	21.579	23.276	25.129
16	17.258	18.639	20.157	21.825	23.657	25.673	27.888
17	18.430	20.012	21.762	23.698	25.840	28.213	30.840
18	19.615	21.412	23.414	25.645	28.132	30.906	33.999
19	20.811	22.841	25.117	27.671	30.539	33.760	37.379
20	22.019	24.297	26.870	29.778	33.066	36.786	40.995
25	28.243	32.030	36.459	41.646	47.727	54.865	63.249

Table A–3. ANNUITY TO FUTURE WORTH,
Compound Sum of a $1 Annuity, Cont'd.

Year n	8%	9%	10%	12%	14%	16%	18%
1	1.000	1.000	1.000	1.000	1.000	1.000	1.000
2	2.080	2.090	2.100	2.120	2.140	2.160	2.180
3	3.246	3.278	3.310	3.374	3.440	3.506	3.572
4	4.506	4.573	4.641	4.770	4.921	5.066	5.215
5	5.867	5.985	6.105	6.353	6.610	6.877	7.154
6	7.336	7.523	7.716	8.115	8.536	8.977	9.442
7	8.923	9.200	9.487	10.089	10.730	11.414	12.142
8	10.637	11.028	11.436	12.300	13.233	14.240	15.327
9	12.488	13.021	13.579	14.776	16.085	17.518	19.086
10	14.487	15.193	15.937	17.549	19.337	21.321	23.521
11	16.645	17.560	18.531	20.655	23.044	25.733	28.755
12	18.977	20.141	21.384	24.133	27.271	30.850	34.931
13	21.495	22.953	24.523	28.029	32.089	36.786	42.219
14	24.215	26.019	27.975	32.393	37.581	43.672	50.818
15	27.152	29.361	31.772	37.280	43.842	51.660	60.965
16	30.324	33.003	35.950	42.753	50.980	60.925	72.939
17	33.750	36.974	40.545	48.884	59.118	71.673	87.068
18	37.450	41.301	45.599	55.750	68.394	84.141	103.740
19	41.446	46.018	51.159	63.440	78.969	98.603	123.414
20	45.762	51.160	57.275	72.052	91.025	115.380	146.628
25	73.106	84.701	98.347	133.334	181.871	249.214	342.603

Table A-3. ANNUITY TO FUTURE WORTH,
Compound Sum of a $1 Annuity, Cont'd.

Year n	20%	24%	28%	32%	36%	40%
1	1.000	1.000	1.000	1.000	1.000	1.000
2	2.200	2.240	2.280	2.320	2.360	2.400
3	3.640	3.778	3.918	4.062	4.210	4.360
4	5.368	5.684	6.016	6.362	6.725	7.104
5	7.442	8.048	8.700	9.398	10.146	10.846
6	9.930	10.980	12.136	13.406	14.799	16.324
7	12.916	14.615	16.534	18.696	21.126	23.853
8	16.499	19.123	22.163	25.678	29.732	34.395
9	20.799	24.712	29.369	34.895	41.435	49.153
10	25.959	31.643	38.592	47.062	57.352	69.814
11	32.150	40.238	50.399	63.122	78.998	98.739
12	39.580	50.985	65.510	84.320	108.437	139.235
13	48.497	64.110	84.853	112.303	148.475	195.929
14	59.196	80.496	109.612	149.240	202.926	275.300
15	72.035	100.815	141.303	197.997	276.979	386.420
16	87.442	126.011	181.87	262.36	377.69	541.99
17	105.931	157.253	233.79	347.31	514.66	759.78
18	128.117	195.994	300.25	459.45	700.94	1064.7
19	154.740	244.033	385.32	607.47	954.28	1491.6
20	186.688	303.601	494.21	802.86	1298.8	2089.2
25	471.981	898.092	1706.8	3226.8	6053.0	11247.0

10,000 →

Table A–4. ANNUITY TO PRESENT WORTH,
Present Worth of a $1 Annuity

Year *n*	1%	2%	3%	4%	5%	6%	7%	8%	9%	10%
1	0.990	0.980	0.971	0.962	0.952	0.943	0.935	0.926	0.917	0.909
2	1.970	1.942	1.913	1.886	1.859	1.833	1.808	1.783	1.759	1.736
3	2.941	2.884	2.829	2.775	2.723	2.673	2.624	2.577	2.531	2.487
4	3.902	3.808	3.717	3.630	3.546	3.465	3.387	3.312	3.240	3.170
5	4.853	4.713	4.580	4.452	4.329	4.212	4.100	3.993	3.890	3.791
6	5.795	5.601	5.417	5.242	5.076	4.917	4.767	4.623	4.486	4.355
7	6.728	6.472	6.230	6.002	5.786	5.582	5.389	5.206	5.033	4.868
8	7.652	7.325	7.020	6.733	6.463	6.210	5.971	5.747	5.535	5.335
9	8.566	8.162	7.786	7.435	7.108	6.802	6.515	6.247	5.985	5.759
10	9.471	8.983	8.530	8.111	7.722	7.360	7.024	6.710	6.418	6.145
11	10.368	9.787	9.253	8.760	8.306	7.887	7.499	7.139	6.805	6.495
12	11.255	10.575	9.954	9.385	8.863	8.384	7.943	7.536	7.161	6.814
13	12.134	11.348	10.635	9.986	9.394	8.853	8.358	7.904	7.487	7.103
14	13.004	12.106	11.296	10.563	9.899	9.295	8.745	8.244	7.786	7.367
15	13.865	12.849	11.938	11.118	10.380	9.712	9.108	8.559	8.060	7.606
16	14.718	13.578	12.561	11.652	10.838	10.106	9.447	8.851	8.312	7.824
17	15.562	14.292	13.166	12.166	11.274	10.477	9.763	9.122	8.544	8.022
18	16.398	14.992	13.754	12.659	11.690	10.828	10.059	9.372	8.756	8.201
19	17.226	15.678	14.324	13.134	12.085	11.158	10.336	9.604	8.950	8.365
20	18.046	16.351	14.877	13.590	12.462	11.470	10.594	9.818	9.128	8.514
25	22.023	19.523	17.413	15.622	14.094	12.783	11.654	10.675	9.823	9.077

Table A-4. ANNUITY TO PRESENT WORTH,
Present Worth of a $1 Annuity, Cont'd.

Year n	12%	14%	16%	18%	20%	24%	28%	32%	36%
1	0.893	0.877	0.862	0.847	0.833	0.806	0.781	0.758	0.735
2	1.690	1.647	1.605	1.566	1.528	1.457	1.392	1.332	1.276
3	2.402	2.322	2.246	2.174	2.106	1.981	1.868	1.766	1.674
4	3.037	2.914	2.798	2.690	2.589	2.404	2.241	2.096	1.966
5	3.605	3.433	3.274	3.127	2.991	2.745	2.532	2.345	2.181
6	4.111	3.889	3.685	3.498	3.326	3.020	2.759	2.534	2.339
7	4.564	4.288	4.039	3.812	3.605	3.242	2.937	2.678	2.455
8	4.968	4.639	4.344	4.078	3.837	3.421	3.076	2.786	2.540
9	5.328	4.946	4.607	4.303	4.031	3.566	3.184	2.868	2.603
10	5.650	5.216	4.833	4.494	4.193	3.682	3.269	2.930	2.650
11	5.988	5.453	5.029	4.656	4.327	3.776	3.335	2.978	2.683
12	6.194	5.660	5.197	4.793	4.439	3.851	3.387	3.013	2.708
13	6.424	5.842	5.342	4.910	4.533	3.912	3.427	3.040	2.727
14	6.628	6.002	5.468	5.008	4.611	3.962	3.459	3.061	2.740
15	6.811	6.142	5.575	5.092	4.675	4.001	3.483	3.076	2.750
16	6.974	6.265	5.669	5.162	4.730	4.033	3.503	3.088	2.758
17	7.120	6.373	5.749	5.222	4.775	4.059	3.518	3.097	2.763
18	7.250	6.467	5.818	5.273	4.812	4.080	3.529	3.104	2.767
19	7.366	6.550	5.877	5.316	4.844	4.097	3.539	3.109	2.770
20	7.469	6.623	5.929	5.353	4.870	4.110	3.546	3.113	2.772
25	7.843	6.873	6.097	5.467	4.948	4.147	3.564	3.122	2.776

Index

Italic numbers refer to pages with illustrations; t = table